Sightseeing Key

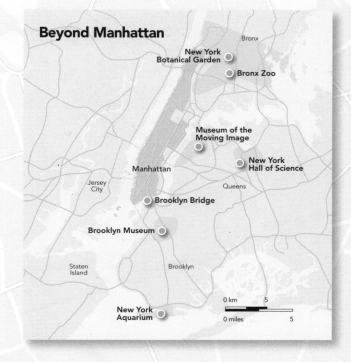

Beyond Manhattan

Bronx

New York Botanical Garden

Bronx Zoo

Museum of the Moving Image

New York Hall of Science

Manhattan

Jersey City

Queens

Brooklyn Bridge

Brooklyn Museum

Staten Island

Brooklyn

New York Aquarium

0 km 5

0 miles 5

EYEWITNESS TRAVEL

FAMILY GUIDE

NEW YORK CITY

EYEWITNESS TRAVEL

FAMILY GUIDE
NEW YORK CITY

DK

MANAGING EDITOR Aruna Ghose

EDITORIAL MANAGER
Sheeba Bhatnagar

DESIGN MANAGER Kavita Saha

DEPUTY DESIGN MANAGER
Mathew Kurien

PROJECT EDITOR Arundhti Bhanot

EDITOR Karen Faye D'Souza

PROJECT DESIGNER
Namrata Adhwaryu

DESIGNER Shruti Bahl

PICTURE RESEARCH MANAGER
Taiyaba Khatoon

PICTURE RESEARCH Sumita Khatwani

DTP DESIGNERS Azeem Siddiqui,
Rakesh Pal

SENIOR CARTOGRAPHIC MANAGER
Uma Bhattacharya

ASSISTANT CARTOGRAPHIC MANAGER
Suresh Kumar

AUTHORS Eleanor Berman, Lee
Magill, AnneLise Sorensen

PHOTOGRAPHY Steven Greaves

CARTOONS Julian Mosedale

ADDITIONAL ILLUSTRATIONS Richard
Draper, Robbie Polley, Arun
Pottirayil, Hamish Simpson,
Pallavi Thakur

DESIGN CONCEPT Keith Hagan at
www.greenwich-design.co.uk

Printed and bound in China

First published in the United States in
2012 by Dorling Kindersley Publishing,
Inc., 345 Hudson Street, New York,
New York 10014. A Penguin Random
House Company

15 16 17 18 10 9 8 7 6 5 4 3 2 1

Reprinted with revisions 2014, 2016

Copyright 2012, 2016 © Dorling
Kindersley Limited, London

Contents

Kids riding hand-carved, painted horses on the Friedsam Memorial Carousel

Macy's Thanksgiving Day Parade

How to Use this Guide

This guide is designed to help families get the most from a visit to New York City, providing expert recommendations for sightseeing with kids along with detailed practical information. The opening section contains an introduction to New York and its highlights, as well as all the essentials required to plan a family holiday (including how to get there, getting around, health, insurance, money, restaurants, accommodations, shopping, and communications), a guide to family-friendly festivals, and a brief historical overview.

The main sightseeing section of the book is divided into areas. A "best of" feature for every chapter is followed by the key sights and other attractions in the area, as well as options for where to eat, drink, play, and have more fun. At the back of the book there are hotel listings and detailed maps of New York.

INTRODUCING THE AREA

Each area chapter opens with a double-page spread setting it in context, with a short introduction, locator map, and a selection of highlights.

Locator map locates the region.

Brief highlights give a flavor of what to see in the area.

Themed suggestions for the best things to see and do with kids.

THE BEST OF...

This planner shows at a glance the best things for families to see and do in each area, with themed suggestions ranging from history, art, and culture to gardens and games.

WHERE TO STAY

Our expert authors have compiled a wide range of recommendations for places to stay with families, from hotels and B&Bs that welcome children to self-catering apartments.

Easy-to-use symbols show the key family-friendly features of places to stay.

Price Guide box gives details of the price categories for a family of four.

SIGHTSEEING IN NEW YORK

Each area features a number of "hub" sights (see below), introduced with a detailed map featuring everything necessary to explore the area. The pages that follow give adults and children a real insight into the destination, focusing on the key sights and what makes them interesting to kids. The sights are balanced by places to let off steam, "take cover" options for rainy days, suggestions for where to eat, drink, and shop with kids, ideas for where to explore next, and all the practicalities, including transportation.

Introductory text focuses on the practical aspects of the area, from the best time of day to visit to how to get around using public transportation.

The Lowdown gives all the practical information you need to visit the area. The key to the symbols is on the back jacket flap.

The hub map identifies the sights featured in the chapter, as well as restaurants, shops, places to stay, transportation, and the nearest playgrounds, supermarkets, and pharmacies.

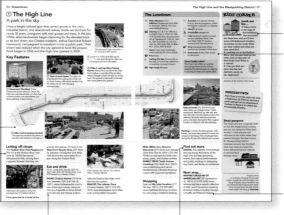

The hub sights are the best places to visit in each area, and use lively and informative text to engage and entertain both adults and children.

Key Features uses illustrated artworks to show the most interesting features of each sight, highlighting elements likely to appeal to children.

Letting off steam suggests a place to take children to play freely following a cultural visit.

Eat and drink lists recommendations for family-friendly places to eat and drink, from picnic options and snacks to proper meals and gourmet dining.

Kids' Corner is featured on all sightseeing pages (see below).

The Lowdown provides comprehensive practical information, including transportation, opening times, costs, activities, age suitability, and how long to allow for a visit.

Next stop... suggests other places to visit, either near the key sight, thematically linked to the sight, or a complete change of pace for the rest of the day.

Find out more gives suggestions for downloads, games, apps, or movies to enthuse children about a place and help them to learn more about it.

More sights near each hub, selected to appeal to both adults and children, are given on the following pages.

Places of interest are recommended, with an emphasis on the aspects most likely to attract children, and incorporating quirky stories and unusual facts. Each one includes a suggestion for letting off steam or taking cover.

Kids' Corners are designed to engage children with the sight, picking out things to look out for, games to play, cartoons, and fun facts. Answers to quizzes are given at the bottom of the panel.

The Lowdown provides the usual comprehensive practical and transportation information for each sight.

Vibrant, colorful graffiti depicting the
Statue of Liberty, painted on a metal
gate in Manhattan, New York City

Introducing
NEW YORK CITY

The Best of New York

The abundance of its cultural treasures, the beauty of its skyline, its many green spaces, and its sheer energy lend New York an iconic identity. The city is full of variety – adventurous and sublime, civilized yet raucous – and there are many ways to experience it. New York is also surprisingly child-friendly, full of museums that focus on kids, plus great parks and playgrounds. Here are just a few ideas to help build the perfect itinerary.

Architectural adventures

New York wouldn't be the same without its dramatic skyline, which changes often and yet somehow remains timeless. The city's love affair with the skyscraper began in about 1890 and shows no signs of abating. Remarkably, three of its most beloved and iconic edifices went up in the space of just three years, between 1930 and 1933 – the **Chrysler Building** (see p95), which became the world's tallest building when it was completed in 1930, the **Empire State Building** (see pp94–5), which surpassed the Chrysler to take the same title in 1931, and the 19-building **Rockefeller Center** (see pp112–13) in 1933, which remains a vibrant cultural hub to this day. They stand just a few blocks away from each other in Midtown.

One of the best ways to appreciate the cityscape is to ascend to **Rockefeller Center's** Top of the Rock, or to the uppermost viewing deck of the **Empire State Building**, and marvel at the forest of towers in every direction. Another unmissable perspective is looking back from the magnificent **Brooklyn Bridge** (see pp196–7), after crossing it on foot.

Above Gilded statue of Prometheus, Rockefeller Center
Below A view of Brooklyn Bridge across the East River, with Manhattan's skyscrapers as a backdrop

Above *Giant Ferris wheel and restaurants along the sandy beach, Coney Island*

Cultural epicenter

One of the most vibrant cultural hubs in the US, New York has an incredible collection of museums. Its art history biggies, such as the **Museum of Modern Art** *(see pp106–107)* and the **Metropolitan Museum of Art** *(see pp150–53)*, will captivate parents and kids alike, as will its cutting-edge centers of contemporary art, which include **PS1** *(see p221)* and the **New Museum** *(see pp74–5)*. Families can also visit a wealth of smaller museums, such as the gallery-cum-studio space at the **Children's Museum of the Arts** *(see p76)*, where kids get to explore their creative side, and the **Museum of the Moving Image** *(see pp218–19)*, which spotlights film and video arts.

Animal attractions

There is plenty to keep kids entertained in the city, from the prehistoric dinosaurs at the **American Museum of Natural History** *(see pp174–5)* to New York's zoos, one in each borough. The intimate **Central Park Zoo** *(see pp128–9)* has excellent penguin and rainforest exhibits, while the highlights at the sprawling **Bronx Zoo** *(see pp236–7)* include an amazing gorilla habitat and a monorail that runs over the Bronx River, passing Asian elephants, red pandas, and Indian rhinos. **Coney Island** *(see p214)* is home to the **New York Aquarium**

(see pp212–13), whose inhabitants include moray eels, penguins, and sea otters, as well as walruses and intelligent California sea lions.

A walk through Central Park's wooded **The Ramble** *(see p136)* reveals the sight and sounds of birds and small mammals. And on a tour of Prospect Park Lake, there is a good chance of spying green and black-crowned night herons.

Hunting the past

New York also has a rich array of places that remember, reveal, and bring history to life. Both the **Ellis Island Immigration Museum** *(see p60)* and the **Tenement Museum** *(see pp72–3)* shed light on the immigrant experience.

Right *Children viewing a majestic black leopard in the Jungle World exhibit at the Bronx Zoo*

The former occupies the building through which millions passed as they were granted entry to the US, while the latter transports visitors back in time for a glimpse of the lives these immigrants led while settling down.

Visiting the **Theodore Roosevelt Birthplace** *(see p83)*, a reconstructed brownstone in Gramercy Park, and **Wave Hill** *(see p232)* in the Bronx is a great way to learn about one of the most fascinating figures in American history. Several preserved houses afford visitors a first-hand peek at their long-ago inhabitants, including the **Edgar Allan Poe Cottage** *(see p232)* and **Lefferts Historic House** *(see p208)* in Prospect Park. Kids who want to know more about the city itself will enjoy a visit to the **Museum of the City of New York** *(see p160)*.

New York on a budget

The city has an abundance of things to do that are free or cost very little. The enormous green spaces of Central Park and **Prospect Park** *(see p208)* are filled with cultural sights and play zones alike. Both host various free walking tours year-round. A visit to Chelsea's **High Line** *(see pp86–7)* is free of charge, as is the entire gamut of New York's extensive parks system. Several museums, zoos, and gardens allow free entry on designated days or mornings. Seeing the **Statue of Liberty** *(see pp58–9)* from the Staten Island Ferry *(see p23)*, exploring architectural gems such as **Grand Central Terminal** *(see pp100–101)*, with its magnificent ceiling, and visiting the various landmarks at **Rockefeller Center** don't cost a dime, either. Come summer, free family-friendly cultural offerings abound, thanks to such events as the **SummerStage** *(see p38)* and the

Below People relaxing along a section of the High Line, an elevated public park created on an old train line

Above *The impressive entrance of Grand Central Terminal, crowned by statues of Mercury, Hercules, and Minerva*

River To River Festival *(see p40)*, whose music, theater, and dance performances are famous, and outdoor kids' film series such as River Flicks.

Green New York

The city's most popular attractions include numerous green oases, foremost among them Central Park. From the **Literary Walk** *(see p131)* to the grand plaza of **Bethesda Terrace** *(see pp134–5)*, and kid-magnets such as the carousel and the zoo, the park is a natural retreat in more ways than one. Central Park also offers rowing, ice-skating, cycling, and walking tours. In Brooklyn, Prospect Park's **Audubon Center** *(see p209)* focuses on the beauty of the park's

Above Cherry trees in blossom in the Japanese Hill-and-Pond Garden, Brooklyn Botanic Garden

diverse terrain and the wildlife that inhabits it. **Brooklyn Botanic Garden** (*see pp206–207*) and the Bronx's **New York Botanical Garden** (*see pp230–31*) offer plenty of child-oriented fun with their vast lawns, flower gardens, deep woods, and even (in the case of the former) a Japanese Hill-and-Pond Garden. The **Hudson River Park** (*see p81*) has basketball, tennis, and beach volleyball courts – all free to use – plus superb playgrounds.

New York by season

Each of New York's four seasons, from its all-too-short summer to its long winter, has its charms. Although the beginning of spring can seem indistinguishable from winter, visits to the **Union Square Greenmarket** (*see pp82–3*), where farmers sell treats such as maple syrup, honey, baby arugula, and goat cheese, and to the **High Line** (*see pp86–7*), which bursts with green plantings from April, show off the season of rebirth to great effect.

Summer is the perfect time to circumnavigate the island of Manhattan by boat, take a kayak out on the Hudson, and experience a baseball game at the **Yankee Stadium** (*see p239*). Nature-lovers can catch an Audubon Center bird-watching boat tour in **Prospect Park**.

The easygoing days of summer start to give way to crisp air and high cultural energy come the fall. Head to the **National Museum of the American Indian** (*see p60–61*) for a primer on the country's original inhabitants. It has great exhibitions, an excellent gift shop and, occasionally, music and dance shows.

Fall is also the perfect season to explore **Chinatown** (*see pp76–7*), make a visit to the **Intrepid Sea, Air & Space Museum** (*see p120*), and take a walk through the wilds of **The Ramble** in Central Park. After the hike, climb up the steps of **Belvedere Castle** (*see pp140–41*) to take in the amazing panorama from one of its three majestic lookouts.

Winter naturally involves spending more time indoors. Besides the city's wealth of museums, Queens' **New York Hall of Science** (*see pp224–5*) is not to be missed. However, a trip to **Trump Rink** (*see p130*) for proper outdoor ice-skating has the potential to delight kids for hours. In December, the tree at **Rockefeller Center** and the lavishly decorated holiday windows of the city's department stores will lend any visit some special seasonal magic.

Right Angel of the Waters sculpture on the Bethesda Terrace in Central Park

New York Through the Year

New York is packed with events all year round. Every season has its own tempo and temptations: ice-skating and expos in winter, blossoms and parades in spring. Summer sports, concerts, and boat rides make the most of the outdoors, while fall ushers in a new Broadway season. Beginning in late November, New York puts on the most glorious Thanksgiving parade and holiday displays in the nation.

Spring

Even before spring has officially begun, the city is filled with activities. As the weather turns warmer, New York's spirit blooms along with its gardens, and parades add to the festive mood.

MARCH

Prize orchids from around the world are on display at the annual **Orchid Show** *(see p229)* in the New York Botanical Garden *(see pp230–31)*.

The **Armory Show** exhibits contemporary art, and the three-week **New York International Children's Film Festival** *(see p38)* screens independent films to delight kids of all ages. Basketball fans focus on the excitement at the **Big East Championship Tournament**.

The **St Patrick's Day Parade** *(see p92)*, on 17 March, gives winter a rousing send-off with a day-long procession of musicians, marchers, and green wearin'in New York's oldest and biggest parade. The annual **Greek Independence Day Parade** (Mar/Apr) features colorful costumes, while **Macy's Flower Show** *(see p95)* turns the store into a floral wonderland.

APRIL

The annual **Sakura Matsuri Cherry Blossom Festival** *(see p201)* is a spectacle of color, with more than 200 blooming cherry trees, plus demonstrations of traditional Japanese arts. The arrival of the **Ringling Bros. and Barnum & Bailey Circus** promises thrills for all ages, while the return of baseball with the Yankees at **Yankee Stadium** *(see p239)* and Mets at Citi Field brings cheering crowds.

New York's gala **Easter Parade and Easter Bonnet Festival**, on Easter Sunday, is a chance to see paraders in their fantastic bonnets. Robert De Niro's prestigious **Tribeca Film Festival** screens more than 1,000 promising new films.

MAY

One of America's finest dance companies, the **New York City Ballet** thrills audiences with its spring shows each year. The **Ninth Avenue International Food Festival** is the city's biggest gathering of food producers from around the world.

Everyone can join in the fun at the **New York Dance Parade**, when dancers performing the samba, waltz, and Irish step dances frolic their way Downtown; this is followed by dancing in Tompkins Square Park. **Fleet Week**, during Memorial Day week, is when thousands of uniformed naval crew arrive in the city and welcome visitors to their ships for free tours.

Below left *One of the many stunning displays at the Orchid Show in New York Botanical Garden*
Below right *Asian elephants performing a balancing act in Madison Square Garden*

Summer

Summer brings free outdoor theater and concerts, craft fairs, boat rides, and dazzling Independence Day fireworks. Baseball is in full swing, nearby beaches beckon, and dragon-boat races bring a festive touch of Asia to the city.

JUNE

Culture buffs can look forward to the annual **Museum Mile Festival**, when nine museums offer free admission and a car-free Fifth Avenue is filled with music and performances. June also sees the colorful **Mermaid Parade** (see p211), which marks the unofficial start of the beach season, with floats and pirates. The **Puerto Rican Day Parade** is the city's biggest Latin celebration, a day-long party that draws millions of spectators.

The **American Crafts Festival**, held over two weekends, brings dozens of artisans to the city to display their creations. The **Lesbian and Gay Pride Day Parade** (see p79) celebrates Gay Pride Week with a rally and street fair in Greenwich Village (see pp80–81).

JULY

The high point of the Independence Day celebrations is **Macy's Fireworks Display** (see p95) on July 4, which lights up the night sky with fantastic pyrotechnics. **Midsummer Night Swing** transforms the outdoor plaza into a dance floor, with live orchestras. Free **Shakespeare in the Park** at the Delacorte Theater (see p141) in Central Park is a summer-long treat, with two productions to entertain audiences. Spectators savor great music and picnic under the stars, when Central Park hosts free **Philharmonic in the Park Concerts** featuring fireworks as an encore. The **Metropolitan Opera** also goes alfresco for a series of concerts. Their Live in HD screenings in the Lincoln Center Plaza and concerts in many city parks are treasured summer events.

AUGUST

Starting in late July, **Lincoln Center Out of Doors** (see p167) puts on three weeks of open-air performances. One of the most unusual events is the **Hong Kong Dragon Boat Festival**, at Flushing Meadows-Corona Park, which sees dragon boats race on Meadow Lake. **Harlem Week** (see p179) has entertainment and cultural events over several days.

The **US Open Tennis Championships** (see p42), which starts at the end of the month, is the year's final Grand Slam event, showcasing the world's best players.

Fall

Labor Day marks the end of the summer, but not the end of outdoor fun, as bright fall days are ideal for festivals and more parades. The Broadway season goes into high gear in fall and museums mount exciting new exhibitions.

SEPTEMBER

Over the Labor Day weekend, the **West Indian Carnival** passes through Brooklyn with one of the city's largest parades, featuring steel bands, floats, and costumes. It attracts over a million spectators. Families flock to the **Richmond County Fair**, also held on Labor Day weekend, where New York's only living-history village offers old-fashioned funfair rides and music.

Early in September, the **Feast of San Gennaro** (see p71), the annual salute to the patron saint of Naples, brings with it 11 days of parades and non-stop Italian food. The **Dumbo Arts Festival** gives this up-and-coming part of Brooklyn an opportunity to show off its arty side with open studios, installations, and street performers. The **New York Film Festival**, which runs into October, gives movie enthusiasts the chance to preview award-winning films and meet their creators.

Below left Participants in the Hong Kong Dragon Boat Festival, Flushing Meadows-Corona Park, Queens
Below right Belly dancers at the annual New York Dance Parade, which features a wide range of dancing styles

OCTOBER

This month features the delightful **St. Francis Day**, celebrated on the first Sunday of the month at the Cathedral Church of St. John the Divine (see pp176–7), when camels, peacocks, and goats line up, along with more familiar pets, for the annual Blessing of the Animals. The **Columbus Day Parade,** on the second Monday of October, salutes Italian-Americans with 35,000 participants and more than 100 bands.

Free tours of interesting buildings and sites, many of which are usually closed to the public, are the highlight of the **Open House New York Weekend**, which celebrates the city's architecture and design. Comic book fans will want to take in the **New York Comic Con**, at the Javits Center, where comics, graphic novels, anime, video games, toys, and movies are on display and for sale.

The city celebrates Halloween in style with the famous **Village Halloween Parade** (see p79) in Greenwich Village, where out-rageous costumes are the norm.

NOVEMBER

As the ice-skating season begins, rented skates are available for hire at the free **Winter Village at Bryant** Park (see p43) or the famous **Rockefeller Center Ice Rink** (see p112). A week or so later **Trump Rink** (see p130) in Central Park opens for the season. While skaters twirl outdoors, the basketball season kicks off indoors as the **New York Knicks** (see p42) go into action at Madison Square Garden. The weather turns colder in November, but that does not deter the thousands of runners who do the 26.2 mile (42.1 km) five-borough run from Staten Island to Central Park in the **New York City Marathon**.

Just for laughs, the five-day **New York Comedy Festival** brings big names in comedy to the stage. Chocoholics wait eagerly for the **Chocolate Expo in Garden City**, where chocolates, baked foods, wine, cheese, and much more, can be tasted and purchased.

The **Macy's Thanksgiving Day Parade** (see p92), on the fourth Thursday of the month, has officially begun the Yule season for over 90 years. Another much-loved tradition is the **Rockefeller Center Tree Lighting** (on the first Wed after Thanksgiving), which sets more than 30,000 lights a-glitter on a giant tree topped with a 550-lb (250-kg) Swarovski crystal star. And the season would not be complete without the aptly named **Christmas Spectacular** at Radio City Music Hall, which thrills with special effects and the high-kicking Rockettes.

From late November to December 24, holiday bazaars at Union Square, Grand Central Terminal (see pp100–101), Bryant Park (see p103), Cathedral Church of St. John, and Columbus Circle (see p169) lure shoppers with big displays of fine crafts that provide inspiration for holiday giving.

The annual **Holiday Train Show** (see p229) at the New York Botanical Garden (pp230–31) runs through January, and sends model trains whizzing through a city of New York landmarks made of bark and plant materials.

Winter

New York is a magical place at Christmas – even the stone lions at the New York Public Library don wreaths for the occasion, and shop windows become works of art. Celebrations abound in the city, and colorful ice-skaters glide in city parks with skyscrapers as a backdrop.

DECEMBER

Christmas is not the only holiday celebrated in December. The Jewish Hanukkah is marked with the lighting of the world's largest

Below left Visitor at the Holiday Train Show at the New York Botanical Garden
Below right Huge SpongeBob SquarePants balloon floating above Macy's Thanksgiving Day Parade

menorah above Fifth Avenue. The annual **Kwanzaa Festival** in late December is a time for African-American music, dance, and crafts at the American Museum of Natural History, Brooklyn Children's Museum, and other venues across the city.

Thousands gather to watch the **New Year's Eve Ball Drop** (see p116) in Times Square (see pp118–19), heralding the start of the new year.

JANUARY

Colder days do not stop the excitement in New York. Organized by El Museo del Barrio, the **Three Kings Day Parade** (see p157), on January 6, is a much-loved procession of children, with camels, sheep, and puppets, as well as adults dressed as the Three Kings. Later in the month, the **New York Boat Show**, a century-old city tradition, offers an eye-boggling display of seafaring craft, from kayaks to yachts.

FEBRUARY

The **Chinese New Year Parade** is usually held in early February, when dazzling dragons dance their way through the streets of Chinatown. Canine-lovers converge to see who will be the top dog at the **Westminster Kennel Club Dog Show** at Madison Square Garden.

The Lowdown

Spring
Armory Show www.thearmoryshow.com
Big East Championship Tournament www.bigeast.org
Easter Parade and Easter Bonnet Festival www.nycgo.com/events/easter-parade-and-easter-bonnet-festival1
Fleet Week fleetweeknewyork.com
Greek Independence Day Parade www.greekparade.org
New York City Ballet www.nycballet.com
New York Dance Parade www.danceparade.org
New York International Children's Film Festival www.gkids.com
Ninth Avenue International Food Festival www.ninthavenuefoodfestival.com
Ringling Bros. and Barnum & Bailey Circus www.ringling.com
Tribeca Film Festival www.tribecafilm.com

Summer
American Crafts Festival www.craftsatlincoln.org
Hong Kong Dragon Boat Festival www.hkdbf-ny.com
Metropolitan Opera www.metoperafamily.org
Midsummer Night Swing www.midsummernightswing.org
Museum Mile Festival www.nycgo.com/events/museum-mile-festival
Philharmonic in the Park Concerts www.nyphil.org
Puerto Rican Day Parade www.nprdpinc.org

Fall
Christmas Spectacular www.radiocity.com
Chocolate Expo in Garden City www.thechocolateexpo.com

New York City Marathon www.tcsnycmarathon.org
New York Comedy Festival www.nycomedyfestival.com
New York Comic Con www.newyorkcomiccon.com
NY Film Festival www.filmlinc.com
Open House New York Weekend www.ohny.org
Richmond County Fair www.historicrichmondtown.org
St. Francis Day www.stjohndivine.org
West Indian Carnival www.wiadca.com

Winter
Chinese New Year Parade www.chinatown-online.com
Kwanzaa Festival amnh.org/calendar/kwanzaa
New York Boat Show www.nyboatshow.com
Westminster Kennel Club Dog Show www.westminsterkennelclub.org

National and New York State holidays
New Year's Day Jan 1
Martin Luther King Day 3rd Mon in Jan
Lincoln's Birthday Feb 12
Presidents' Day (Washington's Birthday) 3rd Mon in Feb
Memorial Day last Mon in May
Independence Day Jul 4
Labor Day 1st Mon in Sep
Columbus Day 2nd Mon in Oct
Election Day 1st Tue in Nov
Veterans' Day Nov 11
Thanksgiving Day 4th Thu in Nov
Christmas Day Dec 25

Below left Chinese New Year in the neighborhood of Sunset Park, Brooklyn Chinatown
Below right New York City Marathon, one of the world's most prestigious annual long-distance running events, Fourth Avenue Brooklyn

Getting to New York

A major gateway to the US for much of the world, New York receives more than 48 million visitors a year. The city terminals can be crowded, but you will receive an efficient and friendly welcome whether arriving by air, sea, or overland. Knowing what to expect on arrival will make entry smoother, so read up on essential requirements and be ready with the necessary credentials when needed, including those for children.

US entry requirements

Citizens of 38 nations, including most European countries, do not need a visa to enter the US, but must submit the Electronic System for Travel Authorization (ESTA) form in advance. The **Transportation Security Administration** is the best source of information on security regulations.

Before landing, overseas visitors need to fill in a **Customs and Border Protection Agency** form, with their passport details, flight number, an address in the US and the value of any gifts being brought in. Visitors can carry $100 in gifts without paying tax. Photos and fingerprints of non-residents between 14 years and 79 years are taken as a security measure.

Arriving by air

John F. Kennedy (JFK) and **Newark Liberty International (EWR)**, in New Jersey, are New York's two main international airports. Both handle some domestic flights as well. The third major airport, **LaGuardia (LGA)**, serves mainly domestic flights. Most major airlines, including **British Airways, Delta, Virgin Atlantic**, and **United Airlines**, offer regular services to New York City. Rates are usually lower mid-week and lowest in the off-season (Nov–Mar), except for holiday periods.

Compare airline rates on websites such as *www.kayak.com, www. expedia.com*, or *www.orbitz.com*. Travelers from smaller European cities may be able to save by flying first to London, where several airlines compete for passengers to the US. The non-stop flight from London to New York takes about 7–8 hours. Visitors from Australia and New Zealand have no non-stop options, but must land in Los Angeles for refueling. The flight to Los Angeles is 14 hours; with lay-over, the total trip is more than 21 hours.

Airport transfers

The **New York Airport Service** operates private cars and shuttle vans between Manhattan and JFK ($15, $27 round trip per person) or LGA ($12, $21 round trip per person). **Olympia Trails Airport Express** runs express buses between Newark Airport and the Port Authority Bus Terminal, Bryant Park, and Grand Central Terminal ($16, $28 round trip per person). Taxis are available near each drop-off point. Door-to-door shared minibus service between all airports and Manhattan is provided by **Super Shuttle** or **Air Link** for about $20 per person, but these take longer. Taxis to Midtown are available from the

Below left Checking train schedules around the four-faced opal clock at Grand Central Terminal
Below right Commuter train at a platform, en route to Penn Station

airports, as are private limo services, such as **Carmel** or **Dial 7**. Ask for a van if you are carrying strollers or heavy baggage.

The **AirTrain** is inexpensive but difficult to manage with luggage. From JFK, it means a train ride from the airport to Howard Beach or Jamaica Station, from where subways A, E, J, and Z go into Manhattan.

Arriving by sea

Cunard has many sailings from England to the US, while Regent, Princess, Carnival, MSC, NCL, Crystal, and Oceania are among those cruising to and from Canada or Mexico. For cruise deals, check *www. cruisecritic.com* or *www.cruises.com*. Most cruise ships land at the main **Manhattan Cruise Terminal** or the growing secondary **Brooklyn Cruise Terminal** in Red Hook.

Arriving by rail

Amtrak is the national rail system. Trains arrive at **Penn Station**, which can be crowded. Commuter trains from upstate and Connecticut arrive at Grand Central Terminal, a much more manageable station. Book in advance online with Amtrak and check for weekly specials.

The Lowdown

US entry requirements
Customs and Border Protection Agency www.cbp.gov
Transport Security Administration www.tsa.gov

Arriving by air
Airports
JFK 718 244 4444; www.panynj.gov/airports/jfk.html
LaGuardia 718 533 3400; www.panynj.gov/airports/laguardia.html
Newark Liberty International 973 961 6000; www.panynj.gov/airports/newark-liberty.html
Airlines
British Airways www.britishairways.com
Delta www.delta.com
United Airlines www.united.com
Virgin Atlantic www.virgin-atlantic.com

Airport transfers
Air Link 212 812 9000; www.goairlinkshuttle.com
AirTrain www.panynj.gov/airports/jfk-airtrain.html; www.panynj.gov/airports/ewr-airtrain.html
Carmel Car Service 212 666 6666; www.carmellimo.com
New York Airport Service www.nyairportservice.com

Olympia Trails Airport Express 877 863 9275; www.coachusa.com/olympia
Super Shuttle 800 258 3826; www.supershuttle.com

Arriving by sea
Brooklyn Cruise Terminal Red Hook Terminal Pier #12; 347 786 1961
Manhattan Cruise Terminal 711 Twelfth Ave at West 55th St; 212 246 5450

Arriving by rail
Amtrak 800 872 7245; www.amtrak.com
Penn Station 234 West 31st St at Eighth Ave; 212 630 6401

Arriving by coach
Bolt Bus 877 265 8287; www.boltbus.com
Greyhound 800 231 2222; www.greyhound.com
Megabus 877 462 6342; www.megabus.com
Port Authority Bus Terminal 625 Eighth Ave; 212 564 8484; www.panynj.gov

Arriving by coach

Greyhound is the largest intercity US bus line, with economical services, across the country. Its newer buses are comfortable. Purchase tickets in advance online and receive them via email. In New York, all long-distance buses are headquartered at the **Port Authority Bus Terminal**, where taxis are usually available. The bargain bus lines such as **Bolt** or **Megabus** from Boston, Philadelphia, Baltimore, or Washington, DC, usually arrive near **Penn Station**.

Below left Cruise ship on Upper Bay, with the Statue of Liberty in the distant background
Below right Passengers arriving at John F. Kennedy International Airport

Getting Around New York

Thanks to the city's extensive and efficient public-transportation system, getting around New York is easy. When traveling by bus or subway, the Metropolitan Transit Authority (MTA) website's Trip Planner can provide maps and directions. Getting around Manhattan is particularly straightforward, as most of the area is laid out in a regular grid pattern. But getting a little bit lost in New York can be a bonus – every block holds interesting discoveries.

Finding your way

Manhattan streets running east-west are numbered – toward Uptown (north), numbers get higher and toward Downtown (south), they get lower. The whole width of the island is only about 12 blocks, divided by avenues running south–north. These avenues may have names instead of numbers, but they too are mostly on a grid. Fifth Avenue divides the "horizontal" streets into "East" or "West" (as in "East 40th St"). It is more challenging to get around in the city's older sections, like Greenwich Village, Chinatown, or the Financial District. The fold-out street map in the Manhattan Yellow Pages phone directory – which will probably be available from your hotel concierge – is very useful for locating street numbers in the city.

The MetroCard

You need a MetroCard to use the subway, and it is convenient on buses too (eliminating the need for exact change). Cards are sold for $1 in all subway stations by booth attendants or vending machines; booths are cash only. A single ride is $2.50. Multi-ride cards may be purchased from $5 up. Up to three children can ride free with an adult, provided they do not exceed 44 inches (112 cm) in height. Put $5 or more on your card and receive a 5 percent bonus amount on the card. Buying a seven-day Unlimited Pass for $30 can amount to substantial savings, even on shorter stays.

Using the subway

The subway is the quickest way to get around the city, but avoid rush hours, before 9:30am and 3:30–8pm, when trains are packed. Train routes are identified by a letter or number and each route also has its own color, so it is easy to follow its path on a subway map – get the children to help out. The main routes run north–south along Lexington, Eighth, Broadway/Seventh, and Sixth avenues. N and R trains travel east–west across mid-Manhattan; an east–west shuttle connects Grand Central Terminal and Times Square on 42nd Street. Signs indicate which direction trains are headed – Uptown (north) or Downtown (south), and whether they are local (making all stops) or express (with limited stops). First and last stops are posted on track signs and in train cars. Large system maps are posted in all stations and free individual maps are available from booth attendants.

Swipe MetroCards at turnstiles to enter the subway; they are not

Below left Swiping a MetroCard on a turnstile at the entance to a New York subway station
Below right An NYC Transit bus in Columbus Circle, Midtown Manhattan

needed to exit. During rush hours, the least crowded cars are at either end of the train. On weekdays, trains run every 2–5 minutes during peak times (6:30–9:30am, 3:30–8pm), and every 20 minutes between midnight and 6:30am. Services are less frequent on weekends.

Stations serving railroad and bus stations and busy stops, such as Rockefeller Center, have elevators and ramps for the disabled and strollers. However, most stations have steep steps and gaps between platform and trains. A list of accessible stations is available on the **MTA** website.

Using buses

Buses are a relaxing way to travel around the city, although slow in heavy traffic. Without a MetroCard or exact change, you can buy a Single Ride ticket for $2.75 at vending machines only (cash and cards accepted). Enter at the front of the bus and use a MetroCard or exact change at the fare box next to the driver. If you need a second bus or subway ride to complete your trip and have paid cash, you must request a transfer; subways will require another fare; you will be given a single-use MetroCard. (Note that MetroCards provide

automatic free transfers to another bus or subway.) You cannot reboard the same bus line with a transfer. "Select Bus Services" (SBS) make limited stops, and is testing a new time-saving system – tickets are purchased at boxes on the sidewalk with MetroCards or cash and passengers can then enter the bus at the front or rear.

Bus stops are marked with round blue signs on a tall post showing a picture of a bus, with route numbers displayed below. Most also have maps giving stops and schedules for each line. There are eight SBS routes along seven corridors, with a ninth route in Manhattan and an SBS corridor in Queens under planning. All Manhattan routes begin with M; B means Brooklyn, Bx means Bronx, Q signifies Queens. Electronic signs at the front of each bus indicate the route number and say "Select Bus Service" when the bus is making fewer stops. Buses do not pick up passengers between designated stops.

To request a stop, press the yellow wall strips between the bus windows. Some buses also have stop buttons on central poles. On request, the driver will call out your stop clearly. Exit from the rear door; press the yellow tape on the door and it will open automatically. Many buses run 24 hours, though

some lines do not operate late at night. Most buses run every 3–5 minutes during morning and evening rush hours, every 7–10 minutes from noon to 4:30pm and after 7pm, every 30–60 minutes from midnight to 6am. Services are reduced on weekends and holidays.

Several bus routes are good for a pleasant and inexpensive sightseeing tour of the city. Among the best sightseeing routes are the M5, which travels Downtown from the Upper West Side along Riverside Drive to Fifth Avenue, then to lower Manhattan on Broadway, before heading back Uptown along Sixth Avenue. The M1 goes Downtown along upper Fifth Avenue from Museum Mile through Midtown to the East Village, then back Uptown via Madison Avenue. The M42 crosstown bus route runs from the United Nations Headquarters past Grand Central Terminal and the New York Public Library to Times Square; this is a two-way street, so you can travel in either direction.

DISABLED ACCESS

All buses have ramp lifts for wheelchair or walker boarding and exit. When the passenger boards, the driver will help to secure wheelchairs and will ask for the stop required.

Below left Street signs at an intersection of routes through the city
Below right Commuters at the Port Authority Bus Terminal subway station

Drivers will also help disabled people to exit the bus at the requested stop. Disabled people pay a reduced fare, but must first apply for a card.

Using taxis

New York taxis, or cabs, are easily identified by their yellow color and distinctive logo. They are convenient, but can be costly, especially when traffic is heavy and the meter keeps ticking. Always use the metered taxis licenced by the city – check the **NYC.gov** website. If you hail a so-called "gypsy cab" – an unlicenced cab – you may end up paying a hefty bill at the end of the trip.

Taxis with their top sign illuminated can be hailed anywhere in the city and will pull up to the curb. No light means the cab is taken; "off-duty" lights mean the cab is not available. Cabs tend to congregate outside hotels and at train and bus stations. When hotel doormen hail a cab for you, a $1 tip is customary.

Taxis accommodate up to four passengers for one fare. The meter begins at $2.50 and increases $0.50 every fifth of a mile (third of a kilometer). A $1 surcharge is added to the meter Monday–Friday, 4–8pm, and a $0.50 surcharge from 8pm to 6am. Tolls are extra, and like surcharges, are added to the fare. All licenced taxis accept both cash and credit cards. There is no charge for luggage. A tip of 10–20 percent at the end of a trip is standard. Limousine services such as **Carmel** and **Dial 7** (see p19) can also provide a car and driver to chauffeur you around town, with stops wherever you choose. For Carmel, the hourly charge within Manhattan is $40 with a minimum of 2 hours. For Dial 7, the charge is $45.

Walking

Given heavy New York traffic, walking is sometimes the quickest way to get around. Cross only at corners and obey the "walk" and "stop" electronic signs. To gauge distances, 20 north–south city blocks equal about 1 mile (1.6 km). Each crosstown (east–west) block is two to three times longer than north–south blocks, so figure 6–10 blocks per mile (1.6 km).

Walking the sidewalks can be hard on the feet – and little legs tire quickly – so be sure to bring comfortable shoes. The city has many places to rest weary legs. Space near both Times Square and Herald Square has been set aside to provide seating areas, and there are plenty of seats around the Lincoln Center as well. Landscaped "vest-pocket" parks in Midtown, such as Paley Park on 53rd Street and Greenacre Park between Second and Third avenues, are also welcome oases, as is Bryant Park. Many of the big office towers on Sixth Avenue also have plazas with seating where you can rest for a spell.

Driving

Driving is the least efficient way to get around New York. Drivers are aggressive, traffic is heavy, street parking is scant (and parking tickets punitive), gas stations are few, and commercial parking lots and garages are extremely expensive. Those lucky enough to find a parking space will need quarters for the meter. Rates are $1–3.50 per hour depending on which part of New York you are in. Meters can be paid with quarters, dollar coins, or NYC Parking Cards. Parking limits vary from 1–12 hours. Meters do not have to be paid on Sunday. For more specific information, call the **Department of Transportation (DOT)**. If a car is truly essential, rentals from major companies, such as Hertz, Avis, and National, are available at all airports and numerous locations in the city.

In order to rent a car, you must be at least 18, have a valid international driver's license, and a

Below left New York's distinctive cheery yellow taxis, driving past Times Square
Below right A ferry docking at the Staten Island Ferry Terminal

major credit card. Expect a surcharge for drivers under 25. Be sure you are properly insured for both collision and personal liability; international visitors can buy insurance from the rental company.

Cycling

The number of bicycle lanes on New York's streets is increasing, but it takes a brave soul to pedal beside heavy traffic, especially with children in tow. Recreational cycle paths in Central Park and along the East and Hudson rivers are more suitable for families. Rent bikes at **Central Park Bicycle Shop** or **Bike Rental NYC**.

Ferries and water taxis

The 50-minute round trip on the **Staten Island Ferry**, between Whitehall Street in Lower Manhattan and St. George, Staten Island, is the best free outing in town, providing great views of Manhattan's skyline, the Statue of Liberty, and Ellis Island. No tickets are required; just show up at the Ferry Terminal and board the next boat. Governors Island's *(see p45)* free ferries are another option.

New York Water Taxi offers free cruises at weekends ($5 on weekdays). These are designed to take shoppers to the Ikea store in Red Hook, Brooklyn, and give visitors a chance to explore a new area. The hop-on, hop-off cruise is $31 per adult and $19 for kids between ages 3–12, and includes the NYWT Express hop-on, hop-off bus. The 90-minute boat ride allows you to get off at any stop and get back on later. Order tickets online, by phone, or buy them on board. Water Taxi also runs commuter routes to Brooklyn, Queens and from Downtown to stops along the East River on a set schedule.

Sightseeing tours

Hop-on, hop-off bus tours allow visitors to see a lot of the city. The routes cover Uptown, Downtown, Harlem, and Brooklyn. You can get off to explore at will. **Gray Line** and **City Sights** are among the leading operators: consult their websites or get a guide to departure points when you buy tickets. Tickets are valid for 48 hours. The Gray Line fare for adults is $54, children is $44, with a $5 discount for those who book online. The City Sights fare for adults is $49, and children is $39.

Neighborhood walking tours are another option, as long as kids are still in strollers or old enough to enjoy a walk. Among the goups offering tours are the **Municipal Art Society** and **Big Onion Tours**.

The Lowdown

Using the subway
Metropolitan Transit Authority (MTA) 511; www.mta.info
Commuter Lines
Long Island Railroad 718 217 5477; www.mta.info/lirr
Metro North 212 532 4900; www.mta.info/mnr
New Jersey Transit 973 275 5555; www.njtransit.com

Using buses
web.mta.info/nyct/bus/howto_bus.htm

Using taxis
311; www.nyc.gov/taxi

Driving
Department of Transportation (DOT) www.nyc.gov/dot

Cycling
Bike Rental NYC 40 West 55th St, 10019; 917 520 2066; www.bikerentalsnyc.com
Central Park Bicycle Shop www.centralparkbicycleshop.com

Ferries and water taxis
New York Water Taxi www.nywatertaxi.com
Staten Island Ferry www.siferry.com

Sightseeing tours
Big Onion Tours 888 606 9255; www.bigonion.com
City Sights 212 812 2700; www.citysightsny.com
Gray Line 212 445 0848; www.newyorksightseeing.com
Municipal Art Society 212 935 3960; www.mas.org

Below left Cycling past colorful foliage in Central Park, Upper West Side
Below right Visitors aboard a Gray Line sightseeing bus, taking pictures

Practical Information

As one of the world's major cities, New York has everything a traveler might need in the way of health facilities, and it offers all modern conveniences, including Wi-Fi, cell-phone connections, and ATMs. Visitors from other countries should be aware, however, that travel insurance is a wise investment. Also be aware that even though the city is now among the safest in the US, a few common-sense precautions are still in order.

Insurance

The high cost of medical care for non-residents in the US, and the difficulties faced in the event of air-travel delays or lost luggage, mean that travel insurance is essential. It is best to buy valid coverage before you travel – your insurance company or travel agent can help you with this and should be able to recommend a suitable policy for your trip. The most important features to look for in an insurance policy are emergency medical and dental care, trip cancellation coverage, and cover for loss of baggage and travel documents. Transportation back home in case of an emergency is another option to consider. If you have coverage for loss of personal property at home, check to see whether it is valid when you travel abroad.

Health

Be sure to pack any prescription medications in your hand baggage and keep medications in their original containers with pharmacy labels so that they will pass easily through airport security. Notify security officials about any special items, such as supplies for diabetics. Unused syringes will be allowed when accompanied by insulin or other injectable prescription medication. Bring medicines for headache, allergies, or stomach upset, as well as sunscreen and hats.

If you need medical assistance while in New York, hotels can usually recommend a doctor, or you can use a service such as **New York Doctor on Call** or **Housecall MD NY**. Be prepared for hefty fees, and note that Housecall MD NY doctors only accept credit cards. Doctor on Call accepts both cash and credit cards.

MEDICAL EMERGENCIES

The locations of hospital emergency rooms can be found in the yellow pages of the NY telephone book. The main Midtown hospitals are **NYU**, **Beth Israel**, and **Roosevelt Hospital**. On the Upper East Side are **Mount Sinai**, **Lenox Hill**, and **NewYork-Presbyterian/Weill Cornell Medical Center**. Pharmacy locations are listed by neighborhood on the map pages in this book. If an ambulance is needed, dial **911**.

FOOD ALLERGIES

Wheat, milk, and butter are staples in American cooking, so be careful if you have special dietary needs. Many restaurants can make vegetarian and gluten-free dishes. If a family member has a nut allergy, do not forget to mention it in advance and keep emergency medication to hand.

Below left A 24-hour pharmacy in New York City
Below right A United States passport, easily identifiable by its blue color and golden, embossed logo

Personal safety

Although New York has become one of America's safest cities, it pays to be alert, especially to pickpockets. Keep your wallet safe in an inside pocket, never in a back pocket. If you are carrying a child, use a cross-body bag; if not, carry your bag in the crook of your elbow, not slung over your shoulder.

Deposit passports in the hotel safe and keep one credit card and a little cash in the safe as well. Laptops can also go into safes. If in doubt about whether to visit a particular neighborhood at night, check with the hotel concierge or clerk before venturing out. If handing luggage over to hotel staff, be sure to get a receipt for it. While out and about, refrain from wearing flashy jewelry or carrying expensive gadgets that might attract muggers.

Call 911 to reach the police or to summon help if you are hurt. If valuables are lost or stolen, get a copy of the police report for your insurance claim at home.

LOST AND FOUND

Grand Central Terminal and Penn Station have lost-and-found rooms. If you leave property on a bus, subway, or taxi, call **311** to report the loss to the taxi commission or the transit authority.

Money

For changing foreign currency into US dollars, bureaus such as **Travelex** can be found at every city airport as well as in Midtown. Most bank ATMs are part of the worldwide Plus or Cirrus network. ATMs usually give the best exchange rates. Bank machines and almost all businesses and restaurants accept popular credit cards, such as MasterCard, Visa, and American Express, although getting cash with a credit card means paying interest fees. To guard against crime, use an ATM inside the bank, rather than machines accessed from the street.

CURRENCY

The basic unit is the dollar, which equals 100 cents. Coins come in 1 cent (penny), 5 cent (nickel), 10 cent (dime), and 25 cent (quarter) denominations; each is a different size and thus easy to tell apart. There is a $1 coin, but it is rarely used. The most common bills are $1, $5, $10, and $20, although $50, $100, and larger denominations exist.

CREDIT CARDS AND TRAVELER'S CHECKS

Major credit and debit cards are widely accepted throughout the US. It is best to use a credit card for expensive purchases, so that you have recourse in case of a problem and also to avoid carrying large sums of cash. Traveler's checks are slowly being replaced by prepaid reloadable travel cards. You pay for these in advance in a denomination of your choice, then draw on the funds when you use the card. There is a fee for this service. Travel cards are issued by major card companies, such as Visa or MasterCard, and are as easily used as any other credit card. They are protected by use of a PIN and/or signature.

Opening hours

Business hours are usually 9am–5pm. Almost all shops in the city open at 10am; smaller shops may close at 6 or 7pm, but department stores stay open till 8:30 or 9:30pm. However, Sunday opening hours are generally from 11am to 6 or 7pm. Banks are generally open 8am–3pm on weekdays, but many stay open later. Saturday hours are usually 9am–3pm.

Visitor information

NYC & Company, the city's official tourist office, has four main visitor centers: at Macy's Herald Square, City Hall, Chinatown, and South Street Seaport.

Below left If buying refreshments from a street vendor in the city, be careful if you have any food allergies
Below right The patch on a New York City Police Department uniform, depicting the department logo

Communications

Dial 1 before making any phone call in New York, even a local one. For example, to make a call within New York, dial 1-212 plus the number. Dial 0 to reach an operator if assistance is needed. To obtain a phone number, dial 411 – but note that there is a fee for this service. Toll-free calls are prefixed by 800, 866, 877, or 888, and you must still begin by dialing 1. To call an overseas number, dial 011, plus the country code, city area code, and number.

CELL PHONES AND INTERNET

Most modern phones are compatible with US services, although you may incur roaming charges, which can be quite high. If your present phone is incompatible with the US system, you may still be able to use it by changing the SIM card. Check with your service provider at home before you leave. It is possible to rent phones from firms such as **Cellhire**. You can also save money by buying one of the prepaid cards that are available at most news-stands; the per-minute rate with these cards is less than that charged by most service providers. Card rates vary, so shop around a bit.

Most hotels offer Internet access and/or Wi-Fi connections, some free, others for a fee. Ask before you book, as fees can be as high as $10 or more per day. day. Free Wi-Fi is available in 20 parks throughout the five boroughs of New York City. A number of Manhattan subway stations also have free Wi-Fi. Visit *www.nycgo.com/articles/wifi-in-nyc* for Wi-Fi maps. In Chelsea, the Google and Chelsea Improvement Company provides free Wi-Fi throughout the neighborhood via CICFreeWiFi.

POSTAL SERVICE

Many hotels sell stamps, and will mail your cards and postcards. Otherwise, you can head for a Midtown post office. The **Main post office** is open 24 hours.

Media

The New York Times is the major daily newspaper in the city, and covers international as well as local news. The newspaper's Friday edition has extensive entertainment listings, including choices for families. The weekly **Time Out New York** magazine gives full coverage of what is happening in the city. **Village Voice**, a weekly alternative newspaper, offers entertainment and news geared to young adults. The three major TV networks are CBS, NBC, and ABC. The two main cable-news outlets are CNN and Fox. Kids will enjoy Nickelodeon, Disney, and the Cartoon Network.

Disabled facilities

All city buses are accessible, as are most restaurants, but only a few major subway stops provide elevators. Most blocks have curb cuts at corners to accommodate wheelchairs, walkers, and buggies or strollers. Disabled travelers can obtain details about special facilities from the **Mayor's Office for People with Disabilities**.

Restrooms

City parks and playgrounds have restrooms, but otherwise public restrooms are not common in New York. Find restrooms at department stores, hotels, train and bus stations, the Time Warner Center, Starbucks, McDonald's, and Barnes & Noble bookstores around town.

Electricity

The standard US electric current is 110 volts. You will need an adapter for European appliances, which run on 220–240 volts.

Below left A shopper browsing at a well-stocked bookstore in the city Below center Distinctive blue letterboxes with the United States Postal Service logo Below right Free Wi-Fi acess is often available at coffee shops in the city

The Lowdown

Health
New York Doctor on Call 212 737 3136; www.doctorcallny.com
Housecall MD NY 877 636 3996; www.housecallmdny.com

Medical emergencies
Mount Sinai Beth Israel First Ave at 16th St, 10003; 212 420 2847
Lenox Hill 100 East 77th St near Lexington Ave, 10075; 212 434 3030
Mount Sinai Madison Ave & 101st St, 10029; 212 241 6639
NewYork-Presbyterian/Weill Cornell Medical Center 525 East 68th St at York Ave, 10065; 212 746 5026
NYU 570 First Ave at 33rd St, 10016; 212 263 5550
Mount Sinai Roosevelt 1000 Tenth Ave at 59th St, 10019; 212 523 4000

Personal safety
Lost and Found on Public Transport 511
Police, Ambulance, Fire 911

Money
Travelex 1271 Broadway at 32nd St, 10001; 212 679 4365.
1578 Broadway at 47th St, 10036; 212 265 6063; www.travelex.com

Visitor information
NYC & Company 810 Seventh Ave, 10019; 212 484 1200; www.nycgo.com
Times Square Alliance 1560 Broadway, 46th St & 47th St, 10036; 212 768 1560; www.timessquarenyc.org

Cell phones
Cellhire 877 244 7242; www.cellhire.com

Postal service
Main post office 421 Eighth Ave at 33rd St, 10001; 212 330 3296

Media
The New York Times www.nytimes.com
Time Out New York www.timeout.com/newyork
Village Voice www.villagevoice.com

Disabled facilities
Mayor's Office for People with Disabilities 100 Gold St, 2nd Floor, 10038; 212 788 2830; www.nyc.gov/html/mopd/home.html

Time
New York is on Eastern Standard Time, 5 hours behind GMT (UK time) and 3 hours ahead of PST (California time). Daylight Saving Time moves the clock forward 1 hour from spring to late fall.

Etiquette
Children are welcomed in most places in the city. Everyone from hotel clerks to bus drivers usually has a friendly smile for young visitors, but it is up to parents to ensure that the welcome remains warm by preparing children in advance to be polite and respectful. If loud crying or noisy squabbles occur in public places, especially in restaurants, parents should take their kids outside until they calm down.

Tipping
Visitors from countries where tipping is not customary should be aware that tips for service personnel are expected in the US. The usual amount is 15–20 percent for waiters and taxi drivers, as well as barbers or hairstylists. Room-service tips can often be added to the bill. Hotel bellhops should receive around $1 per bag, maids $1–2 per day, and coat checks $1 per garment. And while it is not generally required, when waiters or others go out of their way to be helpful with children, a small extra tip is always appreciated.

Below A family enjoying a meal in a New York restaurant, one of the many in the city that caters for, and welcomes, families with children

Where to Stay

There is a wide range of accommodation choices in New York. Many lodgings offer special welcome treats for children and the numerous all-suite properties afford extra space for families. Even "budget" places can cost more than $200 a night, but usually provide all basic facilities, including a TV and Internet access. The listings on pages 240–49 are organized by area, corresponding with the sightseeing section of this guide.

Where to look

Accommodation options are available in every neighborhood of the city, but some areas have special appeal for visitors. Since theater is a major attraction, a large number of hotels are located in the Times Square Theater District, where there are many moderately priced choices. But this is a busy area, and with small children in tow, the Upper East Side and Upper West Side, while less convenient, may appeal for their calm and proximity to parks. They also offer less expensive restaurants and cafés, which are typically more casual than those in Midtown and quite used to serving children.

To save money, choose a hotel in the Financial District on weekends, using public transportation to get to Midtown. Geared mainly to business travelers, hotels here often attract guests on weekends by offering special rates. Here, kids also have access to the parks along the river, where they can run around. Business hotels in Midtown also offer lower rates on weekends.

Midtown also has some of the most exclusive hotels in the city, and for those who can afford the tab, many of these places have special amenities for children, such as mini-bathrobes and slippers.

The Gramercy and Chelsea areas, just below Midtown, are convenient places to stay, but not all the hotels here are of a high standard. Those keen to explore the city's trendier neighborhoods should check out the options on the Lower East Side.

Discounts & extra costs

It may be worth donning a winter coat and coming to New York in the off-season, since by far the best hotel rates are found from January through March (excluding the holiday period). Check with discount booking sites, where rates are lower than those listed by hotels. However, it's worth consulting hotel websites for special packages and discounts.

When calculating the cost of hotels, do not forget about the hefty room tax in New York. City, state, and other taxes add up to 14.75 percent, plus a $3.50 per night occupancy fee. The tip for help with luggage is $1 per bag and $1–2 per night for the maid.

Family rooms and suites may have two full-size beds or one full-size bed and one sofa bed. Some hotels specify that children sharing must be under 12 (sometimes under 17); there may be an added fee for older children or for the use of a cot. Choosing hotels

Below left *Hilton Times Square, located on the famous 42nd Street, close to Broadway*
Below right *Retro comfort at TriBeCa Smyth Hotel's vintage-style bar, with its leather-upholstered sofas*

that include free breakfast, Wi-Fi or Internet access, and cooking facilities, will help the budget considerably, as will using a cell phone instead of the room phone. For information on using a cell phone and finding free Internet access, see page 26.

Hotels

Extra space and cooking facilities are two important considerations when choosing a family hotel in New York. Many hotels do provide handy microwaves and small refrigerators, even if they are not equipped with full kitchens. This is a money-saving bonus, allowing for inexpensive breakfasts and snacks in the room. Also check the availability of cots or cribs, and whether there is a charge for them; if children's menus are offered; and proximity to a park or playground. Most large hotels have a list of reliable babysitters, but it is best to check in advance. Opt for a hotel with an indoor swimming pool, if it fits the budget, as pools are a great outlet for kids, regardless of the weather. Families with cars should consider Skyline Hotel (see p245), which offers parking at $10 per night, or hotels in Brooklyn and Long Island City with lower garage rates.

Apartments

An unhosted, furnished apartment is often less expensive than a hotel room, and provides more space. These might be properties with absent owners, or apartments that are set up for this purpose. Apartments have full kitchens and washing machines, but generally no maid service. Available all over the city, they range from studios to three-bedroom properties. Book through listing agencies, such as **Abode Apartment Rentals** or **Manhattan Getaways**.

Bed & breakfast

New York has only a few bed-and-breakfast establishments, but B&B is available in hosted city apartments. These give a true flavor of the city, but may not allow much privacy and can be tight quarters for young children, so be sure to specify your needs. These can be booked through websites listed on the **Bed and Breakfast Network**.

House-swapping

Many families report success with house-swaps. If you live in Europe, for example, a New York family might be happy to swap their home for yours, saving each of

The Lowdown

Hotel discounts
www.expedia.com, www.travelocity.com, www.quikbook.com, www.hotels.com, www.getaroom.com

Apartments
Abode Apartment Rentals 212 472 2000; www.abodenyc.com; Manhattan Getaways 212 956 2010; www.manhattangetaways.com

Bed & breakfast
Bed and Breakfast Network 800 462 2632; www.bedandbreakfast.com/manhattan-new-york.html

House-swapping
Home Exchange www.homeexchange.com
Home Link www.homelink.org/usa

you a considerable amount of money. Swaps are done through specialized agencies, such as **Home Exchange** and **Home Link**. For a small monthly fee, prospective swappers sign up as members and list their homes. Members can scan listings for the places they want to go, click on likely properties, and send a privacy-protected email directly to the owner. It is a good idea to exchange emails, talk on the phone, ask questions, and trade home photos before signing an agreement.

Below left Modern and stylish Room Mate Grace Hotel, located in Times Square
Below right Visitors in the lobby of the Mandarin Oriental Hotel

Where to Eat

The quality of restaurants in New York is high, but what really sets the city's culinary landscape apart is its incredible diversity. Nearly every country on the planet is represented here. From artisanal ice cream to light-as-a-feather Vietnamese fare, New York cooks and chefs have something for everyone, including young kids. The price categories in this guide allow for a two-course lunch for a family of four, excluding wine but including soft drinks.

Eating out

Most restaurants are open for lunch, dinner, and in between, and there are plenty of 24-hour delis and diners, too. Typically, lunch is served from 11:30am or noon till 2:30 or 3pm – if the place closes before dinner – and dinner from 5:30 or 6pm till 10pm, 11pm, or midnight.

Reservations aren't usually needed for lunch or at budget restaurants, but dinner at a brand-new or popular spot usually requires one. Phoning to book a table is the easiest option, but the online site www.opentable. com is accessible 24/7 and often has exclusive seating options.

Eating out in New York is not cheap. Diners and small Asian or Middle Eastern spots are typically the least expensive eat-in options. Rock-bottom options include street-vendor fare (see p32) and pizza slices. You can peruse menus beforehand at www.menupages. com. If using a stroller, ask ahead about stroller policy, as not all places welcome them. The city's smoking ban is enforced at virtually all restaurants, cafés, and even bars. As is customary anywhere in the US, tipping is considered mandatory at any non-self-service eatery (see p27). The minimum acceptable tip is 15 percent, and the standard tip for good service is 20 percent.

Breakfast & brunch

Delis, especially in Midtown, often have a counter serving up eggs, bagels, sandwiches, and coffee, plus seat-yourself tables and chairs, making them a quick and inexpensive option. Chains such as **Au Bon Pain**, **Le Pain Quotidien** (see p121), and **Sarabeth's Kitchen** specialize in baked goods, including croissants and muffins. New Yorkers prefer the all-American diner, which got its name from dining cars on trains. Here, breakfast staples such as cereal, fruit, French toast, pancakes, and omelets are often available 24/7 and are made to order. Some of the more family-friendly diners in town are **Bubby's**, **Galaxy Diner**, **Tom's Restaurant**, and the **Bel Aire Diner**.

On weekends, many restaurants that don't serve breakfast during the week open for brunch – typically served between 10am and 4pm. Brunches can be found at **Clinton Street Baking Company**, **Dublin 6**, **Joe Allen**, and **Buttermilk Channel**, among many other choice spots.

Southern/soul food

Soul food, which originated in the US south among African-Americans, and Southern cuisine overlap. Both

Below left Facade of the Greek Taverna Kyclades in Astoria, Queens
Below right Colorful interior of La Lucha, a Mexican restaurant in the East Village

involve special methods of cooking, such as using a barbecue or pit smoker, and have specialty dishes, such as cornbread, sweet potatoes, catfish, pulled pork, and collard greens. Among the best soul-food eateries are **Amy Ruth's** (see p181), **Dinosaur Bar-B-Que** (see p182), **Sylvia's**, **Pies 'n' Thighs** and **Red Rooster Harlem**.

New American

A food genre that has taken off in the city is New American – inventive meals made with seasonal, locally sourced ingredients with an emphasis on freshness, flavor, and thoughtful food pairings. Among the more family-friendly exponents are **Tenth Avenue Cookshop** and **The Farm on Adderley**.

Mexican & pan-Latin

New York has some exceptional family-friendly Mexican restaurants. The small plates and tacos at **La Lucha** are terrific. **Maya** serves delicious food and the lauded **Tortillería Nixtamal** (see p226) makes its own tortillas from scratch. The city is home to an array of Central and South American peoples and their cuisines have enhanced the restaurant scene.

Café Cortadito, a Cuban restaurant with a fun atmosphere and Latin music, offers dishes such as churrasco, shrimp in creole sauce, and sweet plantains. Kids will love **Empanada Mama**, with its huge array of super- fresh *empanadas* filled with the likes of mushrooms, cheese, and shrimp.

Greek

Some of the city's finest Greek restaurants can be found in Astoria, Queens. Cross the East River for dinner at **Ovelia** or **Taverna Kyclades**, whose specialty is grilled seafood. Other options include the Flatiron District's **Periyali** and Midtown's **Molyvos**.

Italian

Terrific pasta can be found at **Cacio e Pepe** (see p82) and **Max**, while **Gennaro** has great food at decent prices. For excellent antipasti and wonderful pizza, **Adrienne's Pizza Bar** (see p59) is unbeatable.

Spanish

New Yorkers love Spanish tapas, and the craze shows no signs of abating. **Tía Pol**, a tiny Basque spot, has a tasty array of traditional small

KIDS' CORNER

Do not miss...
1 Egg cream is an invention from the 19th century, originally enjoyed by immigrants on the Lower East Side. It's a kind of fizzy milkshake made with seltzer, chocolate syrup, and milk.
2 The City Bakery's hot chocolate is legendary. It's thick, like a liquid bar of chocolate, and comes topped with a marshmallow if you wish.
3 Once upon a time, hamburgers came in one size – but that was before sliders. Sliders are mini burgers in a tiny soft bun. Now they come in many forms, with crab cakes, veggie burgers, and even lobster inside.
4 Track down Doughnut Plant for a Tres Leches doughnut. It has a crispy sugar layer outside and fluffy cake inside, with soft cream baked inside it, rather than added after baking.

BITE INTO SOUP!
Chinese soup dumplings are not immersed in soup. Instead, the soup is inside and it squirts out when you bite into them.

The more the merrier
There are so many types of delicious ice cream to try in New York. Frozen custard is a thick, creamy ice cream made with egg yolks. Gelato is Italian-style ice cream that's usually made without eggs or added cream. Both are usually heavier, with less air added to them than regular American-style ice cream.

Below Casual outdoor seating at Bubby's, a popular diner in New York's Tribeca neighborhood

plates to try, as does **Boqueria**. **Socarrat Paella Bar** offers inventive meat, seafood, and vegetarian *paella* (rice dishes) and *fideuà* (Spanish noodle dishes).

Ethiopian

Children love food that they can eat with their hands. Ethiopian cuisine fits the bill: *injera* (a spongy bread) is used to scoop up *wat* (vegetable or meat stew). **Meskerem**, **Awash**, and **Meskel** won't disappoint.

Indian

Curry Hill, near Lexington Avenue, and East 6th Street in the East Village, have the highest concentration of Indian restaurants in the city. **Saravanaas** and **Tiffin Wallah** have excellent all-vegetarian options. **Brick Lane Curry House** is a great spot for authentic curry dishes.

Chinese

Head to Chinatown for some of the city's best Chinese eateries. **Golden Unicorn** and **Dim Sum Go Go** are terrific for lengthy, family-friendly dim sum sessions, while **Joe's Shanghai** is famous for its soup-filled dumplings. Seafood is the specialty at **Oriental Garden**,

where the fried shrimp balls, oysters served in a clay pot, and lobster are all superb.

Thai

Thai food is very popular in New York. **Republic** *(see p83)* has a big selection of noodle soups and other traditional Thai fare. **Thai Market** excels at appetizers and classic curries. The most acclaimed Thai spot in the city is **Sripraphai**, which is great for authentic flavors.

Vietnamese

While fans of Vietnam's light, refined cuisine are plentiful, there aren't many restaurants in the city. Among the best are **Nha Trang** *(see p77)* and **Omai**. Both are known for their noodle soups and beef, seafood, and vegetable entrées.

Japanese

Japanese fare of all varieties abounds in the city. For noodles, try **Ajisen Noodle** for ramen and **Cocoron** for soba. For sushi, seek out **Japonica** *(see p83)* or **Jewel Bako**. Kids love the ramen noodles and skewers at **Hana Michi** near Herald Square, and **Naruto Ramen** *(see p152)* near Central Park.

Street food

Some of the tastiest and cheapest food is offered by street vendors. **Calexico** offers burritos, tacos, and grilled corn. **Alan's Falafel** serves up platters of hummus and baba ghanoush. **N.Y. Dosas** offers vegetarian *dosas* (South-Indian crêpes) in several varieties. The roving **Treats Truck**, with assorted brownies and cookies, and the **Van Leeuwen Ice Cream Truck** are ideal for a delicious pick-me-up.

Chocolatiers, ice-cream shops & bakeries

Independent shops with excellent made-in-New-York chocolates may not be plentiful, but are worth tracking down. The confections at **Jacques Torres** *(see p198)*, **Chocolate Bar**, **Li-Lac**, and **Kee's Chocolates** make a perfect treat.

The city has some outstanding ice-cream and *gelato* (soft ice cream) shops, among them **Cones**, **Il Laboratorio del Gelato** *(see p74)*, **Chinatown Ice Cream Factory**, and **L'Arte del Gelato**. For sweet shops, try **Doughnut Plant** *(see p74)*, **Buttercup Bake Shop**, and **Two Little Red Hens** for baked treats, and **Patisserie Claude** for handcrafted French pastries.

Below left A family enjoying a variety of seafood at a Chinese restaurant in Brooklyn
Below right A food vendor near the Grand Army Plaza serving waffles

The Lowdown

Breakfast & brunch
Au Bon Pain www.aubonpain.com
Bel Aire Diner www.orderbelairediner.com
Bubby's www.bubbys.com
Buttermilk Channel www.buttermilkchannelnyc.com
Clinton Street Baking Company www.clintonstreetbaking.com
Dublin 6 www.dublin6nyc.com
Galaxy Diner 665 Ninth Ave at 46th St, 10036; 212 586 4885
Joe Allen www.joeallenrestaurant.com
Sarabeth's Kitchen www.sarabeth.com
Tom's Restaurant www.tomsrestaurant.net

Southern/soul food
Pies 'n' Thighs www.piesnthighs.com
Red Rooster Harlem www.redroosterharlem.com
Sylvia's www.sylviasrestaurant.com

New American
The Farm on Adderley www.thefarmonadderley.com
Tenth Avenue Cookshop www.cookshopny.com

Mexican & pan-Latin
Café Cortadito www.cafecortadito.com
Empanada Mama www.empmamanyc.com
La Lucha www.laluchanyc.com
Maya www.richardsandoval.com/mayany/

Greek
Molyvos www.molyvos.com
Ovelia www.ovelia-nyc.com
Periyali www.periyali.com

Taverna Kyclades www.tavernakyclades.com

Italian
Gennaro www.gennaronyc.com
Max www.max-ny.com

Spanish
Boqueria www.boquerianyc.com
Socarrat Paella Bar www.socarratpaellabar.com
Tía Pol www.tiapol.com

Ethiopian
Awash www.awashny.com
Meskel 199 East 3rd St, 10009; 212 254 2411
Meskerem 124 MacDougal St, 10012; 212 777 8111

Indian
Brick Lane Curry House www.bricklanecurryhouse.com
Saravanaas 81 Lexington Ave, 10016; 212 679 0204
Tiffin Wallah 127 East 28th St, 10016; 212 685 7301

Chinese
Dim Sum Go Go 5 East Broadway, 10038; 212 732 0797
Golden Unicorn www.goldenunicornrestaurant.com
Joe's Shanghai www.joeshanghairestaurants.com
Oriental Garden www.orientalgardenny.com

Thai
Sripraphai www.sripraphairestaurant.com
Thai Market www.thaimarketny.net

Vietnamese
Omai www.omainyc.com

Japanese
Ajisen Noodle www.ajisenusa.com
Cocoron 61 Delancey St, 10002; 212 925 5220; www.cocoron-soba.com
Hana Michi www.hanamichinyc.com
Jewel Bako 239 East 5th St, 10003; 212 979 1012

Street food
Alan's Falafel 140 Broadway, between Cedar St & Liberty St, 10005
Calexico www.calexico.net
N.Y. Dosas 50 Washington Square South, 10014; 917 710 2092
Treats Truck www.treatstruck.com
Van Leeuwen Ice Cream Truck www.vanleeuwenicecream.com

Chocolatiers, ice-cream shops & bakeries
Buttercup Bake Shop www.buttercupbakeshop.com
Chinatown Ice Cream Factory www.chinatownicecreamfactory.com
Chocolate Bar www.chocolatebarnyc.com
The City Bakery www.thecitybakery.com
Cones 272 Bleecker St, 10014; 212 414 1795
Kee's Chocolates www.keeschocolates.com
L'Arte del Gelato www.lartedelgelato.com
Li-Lac www.li-lacchocolates.com
Patisserie Claude 187 West 4th St, 10014; 212 255 5911
Two Little Red Hens www.twolittleredhens.com

Below left Burger and French fries, Bill's Bar and Burger restaurant
Below right Jacques Torres, one of city's best chocolate shops, also serves ice cream

Shopping

New York is a shopper's paradise, full of places that cater to children of all ages, from babies to tweens. Small clothing boutiques, toy stores, art emporiums, and even department stores beckon with unusual, hip, and sometimes unique items. While most kids' shops are found in Manhattan, New York's other packed-with-families borough, Brooklyn, has excellent options too, especially along Smith Street.

Opening hours

Most stores are open seven days a week. Typical department store hours are 10am to 7 or 8pm Monday through Saturday, and noon to 6 or 7pm on Sunday. The opening times of independent shops vary, but most are open from 10 or 11am to 6 or 7pm during the week, with more limited hours on weekends, especially Sunday.

Taxes

The sales tax structure in New York fluctuates constantly, and when it comes to buying clothing, can be confusing even for residents when the next new policy comes along. Non-clothing purchases, including meals, handbags, electronics, and the like, are taxed at 8.875 percent, and clothing and footwear items below $110 are tax-free. For $110 and above, there is 4.5 percent New York City sales tax and 4 percent New York state sales tax.

Returns

Most goods purchased at a department or chain store, including clothing, toys, and outdoor gear, can be returned for a refund within a certain period, provided they have not been used and buyers still have the receipt. Independent stores often offer full refunds as well. However, some shops only offer store credit or exchanges.

Sales

Nearly every clothing shop offers discounts of about 25–40 percent on past-season items in January and June. Higher discounts (50–70 percent off) follow in July, August, February, and March, but the selection is not as extensive. Stores also offers hugely discounted prices on many items on Black Friday (the day after Thanksgiving). Toy stores rarely have large-scale sales, but may mark down certain items.

Where to shop

Carnegie Hill, an Upper East Side neighborhood, is well known for its upscale children's clothing boutiques, such as **Petit Bateau**, **Bonpoint**, and **Catimini**.

Soho, on the southwestern tip of Manhattan, has a handful of kids' stores, including **Giggle**, **Patagonia** (which has a good selection of children's wear, from winter coats to swimsuits), and **Makié**, a Japan-inspired boutique with ultra-minimalist clothing mostly for kids, plus a few things for parents, too.

Below left An abundance of toys and stuffed animals on display inside FAO Schwarz *Below center* Entrance to Toys"R"Us at Times Square, the largest toy store in the world *Below right* Costume jewelry for sale at Hell's Kitchen Fleamarket

Size Chart

Size numbers in Europe and the US are different. Clothes sizes for children go by age in the US.

Women's Clothes			Women's Shoes			Men's Clothes			Men's Shoes			Children's shoes		
UK	Europe	US	UK	Europe	US	UK	Europe	US	UK	Europe	US	UK	Europe	US
4	32	2	3	36	5	34	44	34	6	39	7	7	24	7½
6	34	4	4	37	6	36	46	36	7½	40	7½	8	25½	8½
8	36	6	5	38	7	38	48	38	8	41	8	9	27	9½
10	38	8	6	39	8	40	50	40	8½	42	8½	10	28	10½
12	40	10	7	40	9	42	52	42	9	43	9	11	29	11½
14	42	12	8	41	10	44	54	44				12	30	12½
16	44	14	9	42	11	46	56	46				13	32	13½
18	46	16				48	58	48				1	33	1½
20	48	18										2	34	2½

Tribeca, just below Soho, is an off-the-beaten-path, fun place to explore. Visit **West Side Kids** for an extensive range of toys for children of all ages, and **Babesta**, an excellent toy store and clothing shop. The Flatiron District is home to **Paragon** (see p82), the city's best sporting goods store, and **Union Square Greenmarket** (see p82) as well as a couple of toy stores, **Space Kiddets** (see p82) and **Kidding Around**.

Markets

If browsing artists' work, artisanal crafts, and secondhand collectibles is your passion, get ready to do some walking. The main outdoor market is the seasonal **Hell's Kitchen Fleamarket**, with vendors selling everything from hand-knitted stuffed animals to vintage cameras. Another indoor and outdoor flea-market is **GreenFlea**, which features collectibles of all kinds, including vintage clothing and antiques. **Brooklyn Flea** has a similar set-up, with an indoor market in winter and two outdoor locations. All are family-friendly and provide snacking options. **The Market NYC**, located in the Meatpacking District, is where up-and-coming artists and clothing and jewelry designers sell their work on weekends at direct-to-the-consumer prices.

Toys, games & gadgets

Times Square giant **Toys"R"Us** (see p119) has a huge inventory of board games, LEGO, action figures, and even some pretty cool magic tricks. Plus, it has the only Ferris wheel in Manhattan – inside the store. Far better organized is **FAO Schwarz** (see p109). Its themed areas – baby and toddler toys, Corolle dolls, Thomas trains, science/educational toys, Calico Critters, Breyer horses, play-and-pretend costumes, and the first floor's wonderful stuffed animals – make shopping here enjoyable for everyone. Beyond the stuffed animals is a floor piano and a candy counter.

Below Stalls selling a variety of flowers and fresh produce at Union Square Greenmarket, a well-known farmers' market in the Flatiron District

Many parents prefer the environs of smaller independent toy stores, such as **Kidding Around**, which has a high concentration of European toys and a permanent train set for youngsters to investigate, and **Dinosaur Hill**, a charming spot decorated with marionettes, where kids can find the likes of Ugly Dolls, Slinkys, and beading sets. Chess-lovers won't want to miss the **Village Chess Shop**, where they can play as well as browse unusual chess sets. **Half Pint Citizens** has imaginative craft kits and a great selection of toy cars, trucks, trains, and dolls.

Midtown is home to some mega one-company theme/toy stores, among them the city's sole **Nintendo World** (see p114), where children can try out new DS games; the **LEGO Store** (see p113), also in Rockefeller Center; **Build-A-Bear Workshop**, where kids pick out and stuff their own animals, complete with a red silk heart; and the **Disney Store**, with themed toys, games, and clothing, as well as collectibles such as limited-edition pins.

Toddler & baby gear

Several stores in the city specialize in everything for babies and smaller children, from eco-toys and clothing to cribs, bibs, and strollers. The biggest is **Buy Buy Baby**, with everything parents could possibly need: bottle warmers, kid potties, and Boppys. **Giggle** has an upscale inventory, carrying the likes of Bugaboo strollers, and cherry-picked clothing and books. Less posh but just as useful is **Mini Jake**, with all of the above, plus bikes, books, scooters, mobiles, puppets, plush toys, and dollhouses.

Children's clothing

There is a huge range of clothing options for children in the city, from chains such as **Gap**, with worthy kids' sections, to specialty boutiques, department stores, and even sample sales. **Bundle** (now online only) has designer clothes for babies plus a great selection of onesies, tops, bottoms, dresses, coats, swimsuits, and even jewelry. J.Crew's kids' line, **Crewcuts**, stocks high-quality sweaters, dresses, tees, jeans, sneakers, and shoes. Two favorites with kids and parents alike are **Julian & Sara**, with an inspired range of clothing, and **My Little Sunshine** (see p87), which has a hip selection for boys and girls.

There are also a number of spots that cater to tweens and teens. **Infinity** carries several brands,

including Juicy and J Brand, plus pyjamas and tons of accessories. **B'tween** has girls' clothing from brands such as Tractor and It alongside bathrobes and swimwear.

Several of the city's department stores have very good clothing sections. **Barneys** has the city's best curated and most expensive children's department. Almost as pricey is **Saks Fifth Avenue**. **Bloomingdale's** showcases mainstream brands, such as Lacoste and Levi's, alongside pricier labels like Diesel and Burberry. **Lord & Taylor** and **Macy's** (see p95) are both less fashionista and more affordable, with dependable brands such as Guess, Nautica, and Polo. **Century 21** is a discount megastore, great for families who don't mind braving the crowds and the cramped racks of clothing.

Shoe stores

Sports shoes can be found at stores and chains such as **Skechers**, **David Z**, and **Foot Locker**. If something other than sneakers is in order, several shoe stores will fit the bill. **Ibiza Kidz** carries brands such as Naturino, Primigi, and Geox. **Shoofly**, with many of the same brands, has 50 percent-off sales at the end of June and the beginning

Below left Red and white signage above Macy's, one of the biggest stores in the world
Below right Shopping for secondhand books in the East Village

of January. **Harry's Shoes**, around since 1931, has a good range of quality footware.

Books

Most NYC bookstores carry some books for kids, and national chains such as **Barnes & Noble** have extensive kids' sections with offerings for toddlers, tweens, and teens. **The Strand** offers a variety of books, and over most weekends, has "character visits" from childrens favourites such as Elmo and Peppa Pig. The city's top independent bookshops for kids are **Bank Street Bookstore**, with a huge area for the younger set and a range of storytime offerings, and **Books of Wonder** (see p82), the only store devoted exclusively to children's books that also has a cupcake shop within it.

Art stores

It never hurts to have a stash of drawing materials on hand for rainy days or long journeys. **Blick** has a useful kids' section and an amazing selection of notebooks at good prices. **Michaels** is another haven for creative kids, with art sets and craft materials galore. The store also hosts frequent arts-and-crafts workshops.

The Lowdown

Markets
Brooklyn Flea www.brooklynflea.com
GreenFlea www.greenfleamarkets.com
Hell's Kitchen Fleamarket www.hellskitchenfleamarket.com
The Market NYC 159 Bleecker St, 10012; www.themarketnyc.com

Toys, games & gadgets
Build-A-Bear Workshop 565 Fifth Ave, 10010; www.buildabear.com
Dinosaur Hill 306 East 9th St; 10003; www.dinosaurhill.com
Disney Store 1540 Broadway, 10036; 212 626 2910; www.disneystore.com
Half Pint Citizens 41 Washington St, Brooklyn, 11201; 718 875 4007; www.halfpintcitizens.com
Kidding Around www.kiddingaroundtoys.com
Village Chess Shop 82 West 3rd St, 10012; www.chess-shop.com

Toddler & baby gear
Buy Buy Baby www.buybuybaby.com
Giggle www.giggle.com
Mini Jake www.minijake.com

Children's clothing
Babesta www.babesta.com
Barneys New York www.barneys.com
Bloomingdale's www.bloomingdales.com
Bonpoint www.bonpoint.com
B'tween 354 DeGraw St, Cobble Hill, Brooklyn, 11231; 718 683 7993; www.btweenbklyn.com
Bundle www.bundlenyc.com

Catimini www.catimini.com
Century 21 www.c21stores.com
Crewcuts www.jcrew.com
Gap www.gap.com
Infinity 1116 Madison Ave at 83rd St, 10028; 212 734 0077
Julian & Sara www.julianandsara.com
Lord & Taylor www.lordandtaylor.com
Makié 109 Thompson St, 10012; 212 625 3930; www.makieclothier.com
Patagonia www.patagonia.com
Petit Bateau www.petit-bateau.us
Saks Fifth Avenue www.saksfifthavenue.com
West Side Kids www.westsidekidsnyc.com

Shoe stores
David Z www.davidz.com
Foot Locker www.footlocker.com
Harry's Shoes www.harrys-shoes.com
Ibiza Kidz www.ibizakidz.com
Shoofly www.shooflynyc.com
Skechers www.skechers.com

Books
Bank Street Bookstore www.bankstreetbooks.com
Barnes & Noble www.barnesandnoble.com
The Strand www.strandbooks.com

Art stores
Blick www.dickblick.com
Michaels www.michaels.com

Below left Cheery interior of the LEGO Store, Rockefeller Center
Below right Shoppers with colorful bags from baby and toddler emporium, Giggle

Entertainment

Visiting the landmark sights is a vital part of any trip to New York, but taking in the city's culture via performances, screenings, and fun classes is just as easy, and will let kids feel like honorary New Yorkers. From concerts in Central Park and outdoor summer movies to jewelry-making classes and drawing workshops, there is something for everyone, including plenty of activities that children and their parents can do together.

Practical information

Time Out Kids magazine and its website have pages dedicated to Movies and Music & Stage, with up-to-date reviews. **Mommy Poppins**, run by an NYC mom, is another site devoted to letting parents know what is going on; the two websites often provide links to ticketing sites, too. Some events, such as cooking classes and film-festival screenings, require registration or advance ticket purchase. Likewise, **MoMA's** *(see pp106–107)* family art workshops require pre-registration, while the **Met's** *(see pp150–153)* family activities are first come, first served.

Music

Music concerts for kids take place regularly throughout the city, in venues such as **Joe's Pub** and Uptown's **Symphony Space**, whose Saturday morning family culture series (a mix of film, music, theater, and dance) is excellent. At **Lincoln Center** *(see pp170–71)*, kids can sign up for one of the Chamber Music Society's Meet the Music! sessions, which introduce children to assorted aspects of music.

In summer, the Metropolitan Opera and New York Philharmonic perform free concerts on Central Park's Great Lawn, while the City Parks Foundation's **SummerStage** series brings jazz, pop, and World Music to city parks in all five boroughs – all are free. Other summer festivals include the **River To River Festival** and **Celebrate Brooklyn!**

Cinema

The **New York International Children's Film Festival** (Mar) screens more than 100 films, from mainstream flicks to experimental ones. **BAMkids Film Festival**, at the Brooklyn Academy of Music (typically one weekend in Feb), packs in all sorts of cinematic gems. **Lincoln Square IMAX** brings stories from nature and science – some in 3D – to the (very) big screen.

Art

Many of the city's lauded museums, from **MoMA** and the **Guggenheim** *(see pp158–9)* to the **Metropolitan Museum of Art** *(see pp150–53)*, run children's art programs. **MoMA** offers family gallery talks and art workshops that are free of charge and include museum admission. A visit to the **Children's Museum of the Arts** *(see p76)* is all about kids making art. Admission includes unlimited access to drop-in stations,

Below left Symphony Space, which offers the latest in dance, performance art, and avant-garde music
Below right Kids making colorful cupcakes at a cookery class with Taste Buds

with activities such as collage, clay crafts, and painting. Its rotating exhibitions often feature children's work.

Literature

The **New York Public Library** *(see p102)* has a website with com- prehensive event listings, as do its **Brooklyn** and **Queens** counterparts. Bookshops, including **Bank Street Bookstore**, **Books of Wonder**, and **McNally Jackson**, sometimes host storytimes, as well as frequent author readings and book signings. Symphony Space's **Thalia Kids' Book Club** is a series of one-off events spotlighting a kid-lit author and his or her work.

Crafts

Children can purchase all manner of supplies, and enjoy paper-crafting workshops at **Paper Source** (not all workshops are open to under 16s; check before signing up). **Beads of Paradise** has Sunday afternoon beading classes for ages 12 and up. **Little Shop of Crafts** offers plastercraft and pottery painting, mosaic building, and stuffing your own soft toy, while **La Mano Pottery** has Sunday morning classes for kids aged 6 and up.

The Lowdown

Art Farm in the City 419 East 91st St, 10128; 212 410 3117; *www.theartfarms.org*

BAMkids Film Festival BAM 30 Lafayette Ave, Brooklyn, 11217; 718 636 4100; *www.bam.org/ programs/bam-kids-film-festival*

Bank Street Bookstore 2780 Broadway at West 107th St, 10025; 212 678 1654; *www.bankstreetbooks. com*

Beads of Paradise 16 East 17th St, 10003; 212 620 0642; *www.beads ofparadisenyc.org*

Books of Wonder 18 West 18th St, 10011; 212 989 3270; *www.books ofwonder.com*

Brooklyn Public Library 10 Grand Army Plaza, Brooklyn, 11238; *www.brooklynpubliclibrary.org*

Celebrate Brooklyn! 718 683 5600; *www.bricartsmedia.org*

Institute of Culinary Education 50 West 23rd St, 10010; 800 777 2433; *www.iceculinary.com*

Joe's Pub 425 Lafayette St, 10003; 212 967 7555; *www.joespub.com*

La Mano Pottery 110 West 26th St, 10001; 212 627 9450; *www.lamano pottery.com*

Lincoln Square IMAX 1998 Broadway, 10023; 888 262 4386; *www.imax.com*

Little Shop of Crafts 711 Amsterdam Ave, 10025; 212 531 2723; *www. littleshopny.com*

McNally Jackson 52 Prince St, 10012; 212 274 1160; *www. mcnallyjackson.com*

Mommy Poppins *www.mommypoppins.com*

New York International Children's Film Festival *www.gkids.com*

Paper Source *www.papersource.com*

Queens Public Library *www.queenslibrary.org*

River To River Festival *www.lmcc.net/program/river-to-river*

SummerStage *www. cityparksfoundation.org/summerstage*

Symphony Space 2537 Broadway, 10025; 212 864 5400; *www. symphonyspace.org*

Taste Buds 109 West 27th St, 10001; 212 242 2248; *www.taste budskitchen.com/nyc*

Thalia Kids' Book Club 2537 Broadway, 10025; 212 864 5400; *www.symphonyspace.org*

Time Out Kids *www.timeout.com/new-york-kids*

Culinary arts

The **Institute of Culinary Education** in Chelsea offers classes in pizza-making (ages 9 and up), great cupcakes (ages 11–14), and savory pastries (ages 14–18).

For the younger set, try **Art Farm in the City** (drop-in classes for ages 2–8). **Taste Buds** takes kids to various restaurants in the city, where they learn to cook a simple dish from the staff.

Below left Display window of the Bank Street Bookstore, where children's authors give readings
Below right A young girl works on her latest masterpiece at a crafts class

Theater and Performing Arts

Bright lights and extravagant musicals are both part of Times Square's appeal. A city crazy about its theater, New York has a performing arts scene that extends far beyond the Theater District – Off-Broadway and beyond. Smaller venues mount children's programs all year round, and come summertime, free kids' shows sprout up in all five boroughs. In addition, there are visiting circuses and acrobatic extravaganzas that are sure to enchant kids.

Shows & buying tickets

Time Out Kids magazine and its website, as well as the **Theater Mania** website, list all current shows and have theater reviews too. After choosing a show, check **Broadway Box** for discount codes before buying tickets; they can be used online and at the theater's box office, in person or by phone. One can also go to the show's website, which offers ticketing or redirects the user to **Ticketmaster**. If waiting in line is not a problem, head to one of the three **TKTS booths**, located in Times Square, the South Street Seaport, and Downtown Brooklyn, which sell discounted tickets. Check the TKTS website for details.

Kids' Night on Broadway offers free admission for one child (ages 6–18) with the purchase of one adult ticket. And, during the twice-yearly 20at20 event (*www.20at20.com*), tickets to many **Off-Broadway shows** go on sale for $20, about 20 minutes before the show starts. However, there is no guarantee that tickets to every show will be available.

Free performances

Older kids will love Shakespeare in the Park, the summer-long series at Central Park's **Delacorte Theater** (*see p141*). **TheatreworksUSA** offers a free show at the **Lucille Lortel Theatre** in the West Village, running for about a month each summer. Tickets (four per person) are distributed 1 hour prior to the day's first performance on a first-come, first-served basis. Bryant Park has a Reading Room, where free readings are hosted for kids, and Broadway productions take the stage for **Broadway in Bryant Park**. **New York Classical Theatre** productions take place in Central Park, or as part of the **River To River Festival**, which has other free kids' theater and dance performances as well. There is great family fun to be had at the assorted summer festivals staged in various parks, including SummerStage and Celebrate Brooklyn!

Below left Line outside one of the TKTS booths that sell discounted tickets to Broadway, Off-Broadway, and other venues
Below right Live musical performance at the River To River Festival by the Hudson River

Above Scene from an Off-Broadway production at the DR2 Theatre
Left A TKTS ticket booth in Times Square

Circuses

Each fall, the homespun **Big Apple Circus** sets up its tent at Lincoln Center's Damrosch Park for several months to put on an original show with lots of humor and surprising acts. Two others, **Ringling Bros.** and **Cirque du Soleil**, pay occasional visits to the city. The Brooklyn-based **Streb Lab for Action Mechanics** mounts amazing acrobatic spectacles around the city; some of its rehearsals and workshops are free to attend. Kid-oriented productions that incorporate the likes of juggling and aerial acts frequently take the stage at the **New Victory Theater**.

Broadway

A handful of Broadway productions – the most expensive of all theatrical offerings – are geared toward kids. The most popular are *The Lion King*, a story about the perils and triumphs of a lion cub named Simba; and *Wicked*, an unofficial prequel to L. Frank Baum's *The Wonderful Wizard of Oz*. *Newsies* is another interesting production about young newsboys in turn-of-the-century New York.

Off-Broadway & small theaters

Several Off-Broadway theaters are ideal for families because of their kid-centric orientation. The **New Victory Theater** mounts an array of inventive kids' productions year-round, while the McGinn/Cazale Theatre is home to the **Vital Theatre Company**, which usually has two or three productions playing at any given time. Downtown's **DR2 Theatre**; **Symphony Space**, whose Saturday morning kids' offerings include plays and musicals; the **NYU Skirball Center**, which mounts a family series called the Big Red Chair; and **TADA! Youth Theater**, all cater especially to kids. Do not miss the **Swedish Cottage Marionette Theater** (*see p142*), which makes its own puppets and writes its own shows.

The Lowdown

Big Apple Circus
www.bigapplecircus.org
Broadway Box
www.broadwaybox.com
Broadway in Bryant Park
www.bryantpark.org
Cirque du Soleil
www.cirquedusoleil.com
DR2 Theatre
www.darylroththeatre.com
Kids Night on Broadway
www.kidsnightonbroadway.com
Lucille Lortel Theatre
www.lortel.org
New Victory Theater
www.newvictory.org
New York Classical Theatre
www.newyorkclassical.org
NYU Skirball Center
www.skirballcenter.nyu.edu
Off-Broadway shows
www.newworldstages.com
Ringling Bros. and Barnum & Bailey Circus www.ringling.com
River to River Festival
www.rivertorivernyc.com
Streb Lab for Action Mechanics
www.streb.org
Symphony Space
www.symphonyspace.org
TADA! Youth Theater
www.tadatheater.com
Theater Mania
www.theatermania.com
TheatreworksUSA
www.theatreworksusa.org
Ticketmaster
www.ticketmaster.com
Time Out Kids
www.timeout.com/new-york-kids
TKTS booths
www.tdf.org
Vital Theatre Company
www.vitaltheatre.org

Sporting Events and Activities

Many New Yorkers are big sports fans and enthusiastic supporters of the city's two baseball teams. Watching a home game in warmer weather – or a hockey or basketball game in the winter – is thrilling. The city offers plenty of outdoor activities, from kayaking on the Hudson River to ice-skating in Bryant Park or cycling one of the city's new bike paths. Joining in is not only easy and relatively inexpensive, but also a great way to get off the beaten path.

Spectator sports

BASEBALL

New York is home to two Major League Baseball teams – the **New York Yankees** and the **New York Mets**. Tickets are easy to buy on the official MLB website, or in person on game day, and the two stadiums – Yankee Stadium (see p239) in the South Bronx and Citi Field in Flushing, Queens – are easily reached by subway. Plan to arrive early to beat the last-minute dash.

TENNIS

The **US Open** tennis tournament takes place in Flushing, Queens, in the last week of August and the first week of September. It is best to buy a grounds pass on one of the tournament's first eight days. This affords free access to all field courts, plus the Louis Armstrong Stadium and the Grandstand (but not the huge Arthur Ashe Stadium). Seating is first-come, first-served at these venues so there is no need to buy a ticket in advance, but it is wise to show up early. Use the west entrance; it is farther from the subway station and therefore less crowded.

SOCCER

The popularity of Major League Soccer has grown throughout the US. Fans can take in a game at the Red Bull Arena in Harrison, New Jersey, home to the **New York Red Bulls**, formerly known as the MetroStars. You can buy tickets in family four-packs and the stadium is easily accessible from Manhattan via the PATH train or by bus from the Port Authority in Midtown.

BASKETBALL & HOCKEY

Madison Square Garden is home to the **New York Knicks** basketball team and the ice-hockey team, the

The Lowdown

Spectator sports
New York Knicks
www.nba.com/knicks
New York Mets
newyork.mets.mlb.com
New York Rangers rangers.nhl.com
New York Red Bulls
www.newyorkredbulls.com
New York Yankees newyork.
yankees.mlb.com
US Open www.usopen.org

Family sports & activities
Bike and Roll www.bikeandroll.com
Downtown Boathouse
www.downtownboathouse.org
New York's Waterfront Bicycle
Shop 391 West St; 212 414 2453;
www.bikeshopny.com
The Rink at Bryant Park
West 40th St, between Fifth Ave
& Sixth Ave; www.citipondat
bryantpark.com
Rockefeller Center Ice Skating
Rink 601 Fifth Ave, 212 332 7654;
www.therinkatrockcenter.com
Sky Rink Pier 61, 23rd St & the
Hudson River Park; 212 336 6100;
www.chelseapiers.com

Below Tandem cycling on a bike path through Central Park
Below right Young children ice-skating at the Wollman Rink in winter

Above An aerial view of the Yankee Stadium during a game
Left A basketball game at Madison Square Garden

New York Rangers. If you want good seats, it is wise to book them in advance online. Wear warm clothing for Rangers games.

Family sports & activities

CYCLING

The city's Hudson River Valley Greenway, on the west side of Manhattan, is its most extensive bike path and also its busiest. The section along Battery Park is one of the loveliest, with lawns, playgrounds, and outdoor eateries. Unless you are seasoned urban cyclists, do not venture onto city streets, as drivers can be aggressive. Two bike rental shops right along the Greenway – **New York's Waterfront Bicycle Shop** and **Bike and Roll** – make taking a spin there easy. When renting your two-wheeler, remember that it is mandatory for children aged 13 and under to wear helmets.

KAYAKING

Kayaking is an immensely popular pastime in the city during summer. The **Downtown Boathouse** is an all-volunteer, not-for-profit organization that offers free kayaking to the public at three Hudson River locations. Children under 16 must be accompanied by an adult in a two-person kayak. Check the website for detailed information regarding rules and regulations.

HIKING

Some of New York's most tranquil spots are its forests. The most accessible is Central Park's **The Ramble** *(see p136)*, a mini-wilderness in the middle of the city. Join a tour or explore independently (daytime only). Forest Park in Queens and Van Cortlandt Park, at the northern tip of The Bronx, have extensive trails, gorgeous canopies, and plenty of harmless wildlife.

ICE-SKATING

There are four outdoor rinks and one indoor rink in the city. The most iconic is the **Rockefeller Center Ice-Skating Rink** *(see p112)*, but it is also the priciest. **Trump Rink** *(see p130)*, at the southern end of the Central Park, is a picture-perfect mix of city and country. Each winter, **The Rink at Bryant Park**, a free skating rink, is created in Bryant Park *(see p103)*; early mornings are its least busy time. The **Sky Rink** at Chelsea Piers is a year-round indoor option.

Summer in the City

Add sunshine to New York's amazing array of attractions, and the city becomes an incredibly exciting place to be in the summer. Days are longer, outdoor theater, concerts (see p40), and street fairs abound, and the waters around the isle of Manhattan beckon with the promise of seaside fun and island-hopping adventure. And when the sightseeing gets too much, it is easy to recharge over an alfresco meal or ice cream.

On the water

Though Manhattan and Staten Island are New York's only true islands, all its boroughs have rivers that are worth exploring by boat. One of the most fun excursions is to circumnavigate Manhattan on a mammoth **Circle Line** vessel or aboard the *Manhattan*, a small boat that serves brunch on board. Sailing aboard schooners like the *Adirondack* or the *Shearwater* is an exciting experience that throws the city into a new light. A harbor history tour from **South Street Seaport** (see pp66–7) underscores the city's earlier importance as a maritime hub, and might take in the **Statue of Liberty** (see pp58–9) and the Hudson and East rivers.

Three **Downtown Boathouse** locations along the Hudson provide free, supervised kayaking, while the **Loeb Boathouse** rents rowboats by the hour on Central Park Lake, which is great for wildlife-spotting. Pedal boats and bird-watching tours on Prospect Park Lake are wonderful.

Above Rowing boats on Central Park Lake, with skyscrapers in the background

Wildlife adventures

New York is not exactly known for its wildlife, but there is plenty of it, from exotic migratory birds to bats, turtles, and snails.

The **Audubon Center's** (see p209) family bird-watching tour in Prospect Park may be the most intimate way to glimpse some of the 250 species of birds that call Prospect Park home. Perhaps the most thrilling wildlife adventure, though, is an **Audubon EcoCruise**, a collaboration between the Audubon Center and **New York Water Taxi**. Running on select Sunday evenings in the summer months, the tours are timed to coincide with the return of herons, egrets, and ibises from a day of freshwater fishing to their nesting sites on the uninhabited Brother Islands, in the northern part of the East River.

Island-hopping

Coney Island (see p214) has served as the city's unofficial vacation spot since the late 19th century. Today, New Yorkers flock to Coney (no longer an island) on day trips to enjoy the area's broad wooden boardwalk along the beach, lined with restaurants, and visit **Luna Park** (see p214) with its

The Lowdown

Adirondack Pier 62, Hudson River at 22nd St, 10011; www.sail-nyc.com

Circle Line Pier 83, Hudson River at 42nd St, 10036; www.circleline42.com

Downtown Boathouse Pier 26, Hudson River at Hubert St; Pier 96, Hudson River at 56th St; Pier 101, Governor's Island; www.downtown boathouse.org

Governors Island www.govisland.com

Loeb Boathouse inside Central Park, East 72nd St at Park Dr North; www.thecentralparkboathouse.com

Manhattan Pier 62, Hudson River at 22nd St, 10011; www.sail-nyc.com

New York Water Taxi Audubon EcoCruise, Pier 16 at the South Street Seaport; 212 742 1969; www.nywatertaxi.com

Shearwater 385 South End Ave, North Cove Marina, Battery Park City; www.manhattanbysail.com

Above Visitors at the Water Taxi Beach on Governors Island
Left Lesser yellowlegs flying over shallow water

arcade games, enormous rollercoaster, and Ferris wheel. In June, the Mermaid Parade heralds the start of Coney's summer season, while the **New York Aquarium** *(see pp212–13)* offers kids an up-close look at marine life.

One of the most exciting additions to the city has been the opening of **Governors Island**, in the middle of New York Harbor. Free, frequent ferry services to the island from the Battery Maritime Building run through the summer months *(Fri, Sat & Sun)*. Families can pack a picnic and explore the island on foot, either on their own or on a walking tour, or rent bikes. On weekends throughout the summer, free art workshops for kids, an annual mini-golf installation, and open-air concerts draw many visitors.

It is hard to believe that **City Island** *(see p233)*, a sleepy little town once known for its shipbuilding industry, is part of New York City. Visitors can hire a skiff for an hour or two of fishing or visit the town's small galleries, shops, seafood restaurants, and ice-cream parlors.

Left Fun rides in Luna Park, Coney Island, Brooklyn
Below A Circle Line vessel cruising past the Statue of Liberty

The History of New York

The most populous city in the US is also its oldest, and it is rich in history. New York has witnessed cataclysmic changes during its transformation from an ecologically rich marshland to the first capital of the US. For the past 200 years, the city has been a bastion of hope for the millions of immigrants who have arrived on its shores, and it continues to inspire each new generation with its iconic skyline and the limitless energy of its inhabitants.

Henry Hudson bartering with Native Americans along the Hudson River

Early inhabitants and new settlers

The area was once home to a semi-nomadic group of farmers, fishermen, and hunters known as the Lenape. They foraged the land and sea for food and farmed corn, squash, and climbing beans, moving to different campsites seasonally. The end of the tribe's peaceful existence began with the arrival of Giovanni da Verrazzano in 1524 – he was the first European explorer to encounter the Lenape.

It took another 85 years for the next voyager to arrive, this time an Englishman, Henry Hudson, who sailed to the New World for the

Dutch East India Company in 1609. He became the first non-Native to travel up the river that now bears his name and thanks to his log, the Dutch were able to lay claim to the fertile region, calling it New Netherland, and quickly established strategically placed trading posts. In 1624, 30 Dutch families arrived at what is now Governors Island as the first European settlers. A year later, they moved to the southern tip of Manhattan, a settlement called New Amsterdam. It was secured by the purchase of the isle from the Lenape in 1626 and the construction of a massive fort. That same year, African slaves were brought in by the Dutch West India Company.

New Amsterdam's last governor, Peter Stuyvesant, took control of the city in 1647. After a surprise invasion, the British took possession of the settlement in 1664, and renamed it New York, after the Duke of York. Meanwhile, the Lenape dwindled in number, struck down by infectious, European-borne diseases, and fur-trade wars with the Iroquois tribe. By 1700, just 200 or so remained.

Colonial New York

Post colonialization, the city saw the creation of three new counties – Kings (now Brooklyn), Queens, and Richmond (Staten Island) – two slave rebellions, participation in the Seven Years' War (1756–63), and the tightening of the British Colonial reins on the populace, which resulted in a rebellion against the monarchy across the Atlantic.

In 1689, Jacob Leisler, a German-born merchant, led a rebellion that took control of the city for nearly two years, before he was caught and executed. This was the first instance of insurrection against

A portrait of the last governor of New Amsterdam, Peter Stuyvesant

Timeline

1524	1609	1624	1647	1664	1689	173

Italian Giovanni da Verrazzano discovers New York and its environs — **1524**

English explorer Henry Hudson sails into New York Harbor — **1609**

Thirty Dutch families arrive to settle in New Amsterdam — **1624**

Peter Stuyvesant becomes Director General of New Amsterdam — **1647**

The Dutch surrender to the British, who rename the city New York — **1664**

Leisler's Rebellion takes control of the city from the British — **1689**

The John Peter Zenger trial establishes freedom of the press — **173**

the city's power-mongers. Another landmark event was the 1735 libel trial of John Peter Zenger, publisher of the *New York Weekly Journal*. He was charged with seditious libel for publishing anonymous condemnations of New York's governor. Zenger's defense attorney, Andrew Hamilton, argued that even if the material in thepaper was defamatory, it was based on fact and hence should not be considered libellous. Zenger won the case, and freedom of the press and freedom of speech were both added to the city's roster of human-rights victories.

However, the number of slaves and poor whites continued to grow. The bitter winter of 1741 saw a series of fires across the city, resulting in the arrest of 152 Africans and 20 whites, most of whom were hanged or burnt after a show trial. Called the New York Conspiracy of 1741, this event reflected the growing divide between the upper and lower strata of society.

Revolutionary New York

When the protracted French and Indian War (1754–63) ended with the ousting of the French from the continent, the result was a hugely expanded British territory. Deciding that the colonists should pay for British government and protection, the British Parliament imposed a series of acts that were met with increasing opposition: the 1764

Protestors against the Stamp Act burning stamps in New York City

Sugar Act enforced the collection of a tariff on molasses; the 1765 Quartering Act deemed that colonists must provide food and shelter for British soldiers; and the Stamp Act of 1765 levied taxes on the colonists' use of newspapers, books, contracts, and legal documents, all of which were essential to Colonial commerce.

Reaction to the acts was swift. Two weeks before the Stamp Act was to take effect, representatives from nine of the 13 colonies met in New York as the Stamp Act Congress, most notable as the first organized anti-British assembly. The Congress argued that because the colonists were not represented in Parliament, the British had no right to impose taxation laws upon them. Surprised by the protest, the British repealed the act, but retaliated with a new series of laws to subdue the Colonies.

The Conspiracy of 1741, a slave rebellion, brings harsh retribution

General George Washington loses the Battle of Brooklyn, but saves his troops

| '00 | **1741** | **1765** | **1776** | **1783** |

200 Lenape remain the introduction of pean diseases

The Sons of Liberty protest; the Stamp Act Congress meets in the city

The British depart from New York, defeated by the Revolutionaries

George Washington being sworn in as president

American soldiers and their families lost their lives to disease, hunger, and starvation aboard ships moored in the East River at Wallabout Bay. Finally, in 1783, at war's end, Commander-in-Chief Washington marched into Lower Manhattan in triumph.

The reaction was a boycott of British goods, resulting in a series of violent clashes in Boston that led to the battles of Lexington and Concord in Massachusetts, the effective start of the American Revolution.

Having ousted the British from Boston in March 1776, General George Washington secured Manhattan. However, despite the general's fortifications and forewarning, Washington's Continental Army was surrounded by British troops on the night of August 17, 1776, in what became known as the Battle of Brooklyn, the first military encounter since the signing of the July 4 Declaration of Independence of the same year. Washington ushered his troops back to Manhattan under the cover of fog that night, and eventually retreated with his army to Pennsylvania.

The site of Britain's central command, New York was a haven for the Crown's loyalists for the next seven years. The British also began keeping prisoners of war in the city. More than 10,000

New York in the 18th and 19th centuries

New York became the first capital of the US in 1789, four years after the Continental Congress convened in the city after the successful end of the Revolution. George Washington was sworn in as the country's first president on April 30, 1789. Though the seat of government moved to Philadelphia in 1790, the year that New York held the reins was not

insignificant. The United States Bill of Rights and the Northwest Ordinance, a plan for the westward expansion of the new country, were both drafted here, and the US Congress and Supreme Court assembled for the first time.

The city's population increased dramatically in the mid-19th century with the arrival of Irish immigrants fleeing the Great Famine (1845–52) and Germans escaping the turmoil of the Revolutions of 1848. After the Civil War (1861–65), Ellis Island was established as the only point through which immigrants could gain admittance to New York.

The 20th century

In 1898, five boroughs came together to create a new city. The early 1920s saw the beginning of the Great Migration from the South, primarily that of slaves' descendants. Harlem became a vibrant cultural

Washington's army retreating from Long Island after the Battle of Brookyln (1776)

Timeline

George Washington is inaugurated as the nation's first president	The Erie Canal, connecting the Port of New York to the Great Lakes, opens		The Croton Aqueduct opens, supplying the city's inhabitants with fresh water		Brooklyn Bridge opens after 14 years of construction	
1789	**1811**	**1825**	**1835**	**1842**	**1863**	**18**
	The plan for Manhattan's grid system is proposed		The Great Fire destroys most of Manhattan		New Yorkers protest Civil War conscription in the Draft Riots	

View of Ground Zero – former site of the World Trade Center's Twin Towers

center, spawning literature, music, and visual arts in a movement known as the Harlem Renaissance. During the same period, the city's skyline began to take shape with the building of the Empire State and Chrysler buildings and the Rockefeller Center, even as the Depression took hold.

The city played an important role during World War II: the Brooklyn Navy Yards built battleships, aircraft carriers, and landing craft that could carry tanks abroad for combat.

Soldiers returning from the war in 1945, in addition to countless refugees from Europe, led to another economic and demographic boom. The 1950s and '60s saw a highly creative mix of artists and musicians, such as Allen Ginsberg and Bob Dylan, settle in Greenwich Village. At the same time, racial tensions and poverty gave rise to a mass exodus to the suburbs, and an increase in crime, violence, and public assistance, which reached its peak during the

1970s and '80s. The city only just avoided going bankrupt in 1975. New York's comeback, which began in the 1980s, finally took root in the '90s thanks to nationwide economic growth, the Wall Street stock market boom, and a crackdown on crime.

Modern New York

On September 11, 2001, Al Qaeda terrorists crashed two commercial airliners into the Twin Towers of the World Trade Center. Close to 3,000 people died, most trapped inside the buildings, which toppled within hours of the attack. Today, the city has largely recovered from the emotional shutdown and economic standstill that gripped it for years afterward.

In the last couple of decades, gorgeous parks and recreational facilities have been created or refurbished, and even Times Square has morphed from a seedy, adults-only enclave into a tourist attraction. Rents in Manhattan, however, became exorbitant, making the once free-wheeling city barely affordable for newcomers. On the other hand, New Yorkers are now staying put to raise their children, rather than moving out – strollers are ubiquitous and city schools are feeling the brunt. The recession of 2008 spurred the Occupy Wall Street movement, a massive protest against income inequality. In October 2012, Hurricane Sandy, a powerful tropical storm, devastated large parts of the city.

HEROES & VILLAINS

Modern-day hero
New York's great modern hero is Stephen Siller, a fireman who ran through the Battery Tunnel from Brooklyn to Manhattan in full gear to help those trapped in the World Trade Center on September 11, 2001, after he found out the tunnel was closed to traffic.

Exploring exploits
Englishman Henry Hudson made three attempts to find the Northwest Passage to Asia. Though the passage never existed, Hudson found and explored the river that now bears his name.

Revolutionary martyr
Twenty-one-year-old soldier Nathan Hale, a spy for the Continental Army during the American Revolution, was caught by the British. He gave a valiant, defiant speech on the morning of his hanging.

"Boss" Tweed
The powerful city politician William Magear Tweed was convicted in 1877 of stealing between $25 million and $45 million from New York taxpayers. He died in Ludlow Street Jail.

The Stonewall Riots protest gay discrimination

Terrorists crash two planes into the World Trade Center

| 39 | 1969 | 1977 | 2001 | 2012 |

York hosts the d's Fair

A blackout shuts down power for 25 hours; major looting occurs

Hurricane Sandy devastates the city

People on Bow Bridge, across
Central Park Lake, on a sunny
fall afternoon

Exploring
NEW YORK CITY

Downtown

In the 17th and 18th centuries, New York's city center was at the southernmost tip of Manhattan island, a district known today as Downtown. The nation's first president, George Washington, took oath here in 1789, and this area was the first glimpse immigrants got of their new country. Many of Downtown's sights reflect their story, and the area also offers plenty of green spaces and family-friendly attractions.

Upper
West Side
and Harlem

Central
Park
Upper
East Side

Midtown

Downtown

Highlights

Statue of Liberty & Ellis Island
Climb the 377 stairs to Lady Liberty's crown and then head to neighboring Ellis Island to find out about New York's many waves of immigration (see pp58–60).

Water taxi tour of New York Harbor
Take a boat tour to gain a whole new perspective on the isle of Manhattan, and learn about New York City's history as a world-class port (see p59).

Tenement Museum
Visit this fascinating museum to get a sense of the plight of immigrants living in the most densely populated enclave of the city in the late 19th and early 20th centuries (see pp72–3).

Washington Square Park
Explore the park at the heart of Greenwich Village – it embodies the spirit of this lively neighborhood (see p80).

The High Line
Drop by this reclaimed former freight railroad line, once abandoned and overgrown but now converted into a family-friendly elevated park. Open to the public since 2009, it is in many respects the city's crown jewel (see pp86–7).

Left Lady Liberty stands with a torch in one hand and a stone tablet in the other, Statue of Liberty monument, Liberty Island
Above left Washington Square Arch, on the northern edge of Washington Square Park

The Best of
Downtown

The Downtown district is where New York began, and it remains the heartbeat of the city. At its southernmost tip, boats depart for the iconic Statue of Liberty or for tours of New York Harbor. Farther north lie the charming neighborhoods of the Lower East Side, Greenwich Village and its siblings the East and West Villages, and the Meatpacking District. Its elevated park, the High Line, deserves all the hype it has received.

Shore excursions

One of the best ways to explore New York is via the city's waterways or along the water's edge. The **South Street Seaport** (see pp66–7) is the city's principal maritime hub; its center, Pier 17, is closed for extensive renovations. Head to the northern edge of Pier 16 for a magnificent view of **Brooklyn Bridge** (see pp196–7), then hop aboard a water taxi to tour New York Harbor and learn about the city's historic role as a major port. To the north, **Greenwich Village's** (see pp80–81) Hudson River Park playground, affectionately called the water park or the pirate park, is an ideal place for kids to get wet and cool off in summer. Rent some bikes and ride back downtown along the water. The myriad lawns, playgrounds, and slips along the path through **Battery Park City** (see pp56–7) are enchanting.

Right Water taxi near Brooklyn Bridge
Below Entrance to Ellis Island Immigration Museum

Above *The concrete pathways of the High Line, fringed with greenery, surrounded by highrise buildings*

Time travelers

Unearthing New York's past is well worthwhile. The **Tenement Museum** (see pp72–3) on the Lower East Side, once New York's most densely populated neighborhood, brings the past to life with tours of a restored former tenement building. Some of the area's original retailers, such as Russ & Daughters, are still going strong. The port of entry for many immigrants in the late 19th and early 20th centuries, the Great Hall at the **Ellis Island Immigration Museum** (see p60) brings to mind the plight of the newly arrived. Lastly, stop by the **National September 11 Memorial & Museum** (see p69). Located at the former site of the World Trade Center, it is a poignant reminder of a tragic moment in US history.

Cultural pursuits

The seven-story **New Museum** (see pp74–5) is remarkable for its monumental installations and playful spirit. For a more intimate art experience, make a trip to West 22nd Street between Tenth and Eleventh Avenues in Chelsea; the world-class collection of galleries on this block is eclectic and exceptional. The **National Museum of the American Indian** (see pp60–61) brings the cultures of the country's first inhabitants to life with rotating exhibits and great family programs. And for an insight into the life of a boy who became one of the country's most fascinating presidents, visit the **Theodore Roosevelt Birthplace** (see p83).

Green spaces

New York's parks are far more than oases of green; they are cultural centers where city-dwellers gather, slow their pace, and soak up the serenity. **Tompkins Square Park** (see p75), once the quasi-office of Beat poets such as Allen Ginsberg, is still the heart of the East Village, sprawling under a canopy of rare American elms. Due west, **Washington Square Park** (see p80), once rural farmland and then a potter's field, is today a striking example of urban renewal that pulses with youthful energy. One of the finest corners in the city is Jefferson Market Garden in **Greenwich Village**. This green space, once the site of a women's prison, is entirely community-run and lush with carefully tended plantings. Truly ground-breaking among the city's parks, the **High Line** (see pp86–7) sits atop a formerly abandoned railroad line. Experiencing the city from the 30-ft (9-m) high pathway is incredible.

Left *The lightship Ambrose, Pier 17 on the East River, South Street Seaport*

Statue of Liberty and around

Given that the Statue of Liberty and Ellis Island are among
the most visited sights in New York – and accessible only via
ferry – crowds are virtually unavoidable. Arriving at Battery
Park early in the day can shorten the ferry wait considerably.
Once on Liberty and Ellis islands, visitors can easily reach
the sights on foot. Back in Manhattan, several kid-friendly
attractions beckon, from the Skyscraper Museum to the
unusual Irish Hunger Memorial, plus green spaces such
as Teardrop Park and Bowling Green.

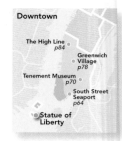

Downtown

The High Line
p84

Greenwich
Village
p78

Tenement Museum
p70

South Street
Seaport
p64

Statue of
Liberty

*A view of New York City's skyscrapers
from across the Hudson River*

The Lowdown

🚗 **Subway** N & R to Whitehall
St; 1 to South Ferry; 4 & 5 to
Bowling Green. **Bus** M5 &
M15; Downtown Connection
– free shuttle service between
Battery Park City and South
Street Seaport with multiple
stops: 10am–7:30pm daily

ℹ **Visitor information** NYC &
Company, 810 Seventh Ave,
10019; 212 484 1200;
www.nycgo.com

🛒 **Supermarket** Gristedes 070,
71 South End Ave & Battery
Park, 10280; 212 233 7770
Market Bowling Green
Greenmarket, at Battery Place
& Broadway; 8am–5pm Tue
& Thu

🎪 **Festival** River to River Festival
– concerts, kids' programs, fairs,
and art exhibits (Jun); *www.lmcc.
net/program/river-to-river*

➕ **Pharmacies** Duane Reade,
67 Broad St, 10004; 212 943
3690; 8am–7pm Mon–Fri.
Battery Park Pharmacy, 327
South End Ave, 10280; 212
912 0555; 8am–8pm Mon–Fri,
9am–7pm Sat, 10am–6pm Sun

🛝 **Nearest playgrounds** Battery
Playspace, Battery Park,
10004. Teardrop Park,
between Warren Street &
Murray Street, east of River
Terrace, 10007

Entrance to the National Museum of the American Indian

*Visitors viewing a scale model of the Burj
Dubai, Skyscraper Museum*

*Children playing on a slide and in
sand at Teardrop Park*

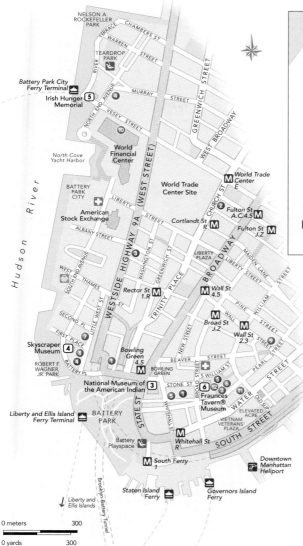

Places of interest

SIGHTS

1. Statue of Liberty
2. Ellis Island Immigration Museum
3. National Museum of the American Indian
4. Skyscraper Museum
5. Irish Hunger Memorial
6. Fraunces Tavern® Museum

EAT AND DRINK

1. Cucina Liberta Market
2. Crown Café
3. Adrienne's Pizza Bar
4. North End Grill
5. Chipotle Mexican Grill
6. Ulysses' Folk House
7. Inatteso Pizzabar Casano
8. 2 West
9. The Country Café
10. PJ Clarke's on the Hudson
11. FIKA
12. Fraunces Tavern®

See also Ellis Island Immigration Museum (p60)

SHOPPING

1. Statue of Liberty Museum Shop

WHERE TO STAY

1. DoubleTree by Hilton Hotel – Financial District
2. Millenium Hilton
3. New York Marriott Downtown
4. The Ritz-Carlton, Battery Park
5. The Wall Street Inn

Ellis Island Immigration Museum, the symbol of America's immigrant heritage

① Statue of Liberty
The symbol of New York

Huge and imposing yet graceful and calming, the Statue of Liberty was a gift from France to the United States in celebration of the 1876 US Centennial. French sculptor Frédéric-Auguste Bartholdi designed and eventually built the masterpiece, putting the entire statue together in Paris, dismantling it for transport to New York City and then putting it all back together again in 1886, the year it was finally unveiled.

Liberty Island Bartholdi deemed this the best site for the statue, since it would be visible to every ship entering the harbor.

The Lowdown

🌐 **Map reference** 1 A6
Address Liberty Island, 10004; www.thestatueofliberty.com

🚗 **Subway** 1 to South Ferry; 4 & 5 to Bowling Green; R & W to Whitehall St. **Bus** M5, M15 & M20. **Ferry** Statue Cruises from Battery Park; check timings at www.statuecruises.com

🕐 **Open** June–Aug: 8am–6pm daily; Sep–May: 9:30am–5pm daily; closed Dec 25

💲 **Price** Ferry fare $45–54 includes entry to Ellis and Liberty islands; under 4s free; crown access additional $3 per person

👥 **Cutting the line** Buy ferry tickets in advance online at www.statuecruises.com

🚩 **Guided tours** Meet at the Liberty Island Flagpole for a free ranger-led tour. Audio tours included in price.

👫 **Age range** 4 plus; children must be 4 ft (1 m) tall to climb to the statue's crown.

👫 **Activities** Junior Ranger Programs for ages 7–12 teach kids about the statue. Print out activities and coloring sheets for kids at www.thestatueofliberty.com

⏱ **Allow** 4 hours

♿ **Wheelchair access** As far as observation deck

☕ **Café** The Crown Café

🛍 **Shop** Statue of Liberty Museum Shop

🚻 **Restrooms** In the monument

Good family value?
Visiting the most iconic symbol of the US is an unparalleled experience and worth the sometimes lengthy wait in line.

Key Features

Crown The seven spikes radiating out of the crown represent the rays of the sun and the world's seven seas and continents.

Dress Lady Liberty is clothed in a gown and cloak in the style seen on Roman goddess statues.

Copper skin The statue's "skin" is made of 2.5-mm (0.1-inch) copper sheets attached to a skeletal framework designed to allow the skin to move in strong winds.

Tablet A book of law held by the statue signifies that the US has a legal system that protects the rights of its citizens.

Pedestal Funded and built by the US, the pedestal is 154 ft (47 m) tall and houses the Statue of Liberty Museum.

The original torch

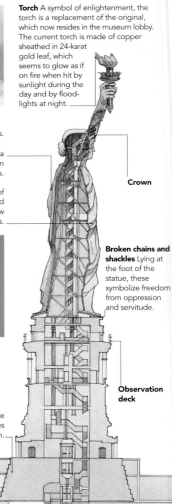

Torch A symbol of enlightenment, the torch is a replacement of the original, which now resides in the museum lobby. The current torch is made of copper sheathed in 24-karat gold leaf, which seems to glow as if on fire when hit by sunlight during the day and by flood-lights at night.

Crown

Broken chains and shackles Lying at the foot of the statue, these symbolize freedom from oppression and servitude.

Observation deck

View of the Elevated Acre, a park with green plantings and plenty of outdoor seating

Letting off steam

After the lengthy trip to Liberty Island, and perhaps Ellis Island (*see p60*) too, head to the **Elevated Acre** (*55 Water St, 10041*), a small but enchanting park that takes a little seeking out. Up a steep flight of stairs, or the escalator if it is operating, await cultivated gardens, a good stretch of Astroturf and fantastic views of the East River and its heliport.

Eat and drink

Picnic: under $20; Snacks: $20–35; Real meal: $35–70; Family treat: over $70 (based on a family of four)

PICNIC Cucina Liberta Market (*17 Battery Pl, 10004; 212 871 6300; www.cucinaliberta.com*), at the north end of Bowling Green, offers deli fare as well as pizza, sushi, and soup, which can be enjoyed in Battery Park or Liberty Island.

SNACKS Crown Café (*Liberty Island, 10079; 212 363 3180*) is a food-court-style dining experience, with seafood platters, burgers, grilled paninis, and wraps.

REAL MEAL Adrienne's Pizza Bar (*54 Stone St, 10004; 212 248 3838; www.adriennespizzabarnyc.com*) is a cozy, grown-up but family-friendly place that boasts top-notch modern

Italian dishes, including excellent antipasti, pastas, salads, and individual pizzas.

FAMILY TREAT North End Grill (*104 North End Ave, 10282; 646 747 1600; www.northendgrillnyc.com*) is an elegant restaurant that uses wood-burning grills and mesquite charcoal ovens to prepare dishes such as Berkshire pork loin and whole free-range chicken. There's also a Sunday night shellfish bake.

Shopping

The **Statue of Liberty Museum Shop** (*www.thestatueofliberty museumstoreonline.com*) stocks souvenirs such as mini replicas of the statue and T-shirts.

Find out more

DIGITAL The website *www.statue ofliberty.net* offers an interactive statue tour and trivia challenge.

FILM *The Statue of Liberty* (1985) is a documentary about the famous statue's history, made by Ken Burns. *An American Tail* (1986) is an animated adventure about a young Russian mouse who becomes separated from his family as they emigrate to the US. For older kids, *The Day After Tomorrow* (2004) shows the statue submerged in snow and ice, the aftermath of a cataclysmic climate shift.

Next stop...

NEW YORK HARBOR Take a boat tour (*www.ny watertaxi.com/HarborTours*) of New York Harbor and the East and Hudson rivers to get a widescreen view of the statue and its setting.

Tucking in at Adrienne's Pizza Bar

KIDS' CORNER

Do you know...

1 Frédéric-Auguste Bartholdi knew from the moment he set eyes on Liberty Island, formerly Bedloe Island, that it would be the perfect place for the Statue of Liberty. Why did he think it was such an ideal spot?

2 At the foot of Lady Liberty are broken chains and shackles that can only be viewed from the air. What do these stand for?

3 How many spikes are there on Lady Liberty's crown and what do they symbolize?

Answers at the bottom of the page.

LONG WAY TO THE TOP

There are 377 steps on the narrow, winding staircase that leads to the crown – roughly the equivalent of 22 floors.

Mamma Mia
The face of the Statue of Liberty was rumored to be a likeness of Bartholdi's mother.

A prolonged wait

After the World Trade Center towers in downtown Manhattan were destroyed in a terror attack in 2001, the statue was closed to the public for three years. And only on July 4, 2009, did Lady Liberty's crown once again open for viewing.

View of Ellis Island Immigration Museum from across the harbor

② Ellis Island Immigration Museum

Former gateway to the United States of America

Tiny Ellis Island was the famous arrival point for millions of immigrants in the late 19th and early 20th centuries. Today, it is home to the Ellis Island Immigration Museum, which tells the stories of the people who made the perilous journey to the shores of the US, why they undertook it, and what awaited them. Between 1892 and 1924, the Ellis Island Immigration Station approved entry to about 12 million people fleeing discrimination, poor economic conditions, religious persecution, and political instability.

The main building of the complex, a Beaux-Arts structure built in 1900, is the only part of the

island open to visitors. The former baggage room on the first floor explains the immigrant experience through exhibits and artifacts; the second floor's inspection center, or Great Hall, is where the fate of the new arrivals was decided. Many were steerage, or third-class, passengers, who had traveled in crowded, unsanitary conditions near the bottom of the steamships. About 2 percent of all arrivals were denied entry, either because they were ill, or because they were deemed likely to engage in illegal pursuits or require public assistance. First- and second-class passengers were spared the process, as the US government believed that those who could afford a more expensive ticket were less likely to become a financial burden on the American people or spread contagious diseases. The sick were sent to the hospital complex on the south side of the island. Some recovered

and later gained entry to the US; others died or were deported to their country of origin.

The facility stopped processing immigrants in 1924 and it became a detention center, before shutting down in 1954. It was not until 1990, after a $160 million restoration, that the Ellis Island Immigration Museum opened to the public. At the Immigration History Center, visitors can access a database to look up information about family members who may have passed through Ellis Island. Today, more than 150 million Americans can trace a branch of their family tree to one of the new arrivals.

Letting off steam
Kids can amble through the Gardens of Remembrance in **Battery Park** (*1 New York Plaza, 10004*). If the weather is warm, they can cool off in the 40-ft (12-m) wide granite spiral fountain, a flat-floored circle with stop-and-start water plumes. If not, let them explore the Battery Labyrinth in the northwest corner of the park, near Pier A.

Exhibits at the National Museum of the American Indian

③ National Museum of the American Indian

Ancient tribes and customs kept alive

Collector George Gustav Heye began collecting Native American artifacts in 1903 and opened the Museum of the American Indian in 1922 on Audubon Terrace in Upper Manhattan. In 1994, the museum moved to its current location where it became the Smithsonian Institution's National Museum of the American Indian. Its mission is not only to preserve the heritage of

The Lowdown

- 🌐 **Map reference** 1 A6
  Address Ellis Island, 10004; 212 561 4588; *www.ellisisland.org*
- 🚇 **Subway** 4 & 5 to Bowling Green; 1 to South Ferry. **Bus** M5, M6 & M15. **Ferry** Statue Cruises to Ellis Island from Battery Park; check timings at *www.statuecruises.com*
- 🕐 **Open** 9am–5pm daily, closed Dec 25
- 💲 **Price** Ferry fee $45–54 (includes access to Ellis Island); under 4s free
- 🎟️ **Cutting the line** Purchase ferry tickets in advance at *www. statuecruises.com* and print them at home or call 877 523 9849.

- 🚩 **Guided tours** Free ranger-guided tours and audio tours; kids' tour narrated by Marty the Muskrat: $31–41. Hard Hat tour (ages 13 plus): $25
- 👫 **Age range** All ages
- 🧒 **Activities** Families can trace their roots at the American Family Immigration History Center. Junior Ranger program available for kids.
- ⏱️ **Allow** 3 hours (6 hours if including trip to the Statue of Liberty)
- ♿ **Wheelchair access** Yes
- 🍴 **Eat and drink** *Real meal* The Ellis Island Café offers burgers, seafood platters, sandwiches, and salads.
- 🚻 **Restrooms** Near the main entrance

Arturo Di Modica's Charging Bull

indigenous peoples across the Americas, but also to foster and support their contemporary cultural pursuits. A huge range of tribes, including nearly all the first nations of the US, most of Canada's, and a large number of Central and South American and Caribbean peoples, are represented by the 850,000 artworks and artifacts, spanning 12,000 years of history.

The museum's primary permanent exhibition, Infinity of Nations: Art and History in the Collections of the National Museum of the American Indian, brings past and present cultures to life by focusing on a selection of artifacts and artworks. It also houses a photographic archive. The museum hosts several events, including American Indian dance and music performances, craft fairs featuring the work of contemporary artisans, and daily workshops for kids.

Do not miss the excellent museum shop, which is chock-full of toys, handmade jewelry, pottery, textiles, and stationery, plus a great selection of books and CDs.

Letting off steam

Take a walk around New York's oldest public park, **Bowling Green** *(between Broadway & Whitehall St, 10004)*, enclosed by its original 18th-century wrought-iron fence, then seek out the famous bronze sculpture *Charging Bull* (1987) by Arturo Di Modica at its northern end.

The Lowdown

- 🌐 **Map reference** 1 D5
  Address 1 Bowling Green, 10004; 212 514 3700; www.nmai.si.edu
- 🚇 **Subway** J, M & Z to Broad St; R to Whitehall St; 4 & 5 to Bowling Green; 1 to South Ferry.
  Bus M5 & M15
- 🕐 **Open** 10am–5pm Fri–Wed, 10am–8pm Thu
- 💲 **Price** Free
- 🚩 **Guided tours** Tours begin at 1pm Mon–Wed, Fri & Sun, and 3pm Mon, Wed & Sun, and leave from the second-floor visitor information desk. Insider tours with cultural interpreters take place daily; for more information, check at the information desk.
- 👫 **Age range** All ages
- 🤸 **Activities** The Storybook Reading and Hands-on Activity program takes place on the second Sat of each month at 1pm.
- ⏱ **Allow** 2 hours
- ♿ **Wheelchair access** Yes
- 🍽 **Eat and drink** Snacks Chipotle Mexican Grill *(2 Broadway, 10004; 212 344 0941)* offers fresh Mexican fare to eat in or take out. *Real meal* Ulysses' Folk House *(95 Pearl St/58 Stone St, 10004; 212 482 0400)* has good pub fare, including a daily "Irish" carvery menu.
- 🚻 **Restrooms** On the first and second floors

Open-air seating at Ulysses' Folk House restaurant

Picnic under $20; **Snacks** $20–35; **Real meal** $35–70; **Family treat** over $70 (based on a family of four)

A young visitor examining an exhibit, Skyscraper Museum

④ Skyscraper Museum

History of highrises

Devoted to the vertical majesty of New York City's architecture, the Skyscraper Museum was founded in 1997, and moved into its permanent home at the southern tip of Battery Park City in 2004. It celebrates the city's architectural heritage with temporary and permanent exhibits. Among these

are several displays that focus on the museum's neighborhood. In the Maps and Photographs of Lower Manhattan exhibit, learn how the mostly abandoned West Side piers in Battery Park City were transformed in the 1960s. The planning and construction of the World Trade Center as well as its tragic destruction are chronicled in the museum, as is Daniel Libeskind's design and the plan for the construction of the Freedom Tower.

Letting off steam

Just north of the nearby ferry landing is the **Robert F. Wagner, Jr. Park** (*between Battery Pl & the Hudson River, 10280*), a mix of manicured lawns and gardens where kids can play tag, fly a kite, or ascend a public roof deck for views of Ellis and Liberty islands.

The Lowdown

🌐 **Map reference** 1 C5
Address 39 Battery Place, 10280; 212 968 1961; *www.skyscraper. org/home.htm*

🚇 **Subway** 1 & R to Rector St; 4 & 5 to Bowling Green. **Bus** M5 & M20

🕐 **Open** Noon–6pm Wed–Sun

💲 **Price** $20

🚩 **Guided tours** Call 212 968 1961 for information on walking tours.

👫 **Age range** 2 plus

🏃 **Activities** Kids' workshops held on some Sat mornings; $5 per child, email education@skyscra per.org or call 212 945 6324 to register.

🕐 **Allow** 1–2 hours

♿ **Wheelchair access** Yes

🍽 **Eat and drink** *Real meal* Inatteso Pizzabar Casano (*28 West St, Battery Park, 10004; 212 267 8000*) serves brick-oven pizzas and meat and fish entrées. *Family treat* 2 West (*Ritz-Carlton Hotel, 2 West St, 10004; 917 790 2525*) has a delightful menu that also includes a "kids' table" with options such as chicken fingers, margherita pizza, and french fries.

🚻 **Restrooms** On the main floor

⑤ Irish Hunger Memorial

In memory of the potato famine

A surprising patch of green amid the skyscraper-strewn confines of Battery Park City, the Irish Hunger

Entrance to the Irish Hunger Memorial

The Lowdown

🌐 **Map reference** 1 A3
Address Vesey St at North End Ave, 10004; 212 267 9700

🚇 **Subway** E to World Trade Center. **Bus** M20 & M22

🕐 **Open** Dawn to dusk daily

💲 **Price** Free

👫 **Age range** All ages

🕐 **Allow** 15–30 minutes

♿ **Wheelchair access** Yes

🍽 **Eat and drink** *Snacks* The Country Café (*60 Wall St, 10005; 212 943 0900*) offers quick eat-in or takeaway options like panini, sandwiches, wraps, and soup. *Real meal* PJ Clarke's on the Hudson (*250 Vesey St, inside the World Financial Center, 10281; 212 285 1500*) serves a variety of food including sandwiches, baby back ribs, and fish tacos.

🚻 **Restrooms** No

Families enjoying a sunny day at Nelson A. Rockefeller Park

Memorial (2002) is a permanent art installation by Brian Tolle. It memorializes the 1 million victims of Ireland's Great Famine of 1845–52 while also addressing current hunger crises around the world. After entering a dark corridor where recorded voices recount the horrors of the famine, visitors emerge onto a concrete path that takes them to an early 19th-century stone cottage from County Mayo. The memorial occupies a beautiful piece of land, designed to evoke the fallow fields of rural Ireland.

Letting off steam

Head west to the edge of the Hudson River and then north to play catch or Frisbee on one of the most popular green spaces in Manhattan: **Nelson A. Rockefeller Park** *(north end of Battery Park City, west of River Terrace, 10282)*.

⑥ Fraunces Tavern® Museum

History and pub grub

This historic tavern was home to the first offices of the Departments of Foreign Affairs, War, and Treasury, following the Revolutionary War. When the federal government moved to Washington, D.C., it was again transformed into a tavern – a boarding house with a bar. After the opening of the Erie Canal in 1825, New York's population grew and the building at 54 Pearl Street housed people who had come to the city for work. The tavern was also a famous meeting place for Patriots, including Alexander Hamilton. The museum has since been restored to its 18th-century appearance and consists of nine galleries and eight dining spaces in five buildings along the same block. The galleries include a collection of maps from the 1700s and 1800s, portraits of George Washington, and early American flags. The Long Room is the site where Washington bid farewell to his surviving officers at the end of the Revolutionary War.

Time your visit to enjoy a meal at "the oldest standing structure in the City of New York."

Letting off steam

Head to the **Elevated Acre** *(55 Water St, 10041; 212 963 7099)* for views of the East River, from the Brooklyn Bridge to Governors Island. The park grounds include an all-season cultivated garden and a good swath of Astroturf.

The Fraunces Tavern® Museum's main building, dating from around 1719

The Lowdown

- 🌐 **Map reference** 2 D5
- **Address** 54 Pearl Street, 10004; 212 425 1778; www.fraunces tavernmuseum.org
- 🚇 **Subway** 2 & 3 to Wall St; 4 & 5 to Bowling Green. **Bus** M5 & M15
- ⏱ **Open** noon–5pm daily, closed Jan 1, Thanksgiving Day & Dec 25
- 💲 **Price** $14–20; under 5s free
- 🏴 **Guided tours** Free guided tours; 2pm on most Sun.
- 👫 **Age range** All ages
- ⏳ **Allow** 1 hour
- ♿ **Wheelchair access** No
- 🍴 **Eat and drink** *Snacks* FIKA *(66 Pearl St, 10004; 646 837 6588)* is a Swedish bakery, named after the traditional Swedish afternoon coffee and sweets break, *fika*. Enjoy truffles, pralines, cakes and other treats, along with high-quality coffee. *Real meal* Fraunces Tavern® *(54 Pearl St, 10004; 212 968 1776; www.frauncestavern.com)* invokes an old-time feel with the Tallmadge Room's shared wooden tables and wide plank floors. The menu is a modern spin on American classics with a strong Irish influence.
- 🚻 **Restrooms** In the restaurant

KIDS' CORNER

Find out more...

1 Which New York City building was the tallest before the construction of the World Trade Center, and once again after 9/11? How many stories does it have?
2 Architect Daniel Libeskind has designed a complex of buildings at Ground Zero. What is the name of his project?
3 In 1783 a treaty was signed, ending the Revolutionary War and recognizing US sovereignty. What is the name of the treaty?

Answers at the bottom of the page.

George Washington
In 2012, the British National Army Museum conducted a poll that resulted in George Washington being declared "Britain's Greatest Military Enemy."

IRISH FAMINE FACTS

A disease called blight destroyed Ireland's potato crop for years, but it was not the only reason for the famine: another was that a lot of food grown in Ireland was exported to England, whose parliament ruled Ireland during that time.

All the way from the Emerald Isle

All the vegetation, stones, and even the dirt that make up the Irish Hunger Memorial was brought over from western Ireland for the project.

Answers: 1 The Empire State Building; it is 102 stories tall. **2** The complex is called the Freedom Tower. **3** The name of the treaty is the Treaty of Paris.

Swedish bakery and espresso bar, FIKA

Picnic under $20; **Snacks** $20–35; **Real meal** $35–70; **Family treat** over $70 (based on a family of four)

South Street Seaport and around

Though many New Yorkers equate the South Street Seaport with Pier 17 – home to a sprawling mall of shops and restaurants, but currently closed for redevelopment – there is a host of other attractions here too. There is lots for families to do in the area, from taking a historical tour of New York Harbor on a water taxi or high-speed motorboat to visiting the fascinating Seaport Museum and the Titanic Memorial Lighthouse along cobblestoned Fulton Street. Walking is one of the most enjoyable ways of exploring this waterfront neighborhood.

Downtown

The High Line
p84
Greenwich
Village
p78
Tenement Museum
p70
South Street
Seaport
Statue of Liberty
p56

Street performer at South Street Seaport

Places of interest

SIGHTS

1. South Street Seaport
2. Federal Reserve Bank of New York
3. Federal Hall
4. National September 11 Memorial & Museum

● **EAT AND DRINK**

1. Fulton Stall Market
2. Cowgirl Sea-Horse
3. Acqua Restaurant & Wine Bar
4. Fresh Salt
5. Zaitzeff

6. Brasserie les Halles
7. Alfanoose
8. Nelson Blue
9. Max Tribeca
10. Trinity Place

● **SHOPPING**

1. Babesta – Threads
2. Midtown Comics

● **WHERE TO STAY**

1. Best Western Seaport Inn
2. Cosmopolitan Hotel
3. Duane Street Hotel

Tribute WTC Visitor Center on Liberty Street, south of National September 11 Memorial & Museum

The Lowdown

🚙 **Subway** 2 & 3 to Fulton St; 4 & 5 to Wall St; J & Z to Broad St; E to World Trade Center.
Bus M1, M6, M9, M15, M109 & M22 crosstown; Downtown Connection (free shuttle bus)

ℹ️ **Visitor information** NYC & Company, 810 Seventh Ave, 10019; 212 484 1200; www. nycgo.com, also see www. southstreetseaport.com

🍽️ **Supermarket** 55 Fulton Market, 55 Fulton St, 10038; 646 581 9260
Market Seaport Youth Market, 19 Fulton St, 10038; 11 Jul–20 Nov: noon–5pm Thu

📽️ **Festival** River To River Festival, with concerts, children's programs, and art exhibits (Jun; www.lmcc.net/program/ rivertoriver)

➕ **Pharmacy** Downtown Pharmacy, 165 William St, 10038; 212 233 0333; 7am–8pm Mon–Fri, 9am–7pm Sat, 10am–8pm Sun

🛝 **Nearest playgrounds** Imagination Playground, Burling Slip, John St at Front St, 10038 (see p68). Washington Market Park, at Chambers St & Greenwich St, 10007 (see p69)

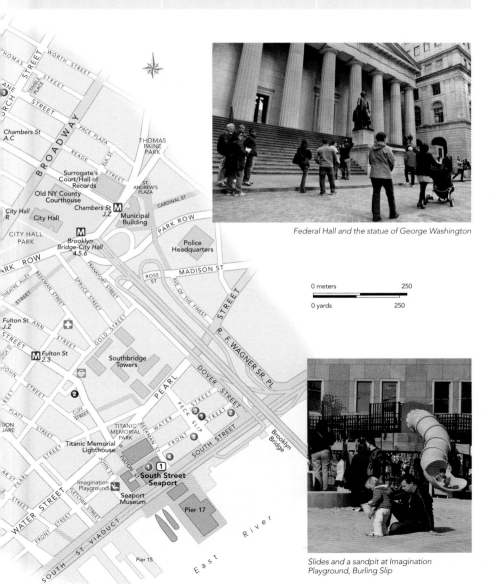

Federal Hall and the statue of George Washington

Slides and a sandpit at Imagination Playground, Burling Slip

① South Street Seaport

Tall ships and other seafaring craft

Few spots in New York are as steeped in history as South Street Seaport, a cobblestoned neighborhood that was the hub of maritime commerce for centuries. It has historic ships to explore, and a memorial to the victims of the *Titanic* attracting streams of visitors. Its piers are home to a flurry of boats, and in summer, open-air markets, a man-made beach, and free concerts add to the charm.

Historic Ships Among the Seaport Museum's ships are the four-masted barque *Peking*, the tugboat *W. O. Decker*, and *Ambrose*, a lightship.

Key Sights

Titanic Memorial Lighthouse The 62-ft (19-m) lighthouse was built in 1913, just a year after the *Titanic* sank. NYC was the intended destination of its maiden voyage.

Schermerhorn Row Built in 1810 by the Schermerhorns, a family of merchants, these brick buildings were leased to hotels and shops. Today, the row is home to the Seaport Museum and several stores.

Seaport Museum New York Partly restored portions of the former Fulton Ferry Hotel form part of the permanent display. It had large saloons on the first and second floors with fine furnishings.

Brooklyn Bridge

Pier 17

Maritime Crafts Center Part of the Seaport Museum, the center is a work-shop for maritime craftspeople, including model-builders who painstakingly create miniature ships and ships-in-a-bottle.

Ambrose

Ambrose Built in 1908, this lightship was used to guide ships safely in from the Atlantic Ocean over the shoals and sandbars of Lower New York Bay.

The Lowdown

🌐 **Map reference** 2 E3
Address Seaport Museum New York, 12 Fulton St, 10038; 212 748 8600; www.southstreetseaportmuseum.org (Pier 17 is currently closed for renovations); please phone for updates or check the museum website for information about visiting the ships and for opening and closing times.

🚇 **Subway** A, C, J, Z, 2, 3, 4 & 5 to Fulton St (3 different stations). **Bus** Downtown Connection, a free shuttle bus, operates 10am–7:30pm daily.

🕐 **Open** Seaport Museum & ships: 11am–5pm daily. Maritime Crafts Center: 11am–7pm daily

💲 **Price** Ships: $40–50, free on third Fri of the month 6–8:45pm

👪 **Cutting the line** Tickets for the ships can be purchased on the website.

👫 **Age range** 4 plus

👫 **Activities** Mini-mates program for 18–36-month-olds on Tue, Wed & Thu. A variety of workshops for ages 12 and up.

⏱ **Allow** 2–4 hours

🛍 **Shop** Bowne Printers, 209 Water St, 11am–7pm daily; Bowne & Co Stationers, 211 Water St, 11am–7pm daily.

☕ **Café** No, but several cafés and restaurants in this historic district.

🚻 **Restrooms** Inside the museum

Good family value?
A visit to one or more of the ships, a stroll around the portside streets, and easy access to good restaurants make this an enjoyable, if not cheap, family day out.

Prices given are for a family of four

Letting off steam

Ambrose Hall (18 Fulton St, 10038; 212 785 0018; noon–10pm Sun–Wed, noon–1am Thu–Sat) is a rustic craft beer hall with a large selection of ales as well as artisanal whiskey, scotch, bourbon, and gin. The menu complements the beer selection with gourmet bar snacks like kettle-cooked chips in melted cheese and baguette sliders.

Eat and drink

Picnic: under $20; Snacks: $20–35; Real meal: $35–70; Family treat: over $70 (based on a family of four)

PICNIC Fulton Stall Market (207A Front St/Cannon's Walk, 10038; 212 981 5157; 10am–5pm Sat, 11am–4pm Sun; www. fultonstallmarket.com) is made up of several different stalls run by local producers like Sun Fed Beef and Beth's Farm Kitchen. It operates an indoor farmers' market on weekends, and a permanent market shop daily. Imagination Playground, just south along South Street, makes a good picnic spot.

SNACKS Cowgirl Sea-Horse (259 Front St, 10038; 212 608 7873; www.cowgirlseahorse.com) like its sister restaurant Cowgirl, has a tasty mix of American comfort food (fried chicken, baby back ribs), Mexican fare (quesadillas, nachos), and seafood (fish tacos, crab cakes).

REAL MEAL Acqua Restaurant & Wine Bar (21 Peck Slip at Water St, 10038; 212 349 4433; www.acqua restaurantnyc.com) is a casual, family-friendly spot with rustic charm and an excellent selection of fresh pasta and pizzas.

FAMILY TREAT Fresh Salt (146 Beekman St, 10038; 212 962 0053; www.freshsalt.com) offers a hearty

Entrance to Acqua Restaurant & Wine Bar

brunch, and their menu has simple dishes kids will enjoy, like pita melt and homemade mac 'n' cheese.

Shopping

Babesta – Threads (66 West Broadway, 10007; 212 608 4522; www.babesta.com) carries a staggering array of hip children's clothing, furniture, and gear. Farther east is the Downtown branch of **Midtown Comics** (64 Fulton St, 10038; 212 302 8192) for comics, action figures, and graphic novels.

Racks full of comics and graphic novels at Midtown Comics

Find out more

DIGITAL For an extensive look at this historic district's past and present, including the lowdown on its fleet of old ships, visit www. southstreetseaportmuseum.org. For updates on concerts and events visit www.southstreetseaport.com

Next stop...

LITTLE AIRPLANE PRODUCTIONS

Stop by Little Airplane Productions (207 Front St, 10038; 212 965 8999; www.littleairplane.com; $40–50), a studio where kids' animated TV programs like Wonder Pets, Go, Baby! and 3rd & Bird are made. The Small Potatoes Animation Factory Tour ($10) introduces children to every aspect of creating an animation show, from writing and drawing to post-production dubbing.

KIDS' CORNER

Look out for...

1 Artisans at the Maritime Crafts Center use wood to create replicas of ship's figureheads. Do you know what they are?

2 While at South Street Seaport, which of New York's bridges can you see?

3 One of the Seaport's ships is a schooner called *Pioneer*. In the days before trucks, she transported heavy loads. Can you see what she is made of?

Answers at the bottom of the page.

SCHOOL ON A BOAT

After she was decommissioned in 1932, the *Peking* spent 40 years serving as a boys' boarding school on the Medway River in England.

Daily reminder

The original home of the Titanic Memorial Lighthouse was on top of the Seamen's Church Institute, which was eventually torn down. It was never a real lighthouse, but it did signal to ships in the harbor. At noon each day, the ball on top used to drop down the pole to signal the time.

Answers: 1 Figureheads are the carved wood decorations found at the prow of a ship. They show the wealth of the owner and often symbolize a quality, or the ship's name – beautiful ladies, Greek gods and ferocious lions. **2** Brooklyn Bridge **3** She has a hull made of steel and frames of iron.

② Federal Reserve Bank of New York

Gold bars and armed guards

The magical sight of bars made of pure gold may seem like something out of a fairy tale, but this huge bank has thousands upon thousands of them. One of 12 branches of the Federal Reserve Bank, the New York location houses about 6,700 metric tons (6,078 tonnes) of gold bullion in its vault, 80 ft (24 m) below the city's streets. In all likelihood it is the largest repository of gold in the world, yet, most of it is owned not by the US but by foreign countries and institutions. The tour, which families can take with advance reservation, begins in the Numismatic (coin) Room. Look out for the famed 1933 Double Eagle, the only such coin in the world on public display. The Mint intended to

Slides, swings, and climbing sets at Imagination Playground

destroy all but two of the Double Eagles made in 1933, but a handful were stolen; this is one of them. An anonymous bidder paid more than $7.5 million for the rarity at an auction in 2002, but agreed to let it be exhibited here.

After watching a short video about the Federal Reserve, take the elevator to the storage vaults. The only way to access them is through a 10-ft (3-m) long hallway; it is part of a 90-ton (80-tonne) steel cylinder that can be closed off at a moment's notice in an emergency. Once inside, see some of the 122 storage vaults – each protected by iron grills and filled with stacks of 27-lb (12-kg) gold bars – as well as a huge scale for weighing gold, and special shoe covers made of magnesium. Costing about $500 a pair, these protect the feet of workers transporting the heavy treasure, in case any bars are

Federal Reserve Bank of New York, built in the style of a Renaissance palace

dropped. One of the Treasury Department's other jobs is to destroy worn-out currency. Get a first-hand look at the results – visitors receive a packet of shredded dollar bills on their way out.

Letting off steam

Surrounded by a curvaceous wooden walkway, **Imagination Playground** *(2 Fulton St, 10038)* offers sand, water, huge foam blocks, wheelbarrows, and buckets for kids to play with.

③ Federal Hall

Where George Washington became America's first president

Almost everyone knows that Washington, D.C. is the capital of the US, but it was not always so. The very first seat of the US government was, in fact, located in New York City, in the building on Wall Street known as Federal Hall. The first Congress met and wrote the Bill of Rights here, and General George Washington took the oath of office on the balcony on April 30, 1789, to become the country's first president.

A grand statue of Washington greets visitors on the front steps of the building, which was modeled after the Parthenon in Athens. Even though the original Federal Hall was demolished in 1812, long after the US Capitol was moved to Philadelphia (in 1790), the historic building that took its place is worth a look with its huge rotunda and exhibits on the history of New York.

The Lowdown

🌐 **Map reference** 1 D4
Address 33 Liberty St (visitor entrance at 44 Maiden Lane), 10045; 212 720 6130; www.newyorkfed.org

🚇 **Subway** A, C, 4 & 5 to Fulton St; 4 & 5 to Wall St. **Bus** M5 & M15

🕐 **Open** Guided tours of the gold vault, 1pm & 2pm Mon & Tue except bank holidays; arrive 20–30 minutes before tour starts for security screening. Printed tickets and a valid government-issued ID are required for entry.

💲 **Price** Free

👫 **Cutting the line** Tours must be reserved ahead of time.

🏷 **Guided tours** Registration for public guided tours opens 30 days prior to the requested date. It is

recommended to book early. Visitors will receive a confirmation number for their booking via email.

👫 **Age range** 16 plus

⏱ **Allow** 1 hour

🍴 **Eat and drink** *Real meal* Zaitzeff *(72 Nassau St, 10038; 212 571 7272)* serves burgers and sandwiches at communal tables. *Family treat* Brasserie les Halles *(15 John St, 10038; 212 285 8585)* offers French bistro classics including *beef bourguignon* (beef braised in red wine) and *moules frites* (mussels and fries).

👫 **Restrooms** On each floor

Letting off steam

Dotted with trees and benches, **Zuccotti Park** *(between Broadway St & Church St, 10006)* is a good place for a picnic or to run around.

The Lowdown

- 🌐 **Map reference** 1 D4
  Address 26 Wall St, 10005; 212 825 6990; *www.nps.gov/feha*
- 🚗 **Subway** J & Z to Broad St; 4 & 5 to Wall St. **Bus** M5 & M15
- 🕐 **Open** 9am–5pm Mon–Fri
- 💲 **Price** Free
- 🚩 **Guided tours** Free ranger-led and self-guided tours available
- 👫 **Age range** 4 plus
- 🏃 **Activities** Walking tours of Downtown start from Federal Hall (Jun–Nov only).
- ⏱ **Allow** 1 hour
- 🍴 **Eat and drink** *Snacks* Alfanoose *(64 Fulton St, 10038; 212 577 8888)* offers delicious, affordable Middle Eastern appetizers and standards like falafel. *Real meal* Nelson Blue *(233–235 Front St at Peck Slip, 10038; 212 346 9090)* prides itself on bringing flavors of New Zealand to New York, from lamb burgers to steamed mussels.
- 🚻 **Restrooms** By the entrance

④ National September 11 Memorial & Museum

In remembrance

After September 11, 2001, when Al-Qaeda terrorists flew two commercial airliners into the Twin Towers of the World Trade Center, there was no place near Ground Zero where visitors could learn about the fateful day that killed nearly 3,000 people. In 2011, the National September 11 Memorial became the first World Trade Center site open to the public since 2001. The museum was dedicated in 2014, and includes photos, video, documents, personal effects, and two steel tridents that formed the entrance to Tower 1.

Two giant square waterfalls-cum-reflecting pools are situated where the towers once stood, surrounded by bronze panels inscribed with the names of those who lost their lives on September 11 and in an earlier WTC attack, in 1993.

Letting off steam

Washington Market Park *(at the intersection of Chambers St & Greenwich St, 10007)* has a huge lawn for playing soccer and a series of playgrounds for all age groups.

The Lowdown

- 🌐 **Map reference** 1 C3
  Address 1 Liberty Plaza, 10006; 212 266 5211; *www.911memorial.org*
- 🚗 **Subway** E to World Trade Center; R to Cortlandt St. **Bus** M5 & M20
- 🕐 **Open** Memorial: 7:30am–9pm daily; Museum: 9am–8pm daily (to 9pm Fri & Sat)
- 💲 **Price** Memorial: free; Museum: $63–78; under 6s free; free on Tue (5–8pm)
- 👫 **Age range** All ages
- ⏱ **Allow** 2 hours
- 🍴 **Eat and drink** *Real meal* Max Tribeca *(181 Duane St, 10013; 212 966 5939)*, a rustic eatery, has authentic pastas. *Family treat* Trinity Place *(115 Broadway, 10006; 212 964 0939)* serves fresh pasta, inventive salads, tuna, and steak tartar.
- 🚻 **Restrooms** In the museum

Signing steel beams used in the construction of the National September 11 Memorial

KIDS' CORNER

Find out more...

1 Billions of dollars' worth of gold is stored at the Federal Reserve Bank. Does all the gold belong to the United States government?
2 Shoe covers made of magnesium can be seen at the Federal Reserve Bank. What are they for, and about how much does one pair cost?
3 Washington, D.C., is the capital of the US today. Where was the capital located when George Washington became the country's first president?

Answers at the bottom of the page.

How much do you weigh?
If each gold bar weighs 27 lb (12 kg), how many gold bars would it take to equal your weight?

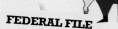

FEDERAL FILE

Every federal officer who works at the Federal Reserve Bank of New York is also a marksman. They practice shooting at a site in the building; and their ability is tested twice a year.

Soaring icon of hope

The Freedom Tower built on the WTC site is 1,776 ft (541 m) tall, a reference to the year America's Declaration of Independence was ratified by the Continental Congress. The tower is the brainchild of architect Daniel Libeskind, whose design won a contest held in 2003 to decide how the site would be rebuilt.

Answers: 1 No, most of it belongs to other countries and their institutions. **2** Their function is to protect workers' feet in case they drop a bar of gold on them; they cost $500 a pair. **3** The capital was New York City.

Tenement Museum and around

Home to New York's largest concentration of immigrants in the late 19th and early 20th centuries, the Lower East Side is a fascinating mix of old and new, traditional and hip. Its historic attractions center on the Tenement Museum, a series of re-created tenement apartments that are open to the public via scheduled tours. Due to its robust nightlife, especially on weekends, the neighborhood is best visited by families during the day.

Downtown

The High Line
p84

Greenwich
Village
p78

Tenement
Museum

South Street
Seaport
p64

Statue of Liberty
p56

La France coal-fired steam engine on display, New York City Fire Museum

Places of interest

SIGHTS
1. Tenement Museum
2. Lower East Side
3. New Museum
4. Little Italy
5. Ukrainian Museum
6. Children's Museum of the Arts
7. Chinatown
8. New York City Fire Museum

🔴 **EAT AND DRINK**
1. Despaña
2. Cheeky Sandwiches
3. Katz's Delicatessen
4. Stanton Social
5. Yonah Schimmel Knishery
6. Cafe Katya
7. Freemans
8. Peasant

9. Vanessa's Dumpling House
10. Balthazar
11. Lombardi's Pizza
12. Blue Ribbon
13. Nha Trang
14. Peking Duck House
15. Ear Inn
16. Mooncake Foods

See also New Museum (pp174–5)

🔴 **SHOPPING**
1. Jane's Exchange
2. Ted's Fine Clothing

See also Tenement Museum (p72)

🔴 **WHERE TO STAY**
1. Blue Moon
2. Bowery Hotel
3. The Gem Hotel SoHo
4. Hotel on Rivington
5. Off SoHo Suites

0 meters   300

0 yards   300

ESSEX STREET
RETAIL MARKET

A store on busy Essex Street

Freshly baked treats on display at the legendary Katz's Delicatessen

The Lowdown

Subway B & D to Grand St; J, M & Z to Delancey St; F to Second Ave; 6 to Spring St (C & E to Spring St by 6th Ave); B, D, F & M to Broadway-Lafayette St. **Bus** M9, M15, M21 & M14A

Visitor information Lower East Side Visitor Center, 54 Orchard St, 10002; 212 226 9010; *www.lowereastsideny.com*; 10am–6pm Mon–Fri; noon–5pm Sat & Sun

Supermarket Key Foods, 52 Ave A, 10009; 212 477 9063 **Market** Essex Street Market, 120 Essex St, 10002; 212 312 3603; 8am–7pm Mon–Sat, 10am–6pm Sun

Festivals The Lower East Side Festival of the Arts (usually on the last weekend of May) features theater and dance performances. Egg Rolls & Egg Creams Festival (usually first or second Sun of Jun). The Feast of San Gennaro has processions, music, dancing, and sideshows (Sep).

Pharmacy Rite Aid, 408 Grand St, 10002; 212 529 7115; 24 hours daily

Nearest playgrounds Seward Park, east of Essex St, between Grand St & East Broadway, 10002. Lillian D. Wald Playground (*see p73*). Hester Street Playground (*see p74*). Desalvio Playground (*see p75*). James J. Walker Park (*see p77*). Tompkins Square Park (*see p75*). Columbus Park (*see p76–7*).

① Tenement Museum
A time capsule discovered

The Tenement Museum transports visitors back to the years between 1863, when the building was constructed, and the 1930s, when its owner sealed it off. Close to 7,000 working-class people lived in the tenement over that period, a time when immigration to the US reached its peak. In 1988, six apartments were discovered intact and painstakingly restored, and they now bring the immigrant experience to life through guided tours and re-enactments. Each tour covers just one or two apartments.

Entrance to the Tenement Museum

Guided Tours

Victoria Confino This 1-hour tour visits the first-floor apartment of Greek Sephardic immigrants. A costumed interpreter plays the role of 14-year-old Victoria Confino, while visitors take on the part of newly arrived immigrants.

Irish Outsiders This apartment was once home to an Irish immigrant family, who moved here in the second half of the 19th century.

Third Floor

Sweatshop Workers This tour explores the life of Jewish immigrants by visiting the garment shop of the Levine family and the apartment of the Rogarshevskys on the third floor.

Hard Times There are two separate tours on the second floor. The 1-hour Hard Times tour visits the apartments of the German-Jewish Gumpertz family, whose father disappeared in the Depression of 1873, and the Baldizzis, who lived through the 1930s Great Depression. A 2-hour version (ages 12 plus) explores the experiences of the two families in more detail.

Second Floor

First Floor

Entrance

The Lowdown

🌐 **Map reference** 5 C5
Address 103 Orchard St, 10002; 212 982 8420; *www.tenement.org*

🚇 **Subway** B & D to Grand St; F to Essex St; J, M & Z to Delancey St

🕐 **Open** 10am–6:30pm daily, till 8:30pm Thu

💲 **Price** $70–90; walking tours are discounted when purchased with an apartment tour (online only).

👫 **Cutting the line** Book tickets at *www.tenement.org/tours.php* or call 877 975 3786 to make bookings in advance.

🚩 **Guided tours** In addition to the tours above, Outside the Home is a 90-minute walking tour for kids aged 8 and above, visiting a public elementary school; Then and Now is a 2-hour tour, also for ages 8 and above, focusing on the history of the Lower East Side and the lives of immigrants who settled here.

👫 **Age range** 5 plus

👫 **Activities** Readings and period re-enactments; free talks at the shop

⏱ **Allow** 2 hours

♿ **Wheelchair access** Limited

🏷 **Shop** The Tenement Museum Shop has children's books about immigration and tenement life.

🚻 **Restrooms** At the Visitors' Center

Good family value?
Despite the somewhat hefty admission price, the Tenement Museum provides an invaluable experience for kids, who will love its interactive approach to living history.

Shooting hoops on a basketball court, Lillian D. Wald Playground

Letting off steam

Named for a woman who pioneered the rights of children, the tree-ringed **Lillian D. Wald Playground** (at Cherry, Gouverneur, Monroe, and Montgomery Streets, 10002) is home to handball, basketball, and volleyball courts, as well as staples such as swings and jungle gyms.

Eat and drink

Picnic: under $20; Snacks: $20–35; Real meal: $35–70; Family treat: over $70 (based on a family of four)

PICNIC Despaña (408 Broome St, between Lafayette St & Cleveland Pl, 10013; 212 219 5050) has Spanish cured meats, cheeses, tortillas and, on weekends, churros (donuts). Pick up supplies and head to the Lillian D. Wald Playground for a picnic.
SNACKS Cheeky Sandwiches (35 Orchard St, near Hester St, 10002) is a no-frills but charming spot serving Cajun and Creole soups and sandwiches, including fried oyster po' boys (submarine sandwiches) and fried chicken on buttermilk biscuits.
REAL MEAL Katz's Delicatessen (205 East Houston St, 10002; 212 254 2246), established in 1888,

continues the immigrant theme with its vintage atmosphere and traditional menu including soups, bagels, and legendary brisket, pastrami, and tasty corned-beef sandwiches.
FAMILY TREAT Stanton Social (99 Stanton St, 10002; 212 995 0099) has a multi-ethnic share plate menu, a raw bar, and 40 other dishes to choose from, like Kobe beef burgers and red snapper tacos. It becomes a party spot at night.

Shopping

Jane's Exchange (191 East 3rd St, 10009; 212 677 0380) is a quality children's and maternity consignment store, with a variety of new and "gently used" clothing. **Ted's Fine Clothing** (155 Orchard St, 10002; 212 966 2029) offers new, vintage-style rocker tees and memorabilia for adults and kids.

Find out more

DIGITAL The museum's website, www.tenement.org, has a section called "Play" with interactive activities such as a virtual walking tour and an immigration game.

Next stop...

ELDRIDGE STREET SYNAGOGUE Just a few blocks away is the magnificent Eldridge Street Synagogue (12 Eldridge St, 10002; www.eldridgestreet.org), which was built by members of the Lower East Side immigrant community in 1887. Reopened in 2007, after an extraordinary 20-year restoration, the synagogue offers tours Sunday through Friday 10am–4pm Sun–Thu, till 3pm Fri. Admission is free on Mondays.

Photographs of famous patrons along the restaurant wall, Katz's Delicatessen

A variety of fruit and vegetables for sale, Essex Street Market

② Lower East Side
Sweet treats and deli delights

Once an enclave teeming with working-class immigrants, the Lower East Side has a cultural identity unlike any other neighborhood in the city. Some of the small, independent stores that sprang up here almost 100 years ago are still going strong today, along with a new crop of businesses crafting everything from *gelato* (soft ice cream) to handmade bagels.

Start by paying a visit to the oldest and most renowned of the originals, **Russ & Daughters** (*179 East Houston St; www.russanddaughters. com*), which has been run by the

Russ family for 100 years, since 1914. The shop specializes in smoked and cured fish, caviar, and other delicacies. Next, head down Essex Street to the revitalized **Essex Street Market** (*120 Essex St*), an indoor collection of food stalls, and seek out Saxelby Cheesemongers. Tasting is encouraged, so try a few samples – all but the parmesan is small batch from domestic farms. Backtrack up to Rivington Street for **Economy Candy** (*108 Rivington St; www.economy candy.com*), the city's ultimate treat emporium, with just about every candy bar known to mankind, plus chocolate by the pound. A couple of blocks back down Essex Street is **Kossar's Bialys** (*367 Grand St; www.kossarsbialys. com*), which since 1936 has been producing a small roll called a bialy, a savory cousin of the bagel with a pat of onion paste in its middle. This New York specialty was once so in demand that the bialy industry had its own union. Continue to **Doughnut Plant** (*379 Grand St; www.doughnut plant.com*), which has elevated the doughnut to an art form with flavored glazes and a core recipe from owner Mark Isreal's grandfather, who baked them in the 1930s. For the last stop, visit **il laboratorio del gelato** (*188 Ludlow St; www.laboratorio delgelato.com*), which offers premium ice cream made on site in nearly 200 flavors.

Letting off steam
At the foot of Sara D. Roosevelt Park is the **Hester Street Playground** (*between Chrystie St & Forsythe St, 10002*). Kids can run through a series of spray showers, play on swings, climb on giant play structures, and try out several sets of rings.

The Lowdown

- 🌐 **Map reference** 5 C4
  Address Houston St to Manhattan Bridge, between Bowery & FDR Drive
- 🚇 **Subway** F to East Broadway, Second Ave or Essex St; J, M & Z to Delancey St; B & D to Grand St. **Bus** M9, M14A, M15 & M103
- 🚩 **Guided tours** A self-guided tour-cum-podcast can be downloaded at *www. lowereastsideny.com*.
- 👫 **Age range** All ages
- ⏱ **Allow** 2–3 hours
- ☕ **Eat and drink** *Snacks* Yonah Schimmel Knishery (*137 East Houston St; 212 477 2858*) specializes in old-world Eastern European fare such as made-on-premises *knishes* (savory or sweet), *blintzes*, and borscht. *Real meal* Café Katya (*79 Orchard St; 212 219 9545*) offers kid-friendly options like burgers and meatballs.
- 🚻 **Restrooms** In Hester Street Playground and various restaurants

③ New Museum
Unique art and architecture

The New Museum is the first newly constructed art museum Downtown has ever had and the only one in the city devoted to emerging artists. Though founded in 1977, the museum rose to prominence in 2007 with the unveiling of its new home, designed by cutting-edge Japanese architectural firm SANAA.

The Lowdown

- 🌐 **Map reference** 5 B4
  Address 235 Bowery 10002; 212 219 1222; *www.newmuseum.org*
- 🚇 **Subway** F to Second Ave; N & R to Prince St; 6 to Spring St. **Bus** M5, M21 & M103
- ⏱ **Open** 11am–6pm Wed, Fri, Sat & Sun, 11am–9pm Thu
- 💲 **Price** $32; under 18s free
- 👫 **Cutting the line** Purchase advance tickets at *www.new museum.org*
- 🚩 **Guided tours** Free docent-led 45-minute tours, 12:30pm Wed–Sun, plus 3pm Sat & Sun.
- 👫 **Age range** 5 plus
- 👫 **Activities** Resource Center offers books, and computers. Free workshop for kids between 3–10 years on the first Sat of the month.
- ⏱ **Allow** 2 hours
- ♿ **Wheelchair access** Yes
- ☕ **Eat and drink** *Snacks* Hester Street Café (*on site*) offers sandwiches, tea, coffee, and baked goods. *Family treat* Freemans (*Off Rivington, between the Bowery & Chrystie, 10002; 212 420 0012*) has a rustic menu of seasonal classics.
- 🚻 **Restrooms** On various floors

Sculptural stack of aluminum-clad cubes, New Museum building

The building comprises seven floors that appear to be precariously stacked one on top of the other – each floor is of a different width and height – and clad in a shimmering, aluminum-mesh skin. One of New York's most contemporary exhibition spaces, it includes innovative digital art and video installations. The museum's bold, large-scale exhibits (all of which are temporary) are often interactive and especially engaging for children.

Letting off steam
In the easternmost part of the East Village is **Tompkins Square Park** (East Seventh St & Ave A, 10009). Graced by huge, rare American elms, three playgrounds, several permanent chess tables, and a dog run, it is perfect for playing and picnicking.

④ Little Italy
Colors and flavors of Italy
Once home to the city's largest concentration of Italian immigrants, today Little Italy has largely disappeared, having either morphed into Chinatown or become gentrified boutique territory such as the neighborhood of Nolita (North of Little Italy). However, vestiges of its cultural identity remain, most prominently in the area along Mulberry Street between Grand and Hester streets, which is very popular and packed with Italian eateries. A number of small Italian grocers retain the old flavor, among them **Piemonte Ravioli** (190 Grand St, 10013), which sells a creative selection of fresh and dried pasta.

An Italian cheese shop, **Alleva** (188 Grand St, 10013), opened in 1892 and has been run by four generations of the same family. Another cheese-centric shop, with about 300 varieties, is **Di Palo Selects** (200 Grand St, 10013), which offers homemade mozzarella and a fantastic selection of imported dried goods. Right across the street is **E. Rossi & Co.** (193 Grand St, 10013), a general store filled to the brim with Italian goods ranging from religious figurines to soccer jerseys.

In September, the San Gennaro Festival takes over Mulberry Street with music, food stalls, amusement rides, and parades, plus a sea of red, green, and white decorations paying tribute to the colors of the Italian flag.

Letting off steam
Desalvio Playground (at the corner of Mulberry St & Spring St, 10002) has modular play equipment, built-in chess tables, and basketball courts.

The Lowdown
- 🌐 **Map reference** 5 A5
- **Address** From Houston St to Canal St, between Bowery and Lafayette St
- 🚇 **Subway** N & R to Prince St; B, D, F & M to Broadway-Lafayette St; 6 to Spring St. **Bus** M21 & M103
- ⏱ **Allow** 1–2 hours
- ☕ **Eat and drink** Real meal The Butcher's Daughter (19 Kenmare St, 10012; 212 219 3434) serves vegetarian (mostly vegan) meals. Family treat Peasant (194 Elizabeth St, 10012; 212 965 9511) features open-fire cooking and an Italian menu.
- 🚻 **Restrooms** Inside various restaurants

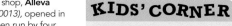

KIDS' CORNER
Find out more…
1 What are the small, family-run shops in the Lower East Side known for?
2 In the 19th century, there were so many bakers making this traditional roll that they formed their own union. What is it called, and how does it differ from a bagel?
3 Why do you think the seven floors of the New Museum are stacked one on top of the other at different angles?
4 This cheese is a traditional part of Italian cooking and it is still made in abundance in New York's Little Italy. What is it called?

⋯⋯⋯⋯⋯⋯⋯⋯⋯⋯⋯⋯⋯⋯

Answers at the bottom of the page.

MILK AND CHEESE
Mozzarella can be made with the milk of cows or, surprisingly, of water buffalo. Their milk has a higher fat content that makes it ideal for making cheese.

A dog's paradise
Tompkins Square Park is known for its lavish dog run, which cost almost $500,000 to renovate. It has three swimming pools for dogs, a bath area with hoses, and picnic tables (for people). It also hosts the biggest dog dress-up Halloween celebration in the country.

⋯⋯⋯⋯⋯⋯⋯⋯⋯⋯⋯⋯⋯⋯

Answers: 1 Many of them specialize in one thing, like doughnuts. **2** The bialy; unlike bagels, bialys have onion paste pressed into their center rather than a hole. **3** So that the sunlight can enter different galleries at different times of the day. **4** Mozzarella.

Relaxing on benches at Tompkins Square Park

Picnic under $20; **Snacks** $20–35; **Real meal** $35–70; **Family treat** over $70 (based on a family of four)

Traditional attire on display at the Ukrainian Museum

⑤ Ukrainian Museum

Costumes and culture

Home to a huge permanent collection of folk and fine art, the Ukrainian Museum moved to its current location in the East Village in 2005. The museum, founded in 1976, showcases a beguiling collection of Ukrainian costumes, lavishly embroidered peasant blouses, colorful sashes, fancy sheepskin, and fur vests, and wedding wreaths of yarn and ribbons. The folk art collection has more than 8,000 objects, making it one of the most important collections outside Ukraine. Exhibits include ceramics, metalwork, carved wooden objects, and Ukrainian Easter eggs.

The Lowdown

- 🌐 **Map reference** 5 A3
- **Address** 222 East 6th St (between 2nd & 3rd Ave), 10003; 212 228 0110; www.ukrainianmuseum.org
- 🚗 **Subway** 6, N, R & F **Bus** M15, M101, M102, M103, M1, M3, M8
- ☺ **Open** 11:30am–5pm Wed–Sun
- Ⓢ **Price** $24–32; under 12s free
- 👫 **Age range** 5 plus
- 👪 **Activities** Family program about Ukrainian culture for ages 5–12. Drop-in workshop $5 per person.
- ♂ **Allow** 1–2 hours
- ♿ **Wheelchair access** Yes
- 🍴 **Eat and drink** *Snacks* Vanessa's Dumpling House *(118A Eldridge St, 10002; 212 625 8008)* serves dumplings and more. *Family treat* Balthazar *(80 Spring St, 10012; 212 965 1414)* offers traditional bistro fare.
- 👫 **Restrooms** On the main floor

Letting off steam

Head west on Houston Street to spot the I. M. Pei and James Ingo Freed-designed **Silver Towers** *(110 Bleecker St, 10012)*. The complex boasts a sculpture designed by Picasso, *Bust of Sylvette* (1967), built by Norwegian artist Carl Nesjär with the maestro's assistance. Kids can run around and look at the artwork from different angles.

⑥ Children's Museum of the Arts

Playacting and art collections

A 2011 renovation tripled the size of this popular rainy-day destination for kids and their families. The 10,000-sq-ft (929-sq-m) space features various large-scale collections of art created by children. Rotating exhibitions have included works by renowned artists such as Keith Haring and Misaki Kawai. Other exhibits include a new media lab featuring a sound booth and a clay bar, as well as video-making and animation equipment to drive CMA's award-winning media programs.

There is also a Fine Arts Studio, where kids can collaborate with artists to create works of art to take home. Kids under 5 years old can visit the WEE Arts Studio for music, storytelling, drumming, and more. The museum also has a 2,000-piece collection of international children's art dating back to the 1930s.

Letting off steam

The museum's Ball Pond is an enclosed area full of giant, multi-colored balls that kids can climb up and fall off to their hearts' content.

Bright signage above the entrance of Chinatown Ice Cream Factory

The Lowdown

- 🌐 **Map reference** 4 E5
- **Address** 103 Charlton St, 10014; 212 274 0986; http://cmany.org
- 🚗 **Subway** 1 to Houston St; C & E to Spring St. **Bus** M20 & M21
- ☺ **Open** Noon–5pm Mon & Wed, noon–6pm Thu & Fri, 10am–5pm Sat & Sun
- Ⓢ **Price** $44; free 4–6pm Thu
- 👫 **Age range** All ages
- ♿ **Allow** 1–2 hours
- ♿ **Wheelchair access** Yes
- 🍴 **Eat and drink** *Real meal* Lombardi's Pizza *(32 Spring St, 10012; 212 941 7994)* serves coal-oven regular and white pies, as well as a selection of salads. *Family treat* Blue Ribbon *(97 Sullivan St, 10012; 212 274 0404)* offers lobster, rack of lamb, and hangar steak. There is also a friendly bar.
- 👫 **Restrooms** On several floors

⑦ Chinatown

Bustling markets and amazing ice cream

Its borders somewhat indistinct, Chinatown is a sprawling, expanding neighborhood with the feel of a totally different city. Ultra-crowded Canal Street teems with vendors hawking fake designer items of all sorts, from sunglasses and handbags to jewelry. Start in Nolita and head south on Mott Street, where the West gradually gives way to the East as one enters Chinatown.

The neighborhood is filled with shoppers stocking up on exotic vegetables, fresh fruit, fish, and rice – at prices far below those at local supermarkets. Continue across Canal Street on Mott to find more shops, as well as teahouses and restaurants. Stop at the **Chinatown Ice Cream Factory** *(65 Bayard St, 10013; www.chinatownicecream factory.com)* for exceptional small-batch ice cream in flavors such as black sesame or lychee, before heading to Columbus Park.

Letting off steam

The fascinating **Columbus Park** *(between Baxter St, Bayard St, Worth St & Mulberry St, 10013)* is a small world unto itself, where locals practice tai chi, play Chinese chess, and just plain people-watch. A playground and some grassy

New York City Fire Museum, which houses a vast collection of firefighting equipment

The Lowdown

🌐 **Map reference** 2 E1
Address Grand St to Worth St, between Lafayette St & the FDR Drive

🚇 **Subway** B & D to Grand St; J & Z to Canal St. **Bus** M22 & M103

👫 **Age range** All ages

🕐 **Allow** 1–2 hours

🍽 **Eat and drink** *Real meal* Nha Trang (87 Baxter St, 10013; 212 233 5948) is a no-frills, family-style Vietnamese restaurant with extremely tasty dishes that can be shared by all the family. *Family treat* Peking Duck House (28 Mott St, 10013; 212 227 1810; www.pekingduckhousenyc.com) is a rare upscale Chinatown find, with specialties ranging from its Peking duck dinner to sizzling prawns.

👫 **Restrooms** At Columbus Park

patches are perfect for kids to run around and play on.

⑧ New York City Fire Museum

Hoses, hydrants, and heroes

Pre-Civil War hand-pumped fire engines, hoses and hydrants, painted leather buckets, and old-fashioned helmets are among the artifacts on view at this museum, which is dedicated to the daily heroism of the city's firefighters. It is housed within a 1904 fire station on Spring Street and full of stories, told through sepia photographs and documents. The entire first floor is an exhibit devoted to the 343 fire personnel who died on September 11, 2001 (see p49), while trying to rescue survivors of the terror attack on the World Trade Center. This includes a glass case with the tools firefighters used to search for survivors, and an interactive computer station.

Letting off steam

Head to **James J. Walker Park** (St. Lukes Pl at Hudson St, 10014), which has swings, climbing equipment and, in summer, sprinklers and benches in the shade. The adjacent public swimming pool, **Tony Dapolito Recreation Center** (1 Clarkson St, 10014), is open from late June through August.

The Lowdown

🌐 **Map reference** 4 F5
Address 278 Spring St, 10013; 212 691 1303

🚇 **Subway** C & E to Spring St; 1 to Houston St. **Bus** M20 & M21

🕐 **Open** 10am–5pm daily; closed Jan 1, Easter, Jul 4, Thanksgiving Day & Dec 25

💲 **Price** $26–36; under 2s free

🎗 **Guided tours** Available for groups of 10 or more, tours include fire-safety training: adults $5, children $3; for reservations, call 212 691 1303.

👫 **Age range** All ages

🕐 **Allow** 1 hour

♿ **Wheelchair access** Yes

🍽 **Eat and drink** *Snacks* Ear Inn (326 Spring St, 10013; 212 226 9060) serves reasonably priced dishes, such as mussels in white wine sauce, burgers, salads, and several entrées. *Real meal* Mooncake Foods (28 Watts St, 10013; 212 219 8888) offers Asian fare, including salads, summer rolls, and chicken wings.

👫 **Restrooms** On the first floor

Greenwich Village and around

With its tree-lined streets and easygoing vibe, Greenwich Village has special appeal even to native New Yorkers. Meandering on foot is a great way to explore the neighborhood, and while the West Village is the historic heart, the East Village and neighboring Flatiron District have their charms too, especially around Union Square and St. Mark's Place. The area is busy day and night, though the Flatiron District tends to empty in the evening once the stores close, so it pays to plan an itinerary carefully.

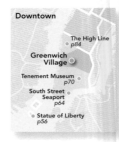

Downtown

The High Line
p84

Greenwich Village

Tenement Museum
p70

South Street
Seaport
p64

Statue of Liberty
p56

Houses along the perimeter of Washington Square Park

0 meters   400

0 yards   400

Places of interest

SIGHTS

1. Greenwich Village
2. East Village
3. Flatiron District & Union Square Greenmarket
4. Theodore Roosevelt Birthplace

EAT AND DRINK

1. Murray's Cheese Bar
2. Mamoun's Falafel
3. Cowgirl
4. Minetta Tavern
5. Artichoke Basille's Pizza
6. Cacio e Pepe
7. Maoz Vegetarian
8. Japonica
9. Rainbow Falafel
10. Republic

SHOPPING

1. Ibiza Kidz
2. Forbidden Planet
3. Strand Bookstore
See also Flatiron District (p82)

WHERE TO STAY

1. Gramercy Park Hotel
2. Hotel 17
3. Inn on 23rd Street
4. Larchmont Hotel
5. Marcel at Gramercy
6. St Marks Hotel
7. The Standard, East Village
8. Union Square Inn
9. W New York Union Square

Entrance of Republic restaurant, opposite Union Square Park

A vendor selling records, East Village

The Lowdown

🚇 **Subway** A, B, C, D, E, F, & M to West 4th St-Washington Sq; N & R to 8th St-NYU; F & M to 14th St; 6 to Astor Place. **Bus** M2, M3, M5 & M8

ℹ️ **Visitor information** NYC & Company, 810 Seventh Ave, 10019; 212 484 1200; *www.nycgo.com*

🛒 **Supermarket** D'Agostino, 790 Greenwich St, 10014; 212 691 9198
Market Union Square Greenmarket, Union Square West, between 14th St & 17th St; 8am–6pm Mon, Wed, Fri & Sat. Abingdon Square Greenmarket, Hudson St, between Eighth Ave & West 12th St; 8am–2pm Sat

🎭 **Festivals** Washington Square Outdoor Art Exhibit (Memorial Day weekend & Labor Day weekend). Halloween Parade (Oct 31). Gay Pride Parade (last Sun of Jun)

➕ **Pharmacy** Duane Reade, 4 West 4th St, 10012; 212 473 1027; 7am–midnight Mon–Fri, 8am–10pm Sat, 8am–9pm Sun

🛝 **Nearest playgrounds** Madison Square Park (see p83). Union Square Park (see pp82–3). Tompkins Square Park (see p75). Washington Square Park West, between West 4th St & Waverly Pl, 10003. Hudson River Park Playground, Pier 51 across West 12th St, 10014

① Greenwich Village
Tiny alleys and winding streets

Beginning as a rural hamlet in the early 18th century, far north of what was then the center of the city, lovely Greenwich Village still has a small-town feel, with its curving alleyways and well-preserved architecture. The height of its bohemian period was the late 1950s and 1960s, when the Beat poets flourished, folk artists such as Bob Dylan emerged on the scene, and the civil rights movement gathered momentum here. Although it has since lost much of its radical edge, its charm has remained.

Washington Square North
The stately row houses in this locality are excellent examples of Greek-Revival architecture.

Key Sights

Bleecker Street Among the area's most fun streets is Bleecker, lined with a colorful mix of music clubs and cafés, plus independent shops such as Murray's Cheese and Amy's Bread.

Washington Square Park A vibrant, laid-back place where musicians stage impromptu concerts and families sprawl out for picnics. The Washington Square Arch here was built for the centennial of George Washington's 1789 inauguration.

Sheridan Square A sculpture here commemorates the 1969 Stonewall Riots, which proved to be the turning point in the struggle for gay rights.

St. Luke's Garden Hidden out of sight but open to the public, this little patch of green has winding pathways, flower gardens, and many birds.

Bedford Street This street is full of historic sites, such as 75 ½ Bedford, the city's narrowest house at 9 ft (3 m) wide. 77 Bedford, a former farmhouse built in 1799, is the Village's oldest building.

Minetta Lane In one of the Village's quietest and most scenic corners, look out for the Minetta Lane Theater, an Off-Broadway House, and Minetta Tavern, the haunt of writers such as Ernest Hemingway, Dylan Thomas, and Eugene O'Neill in the 1930s.

Prices given are for a family of four

The Lowdown

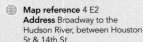

🌐 **Map reference** 4 E2
Address Broadway to the Hudson River, between Houston St & 14th St

🚇 **Subway** A, B, C, D, E, F & M to West 4th St-Washington Sq; 1 to Christopher St-Sheridan Sq. **Bus** M1, M5, M8 & M20

🎯 **Guided tours** Big Onion Walking Tours (*www.bigonion. com*) highlight the area's history and architecture. Foods of New York (*www.foodsofny. com*) tours the city and stops

at restaurants along the way for small bites.

👫 **Age range** All ages

⏱ **Allow** 3–4 hours

🚻 **Restrooms** At Washington Square Park and Starbucks at Sheridan Sq

Good family value?
Greenwich Village is unlike any other part of the city. Families will enjoy its parks and quiet corners, tiny restaurants, quirky shops and, most of all, its easygoing vibe.

Letting off steam

Head west to the Hudson River for **Hudson River Park** *(between Jane St & Spring St, 10014)*, one of the city's best. The stretch flanking the West Village is the nicest, with two piers – one at West 10th Street and the other a block north at Charles Street. The latter has a small Astroturf field used largely by families – and lawns for picnicking or kicking a ball around.

Eat and drink

Picnic: under $20; Snacks: $20–35; Real meal: $35–70; Family treat: over $70 (based on a family of four)

PICNIC Murray's Cheese Bar *(264 Bleecker St, 10014; 646 476 8882)* stocks farmhouse cheeses, olives, and baguettes. Pick up supplies and stake out a bench or a patch of grass in Washington Square Park.
SNACKS Mamoun's Falafel *(119 MacDougal St, 10012; 212 674 8685; www.mamouns.com)* is renowned for its tasty, inexpensive Middle-Eastern fare, including falafel, hummus, and pita. It is small, so takeout is a good idea.
REAL MEAL Cowgirl *(519 Hudson St at West 10th St, 10014; 212 633 1133; www.cowgirlnyc.com)* serves delicious Southern-inspired comfort food in a cozy space with Wild West decor. It also has a kids' menu.
FAMILY TREAT Minetta Tavern *(113 MacDougal St, 10012; 212 475 3850; www.minettatavernny.com)* is an upscale bistro with a menu based on ultra-fresh ingredients. Try the mesclun salad, brioche French toast, dressed prawns, and signature prime, dry-aged burger.

Cozy and comforting Cowgirl restaurant

Young children experimenting with paint, Children's Museum of the Arts

Shopping

Ibiza Kidz *(830 Broadway, 10003; 212 228 7990)*, a shoe store-cum-toy shop, and **Forbidden Planet** *(832 Broadway, 10003; 212 473 1576)*, a comics and manga destination, are worth a stop. **Strand Bookstore** *(212 473 1452; www.strandbooks.com)*, stocks a large number of new, used, rare, and out-of-print books.

Find out more

FILM Alfred Hitchcock's *Rear Window* (1954) was set here, as were parts of the NBC sitcom *Friends*: 90 Bedford Street was the apartment where the gang spent much of their time.

Take cover

Head to the **Children's Museum of the Arts** *(see p76)*, where kids can let their imaginations run wild with a variety of art projects, and participate in theatrical performances.

Next stop...

MERCHANT'S HOUSE MUSEUM This red-brick and marble row house *(29 East 4th St, 10003; 212 777 1089; www.merchants house.org)*, bought by merchant Seabury Tredwell in 1835, is an authentic time capsule and a rare glimpse into mid-19th-century life in New York City. All the furnishings, decorative objects, and personal memorabilia are original.

Swings and other play equipment at Union Square Park playground

② East Village
Little Tokyo and home of punk

Also known as EVill, the East Village is a sprawling offshoot of Greenwich Village once known for its artistic residents, from hippies and musicians to actors and Beat poets, and its relatively cheap rents – as portrayed in the successful Broadway musical *Rent* (1996). Its southeastern end, known as Alphabet City, overlaps with the Lower East Side.

Two must-visit spots are Tompkins Square Park (*see p75*) and St. Marks Place (*East 8th St, between Second Ave & Ave A*), a street that retains more than a few remnants of its 1970s punk rock heyday, including tattoo parlors, quirky shops and record stores, plus tiny, tucked-away cafés. The small patch called **Little Tokyo**, on East 9th Street between Second and Third avenues, has the feel of another city altogether, thanks to its Japanese groceries, restaurants,

and shops. Just a block north, the historic **St. Mark's Church in-the-Bowery** (*131 East 10th St, 10003*) transports visitors not to another country, but to another century, with its fieldstone Georgian architecture and spacious grounds. The land it sits on was once farmland owned by the Dutch Stuyvesant family.

Visitors may stumble across 24-hour poetry readings and dance and theater performances, as the East Village is now home to more than one celebrated arts

Shops lining St. Mark's Place, a popular street in the East Village

organization. Although the neighborhood is a lot tamer than it used to be, its scruffy, laid-back feel has made it a popular place to live for families seeking an authentic Downtown vibe.

Letting off steam
Stuyvesant Square (*Second Ave & 15th St, 10003*) is a public park built on farmland given to the city by Peter Gerard Stuyvesant in 1836. A playground, numerous statues, and wide paths make it perfect for kids.

③ Flatiron District and Union Square Greenmarket
A towering triangle and a foodie haven

Anchored by and named for the impossibly tall, triangle-shaped 1902 **Flatiron Building** at the intersection of Broadway and Fifth Avenue at 23rd Street, the Flatiron District is small but bustling with commerce. Several shopping destinations are located here, such as Paragon Sports (*867 Broadway, 10003; 212 255 8889*), the city's premier sports outfitter, with sneakers and gear in all sizes, and Books of Wonder (*18 West 18th St, 10011; 212 989 3270*), a kids' bookstore. Another shop worth checking out is Space Kiddets (*26 East 22nd St, 10010; 212 420 9878*), a toy store with an amazing collection of vintage and vintage-inspired playthings.

Just a few blocks south is the famous **Union Square Greenmarket** on the west side of Union Square Park, between 14th and 17th streets, where food purveyors from upstate New York, Pennsylvania, and Connecticut come to sell their products to top New York chefs and regular folks alike. Among the ultra-fresh offerings are all manner of fragrant produce, including apples and apple cider, home-made bread, cheese, eggs, meat and poultry, maple syrup, pretzels, flowers, greenhouse plants, and even wine.

Letting off steam
The extensively refurbished **Union Square Park playground** (*between Broadway & Fourth Ave, East 14*

The Lowdown

🌐 **Map reference** 5 B2
Address Broadway to the East River, between Houston St & East 14th St

🚇 **Subway** L to Third Ave or First Ave; N & R to 8th St-NYU; 6 to Astor Pl. **Bus** M8, M9, M14A, M15 & M103

🚩 **Guided tours** Big Onion Walking Tours (*www.bigonion.com*) offers an East Village walking tour, which lasts for about 2 hours: $60–80 register online or call the tour hotline 888 606-WALK (9255).

🚹🚺 **Age range** All ages
⏱ **Allow** 2 hours

🍽 **Eat and drink** Real meal Artichoke Basille's Pizza (*328 East 14th St, 10012; 212 228 2004; www. artichokepizza.com*) offers down-home Italian-American fare: pizza mostly, but also improvised, off-the-menu dishes that might include meatballs-on-a-stick and cauliflower fritters. *Family treat* Cacio e Pepe (*182 Second Ave, 10003; 212 505 5931; www.cacioe pepe.com*) is a trattoria with fine antipasti and excellent pasta dishes.

🚹🚺 **Restrooms** In the various parks and restaurants

The Lowdown

- **Map reference** 9 A6
- **Address** Sixth Ave to Park Ave, between 14th St & 23rd St
- **Subway** L, N, Q, R, 4, 5 & 6 to 14th St–Union Sq; F & M to 14th St; N & R to 23rd St. **Bus** M1–M3, M5, M6, M8, M14A & M23
- **Age range** All ages
- **Allow** 2 hours
- **Eat and drink** Snacks Maoz Vegetarian (38 Union Sq East, 10003; 212 260 1988) has a salad bar, falafel sandwiches, and Belgian fries. Family treat Japonica (90 University Pl at 12th St, 10003; 212 243 7752) serves everything from soba noodles and tempura to ultra-fresh sushi and sashimi.
- **Restrooms** In the various parks and restaurants

Manicured flowerbeds and trees surrounding Madison Square Park

wife to purchase the site and rebuild the home in Teddy's honor, decorating it with many objects and furnishings from the original. The reconstructed house contains five period rooms, two galleries – one of which exhibits cartoons of Roosevelt, giving visitors a quirky look at the former president – and a bookstore.

Letting off steam

Head several blocks north to **Madison Square Park** (10 Madison Ave, 10010; 212 538 1884). This lush park has a fountain, numerous wide pathways to amble on, and a fun playground at the northern end with sprinklers in summer.

The Lowdown

- **Map reference** 9 A6
- **Address** 28 East 20th St, between Broadway & Park Ave South
- **Subway** L, N, Q, R, 4, 5 & 6 to 14th St-Union Sq; N, R & 6 to 23rd St. **Bus** M1–M3, M5 & M23
- **Open** 9am–5pm Tue–Sat
- **Price** Free
- **Guided tours** 40-minute period-room tours; on the hour from 10am–4pm (no tour at noon)
- **Age range** All ages
- **Allow** 1 hour
- **Wheelchair access** No
- **Eat and drink** Snacks Rainbow Falafel (26 East 17th St, 10003; 212 691 8641) is perfect for a light meal, specializing in falafel. Also vegetarian platters, babaganoush, and soups. Real meal Republic (37 Union Sq West, 10003; 212 627 7172) serves Southeast Asian fare, including seafood, noodle soups, and various rice bowls.
- **Restrooms** On the first floor

to East 17th St, 10003) is filled with hi-tech equipment, such as rubber floor tiles, a shiny silver metal dome that kids can try to scale, and a futuristic spinning teacup.

④ Theodore Roosevelt Birthplace

Frail child, great president

Probably the most colorful personality to make the White House his home, Theodore Roosevelt Jr. was vice president when President William McKinley was assassinated in 1901. Thus becoming the 26th president, he was the youngest ever, at age 42. Known to his family and the nation as Teddy, Roosevelt was a noted historian and peacemaker – he won the Nobel Peace Prize for brokering peace between Japan and Russia in 1905 – a prolific writer, a nature lover and conservationist, and a family man. He is the only US president to hail from New York City.

Roosevelt was born in a townhouse at 28 East 20th Street on 27 October 1858, and lived there until the age of 14. He was a sickly child and was therefore home-schooled. The historic landmark house at the same address today is not the family original – that was demolished in 1916. But Roosevelt's death in 1919 prompted his sisters and his

---

The High Line and the Meatpacking District

Downtown

○The High Line

Greenwich Village
p78

Tenement Museum
p70

South Street
Seaport
p64

● Statue of Liberty
p56

Once a kind of no man's land, the Meatpacking District and West Chelsea now house Manhattan's premier galleries. The area is also dotted with trendy clubs, chic lounges, and boutique hotels, which throng with New Yorkers out for a good time. The opening of the High Line, an elevated park along a former railroad line, has made this part of the city even more of a cultural magnet. The High Line has nine access points spaced out between Gansevoort Street and West 30th Street.

Benches scattered along the High Line offer spots to sit down and relax

The Lowdown

🚗 **Subway** A, C, E & L to 14th St-Eighth Ave; 1, 2 & 3 to 14th St. **Bus** M11, M14, M20, M23 & M34

ℹ️ **Visitor information** NYC & Company, 810 Seventh Ave, 10019; 212 484 1200. For information on the High Line call 212 206 9922 or check *www.thehighline.org*

🛒 **Supermarket** Western Beef, 431 West 16th St, between Ninth Ave & Tenth Ave, 10011; 212 924 1401
Markets Abingdon Square Greenmarket, Hudson St, between Eighth Ave & West 12th St, 10014; 8am–2pm Sat year-round. Chelsea Market, 75 Ninth Ave, between

15th St & 16th St, 10011; 7am–9pm Mon–Sat, 8am–8pm Sun

➕ **Pharmacy** CVS/pharmacy, 272 Eighth Ave at 24th St, 10011; 212 255 2592; open 24 hours

🧒 **Nearest playgrounds** Hudson River Park playground, Pier 51 at the Hudson River, near Jane St, 10014 (*see p86*). Chelsea Park, Ninth Ave & Tenth Ave, between West 27th St & West 28th St, 10001. Chelsea Waterside Park, West 23rd St, 10011

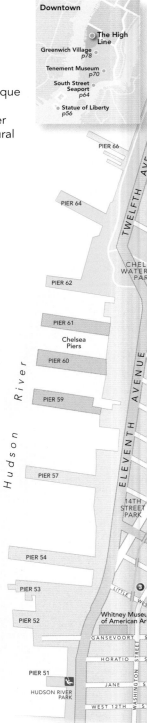

PIER 66

TWELFTH AVE

PIER 64

CHEL WATER PAR

PIER 62

PIER 61

Chelsea Piers

PIER 60

AVENUE

PIER 59

Hudson River

PIER 57

ELEVENTH AVENUE

14TH STREET PARK

PIER 54

PIER 53

LITTLE WE

PIER 52

Whitney Museu of American Ar

GANSEVOORT S

HORATIO S

PIER 51

JANE S

HUDSON RIVER PARK

WASHINGTON ST

WEST 12TH S

The Lobster Place, a popular seafood retailer in Chelsea Market

Places of interest

SIGHTS
1. The High Line

● **EAT AND DRINK**
1. Chelsea Market
2. The Lobster Place
3. Don Giovanni Ristorante
4. Tenth Avenue Cookshop

● **SHOPPING**
1. My Little Sunshine

● **WHERE TO STAY**
1. Chelsea Lodge
2. Hotel Gansevoort
3. The Standard, High Line

0 meters 250
0 yards 250

Visitors strolling among the stores at Chelsea Market

① The High Line
A park in the sky

Once a freight railroad spur that carried goods to the city's industrial district, this abandoned railway trestle sat dormant for nearly 30 years, overgrown with wild grasses and trees. In the late 1990s, when landowners began clamoring for the elevated track to be torn down, two Chelsea residents, Joshua David and Robert Hammond, campaigned to transform it into a public park. Their dream was realized when the city agreed to fund the project. Work began in 2006 and the High Line opened in 2009.

The elevated High Line park is an unusual public space

Key Features

③ Tenth Avenue Square The open-air, amphitheater-like seating here looks out on Tenth Avenue, effectively transforming the street into an ever-changing moving image.

④ Lawn This 4,900-sq-ft (455-sq-m) lawn is the only spot along the High Line where people can sit on the grass.

⑤ Philip A. and Lisa Maria Falcone Flyover About 8 ft (3 m) above the High Line's surface, a woodland flyover takes visitors through a forest of trees at canopy level. The ground underneath is covered with mossy plants and grasses.

① Gansevoort Woodland At the Gansevoort Street entrance, where the High Line was dramatically cut when the southern portion was demolished, is a dense planting of gray birches.

② Diller–von Furstenberg Sundeck This spacious sundeck has plenty of benches and recliners to lounge on.

Letting off steam

The **Hudson River Park Playground** *(Pier 51 at the Hudson River, near Jane St, 10014)* has several attractions for kids, among them a gigantic fountain that they can

Halloween decorations lining the passageways of Chelsea Market

Prices given are for a family of four

activate themselves. Or head to the **Waterfront Bicycle Shop** *(391 West St, between Christopher St & West 10th St)* and rent some bikes for a spin along the Hudson River.

Eat and drink

Picnic: under $20; Snacks: $20–35; Real meal: $35–70; Family treat: over $70 (based on a family of four)

PICNIC Chelsea Market *(75 Ninth Ave, between 15th St & 16th St, 10011; www.chelseamarket.com)* is one of the city's culinary treasures. Pick up a baguette at Amy's Bread and cold cuts and cheese at Buon

Italia, and head to the High Line's benches for a picnic.
SNACKS The Lobster Place *(Chelsea Market, 10011; 212 255 5672; www.lobsterplace.com)* offers sushi and excellent chowders.

Fresh lobsters for sale at The Lobster Place, Chelsea Market

The Lowdown

Map reference 3 C1
Address Gansevoort St to 30th St, between 10th & 11th Ave; *www.thehighline.org*

Subway A, C & E to 14th St; L to Eighth Ave; 1, 2 & 3 to 14th St & Seventh Ave; access points are at Gansevoort, 14th St, 16th St, 18th St & 20th St, 23rd St, 26th St, 28th St & 30th St. **Bus** M11, M14, M23 & M34

Open hours vary seasonally; check website for more details.

Price Free

Cutting the line Arrive early in the day, or in the late afternoon or evening, to avoid crowds.

Age range All ages

Activities For garden, family, history, and art programs, check the Events Calendar on website.

Allow 1–2 hours

Wheelchair access Yes

Café Seasonal vendors in park section between West 15th and West 16th St; Santina restaurant at Gansevoort St

Shop Seasonal kiosk where vendors are located; online store

Restrooms At the 16th Street access point

Good family value?
The High Line offers an entirely new perspective on the historic neighborhoods beneath it, making it exciting for kids and adults alike.

Railroad trestle The 30-ft (9-m) high steel trestle was stripped down, made waterproof, filled back up with soil, and then laid with concrete planks to form the walkway. All tracks were removed and some were later returned to their original location, to blend in with the plantings.

Plantings A variety of prairie grasses, wildflowers, and trees were planted to mimic the overgrown landscape that developed here during the 30 years the railroad went unused.

Dual purpose
The High Line was originally built so that freight trains coming into the city along the West Side wouldn't crush people and vehicles on the street when they passed through. Another bonus for Meatpacking District business-owners was that theft went way down because the trains delivered goods directly to second-floor storage areas.

REAL MEAL Don Giovanni Ristorante *(214 Tenth Ave, between 22nd St & 23rd St, 10011; 212 242 9054)* is a cozy spot for brick-oven pizzas, pasta, and chicken entrées.
FAMILY TREAT Tenth Avenue Cookshop *(156 Tenth Ave, 10011; www.cookshopny.com)* serves Mediterranean-inflected American cuisine with seasonal ingredients.

Shopping
Seek out **My Little Sunshine** *(177 9th Ave, 10011; 212 929 0887; www.mylittlesunshinenyc.com)* for fun and unique children's clothing.

Find out more
DIGITAL The website *www.thehighline.org* traces the history of the High Line and lists upcoming events, from dance performances and poetry readings to stargazing, bug hunts, and family art workshops.

Next stop...
WHITNEY MUSEUM OF AMERICAN ART *(99 Gansevoort St, 10014; 212 570 3600; www.whitney.org)* has a superb collection of 20th- and 21st-century works by American artists, including Georgia O'Keeffe and Edward Hopper.

Midtown

Midtown is the quintessential Manhattan neighborhood, with its looming skyscrapers (among them the Chrysler and Empire State buildings), the dazzling lights of Times Square, and historic Grand Central Station. It also has a mix of sights and activities to entertain children, from Rockefeller Center and riding the antique carousel in leafy Bryant Park to zipping to the top of New York's tallest building.

Upper
West Side
and Harlem

Central
Park
Upper
East Side

Midtown

Downtown

Highlights

Empire State Building
Board a high-speed elevator to the top of the world's most famous skyscraper and gaze down at the city lights far below (*see pp94–5*).

Grand Central Terminal
Visit the city's best-known train station, with its magnificent early 20th-century architecture (*see pp100–101*).

New York Public Library
Browse through the massive collection of books and manuscripts at one of the city's most beloved institutions (*see p102*).

The Museum of Modern Art
Admire the world's largest collection of modern art and sculpture in MoMA's unique and contemporary building (*see pp106–107*).

Rockefeller Center
Discover the center's famous attractions and artworks. In winter, its towering Christmas tree and glittering ice-skating rink enchant children (*see pp112–13*).

Times Square
Explore this vibrant square, with its flashing neon lights and lively restaurants and shops (*see pp118–19*).

Left *Ice-skating in front of the impressive gilded statue of the mythical god Prometheus, Rockefeller Center*
Above left *Reading Room at the New York Public Library*

The Best of
Midtown

Midtown offers the classic Manhattan experience: towering buildings, superb museums, lovely urban parks, bustling train stations, and the razzle-dazzle of Times Square. There is plenty to excite children, from a ride up the elevator to Top of the Rock in the Rockefeller Center to thumbing through children's books at New York Public Library or roaming the colorful aisles of toy stores such as FAO Schwarz and Toys"R"Us.

Architectural wonderland

Midtown is a celebration of New York's famous architecture, including the soaring **Empire State Building** (see pp94–5), the city's tallest skyscraper, which even has its own ZIP code. High-speed elevators whisk visitors to the top for marvelous 360-degree views. Less tall, but equally impressive, is **Grand Central Terminal** (see pp100–101), a masterpiece of early 20th-century architecture. One of New York's busiest transportation hubs, the station is also beautifully maintained, with an elegant ceiling covered in constellations of stars, and a four-faced clock that presides over the concourse. Another famous landmark, **Rockefeller Center** (see pp112–13), features beautiful Art Deco design, a breezy public plaza, and **Top of the Rock** (see p112), one of the best vantage points for aerial views of the city.

Shop till you drop

Midtown is full of top-notch places to shop, including several of New York's finest toy stores. Enter another world at **FAO Schwarz** (see p109), where buckets of rainbow-colored candy, giant stuffed animals, and board games of all kinds await. At **Rockefeller Center**, the massive LEGO Store delights kids with its innovative displays, lively play areas, and events. Video gamers flock to **Nintendo World** (see p114) to try their hand at the latest games and some classics as well. Macy's shines the

Below Brooklyn Bridge and the Midtown Manhattan skyline at dusk

Above Shops and neon lights along a busy street, Times Square *Middle* Children enjoying a ride on the brightly colored Ferris wheel at Toys"R"Us *Below* Kids waiting to see a show, New Victory Theater, Times Square

brightest of the many stores on **Herald Square** (see p97), while **Times Square** (see pp118–19) is also lined with diners and shops the kids will love, including Toys"R"Us and the Disney Store.

Art matters

Midtown's art scene is anchored by the excellent **Museum of Modern Art (MoMA)** (see pp106–107). Its collection features a slew of superstar paintings, from Picasso's *Les Demoiselles d'Avignon* to Vincent van Gogh's *The Starry Night*, while the eye-catching building features sky-lit galleries and an outdoor Sculpture Garden. **The Morgan Library and Museum** (see p96) is one of the city's finest small museums, showcasing rare manuscripts and classic children's books. Also in this neighborhood is **New York Public Library** (see p102). Set in a splendid Beaux-Arts building, it's a great place to spend a rainy day.

Sassy shows and TV tours

From TV to theater, Midtown Manhattan has it all. Take in an entertaining show at the **New Victory Theater** (see p118), the city's premier children's theater, or pay a visit to the **Paley Center for Media** (see p115) to watch popular TV shows. Tour the cutting-edge TV studios of **NBC** (see p113) at its home in **Rockefeller Center**, or pose for a photo outside the iconic facade of the **Radio City Music Hall** (see p112), which hosts one of New York's most popular high-kicking holiday dance shows, performed by the Rockettes.

Empire State Building and around

The Empire State Building is one of New York's most popular sights, and consequently this neighborhood fills with crowds every day, particularly on the streets around the skyscraper. The area is also packed with shops, which draw a steady stream of locals and tourists. This part of Midtown is well connected to the rest of the city by subway: arrive at 34th Street station, and explore the area on foot. Aim to come in the early afternoon after the lunch hour, or early evening if possible, when the crowds tend to thin out a little.

Midtown

Rockefeller Center
p110

MoMA
p104

Times Square
p116

Grand
Central
Terminal
p98

Empire State
Building

The Lowdown

🚇 **Subway** B, D, F, M, N, Q & R to 34th St-Herald Sq.
Bus M1–5, M16, M34 & Q32; www.mta.info

🛒 **Supermarket** D'Agostino 578 Third Ave, 10016; 212 972 4892
Markets Various street fairs during the year, with food and craft vendors

🎊 **Festivals** Saint Patrick's Day Parade (Mar). Columbus Day Parade (Oct). Macy's Thanksgiving Day Parade (Nov)

➕ **Pharmacy** Duane Reade, 1350 Broadway, 10018; 212 695 6346; store open 24 hours, pharmacy 8am–9pm Mon–Fri, 9am–6pm Sat

🛝 **Nearest playground** Madison Square Park, between Madison Ave & 23rd St, 10010

Clothing and home decor, The Shop @ Scandinavia House

View of the Empire State Building from across the East River

Places of interest

SIGHTS
- ① Empire State Building
- ② Scandinavia House
- ③ The Morgan Library and Museum
- ④ Herald Square

● **EAT AND DRINK**
1. 'wichcraft
2. Shake Shack
3. Circa
4. Heartland Brewery
5. El Rio Grande
6. 2nd Avenue Deli
7. Stella 34 Trattoria
8. Keens Steakhouse

See also Scandinavia House (p96) & The Morgan Library and Museum (p96)

● **SHOPPING**
1. Manhattan Mall
2. Macy's

● **WHERE TO STAY**
1. 70 Park Avenue Hotel
2. Affinia Dumont
3. Affinia Manhattan
4. Affinia Shelburne
5. Carlton Arms Hotel
6. DoubleTree by Hilton Hotel New York City – Chelsea
7. Eventi
8. The Evelyn
9. Hotel Giraffe
10. Hotel Metro
11. Martha Washington Hotel
12. nyma, the new york manhattan hotel
13. Ramada Eastside
14. Residence Inn by Marriott
15. The MAve

Shrek looms large at Macy's Thanksgiving Day Parade

① Empire State Building
Up, up, and up

Rising to a whopping 1,454 ft (443 m) – 102 stories – the Empire State Building is the tallest skyscraper in New York City. Built in 1931, it was the world's highest building until it lost that title in the 1970s. The high-speed elevator ride to the observation deck is as memorable as the panoramic view upon arrival, especially at night, with twinkling lights all around. On a clear day, it's possible to see the states of New Jersey, Pennsylvania, Connecticut, Massachusetts, and New York.

Key Features

Manhattan skyline One of the best views of the city's star skyscraper is from the East River State Park.

204-ft (62-m) tall mooring mast Designed as a landing for airships, today the mast transmits radio and TV signals.

Colored lighting LED tower lights on the top 30 floors mark special days; at Christmas they sparkle in red and green.

Observation deck

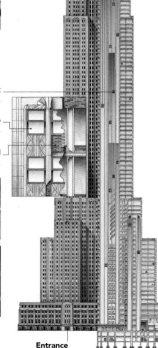

The Lowdown

- 🌐 **Map reference** 8 H3
  Address 350 Fifth Ave, 10118; 212 736 3100; www.esbnyc.com
- 🚗 **Subway** B, D, F, M, N, Q & R to 34th St-Herald Sq. **Bus** M4, M16, M34 & Q32
- 🕐 **Open** 8am–2am daily; last elevator at 1:15am
- 💲 **Price** $90–116; under 6s free; Main Deck Express Pass ($55 per person) allows visitors to move to the front of each line.
- 👥 **Cutting the line** The best times to visit are early in the morning, mid-afternoon, or after midnight.
- 🚩 **Guided tours** New York Skyride is a 30-minute simulated flight over the city's landmarks; 8am–10pm daily; adults $42; under 13s $33; 212 279 9777; www.skyride.com
- 👫 **Age range** 5 plus
- ⏱ **Allow** 2 hours
- ♿ **Wheelchair access** Yes
- ☕ **Café** State Grill & Bar and Starbucks on main lobby level
- 👫 **Restrooms** On the main deck

Good family value?
The fun elevator rides and incredible views make this a memorable experience.

Observation deck Marvel at the fantastic views over Manhattan, from the Chrysler Building to Rockefeller Center, from the observatory on the 86th floor.

High-speed elevators Zip to the top at speeds up to 1,000 ft (305 m) a minute.

Windows Aluminium panels were used to surround the 6,500 windows.

Brickwork Ten million bricks were used to line the entire building.

Lobby mural The main lobby houses an Art Deco relief depicting the Empire State in steel, aluminum, and gold leaf.

Entrance

Letting off steam

Just a 10-minute stroll from the Empire State Building, **Madison Square Park** (see p83) is a great place to unwind. This leafy area has lots of benches and plenty of space for kids to play. Afterwards, stop for creamy gelato at **Eataly** (200 Fifth Ave, 10010; www.eataly ny.com; 10am–11pm daily).

Visitors tucking in at Shake Shack, a popular café in Madison Square Park

Eat and drink

Picnic: under $20; Snacks: $20–35; Real meal: $35–70; Family treat: over $70 (based on a family of four)

PICNIC 'wichcraft (11 East 20th St, between Fifth Ave & Broadway, 10003; 212 780 0577; www.wichcraftnyc.com) offers fat sandwiches that can be enjoyed outdoors in nearby Madison Square Park.
SNACKS Shake Shack (Southeast corner of Madison Square Park, near Madison Ave & East 23rd St, 10010; 212 889 6600; www.shakeshack. com) has shaded outdoor seating and serves inexpensive juicy burgers and delicious custards for dessert.
REAL MEAL Circa (22 West 33rd St, 10001; 212 244 3730; www. circa-ny.com; closed Sun) features everything from paninis and pasta to sushi, salads, and soups.
FAMILY TREAT Heartland Brewery (350 Fifth Ave at 34th St, 10118; 212 563 3433; www. heartlandbrewery.com; 11am– 9:30pm Sun–Tue, till 10:15pm

Warm interiors with wood-paneled floors at the Heartland Brewery

Wed–Sat) is a restaurant-brewpub that offers frothy pints of beer, steaks, and Maine crab cakes.

Shopping

Manhattan Mall (100 W. Broadway at 33rd St, 10001; 212 465 0500; www.manhattanmallny.com; 9am– 9:30pm Mon–Sat, 10am–8:30pm Sun) houses several stores, from JCPenny, Hallmark, Gamestop, and Toys"R"Us to shops selling leather goods. **Macy's** (151 West 34th St, between Broadway & Seventh Ave; www.macys.com) is one of the world's largest stores, with ten-and-a-half floors selling everything from food and toys to clothing and jewelry.

Find out more

DIGITAL The official site, www. esbnyc.com, includes links to videos and a list of children's books about the Empire State Building.
FILM Savor an iconic moment in movie history, when the great ape escapes his captors and climbs to the top of the Empire State Building in King Kong (1933). Go on an adventure around the world, including the Empire State Building, with a trouble-prone teenager in Percy Jackson & the Olympians: The Lightning Thief (2010).

Terraced arches with triangular windows on the spire of the Chrysler Building

Next stop...

HEAD FOR HEIGHTS For more great views, head to **Rockefeller Center** (see pp110–11), which offers a 360-degree panorama of New York City. Visit the **Chrysler Building** (405 Lexington Ave, 10174) and admire its spire, which looks like a car-radiator grille. The building's gargoyles were designed to look like hood ornaments from a 1929 Chrysler Plymouth. Later, explore the **Grand Central Terminal** (see pp100–101).

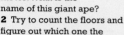

KIDS' CORNER

Look out for...

1 Can you see the spire of the Empire State Building, where an ape battled army airplanes in a famous 1933 movie. What is the name of this giant ape?
2 Try to count the floors and figure out which one the observation deck is on.
3 Can you guess how many steps there are to the very top of the Empire State Building?
4 Do you know how many windows the Empire State Building has?
5 How many states can you see from the top of the Empire State Building? Can you name them?

Answers at the bottom of the page.

RACE TO THE TOP
The Empire State Building Run-Up, held annually since 1978, is a foot race from ground level to the 86th floor observation deck. The record time is 9 minutes and 33 seconds.

Lightning strikes
The Empire State Building is designed to serve as a natural lightning rod for the surrounding area. It is struck by lightning around 100 times per year. The observation deck is closed during unfavorable weather.

Massachusetts.
Pennsylvania, Connecticut, and
5 Five: New Jersey, New York,
street level to the 102nd floor. **4** 6,500.
floor. **3** There are 1,860 steps from
Answers: 1 King Kong. **2** The 86th

② Scandinavia House

LEGO, fairytales, and elves

A row of Nordic flags – representing Denmark, Sweden, Iceland, Norway, and Finland – mark Scandinavia House. The playful, warm interior seems to have been designed with kids in mind. Look up to the ceiling to see the famous "artichoke lamps." Like many Scandinavian creations, their design is rooted in simplicity and functionalism. The same can be said for Denmark's most famous export, those little plastic building blocks in primary colors – LEGO! Children can play with LEGO in a romper room, which also hosts a Hans Christian Andersen storytelling hour.

Scandinavia House is at its most alluring at Christmas, when it fills with red, green, and gold ribbons, snowflake decorations, and plenty of naughty little *nissar* (elves), who are often seen in the gift shop, dressed in pointy red caps.

Letting off steam

Sit under shady trees and watch the world go by at **Madison Square Park** (*see p83*). Its playground offers lots of games and activities for kids.

The Lowdown

- 🌐 **Map reference** 9 B2
- **Address** 58 Park Ave, 10016; 212 779 3587; www.scandinavia house.org
- 🚇 **Subway** 6 to 33rd St. **Bus** M1–M4, M16, M34, M101–M103
- 🕐 **Open** 11am–10pm Mon–Sat, 11am–5pm Sun; Children's Center: noon–5pm Sat; galleries: noon–6pm Tue–Sat (7pm Wed)
- 💲 **Price** Free; Children's Center $15
- 👫 **Age range** 2 plus
- **Activities** Storytelling on Sat mornings; weekly kids' workshops; puppet playtime; Scandinavian sing-along hour
- ⏱ **Allow** 1 hour
- ♿ **Wheelchair access** Yes
- **Eat and drink** *Picnic* El Rio Grande (160 East 38th St, between Lexington and Third, 10016; 212 867 0922) serves Mexican and American fare. *Real meal* Smörgås Chef (on site) offers juicy Swedish meatballs, fresh salmon, and delicious Danish pastries.
- 👫 **Restrooms** On level B

High-ceilinged interior of J.P. Morgan's Study at the Morgan Library

③ The Morgan Library and Museum

Find the Mad Hatter

The legendary financier Pierpont Morgan (1837–1913) founded the Morgan Library and Museum to showcase his one-of-a-kind collection of more than 10,000 drawings, and manuscripts, illuminated books, and ancient seals. Among the exhibits are some of the earliest examples of writing in the world, including tablets, seals, and papyrus fragments from Egypt and the Near East. Keep an eye out for the original manuscripts of many famous children's books, including *The Story of Babar the Little Elephant*, and delightful drawings from *Alice in Wonderland*. Also on display are the famous Gutenberg Bibles (the museum owns three out of 11 surviving originals); drawings

by Rembrandt and Degas; original scores by Beethoven; and handwritten manuscripts by Dickens. Equally impressive is the library's stunning glass and steel atrium.

Letting off steam

Discover a hidden gem smack in the middle of Manhattan – at 150–58 East 36th Street. Step back in time in this charming courtyard with its ten Romanesque-style carriage houses from the 1850s.

The Lowdown

- 🌐 **Map reference** 9 A2
- **Address** 225 Madison Ave, 10016; 212 685 0008; www.themorgan.org
- 🚇 **Subway** 6 to 33rd St. **Bus** M1–M5 crosstown M16, M34
- 🕐 **Open** 10:30am–5pm Tue–Thu, 10:30am–9pm Fri, 10am–6pm Sat & 11am–6pm Sun
- 💲 **Price** $48–60; under 12s free; free on Fri (7–9pm)
- **Cutting the line** Tickets can be bought online, although there is rarely a long wait to enter.
- **Guided tours** Audio guides are free with admission; complimentary exhibition and tours.
- 👫 **Age range** 6 plus
- **Activities** Museum sometimes organizes events for kids. Stroller tour for parents with pre-toddlers.
- ⏱ **Allow** 2 hours
- ♿ **Wheelchair access** Yes
- **Eat and drink** *Snacks* 2nd Avenue Deli (162 East 33rd St, 10016; 212 689 9000) features pastrami and beef sandwiches and creamy potato salad. *Real meal* Morgan Café or Morgan Dining Room (central court) for sit-down meals.
- 👫 **Restrooms** On the main floor

A playroom with LEGO blocks in the Children's Center, Scandinavia House

Massive helium balloon of Snoopy, Macy's Thanksgiving Day Parade

④ Herald Square

Retail therapy

A walk around this busy square will reveal that it is actually triangular. Herald Square is named after a famous newspaper – *The New York Herald* – which had its offices here from 1894 to 1921. In fact, a piece of history from those days still remains here – the historic clock from the Herald building now stands where Broadway meets Sixth Avenue.

These days, the square features a lively mix of crowds, honking taxis, and, most popularly, shops. The queen bee of the square is Macy's *(151 West 34th St, 10001)*, the world's largest department store, where shoppers roam aisle upon aisle of everything from shoes, clothing, and accessories to pots and pans, drum sets, and coloring books. In November, Macy's Thanksgiving Day Parade fills the streets with huge helium balloons and marching bands.

A vivid mix of neighborhoods adjoin Herald Square: Little Korea, on West 31st Street and 32nd Street, is filled with Korean shops, hotels, and restaurants. Fashion Avenue is the name given to the stretch of Seventh Avenue, around 34th Street, that marks the heart of New York's garment district. It is home to fashion showrooms, famous designers, and wholesalers.

Letting off steam

Escape the shopping masses by ducking into tiny **Greeley Square Park** *(Sixth Ave, between West 32nd St & West 33rd St, 10001)*. It is well tended and wonderfully leafy, offering respite from the bustle of the city's streets.

The Lowdown

- 🌐 **Map reference** 8 G3
- 📍 **Address** At the intersection of 34th St, Broadway & Sixth Ave, 10001. Macy's: 212 695 4400; www.macys.com
- 🚇 **Subway** B, D, F, M, N, Q, R to 34th St-Herald Square. **Bus** M1–M5, M7, M16, M20 & M34
- 🕐 **Open** 9am–9:30pm Mon–Thu, 9am–10pm Fri, 9am–11pm Sat, 11am–8:30pm Sun
- 💲 **Price** Free
- 🚶 **Cutting the line** Macy's – and all of Herald Square – is packed with crowds. Shop in the early morning or early afternoon to avoid the masses.
- 👫 **Age range** 4 plus
- ⏱ **Allow** 2 hours
- 🍴 **Eat and drink** *Snacks* Stella 34 Trattoria *(Macy's 6th floor, 151 West 34th St, 10001; 212 967 9251) Real meal* Keens Steakhouse *(72 West 36th St, 10018; 212 947 3636; www.keens.com)* offers juicy steaks, and burgers.
- 🚻 **Restrooms** On several floors

Greeley Square Park, a peaceful retreat from the busy streets

Grand Central Terminal and around

A busy commercial district, Midtown Manhattan is invaded by an army of office workers on weekdays, many of them gushing out of Grand Central Terminal. Midtown's main station, it is served by several subway lines as well as commuter rail. The area is also well-connected by bus, but as most sights are within walking distance of the terminal, it can be explored on foot. The best time to come here is in the evening and on weekends, when the crowds lessen considerably.

Midtown

Rockefeller Center _p110_
MoMA _p104_
Times Square _p116_
Empire State Building _p92_
Grand Central Terminal

Sculptures of Mercury, Hercules, and Minerva, Grand Central Terminal

Places of interest

SIGHTS
1. Grand Central Terminal
2. Library Way
3. New York Public Library
4. Bryant Park

● **EAT AND DRINK**
1. Grand Central Market
2. Magnolia Bakery
3. La Fonda del Sol
4. Oyster Bar & Restaurant
5. Sarabeth's
6. Café Zaiya
7. Hale & Hearty
8. DB Bistro Moderne
9. Bryant Park Café
10. Koi

● **SHOPPING**
1. Grand Central Market
2. Kinokuniya Bookstore

● **WHERE TO STAY**
1. Best Western Plus Hospitality House
2. Fifty NYC
3. Kimberley Hotel
4. Library Hotel
5. Mansfield Hotel
6. Roger Smith Hotel
7. Room Mate Grace Hotel
8. The International New York Barclay
9. The Muse Hotel
10. Waldorf Astoria
11. Wyndham Midtown 45

Tree-lined Bryant Park, a popular outdoor space

Hale & Hearty restaurant on West 42nd Street

The Lowdown

🚗 **Subway** S, 4, 5, 6 & 7 to
Grand Central-42nd St.
Bus M1–M5, M42, M9,
M101–M103 & Q32

🍽 **Supermarket** Grand
Central Market, 89 East
42nd St, 10017
Market Zeytinz, 24 West
40th St, between Fifth Ave &
Sixth Ave, 10018; 212 575
8080; 6:30am–7pm Mon–Fri,
8am–4pm Sat

✚ **Pharmacies** Duane Reade,
1471 Broadway, 10036;
212 302 0552; store open
24 hours, pharmacy open
8am–10pm Mon–Fri,
9am–6pm Sat, 10am–6pm
Sun. Duane Reade, 535 Fifth
Ave, 10017; 212 687 8641;
8am–7pm Mon–Fri

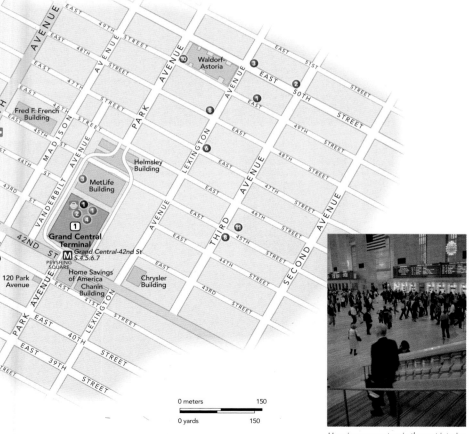

Hurrying commuters in the vast interior
of Grand Central Terminal

① Grand Central Terminal
All aboard!

New York's most famous train station is also one of its busiest transport hubs. All it takes is a stroll through the buzzing terminal to understand why it has given rise to the popular phrase: "It's as busy as Grand Central!" Built between 1903 and 1913, the station is known as much for its splendid Beaux-Arts architecture as its transportation links. Gaze up at the star constellations illuminating the vaulted ceiling, and discover secret subterranean passageways between floors.

Statue of rail magnate Cornelius Vanderbilt

Key Features

Statuary A sculpture of Mercury flanked by Hercules and Minerva crowns the main entrance.

Huge arches Three arched windows, 60 ft (18 m) high, tower over the crowds.

Vanderbilt Hall Named for the family who built the station, this hall is decorated with pink marble and gold chandeliers.

Subway

Celestial ceiling More than 2,500 gold-leaf stars form well-known constellations, including Pisces, seen here.

Main concourse More than half a million people, mostly commuters, pass through this massive hall each day.

Four-faced clock Perched on top of the information booth on the main concourse, this iconic clock, with its four opal faces, presides over the center of the terminal.

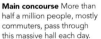

The Lowdown

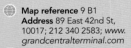

🌐 **Map reference** 9 B1
Address 89 East 42nd St, 10017; 212 340 2583; www. grandcentralterminal.com

🚗 **Subway** S, 4, 5, 6 & 7 to Grand Central-42nd St. **Bus** M1–M5

🕐 **Open** 5:30–2am daily

💲 **Price** Free

Cutting the line Come in the late morning or mid-afternoon on weekdays, early morning on weekends, or on Sat evening.

🚩 **Guided tours** The Municipal Arts Society offers tours ($70–80) daily at 12:30pm; buy tickets at the ticket window in the Main concourse. Grand Central Partnership conducts free walking tours at 12:30pm on Fri; meet in the street-level atrium at 120 Park Ave.

👫 **Age range** 4 plus

Activities In the Whispering Gallery on the lower concourse, (outside Oyster Bar & Restaurant)

murmur secrets to someone in the opposite corner of the room.

⏱ **Allow** 1 hour

♿ **Wheelchair access** Yes

☕ **Café** In the market and food court

🚻 **Restrooms** Near the foodcourt

Good family value?
Free tours and delights such as the Whispering Gallery make Grand Central superb value for the family.

Prices given are for a family of four

Letting off steam

Escape the Grand Central crowds by heading to **Bryant Park** (see p103), which offers lush lawns, plenty of shaded seating, and an antique carousel.

Visitors enjoying a summer's day around a fountain in Bryant Park

Eat and drink

Picnic: under $20; Snacks: $20–35; Real meal: $35–70; Family treat: over $70 (based on a family of four)

PICNIC Grand Central Market (Lexington Ave, 10017; 212 340 2583) boasts a wide range of excellent specialty shops offering tasty supplies. Pick up crusty bread or *rugelach* (stuffed pastry) at **Zaro's Bakery**, fresh fruit at **Eli Zabar's Farm to Table**, and pungent cheeses at **Murray's Cheese** before heading to nearby Bryant Park for a picnic.

SNACKS Magnolia Bakery (Dining Concourse, Lower Level; 212 682 3588; www.magnoliabakery.com; 7:30am–10pm Mon–Fri, 9am–10pm Sat, till 8pm Sun) is famous for its delicious cupcakes topped with colorful butter icing, as well as for other classic American desserts.

Oyster Bar & Restaurant, a New York seafood institution

REAL MEAL La Fonda del Sol (Time-Life Building, 200 Park Ave, 10166; 212 867 6767; 11:30am–10:30pm Mon–Fri, 5–10pm Sat) serves Spanish cuisine, from tapas to hearty dishes such as garlic shrimp, tuna tacos, and paella.

FAMILY TREAT Oyster Bar & Restaurant (Lower Level, 212 490 6650; www.oysterbarny.com; 11:30am–9:30pm Mon–Sat) is one of New York's best-known seafood restaurants, with more than 30 varieties of oyster and almost as many types of fresh fish.

Shopping

Grand Central (www.grandcentral terminal.com) has an array of fine shops, particularly in Lexington Passage. Check out **Tia's Place** for creative accessories and gifts, from lovely handbags to chunky jewelry, funky hats, and scarves. **LaCrasia Gloves and Creative Accessories** sells soft gloves, hats, handbags, scarves, sarongs, and umbrellas.

Freshly baked loaves at Zaro's Bakery, Grand Central Market

Find out more

FILM Grand Central has been featured in numerous films, including *Madagascar* (2005) and *Superman* (1978), in which the villain Lex Luthor had his subterranean den beneath the station.

Next stop…

NEW YORK TRANSIT MUSEUM
The annex of the New York Transit Museum (see p199), near Grand Central's shuttle passage, has fun exhibits on the transportation history of the city. Its shop sells everything from T-shirts to magnets with transportation logos.

KIDS' CORNER

Find out more…

1 Grand Central Terminal has more platforms than any other train station in the world. Count them – how many are there?
2 Tick, tock: Look for the famous four-faced clock in the center of the main hall. Which sides face north, south, east, and west?
3 It's not just trains at Grand Central. Look around: What other types of transportation do you see?

Answers at the bottom of the page.

Missing?
Grand Central has one of the world's largest Lost and Found departments, with 80 percent of things finding their way back to their owners.

WHISPER A SECRET
Whisper to someone – from across the room! Find the terminal's Whispering Gallery, face a corner and whisper something. The person in the diagonally opposite corner will hear it clearly.

Hole in the sky
Grand Central's famous ceiling is covered in constellations, but a closer look reveals a strange hole in the middle of all the stars. A Redstone rocket was put on display in the terminal in 1957. Unfortunately, the rocket was too tall for the terminal and the ceiling was punctured by its tip.

Answers: 1 44 platforms – and 67 rail tracks. **2** The clock face that looks in the direction of 42nd Street is north, and from there you can figure out the rest! **3** Subway, bus, taxi – and even bicycle rickshaws.

Grand chandeliers hanging from the ceiling of New York Public Library

Visitors enjoying their meals at cozy Café Zaiya, Midtown Manhattan

② Library Way
The way to the lions

East 41st Street has been transformed into "Library Way," an entertaining promenade leading to New York Public Library. It displays 96 bronze sidewalk plaques with famous quotes about literature from writers as diverse as Dylan Thomas and Virginia Woolf. The street is a wonderful introduction to the library: start at the far end, and while walking to the library, read the quotes along the way. Library Way leads to two famous lions seated at the entrance to the library, named "Patience" and "Fortitude."

Take cover
Head to the **Algonquin Hotel** (59 West 44th St, between Fifth Ave & Sixth Ave; 212 840 6800; www. algonquinhotel.com; see p246) to meet Matilda the cat, who is often

seen lurking around the lobby. Matilda is a resident at this sumptuous, Edwardian-style hotel. Sink into comfy couches and order a freshly squeezed orange juice.

③ New York Public Library
The world's largest library

With its proud lions guarding the entrance, and a labyrinth of shelves groaning under a mind-boggling collection of books, New York Public Library is one of the city's premier institutions. The library, housed in a Beaux-Arts building, opened in 1911. Its collections easily measure up to those of the Library of Congress in Washington, D.C. and the British Library in London. They include venerable pieces such as Thomas Jefferson's manuscript copy of the Declaration of Independence, along with classic kids' books and first editions.

Also on display are the original Winnie-the-Pooh toys that belonged to Christopher Robin

Milne. The toys inspired his father, A.A. Milne, to write his famous book about the honey-loving bear.

The colorful NYPL children's center delights kids of all ages with a wonderful array of books, music CDs, storytelling, live theatrical performances, and events such as "Game On" when children get to play Wii in the library.

Letting off steam
After a literary adventure through the library, head for some outdoor action at the carousel in **Bryant Park** (see right), just behind the

The Lowdown

🌐 **Map reference** 8 H1
🏠 **Address** 455 Fifth Ave, between 40th St & 42nd St, 10016; 212 340 0863; www.nypl.org
🚗 **Subway** B, D, F & M to 42nd St-Bryant Park; 7 to Fifth Ave
🕐 **Open** 8am–11pm Mon–Thu, 8am–8pm Fri, 10am–6pm Sat & Sun; closed Sun in summer
💲 **Price** Free
🚶 **Cutting the line** Lines are rare.
🚩 **Guided tours** Free 1 hour tours; 11am & 2pm Mon–Sat, 2pm Sun
👫 **Age range** 4 plus
🎨 **Activities** Story hour, arts and crafts, and movies. Check the library website, www.nypl.org, for details of events program.
⏱ **Allow** 1½ hours
♿ **Wheelchair access** Yes
🍽 **Eat and drink** Snacks Hale & Hearty (49 West 42nd St, 10036; 212 575 9090) serves soups and sandwiches. Real meal DB Bistro Moderne (55 West 44th St, 10036; 212 391 2400) offers fine French fare.
🚻 **Restrooms** On several floors

The Lowdown

🌐 **Map reference** 9 A1
🏠 **Address** East 41st St, between Park Ave South & Fifth Ave, 10018; 212 930 0800; www.nypl.org
🚗 **Subway** S, 4, 5, 6 & 7 to Grand Central-42nd St; 7 to Fifth Ave
🕐 **Open** 24 hours daily
💲 **Price** Free
👫 **Age range** 4 plus
⏱ **Allow** 30 minutes
🍽 **Eat and drink** Snacks Sarabeth's (424 Fifth Ave, 10018; 212 827 5068) serves muffins, croissants, salads, and more. Real meal Café Zaiya (18 East 41st St, 10017; 212 779 0600) offers Japanese bento-box lunches and baked goods.
🚻 **Restrooms** No, but nearby in the New York Public Library

Entrance to the Algonquin Hotel, one of the city's most historic landmarks

library. Climb on the vintage horses and spin around to the sounds of French cabaret music.

④ Bryant Park

Flying horses

The antique carousel is the main draw for kids at Bryant Park, one of Midtown Manhattan's most charming public spaces. Leafy, elegant, and beautifully maintained, the park features lush lawns, slender trees, twin promenades, and pebbled pathways dotted with green folding chairs.

There are a host of other fun activities for children here too, including chess, ping-pong and, in winter, ice-skating. In summer, the park hosts dance classes in the mornings and movie nights at sunset, where contemporary and classic favorites are shown on an outdoor screen.

Above Stacks of books in Japanese and English at Kinokuniya Bookstore
Below The carousel, Bryant Park

Take cover

Browse through three floors of Japanese comics (manga), books, dolls, DVDs, and action figures – plus fascinating stationery such as origami paper – at the colorful **Kinokuniya Bookstore** (1073 Avenue of the Americas; 212 869 1700; www.kinokuniya.com/us).

The Lowdown

🌐 **Map reference** 8 G1
Address Behind New York Public Library, between 40th St and 42nd St & Fifth Ave and Sixth Ave, 10018; www.bryantpark.org

🚇 **Subway** B, D, F & M to 42nd St-Bryant Park; 7 to Fifth Ave

🕐 **Open** Hours and timings are subject to change monthly and seasonally; check website for timings. The park may remain closed during bad weather days.

💲 **Price** Park free; ice-skate rentals $60 (family of four); carousel ride $3; chess free

🚻 **Cutting the line** Busiest during lunch hour; relatively quiet in late morning or mid-afternoon.

👫 **Age range** 3 plus

Activities Carousel rides, ice-skating, and free dance classes

☕ **Allow** 1 hour

☕ **Eat and drink** Picnic Bryant Park Café (42nd St side of the Upper Terrace, 10018; 212 840 6500) has salads and sandwiches. **Family treat** Koi (40 West 40th St, 10018; 212 921 3330; www. koirestaurant.com) features superb Japanese cuisine.

👫 **Restrooms** Near the west end of the park

KIDS' CORNER

Look out for...
1 Wander past shelves upon shelves of books in New York Public Library: Can you guess how many miles of books there are?
2 The lions that guard the library each have a special name that describes a quality. What are they?
3 What is Winnie-the-Pooh's favorite food?

Answers at the bottom of the page.

CHILLS AND THRILLS
Every winter, The Rink – the ice-skating rink in Bryant Park – opens to the public along with a host of annual Holiday Shops.

Medieval origins
The carousel can trace its roots to a 12th-century Arabian exercise game, which strengthened riders and prepared them for combat. European crusaders brought the idea back to Europe. In Spain it came to be known as carosella, meaning "little battle." In the 16th century, the game spread to France, where artisans began carving horses for riders to practice on. Later, the horses became fixtures on carousels such as deer and pigs.

Picnic under $20; **Snacks** $20–35; **Real meal** $35–70; **Family treat** over $70 (based on a family of four)

The Museum of Modern Art and around

Located in the heart of the Midtown neighborhood, The Museum of Modern Art sits within easy strolling distance of many major attractions, including the high-end shops on Fifth Avenue, Rockefeller Center, and leafy Central Park. The area bustles throughout the day with a mix of locals and shoppers, with crowds generally only thinning out later in the evening. Arrive by subway – several stations are in striking range of the museums.

The Lowdown

Subway E & M to Fifth Ave-53rd St; B, D & E to Seventh Ave. **Bus** M1–M5, M7, M31 & M57

Supermarket Gristedes, 907 Eighth Ave & 54th St, 10019; 212 582 5873

Pharmacy Duane Reade, 100 West 57th St, 10019; 212 956 0464; 7:30am–8pm Mon–Fri, 9am–6pm Sat, 10am–5pm Sun

Nearest playground Heckscher Playground, between 61st St & 63rd St, Central Park Conservancy 10022; 212 310 6600; www.centralparknyc.org; 8am–dusk daily

Entrance to the famous Carnegie Deli on Seventh Avenue

Kids enjoying a splash at Heckscher Playground, Central Park

Places of interest

SIGHTS

1. The Museum of Modern Art
2. Carnegie Hall
3. Apple Store Fifth Avenue
4. FAO Schwarz

EAT AND DRINK

1. Carnegie Deli
2. Burger Joint
3. China Grill
4. Aquavit
5. The Halal Guys
6. A Voce
7. The Todd English Food Hall
8. Landmarc
9. La Bonne Soupe
10. The Modern

SHOPPING

1. Henri Bendel
2. Gap

WHERE TO STAY

1. Courtyard by Marriott
2. The Shoreham Hotel
3. Four Seasons Hotel
4. Hotel Elysée
5. The London NYC
6. The Peninsula New York
7. Warwick New York Hotel

0 meters 200

0 yards 200

Traditional horse-and-buggy carriage at Grand Army Plaza, Central Park

① The Museum of Modern Art

An explosion of shapes and colors

The Museum of Modern Art (MoMA) offers a double draw: the world's largest collection of modern art and sculpture, and a unique building, which is a contemporary masterpiece in itself. The museum was founded in 1929, and the building it occupies (designed by Japanese architect Yoshio Taniguchi and built in 2004) features a sculpture garden, skylights, and galleries with soaring ceilings. On display are famous paintings by artists including Pablo Picasso, Vincent van Gogh, and Salvador Dalí.

Key Features

① **Sculpture Garden** The peaceful Abby Aldrich Rockefeller Sculpture Garden has not just eye-catching sculptures, but trees and a soothing reflecting pool.

② **Hope, II** (1907) Depicting a pregnant woman with her head bowed towards her belly – in prayer or in mourning – Gustav Klimt originally called his artwork *Vision*.

■ **Sixth Floor** Special exhibitions
■ **Fifth Floor** Paintings and sculpture
■ **Fourth Foor** Paintings and sculpture
■ **Third Floor** Architecture and design, drawings, photography, and special exhibitions
■ **Second Floor** Prints, media, illustrated books, and contemporary art
■ **First Floor** Sculpture Garden

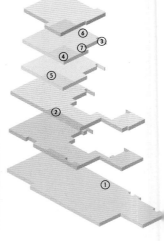

③ **The Starry Night** (1889) Vincent van Gogh's turbulent night scene, depicting the view outside his sanatorium window, is often considered his masterpiece.

④ **Christina's World** (1948) Andrew Wyeth's affecting painting contrasts the vast American landscape with a tenderly drawn close-up portrait of his neighbor, who suffered from polio.

The Lowdown

🌐 **Map reference** 12 H5
Address 11 West 53rd St, 10019; 212 708 9400; *www.moma.org*

🚇 **Subway** E, M to Fifth Ave-53rd St. **Bus** M1–M5, M31 & M57

🕐 **Open** 10:30am–5:30pm daily, till 8pm Thu; closed Thanksgiving Day and Dec 25

💲 **Price** $50–60; under 16s free; 4pm–8pm Fri, free

👪 **Cutting the line** Visit mid-week to beat the rush. Tickets can be bought online to avoid the long wait on arrival.

🚩 **Guided tours** Art historians and curators offer guided tours; for more information and booking, check the museum website.

👫 **Age range** 6 plus

👬 **Activities** The museum offers children's workshops, gallery talks, and movies.

🕐 **Allow** 2–3 hours

♿ **Wheelchair access** Yes

☕ **Cafés** Café 2, Terrace 5 restaurant, and The Modern restaurant

🛍 **Shop** MoMA Design and Book Store on the first floor

👫 **Restrooms** On every floor

Good family value?

Lots of bold and colorful art, plus airy spaces and a wide choice of restaurants, make this a good outing.

⑤ **Campbell's Soup Cans** (1962) One of America's greatest pop artists, Andy Warhol first exhibited his Campbell's series on a shelf mounted on the wall, like groceries in a store.

⑥ **Les Demoiselles d'Avignon** (1907) Picasso's Cubist work depicts five women in Barcelona, and is partly influenced by the Iberian sculpture of his native Spain.

⑦ **The Persistence of Memory** (1931) Watches melt against an eerie landscape of leafless trees and stark cliffs in this arresting work by the Surrealist painter Salvador Dalí.

Entrance to the Museum of Modern Art

Letting off steam

The museum's shaded Sculpture Garden offers pleasant outdoor respite for kids after viewing the art indoors. A lovely spot, children are free to run about here or stroll around the reflecting pool. The garden also features sculptures and installations by artists such as Hector Guimard, Alexander Calder, and Alberto Giacometti. It often hosts jazz and classical concerts.

Eat and drink

Picnic: under $20; Snacks: $20–35; Real meal: $35–70; Family treat: over $70 (based on a family of four).

PICNIC Carnegie Deli (854 Seventh Ave at 55th St, 10019; 212 757 2245; www.carnegiedeli.com; 6:30am–2am daily) sells towering pastrami sandwiches and creamy cheesecake for dessert, which can be enjoyed in Central Park.

SNACKS Burger Joint (119 West 56th St, 10019; 212 708 7414; www.parkerhotel.com; 11am–11:30pm Sun–Thu, 11am–midnight Fri–Sat), is a delightful restaurant in the Le Parker Méridien hotel, serving juicy burgers and thick-cut fries.

REAL MEAL China Grill (60 West 53rd St at Sixth Ave, 10019; 212 333 7788; 11:45am–10:30pm Tue–Thu, 11:45pm–10pm Sun & Mon, 11:45pm–1:30pm Fri & Sat) serves Pan-Asian cuisine, from spicy chicken to hot noodle soup.

FAMILY TREAT Aquavit (65 East 55th St, 10022; 212 307 7311; www.aquavit.org; 11:45am–2:30pm & 5:30–10:30pm Mon–Fri, 5:30–10:30pm Sat) has separate dining areas and a Scandinavian menu including modern and traditional dishes, with everything from Swedish meatballs to cold-smoked Scottish salmon, plus some more exotic reindeer specialties.

Shopping

A short walk from MoMA, Fifth Avenue is lined with some of the best shops in the city. The multi-level **Henri Bendel** (712 Fifth Ave, 10019; 212 247 1100; www.henribendel.com) has designer clothes, including children's clothing. For colorful kids' clothes and accessories, pop into the **Gap** store (680 Fifth Ave, 10019; 212 977 7023), which has both GapKids and babyGap. The superb toy store **FAO Schwarz** (see p109) lies a couple of blocks north of MoMA.

Find out more

DIGITAL The museum's informative website, www.moma.org, has an interactive section where families can sign up for workshops, gallery walks, and art classes.

Next stop…

SONY WONDER TECHNOLOGY LAB Go on a digital adventure at the Sony Wonder Technology Lab (550 Madison Ave at 56th St, 10022; 212 833 8100; www.sonywondertechlab.com; free), a four-story technology and entertainment center that appeals to all ages. Play video games or perform dance moves with animated characters. Reservations are recommended.

Kids trying their hand at one of the exhibits at Sony Wonder Technology Lab

see p109

KIDS' CORNER

Look out for…

1 Among MoMA's many works of art, can you spot the one with melting watches? Do you know the name of the artist who painted it?

2 Take a stroll around the lovely Sculpture Garden. What do you see in the middle? Where can you catch a glimpse of your reflection?

3 In the paintings and sculpture section, find Vincent van Gogh's painting of a swirling sky filled with bright stars. Do you know what town it depicts?

Answers at the bottom of the page.

LOSING COUNT

The Museum of Modern Art began with an initial gift of just eight prints and one drawing. Since then, MoMA has amassed 150,000 paintings, sculptures, prints, and photographs, and 300,000 books and periodicals.

Day-to-day art

MoMA was the first museum in the world to include everyday objects in its collection, including household appliances, radios, glassware, cutlery, and furniture.

Answers: 1 It's Salvador Dalí's famous *The Persistence of Memory.* **2** A reflecting pool. **3** Van Gogh's *The Starry Night* shows the French town of Saint-Rémy, as seen from the window of the sanatorium where Van Gogh was a patient.

Carnegie Hall, New York's great concert venue

② Carnegie Hall
Music, music, everywhere!

Celebrate music, from classical to contemporary, at the splendid 19th-century Carnegie Hall, one of the world's greatest concert venues. Prominent figures of the music world – from George Gershwin, The Beatles, and Maria Callas to Frank Sinatra, Arturo Toscanini, and Mahler – have performed here.

Performances range from jazz, pop, and world music to operas and classical music concerts. Take a one-hour tour to peek behind the scenes, exploring the palatial stage, discovering the inner workings of the theater, and learning all about Carnegie Hall's amazing history.

In 1991, a museum opened next to the first-tier level, telling the story of the first 100 years of "The House that Music Built." Top orchestras and performers from around the world still fill Carnegie Hall, and the corridors are lined with memorabilia of artists who have performed here.

Letting off steam
Enjoy the urban outdoors by heading to **The Pond** in Central Park. It makes a wonderful place to wind down, with bridges arching over the water, and ducks floating peacefully along the shaded edges of the pond.

The Lowdown

- 🌐 **Map reference** 12 G4
  Address 57th St at Seventh Ave, 10019; 212 903 9765; *www.carnegiehall.org*
- 🚗 **Subway** N, Q & R to 57th St; B, D & E to Seventh Ave. **Bus** M5–M7, M20, M30 & M31
- 🕐 **Open** Tours Oct–late Jun: 11:30am, 12:30pm, 2pm & 3pm Mon–Fri, 11:30am & 12:30pm Sat, 12:30pm Sun
- 💲 **Price** $40–60; $10 for students; $5 for under 12s
- 👥 **Cutting the line** There is rarely a line to get in
- 👫 **Guided tours** The hall & museum offer guided tours (see above).
- 👪 **Age range** 8 and up
- **Activities** The hall occasionally hosts special children's concerts; check the website for details and updates.
- ⏱ **Allow** 2 hours
- ♿ **Wheelchair access** Yes
- 🍽 **Eat and drink** *Snacks* The Halal Guys (*53rd & 6th St, 10019; www.53rdand6th.com*) serves up tasty street food. The most popular dish here is the platter of rice and chicken. *Real meal* A Voce (*10 Columbus Circle, 3rd Floor, 10019; 212 823 2523; www.avocerestaurant.com*) serves up gourmet Italian cuisine in a gorgeous setting.
- 👪 **Restrooms** Off the main hall

The busy Landmarc restaurant, part of the Time Warner Center (see p170)

③ Apple Store Fifth Avenue
All things Mac

With a giant, illuminated glass cube for an entrance, the Apple Store on Fifth Avenue is easy to spot. On entering the 32-ft (10-m) tall block, take the circular elevator or spiral staircase down to a massive space filled with laptops, desktops, iPhones, and iPods. Here, the ever-popular Genius Bar information desk buzzes around the clock with savvy staff answering all questions related to Macs. A children's nook caters to young Mac-lovers, with a

The striking glass-cube entrance to the Apple Store on Fifth Avenue

The Lowdown

- 🌐 **Map reference** 12 H3
  Address 767 Fifth Ave at 59th St, 10153; 212 336 1440; *www.apple.com*
- 🚗 **Subway** N, Q & R to Fifth Ave-59th St. **Bus** M1, M2, M4 & M5
- 🕐 **Open** 24 hours
- 💲 **Price** Free
- 👥 **Cutting the line** It is best to visit early in the morning or later at night to avoid crowds.
- 👪 **Age range** 5 plus
- **Activities** For Youth Programs, check *www.apple.com/retail/youth*
- ⏱ **Allow** 1 hour
- ♿ **Wheelchair access** Yes
- 🍽 **Eat and drink** *Real meal* The Todd English Food Hall (*One West 59th St, Concourse Level, 212 986 9260*) serves a variety of cuisine, from steaks to sushi. *Family treat* Landmarc (*10 Columbus Circle, 3rd Floor, 10019; 212 823 6123; www.landmarc-restaurant.com*) offers salads, steaks, and pasta dishes.
- 👪 **Restrooms** On the ground floor

Arched stone bridge and duck pond in Central Park during fall

range of products for kids to try out. Visitors can also play computer games here all day long.

Letting off steam

Children can try spotting water birds, such as sheldrake, teals, and pintails, among others at the landscaped **Pond** in Central Park. It's a picturesque place to spend an afternoon.

④ FAO Schwarz

Toys, toys, and more toys

The massive FAO Schwarz store sells every toy imaginable, with a mix of classic and contemporary choices, from old-school board games and plush stuffed animals to the latest video games and electronic gadgets. The Outdoor Play section includes powered scooters, skateboards, and trampolines, while Arts & Crafts features colorful beads, clay, and easels. Kids can choose from a variety of confectionery in the candy section, which is lined with buckets of Jelly Bellys,

chewing gum, and chocolate-coated goodies. However, the biggest draw is the giant floor piano, where kids can bang out their favorite tunes with their feet – à la Tom Hanks in the movie *Big* (1988).

Letting off steam

Stroll around or just watch the world go by at the nearby **Grand Army Plaza** *(at the intersection of 59th St & Fifth Ave, 10153)*. Completed in 1916, the oval-shaped Beaux-Arts plaza features a golden equestrian statue of American Civil War hero General William Tecumseh Sherman, with Lady Victory holding a palm frond showing him the way.

The Lowdown

- 🌐 **Map reference** 12 H3
- **Address** 767 Fifth Ave at 58th St, 10153; 212 644 9400; www.fao.com
- 🚗 **Subway** N, Q & R to Fifth Ave-59th St. **Bus** M1, M2, M4 & M5
- 🕐 **Open** 10am–7pm Sun–Thu, 10am–8pm Fri & Sat
- 💲 **Price** Free
- 🧍 **Cutting the line** The store gets most crowded during holidays, Christmas, and New Year.
- 👫 **Age range** 3 plus
- ♿ **Wheelchair access** Yes
- 🍴 **Eat and drink** *Real meal* La Bonne Soupe *(48 West 55th St, 10019; 212 586 7650)* dishes out hearty bistro fare, from crepes and sandwiches to soups, and has a "Junior Menu." *Family treat* The Modern *(9 West 53rd St, 10019; 212 333 1220; www.themodernnyc.com)* serves French-American cuisine inspired by the native Alsace chef.
- 🚻 **Restrooms** On the top floor

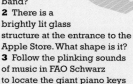

TOY STORY

Created in 1862, FAO Schwarz is not only the oldest toy store in the United States, but also one of the oldest retail shops in the country. It was founded in Baltimore by German immigrant Frederick August Otto Schwarz.

The Sound of Music

The story of Carnegie Hall began with a simple conversation on a big ship. In 1887, on a ship from New York to London, the 25-year-old conductor, Walter Damrosch, met the famous and very wealthy industrialist Andrew Carnegie – and the idea for Carnegie Hall was born.

Children playing the giant piano in FAO Schwarz

Picnic under $20; **Snacks** $20–35; **Real meal** $35–70; **Family treat** over $70 (based on a family of four)

Rockefeller Center and around

Brimming with shops, restaurants, and offices, and home to a bustling plaza and a popular rooftop observation deck, Rockefeller Center is a draw for locals and visitors alike. Kids are well catered for too, thanks to Nintendo World and a giant LEGO store. The area can get busy with commuters during rush hours (morning and late afternoon), so drop by in mid-afternoon to dodge the crowds. It's best to arrive by subway, then explore on foot.

Places of interest

SIGHTS
1. Rockefeller Center
2. Nintendo World
3. St. Patrick's Cathedral
4. Paley Center for Media

● EAT AND DRINK
1. Rockefeller Center Concourse and Food Court
2. Burger Heaven
3. American Girl Café
4. The Sea Grill
5. Bill's Bar and Burger
6. Rock Center Café
7. Xi'An Famous Foods
8. Oceana
9. Cosi
10. Ellen's Stardust Diner

● SHOPPING
1. LEGO Store
2. NBC Experience Store

● WHERE TO STAY
1. DoubleTree Guest Suites
2. Novotel
3. Omni Berkshire Place
4. Renaissance New York Times Square
5. broadway @ times square
6. The Jewel
7. The New York Palace

Midtown

Rockefeller Center
Times Square p116
Empire State Building p92
MoMA p104
Grand Central Terminal p98

0 meters 150
0 yards 150

Huge Christmas tree outside Rockefeller Center

CENTRAL
PARK

Duck
Pond

CENTRAL PARK SOUTH (OLMSTED WAY)

58TH STREET

57TH

Plaza
Hotel

WEST 58TH STREET

Fifth Ave-
59th St
N Q R **M**

GRAND
ARMY
PLAZA

Apple Store
Fifth Avenue

City Center of
Music and
Dance

M
57th St
F

STREET

FAO
Schwarz

WEST 56TH STREET

WEST 55TH STREET

Trump
Tower

IBM
Building

WEST 54TH STREET

FIFTH AVENUE

Museum of
Modern Art

WEST 53RD STREET

MADISON

WEST 52ND STREET

4 Paley Center
for Media

M Fifth Ave-53rd St
E M

6

EAST 52ND STREET

3

Villard
Houses

5
International
Building

EAST 51ST

6

The British
Empire Building

3 St. Patrick's
Cathedral

EAST STREET

2
La Maison
Francaise

EAST 50TH STREET

7

ufacturers
over Trust
uilding

EAST 49TH STREET

2

STREET

EAST 48TH STREET

EAST 47TH STREET

Fred F. French
Building

AVENUE

VANDERBILT AVENUE

MADISON

The Lowdown

🚇 **Subway** E & M to Fifth
Ave-53rd St; B, D, F & M to
47-50th St-Rockefeller Center;
N, Q & R to 49th St.
Bus M1–M5, M7 & M50

🚢 **Supermarket** Ernest Klein
& Co Supermarket, 1366
Avenue of the Americas,
10019; 212 245 7722; www.
ernestklein.net

➕ **Pharmacies** Duane Reade,
1150 Avenue of the Americas,
10036; 212 221 3588;
8am–8pm Mon–Fri, 9am–6pm
Sat, 10am–5pm Sun. Duane
Reade, 1627 Broadway,
10019; 212 586 0374;
7am–9pm Mon–Fri,
8am–8pm Sat & Sun

Entrance to the Paley Center for Media

Children playing games inside the LEGO store

① Rockefeller Center
Jaw-dropping views and Deco sculptures

A gem of urban planning, Rockefeller Center® has long occupied a special place in the hearts of New Yorkers. Built in the 1930s by philanthropist John D. Rockefeller Jr., the Art Deco complex is full of impressive sculptures and works of art, excellent restaurants, and souvenir shops, all set around a breezy plaza. Enjoy a backstage tour of the famous NBC TV Studios or take the trip up by elevator to Top of the Rock, one of the best vantage points for views of the city.

Atlas shouldering the world

Key Features

Top of the Rock Observation Deck®

Radio City Music Hall This Art Deco building on the Sixth Avenue side of the Center is the most famous theater in New York – if not in the entire USA.

Ice-skating rink Open during the winter, this draws skaters from beginner to professional, who twirl around in the shadow of Midtown buildings.

GE building artworks One of the center's main structures, the towering GE building features Lee Lawrie's famous bas-relief, *Wisdom*, and José Maria Sert's faded yet grand murals, *Time* and *American Progress*.

Main promenade Separating the French and British Empire buildings on either side, the center's tree-shaded Channel Gardens are named for the English Channel.

Statue of Prometheus Paul Manship's famous gilded statue of the Greek god bringing fire to mankind rises over the lower plaza.

Top of the Rock Observation Deck® Speedy elevators zip up to the viewing deck, which has incredible views of New York City's skyline.

The Lowdown

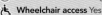

🌐 **Map reference** 12 H5
Address Between Fifth Ave & Sixth Ave and 48th St & 51st St, 10020; 212 332 6868; www.topoftherock.com; Top of the Rock, entrance on 50th St, 10020; 212 698 2000

🚕 **Subway** B, D, F, & M to 47-50th St-Rockefeller Center. **Bus** M1–M5, M7 & M50

🕐 **Open** Plaza: 24 hours daily; Top of the Rock: 8am–midnight daily, last elevator at 11pm

💲 **Price** Entrance to the Rockefeller Center and its buildings is

free; Top of the Rock $82–92; NBC Tour $90–100

👬 **Cutting the line** Top of the Rock sells time-stamped tickets, so visitors enter at designated times. Buy tickets online or at Rockefeller Center.

🚩 **Guided tours** Self-guided podcast tours of Top of the Rock are available with purchase of tickets online.

👫 **Age range** 5 plus

👫 **Activities** Ice-skating in winter and Top of the Rock Breezeway

⏱ **Allow** 3 hours including tour

♿ **Wheelchair access** Yes

☕ **Café** At the food court on the lower level

🛍 **Shops** A wide range of shops in the center

🚻 **Restrooms** On several levels

Good family value?
Attractions that appeal to both adults and kids, from a rooftop observation deck to an ice-skating rink, make this a prime location for the whole family.

Prices given are for a family of four

Colorful lighting in the Top of the Rock Breezeway

Letting off steam

Connecting the observation decks at Top of the Rock, the Target Interactive Breezeway is a motion-detecting walkway with a glowing ceiling and walls that are entirely lit by LED systems. Kids will love jumping around in front of the sensors as they watch the colors follow their every movement.

Eat and drink

Picnic: under $20; Snacks: $20–35; Real meal: $35–70; Family treat: over $70 (based on a family of four)

PICNIC Rockefeller Center Concourse and Food Court *(212 332 6868; www.rockefellercenter. com/food-and-drink; 7am–midnight daily)* offers sandwiches, burritos, and baked goods that can be enjoyed as a picnic on the shaded benches in Rockefeller Plaza.

SNACKS Burger Heaven *(20 East 49th St, near Madison Ave, 10019; 212 755 2166; www.burgerheaven. com; 7am–7:30pm Mon–Fri, 8am–5:45pm Sat, 9:30am–4:30pm Sun)* specializes in big, tasty burgers, topped with everything from bacon to avocado.

REAL MEAL American Girl Café *(609 Fifth Ave at 49th St, 10017; 877 247 5223; call ahead for specific seating times)* is located inside

Facade of the popular American Girl Place, home of American Girl Café

a doll emporium. It offers prix fixe brunch, lunch, afternoon tea, and dinner. The menu includes macaroni and cheese, and grilled mahi-mahi.

FAMILY TREAT The Sea Grill *(Rockefeller Plaza, 19 West 49th St, 10020; 212 332 7610; www. theseagrillnyc.com; 11:30am–3pm & 5–10pm Mon–Sat)* is a stylish restaurant that serves a range of choice seafood, from crab, lobster, and oysters, to salmon and swordfish.

Shopping

Rockefeller Center has several shops, including a massive **LEGO Store** *(620 Fifth Ave, 10020; 212 245 5973; http://stores.lego.com)*, souvenir shops, and clothing stores such as Anthropologie, Ann Taylor, and Brooks Brothers. TV fans will enjoy the **NBC Experience Store** *(30 Rockefeller Plaza, 10112; 212 664 3700)*, which sells branded goods, from mugs and magnets to sweatshirts.

Shoppers inside the LEGO Store at the Rockefeller Center

Find out more

DIGITAL Browse *www.rockefeller center.com*, which has detailed sections on the center's art, special events, shops, and restaurants.

Next stop...

NBC STUDIO TOUR The daily, hour-long NBC Studio Tour *(www. nbcstudiotour.com)* gives visitors a backstage look at the NBC Studio and its hit shows, such as *Saturday Night Live* and *Football Night in America*. For a free early-morning TV thrill, join the crowds to watch the audience for NBC's popular *Today Show*.

② Nintendo World

Gaming paradise

Video gamers will delight in Nintendo World, the largest Nintendo store in the US. Over 10,000 sq ft (930 sq m) in size, the massive outlet features a wide array of console games, involving the phenomenally popular Wii system, from Just Dance to Donkey Kong. There is also a large section dedicated to Pokémon, filled with lively games and colorful cards and accessories.

Letting off steam

After a few hours of gaming, walk to nearby Fifth Avenue and window-shop along the way to

Entrance of the Nintendo Store facing Rockefeller Plaza

The Lowdown

🌐 **Map reference** 12 H6
Address 10 Rockefeller Plaza, 10020; 646 459 0800; www.nintendoworldstore.com

🚗 **Subway** B, D, F & M to 47-50th St-Rockefeller Center. **Bus** M1 & M5

🕐 **Open** 9am–8pm Mon–Thu, 9am–9pm Fri–Sat, 11am–6pm Sun

💲 **Price** Free

👫 **Age range** 4 plus

Activities A fantastic range of games to keep kids occupied

⏱ **Allow** 1 hour

♿ **Wheelchair access** Yes

☕ **Eat and drink** *Real meal* Bill's Bar and Burger (*16 West 51st St, Fifth Ave, 10019; 212 705 8510*) has juicy burgers and hot dogs. *Family treat* Rock Center Café (*20 West 50th St, 10020; 212 332 7620*) serves Italian and American fare.

👫 **Restrooms** On the first floor

Booth at Bill's Bar & Burger restaurant on Fifth Avenue

Central Park South. Take a look at the horses and carriages parked on the edge of the park. Children will delight in seeing the animals up close and some carriage owners may even let them pet the horses.

③ St. Patrick's Cathedral

Towering basilica in the heart of the city

Looming majestically over glamorous Fifth Avenue, the Gothic Revival St. Patrick's is the largest Catholic cathedral in the country, and one of the most important – serving as a hub for generations of Irish, Italian, and other Catholic immigrants. Walk the circumference of the cathedral and take in the imposing white-marble facade and massive bronze doors, which weigh an impressive 20,000 lb (9,000 kg) and are decorated with religious figures. For a quiet

moment away from the bustling crowds, head to the simple and peaceful Lady Chapel at the back of the cathedral.

Letting off steam

Head to the nearby **LEGO Store** (*see p113*), which is filled from top to bottom with Denmark's most famous export. The store features a towering pick-a-brick wall and the popular Master Builder Bar, where LEGO fans can play games, build models, and participate in trivia quizzes.

The Lowdown

🌐 **Map reference** 12 H5
Address 460 Madison Ave, 10022; 212 753 2261; www.saintpatrickscathedral.org

🚗 **Subway** E & M to Fifth Ave-53rd St. **Bus** M1–M5, M27 & M50

🕐 **Open** 6:30am–8:45pm daily

💲 **Price** Free

Guided tours For groups of ten or more at 10am; call in advance

👫 **Age range** 5 plus

Activities Concerts and performances held throughout the year; check website for details

⏱ **Allow** 1 hour

♿ **Wheelchair access** Yes

☕ **Eat and drink** *Snacks* Karam II Restaurant (*24 West 45th St, near Fifth Ave, 10036; 212 354 7400; www.karam2restaurant.com*) has tasty Middle Eastern cuisine, including hummus platters and grilled lamb. *Family treat* Oceana (*120 West 49th St, near Sixth Ave, 10020; 212 759 5941; www.oceanarestaurant.com*) serves the freshest seafood in Midtown.

👫 **Restrooms** Off the main chapel

Sunday mass in progress at St. Patrick's Cathedral

Fountains in front of Radio City Music Hall, Rockefeller Center

④ Paley Center for Media

Small-screen chronicles

There is no place better in Manhattan for small-screen aficionados than the Paley Center for Media, which documents the entire history of American television under one roof. The center holds an archive of more than 150,000 TV shows, radio broadcasts, and commercials, right from the 1950s sitcom *I Love Lucy* to contemporary dramas, most of which are available for viewing on personal TV consoles. Children's televison is also well represented. Kids will enjoy watching a range of shows from the past and present, including *Sesame Street*, as well as televised question-and-answer sessions with children, hosted by former US presidents.

Seating for visitors in the lobby, Paley Center for Media

The Lowdown

- 🌐 **Map reference** 12 H5
- **Address** 25 West 52nd St, between Fifth Ave & Sixth Ave, 10019; 212 621 6600; www.paleycenter.org
- 🚗 **Subway** E & M to Fifth Ave–53rd St. **Bus** M1–M5 & M7
- 🕐 **Open** Noon–6pm Wed–Sun, until 8pm Thu
- 💲 **Price** $30–40
- 👫 **Age range** 4 plus
- 👫 **Activities** The center hosts many events, from media panels to sitcom screenings; the center's interactive website is packed with videos and a daily TV quiz. Media savvy kids can send in questions for selection on the site.
- ⏱ **Allow** 1 hour; longer for an event or performance
- ♿ **Wheelchair access** Yes
- 🍴 **Eat and drink** *Real meal* Cosi (1633 Broadway, at 51st St, 10036; 212 397 9838; www.getcosi.com) serves creative sandwiches and soups. *Family treat* Ellen's Stardust Diner (1650 Broadway, at 51st St, 10019; 212 956 5151; www.ellensstardustdiner.com) offers comfort food, such as chicken pot pie, in a vintage diner setting.
- 👫 **Restrooms** On the first floor

Letting off steam

Cool off in the spray of the large fountain across from the Radio City Music Hall, at the corner of Avenue of the Americas (Sixth Ave) and 50th Street. It is a prime spot to watch the world go by at one of New York's busiest intersections.

Picnic under $20; Snacks $20–35; Real meal $35–70; Family treat over $70 (based on a family of four)

Times Square and around

The busiest crossroads in New York City, Times Square is alive with activity throughout the day and night. Right in the heart of the "city that never sleeps," there is no place better for people-watching than here. Broadway, the city's longest street, is also dubbed the "Great White Way" because it was one of the first areas lit by electronic advertisements in the US. Times Square is served by many subway lines, while the sights along the Hudson River can be reached on foot or by bus.

Midtown

Rockefeller Center
p110

MoMA
p104

Times Square

Grand
Central
Terminal
p98

Empire State
Building
p92

The Lowdown

🚃 **Subway** B, D, F & M to 42nd St-Bryant Park; 1, 2 & 3 to Times Sq-42nd St; A, C & E to 42nd St-Port Auth. **Bus** M5, M7, M11 & crosstown M42

🍴 **Supermarket** Food Emporium, 810 Eighth Ave at 49th St, 10019; 212 977 1710

🎭 **Festivals** Times Square hosts the largest New Year's Eve celebration in the US, when swarms of revelers gather to watch the famous crystal ball descend on a lighted pole at the stroke of midnight.

➕ **Pharmacy** Rite Aid, 301 West 50th St, 10019; 212 247 8384; 24 hours daily

🛝 **Nearest playground** De Witt Clinton Park, between West 52nd St to West 54th St and 11th Ave to 12th Ave

Striking ruby-red stairs above the TKTS booth, Times Square

Diners enjoying their meals, Angus McIndoe restaurant

Places of interest

SIGHTS
1. Times Square
2. Intrepid Sea, Air & Space Museum
3. Circle Line Cruise
4. The Town Hall

● EAT AND DRINK
1. Carve
2. Virgil's Real Barbecue
3. Angus' Café Bistro
4. Aureole
5. Five Napkin Burger
6. Joe Allen
7. West Bank Café
8. Becco
9. Le Pain Quotidien

See also International Center of Photography (p121)

● SHOPPING
1. Toys"R"Us
2. Mud Sweat Tears
3. Hershey's
4. M&M's World

● WHERE TO STAY
1. 414 Hotel
2. Algonquin Hotel
3. Belvedere Hotel
4. Best Western President Hotel
5. Edison Hotel
6. Hilton Garden Inn Times Square
7. Hilton Times Square
8. Intercontinental New York Times Square
9. Skyline Hotel
10. The Hotel @ Times Square
11. The Westin New York at Times Square

0 meters 200

0 yards 200

WEST 57TH STREET
WEST 56TH STREET
WEST 55TH STREET
WEST 54TH STREET
WEST 53RD STREET
WEST 52ND STREET
WEST 51ST STREET

MONY Tower
57th St
N.Q.R

WEST 55TH ST
WEST 54TH ST
WEST 53RD ST

Seventh Ave
B.D.E

Museum of Modern Art

50th St
C.E

W. C. HANDY'S PLACE
50th St
WEST 51ST STREET
WEST 50TH
49th St
N.Q.R
47th-50th St-Rockefeller Center
B.D.F.M

Paley Center for Media

Radio City Music Hall

W 52ND ST

Rockefeller Center

TKTS Booth

DUFFY SQUARE

Lyceum Theater

SHUBERT ALLEY

WEST 48TH STREET
WEST 47TH STREET
WEST 46TH STREET
WEST 45TH STREET
WEST 44TH STREET

Times Sq-42nd St
1.2.3

Times Sq-42nd St
7.N.Q.R.S

The Town Hall

Times Square

42nd St-Bryant Park
B.D.F.M

42ND STREET

Fifth Ave
7

BRYANT PARK

New York Public Library

WEST 39TH STREET
WEST 38TH STREET
WEST 37TH STREET

Macy's

34th St-Herald Sq
B.D.F.M.N.Q.R

HERALD SQUARE

Shaw Lowell Memorial Fountain in Bryant Park

① Times Square
Bright lights, big fun

The neon-lit heart of New York, Times Square is an unstoppable whirl of activity, ever busy with crowds, cabs, double-decker tourist buses, and street vendors. Stretching between 42nd Street and 47th Street, it is one of the liveliest intersections in the world. Home to the dazzling playground of Toys"R"Us, towering candy stores such as the fragrant Hershey's and colorful M&M's, plus the jaw-dropping Ripley's Believe it or Not! museum and the New Victory Theater, the square offers plenty to engross kids, big and small.

Key Features

Ripley's Believe It or Not! museum View the weird and wonderful, from an albino giraffe to a collection of shrunken heads at this museum of oddities.

One Times Square At the southernmost edge rises the 25-story building, originally the headquarters of the *New York Times* newspaper.

Madame Tussauds New York Greet wax doubles of the stars, from Beyoncé and The Beatles to Muhammad Ali, as well as popular comic-book characters such as the Incredible Hulk.

New Victory Theater Times Square sits in the middle of the theater district, whose many historical playhouses include the New Victory Theater (*see p41*), the city's premier children's theater.

Electronic tickertape One of the Square's many eye-catching neon signs, the figures on the Morgan Stanley LED tickertape are 10 ft (3 m) high.

Red steps Rising over the TKTS booth on Duffy Square, 27 ruby-red glass steps fill with hundreds of people at a time and offer a unique, panoramic view of the brightly lit street.

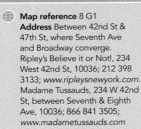

New Victory Theater

Madame Tussauds New York

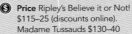

Ripley's

W 48TH ST
W 47TH ST
BROADWAY
AVENUE
W 47TH ST
SEVENTH
W 46TH ST
W 45TH ST
W 44TH ST
W 44TH ST
W 43RD ST
W 43TH ST
W 42ND ST

The Lowdown

🌐 **Map reference** 8 G1
Address Between 42nd St & 47th St, where Seventh Ave and Broadway converge. Ripley's Believe it or Not!, 234 West 42nd St, 10036; 212 398 3133; www.ripleysnewyork.com. Madame Tussauds, 234 W 42nd St, between Seventh & Eighth Ave, 10036; 866 841 3505; www.madametussauds.com

🚇 **Subway** B, D, F & M to 42nd St-Bryant Park; 1, 2, 3 to Times Sq-42nd St; 7, N, Q, R & S to Times Sq-42nd St; A, C & E to 42nd St-Port Auth. Bus Terminal

🕐 **Open** Ripley's Believe it or Not!: 9am–1am daily. Madame

Tussauds: 10am–8pm Mon–Thu & Sun, 10am–10pm Fri–Sat

💲 **Price** Ripley's Believe it or Not! $115–25 (discounts online). Madame Tussauds $130–40

👫 **Cutting the line** The TKTS booth, Father Duffy Square, under the "red steps," Broadway & 47th St, 10036; 212 912 9770; 3–8pm Mon, Thu & Fri, 2–8pm Tue, 10am–2pm & 3–8pm Wed & Sat, 11am–7pm Sun; www.tdf. org, where cut-price theater tickets are sold daily, has some of the longest lines in Times Square. The best time to arrive is right after opening or just before closing.

🚻 **Age range** 3 plus

⏱ **Allow** 1 hour or more

♿ **Wheelchair access** Yes

☕ **Café** On site

🛍 **Shops** Times Square is lined with many stores, from Toys"R"Us to souvenir shops.

🚻 **Restrooms** In many of the attractions, shops, and restaurants around the square, including Toys"R"Us

Good family value?
Although expensive, super-commercial, and crowded, Times Square offers plenty of fun and entertainment for kids.

Prices given are for a family of four

Children on the Ferris wheel inside Toys"R"Us

Take cover

Kids and adults will enjoy a romp through **Toys"R"Us**, the largest in the world, which features a 60-ft (18-m) high Ferris wheel, an animatronic dinosaur, and, to the delight of little girls, a life-sized Barbie dollhouse.

Eat and drink

Picnic: under $20; Snacks: $20–35; Real meal: $35–70; Family treat: over $70 (based on a family of four)

PICNIC Carve *(760 Eighth Ave at 47th St, 10036; 212 730 4949; open 24 hrs)* has a variety of sandwiches made with freshly carved meats, along with fruits and organic chocolate bars. Afterward, head to the "red steps" or Times Square's pedestrian area, which is filled with tables and chairs.

SNACKS Virgil's Real Barbecue *(152 West 44th St, 10036; 212 921 9494; 11:30am–11pm Mon, 11am–midnight Tue–Sat, 11am–11pm Sun)* is a good place to refuel with a Texas-style BBQ. Coloring books are handed out to keep the little ones occupied.

REAL MEAL Angus' Café Bistro *(258 West 44th St, near Eighth Ave, 10036; 212 221 9222; www.angus cafebistro.com; noon–11pm Mon & Tue, till 11:30pm Wed & Thu, till 11:45pm Fri & Sat, till 10:30pm Sun)* features hearty, high-end American fare, from sirloin steak to steamed mussels with smoked bacon. Kids especially like the thick-cut fries.

FAMILY TREAT Aureole *(135 West 42nd St, between Sixth Ave & Broadway, 10036; 212 319 1660; 11:45am–2:15pm Mon–Fri, plus 5–10:30pm daily (till 11pm Fri & Sat, till 10pm Sun & Mon)* serves Mediterranean-accented American fare, from pork-belly sliders to chilled gazpacho soup.

Shopping

The multistoried **Toys"R"Us** *(1514 Broadway, 10036; 646 366 8800; www.toysrus.com)* rises over the square, along with the sparkling **Sanrio** *(233 West 42nd St, 10036; 212 840 6011; www.sanrio.com)*, showcasing the big-eyed Hello Kitty. **Hershey's** *(1593 Broadway, 10036; 212 581 9100; www.hersheys.com)* fills with the aroma of chocolate, as does **M&M's World** *(1600 Broadway, 10019; 212 295 3850; www.mymms.com)*, where candy can be bought by color. There is an interactive play area here, too.

Find out more

DIGITAL Times Square's official website, *www.timessquarenyc.org*, is an excellent source for current events, fun facts, and recommendations.

Next stop...

NEW VICTORY THEATER Brighten up the evening with a show at the New Victory Theater *(209 West 42nd St, 10036; 646 223 3010; www.newvictory.org)*, New York's first and only performing arts theater dedicated to kids. The theater, housed in a historic building dating back to 1900, presents a diverse season of theater, dance, vaudeville, puppetry, and music from around the globe.

Entrance to Angus' Café Bistro, Times Square

② Intrepid Sea, Air & Space Museum

Space craft and spy planes

At Pier 86 on the Hudson River looms the massive USS *Intrepid*, which houses the Intrepid Sea, Air & Space Museum. This old aircraft carrier has a distinguished history, including hauling space capsules out of the ocean after the Mercury and Gemini space missions (1956–63). On board is a collection of air and sea craft, including an A-12 Blackbird, the world's fastest spy plane. Kids will enjoy the 3D movies that take visitors "flying" through space, and simulators such as the "G-force." In 2012, the museum added the original NASA orbiter *Space Ship Enterprise* to the flight deck as part of its permanent exhibition. Explore the crew's quarters and view navigational gadgets in the lower levels. During Fleet Week (*see p14*), ships and their crew members gather here from all over the world.

Letting off steam

At Piers 40 and 96, the **Downtown Boathouse** (*www.downtownboat house.org; mid-May–mid-Oct*) offers

Exterior of Five Napkin Burger restaurant, a popular burger joint

free kayaking lessons along the Hudson River. The only requirement to join a class is to be able to swim. Kayakers can go on a short trip around the protected embayment in front of the boathouse, enjoy the river scene, and get a new perspective on New York City.

③ Circle Line cruise

Sailing along the shore

The best views of Manhattan are from the water. Embark on a popular Circle Line cruise along the shores of Manhattan, take in the city skyline, and float past the magnificent Statue of Liberty (*see pp58–9*). Full-island sight-seeing tours feature all of New York Harbor's greatest sights, from the elegant Brooklyn Bridge (*see pp196–7*) to views of leafy Staten Island. The Circle Line also offers lively musical cruises and sunset trips.

Those looking for an adrenaline rush should jump aboard the "The Beast"(*2 May–27 Sep*), a speedboat painted with shark's teeth that offers a wet and wild ride on the Hudson River.

The Lowdown

🌐 **Map reference** 7 B1
Address Pier 83, West 42nd St & Twelfth Ave, 10036; 212 563 3200; *www.circleline42.com*

🚇 **Subway** 1, 2, 3, 7, N, Q & R to Times Sq-42nd St; B, D & F to Fifth Ave & 42nd St. **Bus** M42

🕐 **Open** Daily all year round; The Beast & Harbor Lights times vary

🚩 **Guided tours** Timings for tours vary; check website for timings and details

💲 **Price** Full Island Cruise $132; under 3s free; The Beast $100

👫 **Cutting the line** Book tickets online during the summer high season. Visitors will still have to stand in a line to board the boat.

👫 **Age range** 3 plus; **Beast:** Kids must be at least 40 inches (100 cm) tall to ride the speedboat

⏱ **Allow** Full Island Cruise: 3 hours; The Beast: 30 minutes

♿ **Wheelchair access** Yes

🍽 **Eat and drink** *Real meal* West Bank Café (*407 West 42nd St, near Ninth Ave, 10036; 212 695 6909;*) features American and French dishes. *Family treat* Becco (*355 West 46th St, near Ninth Ave, 10036; 212 397 7597*) serves robust Italian specialties.

🚻 **Restrooms** On the lower deck of the boat

Letting off steam

Walk south beside the Hudson River and look out for people flying through the air. This is the **Trapeze School of New York** (*353 West St, 10014; 212 242 8769*), which offers flying trapeze classes right on the banks of the river. Providing a couple of hours of unique fun, the school is open to nearly all age groups; 4-year-olds and above can participate.

The Lowdown

🌐 **Map reference** 11 B6
Address Pier 86, West 46th St & Twelfth Ave,10036; 212 245 0072; *www.intrepidmuseum.org*

🚇 **Subway** A, C & E to 42nd St-Port Auth. Bus Terminal. **Bus** M42 & M50

🕐 **Open** Apr–Oct: 10am–5pm Mon–Fri, 10am–6pm Sat, Sun & hols; Nov–Mar: 10am–5pm daily

💲 **Price** $96–110; kids 3–6 $17;; under 3s free

🚩 **Guided tours** Audio tour $5; tickets available at the entrance.

👫 **Age range** 3 plus

⏱ **Allow** 1 hour

♿ **Wheelchair access** Yes

🍽 **Eat and drink** *Snacks* Five Napkin Burger (*630 Ninth Ave, between 44th St & 45th St, 10036; 212 757 2277*) offers good burgers. *Real meal* Joe Allen (*326 West 46th St, near Ninth Ave, 10036; 212 581 6464*) serves Italian specialties and sandwiches.

🚻 **Restrooms** Every floor except the flight deck

Visitors aboard a Circle Line cruise ship taking in views of Manhattan

Prices given are for a family of four

The Town Hall's brick facade

④ The Town Hall

History buffs and culture vultures

Founded by a group of suffragists (The League for Political Education) in 1921, The Town Hall is a National Historic site in the heart of New York's theater district. Intended as a meeting space to educate people on the important issues of the day, McKim, Mead & White architects designed the building to reflect the democratic principles of the League. All seats had an unobstructed view, giving rise – legend has it – to the phrase "Not a bad seat in the house."

These days The Town Hall hosts an impressive program of events and festivals, ranging from world music to show tunes, political theater to dance. The venue is also committed to instilling cultural awareness in children from a young age. Children's shows include kid-friendly versions of the World Music and Dance Festival and the Annual Black History Month Celebration.

Free hour-long tours take place on Friday at 10:30am. Sign up by the previous Wednesday.

Letting off steam

Head two blocks west to the **McCaffrey Playground**, where kids can clamber about the sturdy playground's swings and slides. There is also a handball court and a basketball court. The playground is fenced in, giving parents peace of mind as children play and explore the area.

The Lowdown

🌐 **Map reference** 8 G1
Address 123 West 43rd St (between 6th Ave & Broadway), 10036; www.thetownhall.org

🚇 **Subway** B, D, F & M to 42nd St-Bryant Park; 1, 2, 3, 7, N, Q, R & S to Times Sq-42nd St; A, C & E to 42nd St-Port Authority Bus Terminal. **Bus** M5, M7, M20 & M42

🕐 **Open** Box office:10am–6pm Mon–Sat

💲 **Price** shows vary

🎫 **Guided tours** Free, 10:30am Fri

👫 **Age range** 7 plus

⏱ **Allow** 1 hour for tours

♿ **Wheelchair access** Yes

🍽 **Eat and drink** *Real meal* Le Pain Quotidien *(70 West 40th St, at Sixth Ave, 10018; 212 354 5224)* offers soups, Mediterranean platters, and salads to go with its handmade organic breads.

👫 **Restrooms** Downstairs (men) and on the mezzanine (women and disabled access)

THE 19TH AMENDMENT

The League for Political Education fought for the 19th Amendment (women's right to vote), which passed in 1921.

Arrest of Margaret Sanger

Margaret Higgins Sanger (1879–1966) was a nurse and sex educator who became an iconic figure in the American reproductive rights movement. Sanger founded the American Birth Control League, now known as Planned Parenthood, and was once dramatically arrested on stage at The Town Hall during a public meeting on birth control, held on November 13, 1921.

Outdoor seating with umbrellas at Le Pain Quotidien

Central Park

Enormous swaths of pastoral hills, woods, lakes, and streams – stretching out along 50 blocks – make up New York's most treasured green space, Central Park. Opened in 1860, it was the city's first major public park and is known as the backyard of all New Yorkers. Among the greenery there is plenty to explore, including Belvedere Castle and Bethesda Terrace, as well as a zoo and several excellent playgrounds.

Upper
West Side
and Harlem

**Central
Park**

Upper
East Side

Midtown

Downtown

Highlights

Central Park Zoo
Marvel at speedy penguins, grizzly bears, and stealthy snow leopards from the Himalayas at this zoo, perfectly sized for kids (see pp128–9).

Friedsam Memorial Carousel
Spin around on colorful, handcrafted horses to cheerful tunes on this carousel, built in 1908 (see pp130–31).

Bethesda Fountain
Admire the park's crown jewel, the elegant *Angel of the Waters* fountain, from Bethesda Terrace or from a rowing boat on the adjoining lake (see pp134–5).

Conservatory Water
Rent mini remote-controlled boats by the hour on the lake made famous by the book *Stuart Little (see p136).*

Belvedere Castle
Explore a castle right out of a fairy tale – faux-medieval Belvedere is not only pretty to look at, but offers spectacular views (see pp140–41).

Swedish Cottage
Drop by this charming wooden cottage, brought here from Sweden in 1876, for wonderful marionette shows for children (see p142).

Left Sea lions atop a rocky outcrop in their enclosure, Central Garden and Sea Lion Pool, Central Park Zoo
Above left The fairy-tale facade of Belvedere Castle, Central Park

The Best of
Central Park

As essential to the identity of New York City as its skyline, Central Park combines idyllic natural beauty with cultural attractions. Nearly every corner of the park has something to offer. Take a hike, go looking for wildlife, or check out family-friendly sights such as the zoo. Children will enjoy a turn around the skating rink, which becomes an amusement park in summer. There is even a children's theater offering puppet shows.

Eco explorers

Begin at the Henry Luce Nature Observatory, inside **Belvedere Castle** (see pp140–41), to learn about the park's flora and fauna, then borrow a nature kit and go bird-watching at nearby Turtle Pond. Next, head out for a hike through **The Ramble** (see p136), a wooded nature preserve strewn with trails that wind through forest, glades, and along a stream. Stop for a bite at any of the hot-dog carts sprinkled throughout the park, then continue on to the Tisch Children's Zoo (see p128) and feed pot-bellied pigs, sheep, and goats. Finish by exploring the main **Central Park Zoo** (see pp128–9), whose inhabitants include sea lions, grizzly bears, snow monkeys, and penguins.

Left Gentoo penguins in Central Park Zoo
Below Bethesda Terrace, with its famous fountain

Above *Elegant Bow Bridge stretching across Central Park Lake, with rowboats on the water*

Monumental markers

Tributes to notable events, cultures, people, and even a heroic dog are sprinkled throughout the park. Visit **Bethesda Terrace** *(see pp134–5)*, a regal plaza with a fountain crowned by the lovely *Angel of the Waters* sculpture. Then head southwest to **Strawberry Fields** *(see p135)*, a small corner of the park dedicated to former Beatle John Lennon. Stroll due east to the **Literary Walk** *(see p131)*, then south to the statue of **Balto** *(see p131)*, the canine dogsled leader who completed the final leg of the 1925 serum run in blizzard conditions, saving the children of a small town in Alaska from diphtheria. Afterward, head north to the **Obelisk** *(see p143)*. This 71-ft (22-m) high monument was built in Egypt in 1450 BC, and its hieroglyphs praise the dominion of a pharaoh. The Egyptian government gifted it to New York City in 1880.

Water worlds

Water lends any landscape a natural and calming effect and, with this in mind, Frederick Law Olmsted, one of Central Park's designers, carefully positioned ponds, lakes, and streams throughout the park, the largest of which is Central Park Lake. It is best explored on a rowboat rented at the Loeb Boathouse. Next, walk east to **Conservatory Water** *(see p136)* to rent a remote-controlled sailboat or just to watch the nautical pursuits of others, before heading north to the **Jacqueline Kennedy Onassis Reservoir** *(see p143)* to take in the breathtaking views from its waterside pathways. Look out for some of the animals and birds that make the lake their home.

Theatrical endeavors

Embark on a journey that explores the park's dramatic side. Start by taking in a marionette show at the **Swedish Cottage Marionette Theatre** *(see p142)*. Nearby, the medieval-looking Belvedere Castle is the perfect setting for kids to undertake some make-believe play of their own; it served as Count von Count's home on *Sesame Street*. Theater aficionados visiting during the summer should do whatever is takes to snag seats for a Shakespeare play at the open-air **Delacorte Theater** *(see p141)*, including lining up early in the morning for free tickets, which are distributed at noon on the day of the performance.

Right *A visitor walking past the rustic home of the Swedish Cottage Marionette Theatre*

Central Park Zoo and around

The lovely, southernmost band of Central Park is also the busiest – full of attractions including the zoo, Wollman Rink, and the carousel, plus nature spots such as Sheep Meadow and the Literary Walk. Its open spaces are good for picnics but mostly devoid of shade, so they can get very hot on a sunny day. On the weekend, come here early morning to escape the crowds, and avoid major parade days, when the stretch along Fifth Avenue throngs with people. Roads are closed to cars outside rush hours, but watch out for cyclists and skaters.

Central Park

Belvedere Castle
p138
Bethesda
Terrace
Central p132
Park Zoo

Wide pedestrian pathway lined with trees, on the Literary Walk, Central Park

Places of interest

SIGHTS
1. Central Park Zoo
2. Trump Rink
3. Friedsam Memorial Carousel
4. Balto Statue and Literary Walk

EAT AND DRINK
1. Carnegie Deli
2. Dancing Crane Café
3. Viand Coffee Shop
4. Bistro Chat Noir
5. Trattoria Dell'Arte
6. Le Pain Quotidien
7. Le Charlot

See also Trump Rink (p130)

SHOPPING
1. Zootique

WHERE TO STAY
1. Loews Regency
2. Le Parker Meridien
3. Plaza Hotel
4. Salisbury Hotel

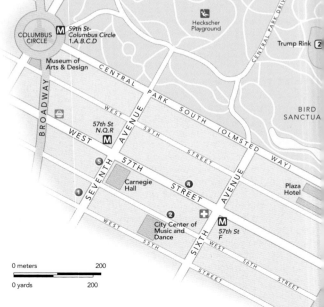

Tavern on the Green

Mineral Springs

SHEEP MEADOW

65TH ST TRANSVERSE

HECKSCHER BALLFIELDS

Friedsam Memorial Carousel 3

CENTRAL PARK

Heckscher Playground

Trump Rink 2

COLUMBUS CIRCLE
M 59th St-Columbus Circle 1.A.B.C.D

Museum of Arts & Design

CENTRAL PARK SOUTH (OLMSTED WAY)

BIRD SANCTUA

BROADWAY

WEST 57th St N.Q.R
M

Carnegie Hall

57TH STREET

Plaza Hotel

City Center of Music and Dance

M 57th St F

SIXTH AVENUE

0 meters 200
0 yards 200

Kids in the rain forest habitat, Central Park Zoo

The Lowdown

🚗 **Subway** N, Q & R to Fifth Ave-59th St; F to 57th St. **Bus** M1, M2, M3, M4, M5 & M66

ℹ️ **Visitor information** The Dairy Visitor Center, mid-park at 65th St, Central Park, 10065; 212 794 6564; 10am–5pm Mon–Sun; *www.centralparknyc.org*

🍴 **Supermarket** Morton Williams Supermarket, 140 West 57th St, 10019; 212 315 4434 **Market** 57th St Greenmarket, Ninth Ave, between 56th St & 57th St, 10019; May–Dec: 8am–5pm Wed & Sat

➕ **Pharmacy** Duane Reade, 100 West 57th St, 10019; 212 956 0464; 7:30am–8pm Mon–Fri, 9am–6pm Sat, 10am–5pm Sun

🎠 **Nearest playgrounds** Billy Johnson Playground, Fifth Ave at 67th St, 10065 (see p129). Heckscher Playground, (see p131)

Ice skating at Trump Rink, a popular spot in winter, Central Park

The outdoor terrace at Le Pain Quotidien, Central Park

① Central Park Zoo
Torpedoing penguins and snow monkeys

Operated by the Wildlife Conservation Society, Central Park Zoo is very popular with children. The city's first zoo, it began as an informal menagerie of donated animals in the 1860s, and even after two makeovers (in 1934 and the mid-'80s), retains a kind of backyard intimacy. More than 100 species can be seen, grouped into three climatic zones – the Tropic Zone, the Temperate Territory, and the Polar Circle.

A golden weaver nesting

Star Attractions

① **Tropic Zone** Spot huge tortoises, colorful birds, colobus monkeys, and tiny lion-headed tamarins inside this steamy tropical zone, teeming with African and South American flora and fauna.

Entrance to Central Park Zoo

Entrance to Tisch Children's Zoo

④ **Grizzly bears** These massive bears were taken in as rescues because they had grown too accustomed to people in the wild. Watch them play in their habitat, which includes a waterfall and stream.

⑤ **Penguins** The Polar Circle exhibit is home to four penguin species: gentoo, chinstrap, rockhopper and king. See these Antarctic birds being hand-fed fish or torpedoing through the water gracefully.

③ **Snow leopards** Occupying a rugged evergreen habitat that re-creates the environment of their Central Asian home, these cats are most active in the early morning and late afternoon.

⑥ **Central Garden and Sea Lion Pool** Watch California sea lions swim elegantly in their glass-enclosed habitat. Do not miss feeding time, when they show off their diving and other fish-earning skills.

② **Snow monkeys** Native to Japan, they live on a rocky island here in large groups of 500. The average group size falls between 40 to 200. The zoo features a hot tub and pond as part of its snow monkey exhibit.

⑦ **Tisch Children's Zoo** Part of Central Park Zoo, the tiny pond here is bursting with turtles, koi, and ducks. In the eastern part of the zoo, kids get to pet and feed the friendly sheep and llamas.

The Lowdown

🌐 **Map reference** 12 H2
Address East 64th St at Fifth Ave, 10065; 212 439 6500; www.centralparkzoo.com

🚗 **Subway** N, Q & R to Fifth Ave-59th St; F to 57th St.
Bus M57 (runs crosstown), M1, M2, M3, M4 & M5

🕐 **Open** Nov–Mar: 10am–4:30pm daily; Apr–Oct: 10am–5pm Mon–Fri, 10am–5:30pm Sat & Sun

💲 **Price** $38; child $7; under 3s free

👫 **Cutting the line** Tickets can be purchased online; be sure to print them out beforehand.

🚩 **Guided tours** For family programs and guided tours, check the park website.

👫 **Age range** All ages

👫 **Activities** Sea lion feedings, harbor seal feedings, and penguin feedings take place two or three times a day. Check the website for feeding times, as the schedule is subject to change.

⏱ **Allow** 2 hours

♿ **Wheelchair access** Yes

☕ **Café** The zoo's Dancing Crane Café offers affordable basics for lunch.

Prices given are for a family of four

Marble slide at Billy Johnson Playground

Letting off steam

The **Billy Johnson Playground** (off Fifth Ave at 67th St, Central Park, 10022) is a great favorite with locals. Its most popular feature is an amazing marble slide set into a hill. Don't be shy about picking up one of the pieces of cardboard lying around to sit on – it adds speed to the ride down. The park also has bucket swings and a small amphitheater.

Eat and drink

Picnic: under $20; Snacks: $20–35; Real meal: $35–70; Family treat: over $70 (based on a family of four)

PICNIC Carnegie Deli (854 Seventh Ave at 55th St, 10019; 212 757 2245; www.carnegiedeli.com) is a classic Jewish New York deli. Its most famous sandwich is the corned beef and pastrami, "Broadway Danny Rose". Eat at an outside table at Central Park Zoo's café.
SNACKS Dancing Crane Café (East 64th St at Fifth Ave, 10065; 212 439 6500), open year-round, is a convenient spot for lunch inside the zoo. It serves pizzas, hot dogs, soups, and salads, and has both indoor and outdoor seating.

💷 **Shops** The extensive gift shop is outside the zoo; tickets are not required to enter.

🚻 **Restrooms** By the cafeteria

Good family value?
Despite the somewhat steep admission price, the zoo is ideal for children. It is relatively small, but has a great selection of animals.

REAL MEAL Viand Coffee Shop (673 Madison Ave at 61st St, 10021; 212 751 6622) is an old New York diner serving all-day breakfast, hamburgers, and even egg creams – a fizzy milk shake made with soda water, milk, and chocolate syrup – a beverage that has been on its menu for 100 years.
FAMILY TREAT Bistro Chat Noir (22 East 66th St, 10065; 212 794 2428) offers French classics such as onion soup and goat cheese soufflé alongside well-prepared fish, beef, and lamb main courses.

Shopping

The zoo gift shop, **Zootique**, is worth a look for T-shirts and novelties the kids are bound to love, such as animal masks, mini animal sets, and squishy amphibian toys.

Find out more

DIGITAL The zoo's website, www. centralparkzoo.com, is full of exhibit information, animal profiles, and videos to download.
FILM The zoo is featured in all three Madagascar (2005, 2008, and 2012) movies, as well as the animated television series The Penguins of Madagascar (2008).

Children heading to the Dancing Crane Café, Central Park Zoo

Next stop...

AMERICAN MUSEUM OF NATURAL HISTORY Kids can explore the world's wealth of animal species with a visit to the American Museum of Natural History (see pp174–5). Its dioramas are filled with everything from African elephants to huge Alaskan bears.

KIDS' CORNER

Find out more...
1 Polar bears and penguins live on opposite sides of the Earth, yet their environments are very similar. How can this be?
2 The zoo has harbor seals and California sea lions, both of which are found in the oceans of the Northern Hemisphere. Which of the animals is being described in each of the following points:
a They grow to be about 7 ft (1.85 m) long.
b They've got thick brown fur.
c They're found only in the waters of the Pacific along the west coast of North America.
d They have small ear canals behind their eyes.

Answers at the bottom of the page.

Diving enthusiasts
Gentoo penguins dive up to 400 times a day to forage for crustaceans, krill, squid, and small fish.

UNDER COVER
Polar bears have yellowish-white fur – which helps them hunt for seals in camouflage against the snowy ice floes – but their skin is actually black, enabling them to absorb as much of the sun's heat as possible during the day.

Winter wear
Because of their high-altitude habitat, snow leopards are the furriest of all big cats. The thick padding on the bottom of their paws insulates them from the cold, like snow boots.

Answers: 1 They both live in polar environments – penguins in the Antarctic and polar bears in the Arctic. **2 a** Harbor seals; **b** California sea lions; **c** California sea lions; **d** Harbor seals.

Trump Rink in winter, with the Central Park South skyline beyond the trees

② Trump Rink

Skating, rides, and games

During the late fall and in winter, Trump Rink is the city's best place to skate. It is larger, not as crowded, and less expensive than the rink at Rockefeller Center *(see pp112–13)*. Trump Rink's mix of pastoral and urban appeal makes a nice change from the city's other rinks and the views of the skyscrapers on Central Park South are unbeatable.

Starting on Memorial Day, the last weekend in May, the spot transforms into an amusement park called Victorian Gardens, with rides, a giant slide, game booths, and live entertainment including clowns and magicians. The rides are tame compared with those at Coney Island *(see p214)* – there are no roller coasters or Ferris wheels – but kids up to about age 12 will enjoy the speed rush and the challenge of traditional games, such as Whac-A-Mole, which involves pounding as many (fake) moles as possible in the shortest time.

Letting off steam

Just southeast of the rink complex is a lovely pond surrounded by trees. Stroll around the edge of the water and let the kids keep track of how many ducks, swans, and turtles they can spy.

The Lowdown

🌐 **Map reference** 12 G3
Address Southeast corner of Central Park, between 62nd St & 63rd St, 10065; 212 439 6900; www.wollmanskatingrink.com

🚇 **Subway** N, Q & R to Fifth Ave-59th St; F to 57th St. **Bus** M5, M7 & M31

🕐 **Open** Skating: (end Oct–early April) 10am–2:30pm Mon & Tue, 10am–10pm Wed & Thu, 10am–11pm Fri & Sat, 10am–9pm Sun. Amusement park: (end May–mid-Sep) daily, but hours vary; check website for schedule.

💲 **Price** Skating: Mon–Thu $34–44, Fri–Sun $46–56; skate rental $8 per person. Victorian Gardens: Mon–Fri $24–32, Sat & Sun $27–36; plus $1 per ticket (4 tickets per ride/game; pay-as-you-go); unlimited rides wristband: Mon–Fri $23, Sat & Sun $26 per person. Kids below 36 inches (91.44 cm) free with adult.

🏃 **Activities** Private skating lessons (extra $70 for 30 minutes) may be available; inquire online about the availability of an instructor.

👫 **Age range** 2 plus

⏱ **Allow** Skating: 1–2 hours; Victorian Gardens: 2–3 hours

🍴 **Eat and drink** Snacks The on-site concession stand offers burgers, snacks, and beverages; there's seating ($5) so visitors can watch the skaters while they eat. Family Treat Trattoria Dell'Arte (900 Seventh Ave, between 56th St & 57 Fifth St, 10106; 212 245 9800) serves antipasti, risotto, pasta, and top-notch thin-crust pizza.

🚻 **Restrooms** In the main building

③ Friedsam Memorial Carousel

Speed, music, and noisy fun

Among the biggest child magnets in the park, this lovely carousel is loud and seriously fast as carousels go, and is also one of the largest in the US. Crafted in 1908, in a Brooklyn carousel workshop, it did not find its way to the park till 1950, when its predecessor burned down. Nearly 50 ft (15 m) in diameter, the spinning wonder sports 58 horses and two chariots, all hand-carved and hand-painted by artists Sol Stein and Harry Goldstein. Some of the horses go up and down during

The Lowdown

🌐 **Map reference** 12 G2
Address Mid-Park, south of 65th St, 10065

🚇 **Subway** F to 57th St; N & R to Fifth Ave-59th St. **Bus** M10 & M20

🕐 **Open** Apr–Oct: 10am–6pm daily (weather permitting); Nov–Dec: call in advance (212 439 6900 ext 12)

💲 **Price** $3 per ride; cash only

👫 **Age range** All ages

⏱ **Allow** 30 minutes

🍴 **Eat and drink** Real meal Le Pain Quotidien (in the Mineral Springs Pavilion, north of Sheep Meadow at 69th St, 10023) offers salads, sandwiches, and a great cheese plate. Family Treat Trattoria Dell'Arte (see Trump Rink)

🚻 **Restrooms** In Heckscher Playground

Riding hand-carved, colorful horses on the Friedsam Memorial Carousel

the ride, while others are stationary, so choose carefully. Upbeat pop tunes played by an organ lend this horseback-riding adventure an old-time thrill.

Letting off steam

Heckscher Playground (61st St to 63rd St, 10022) is an ideal place for kids to jump around. Most of the park's flooring is rubber, so it is safe for full-speed running. A tall, old-fashioned slide and a large climbing boulder called Umpire Rock are especially popular features.

Children enjoying a day out in the lush expanse of Sheep Meadow

4 Balto Statue and Literary Walk

Tributes to a heroic husky, poets, and writers

Just northwest of Central Park Zoo (see pp128–9), up a small hill, is a statue of Balto, a Siberian husky. In January 1925, he completed the final leg of a heroic journey to transport medicine in blizzard conditions to Nome, Alaska. A deadly diphtheria outbreak had begun several weeks earlier, and a relay of dogsled teams was thought to be the quickest and most reliable means of getting the serum to the remote town. Of course, it was not just Balto who pulled off the amazing feat, but as he was the lead dog of the pack that delivered the medicine to its final destination, he and his Norwegian driver, Gunnar Kaasen, received the most attention. When Frederick Roth's statue of Balto was unveiled in the park in December 1925, both Balto and Kaasen were present for the honor. A path from Balto leads

through a tunnel beneath Park Drive East, and emerges onto the north-south Mall, the park's wide pedestrian promenade. The southern end of the tranquil pathway, known as the Literary Walk, is flanked by four rows of regal American elms and a number of statues commemorating poets, writers, and also, somewhat oddly, Christopher Columbus. The extraordinary trees are one of the largest and last remaining stands of the species in North America.

Follow the pathway north to the Central Park Bandshell for a look at statues of composers Ludwig van Beethoven and Victor Herbert, plus *The Indian Hunter* by John Quincy Adams Ward, and Christopher Fratin's *Eagles and Prey*.

Letting off steam

Sheep Meadow (West side, between 66th St & 69th St, 10023) is a great place for kids to kick around a soccer ball or fly a kite. From the park's inception in 1864 until 1934, the tree-encircled lawn here was a meadow where sheep grazed.

The Lowdown

🌐 **Map reference** 12 H2

Address Balto: east of East Drive at about 67th St; Literary Walk, The Mall: just West of East Drive from 66th St to 72nd St

🚗 **Subway** N & R to Fifth Ave-59th St; F to 57th St. **Bus** M1–M5, crosstown M66 & M72

👫 **Age range** All ages

⏱ **Allow** 1 hour

☕ **Eat and drink** *Snacks* Le Charlot (19 East 69th St, 10021; 212 794 6419) is a classic French bistro serving up delectable mussels. *Real meal* Le Pain Quotidien (see Friedsam Memorial Carousel)

🚻 **Restrooms** Dairy Visitors' Center

Posing with the statue of Balto, Central Park

Bethesda Terrace and around

The centerpiece of Central Park is the grand open-air plaza by Central Park Lake, showcasing Bethesda Fountain. Whether descending the sweeping staircase from the 72nd Street Transverse Road or entering the plaza via the arcaded tunnel from the Bandshell, the view is magnificent. Equidistant between Fifth Avenue and Central Park West, it is easily accessible from either side of the park. The roads are closed to traffic on weekends (72nd Street Transverse Road opens 8am to 10am, East Drive 3pm to 7pm).

Central Park

Belvedere Castle
p138

Bethesda Terrace

Central Park Zoo
p126

Visitors relaxing around Bethesda Fountain

The Lowdown

🚇 **Subway** B & C to 72nd St; 6 to 68th St. **Bus** M10, M66, M72 & M79

🛒 **Supermarket** Pioneer Supermarket, 289 Columbus Ave, 10023; 212 874 9506 **Market** 79th Street Greenmarket, Columbus Ave, between 78th St & 81st St 10024; 9am–5pm Sun

🎭 **Festival** SummerStage: dance, theater, and music shows take place at the Main Stage, near Rumsey Playfield (www.summerstage.org).

➕ **Pharmacy** Duane Reade, 325 Columbus Ave, 10023; 212 580 2017; 8am–9pm Mon–Fri, 9am–7pm Sat, 9am–6pm Sun

🛝 **Nearest playgrounds** East 72nd Street Playground, between 71st St & 72nd St, 10065 (see p136). James Michael Levin Playground, East 77th St, 10075 (see p137). Billy Johnson Playground, Fifth Ave at 67th St, 10065

Part of Central Park Lake, as seen from Bow Bridge

Remote-controlled sailboats on Conservatory Water

Places of interest

SIGHTS

1. Bethesda Terrace
2. The Ramble
3. Conservatory Water
4. Alice in Wonderland and Hans Christian Andersen statues

● **EAT AND DRINK**

1. Gourmet Garage
2. Express Café
3. Candle Cafe
4. Lakeside Restaurant
5. Le Charlot
6. Patsy's Pizzeria
7. Outside Bar at the Loeb Boathouse
8. Sant Ambroeus

● **WHERE TO STAY**

1. The Carlyle

① Bethesda Terrace
Splashing angel and boats to row

An architectural masterpiece, Bethesda Terrace is also a popular meeting place, full of life. In the center of the plaza is a stunning sculpture of a winged angel atop a grand fountain. Its name is the *Angel of the Waters*, although New Yorkers simply call it Bethesda Fountain. Sweeping views of the lake, across Bow Bridge to the woods on the other side lend this area an almost magical quality.

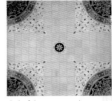
Colorful mosaic on the ceiling of Bethesda Arcade

Key Features

① **Central Park Lake** Created from swampland and excavated by manual labor, this lake was designed to look natural, and is great to explore by boat.

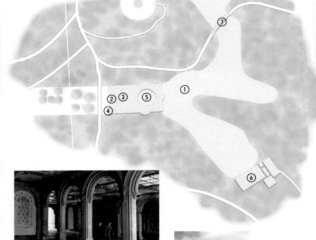

The Lowdown

🌐 **Map reference** 12 G1
Address Mid-Park at 72nd St, 10021; 212 310 6600; *www.centralparknyc.org*

🚗 **Subway** B & C to 72nd St; 6 to 68th St-Hunter College. **Bus** M1, M2, M3, M4 & M72

🕐 **Open** 6am–1am daily

💲 **Price** Free

🎫 **Guided tours** The Central Park Conservancy offers a variety of tours, some free; call 212 772 0210 for more information and details.

👫 **Age range** All ages

👫 **Activities** Rowboats and bicycles can be rented at the Loeb Boathouse.

⏱ **Allow** 2–3 hours

☕ **Café** Express Café in the Loeb Boathouse

🚻 **Restrooms** In the Loeb Boathouse

Good Family Value?
The terrace is ideal for families thanks to its idyllic setting and the wealth of ways they can enjoy its plaza, fountain, lake, and Moorish passageway: by boat, by bike, or on foot.

② **Bethesda Arcade** Decorated in Moorish style with an ornate tiled ceiling, this covered passageway, which runs under the 72nd Street Transverse Road, connects the lower terrace with the Mall.

③ **Lower terrace** The plaza on the lower terrace is paved with Roman-style bricks in a herringbone pattern.

④ **Upper terrace** Flanking the 72nd Street Transverse, this terrace offers fine vistas of the plaza and the fountain below.

⑤ *Angel of the Waters* The fountain's striking angel was unveiled in 1873. The pool is populated with papyrus, water lilies, and lotus in summer.

⑥ **Loeb Boathouse dock** Just behind the Boathouse is a long wooden dock filled with rowboats for rent.

⑦ **Bow Bridge** The majestic cast-iron bridge over Central Park Lake, co-designed by Jacob Wrey Mould and Calvert Vaux, was completed in 1862. It connects Cherry Hill on one side with the woodlands known as The Ramble on the other.

Imagine, *a mosaic dedicated to John Lennon, in Strawberry Fields, Central Park*

Letting off steam

Rowing a small skiff with wooden oars anywhere on the lake is the perfect way to satisfy children's thirst for adventure. Rowing is hard work, but sitting back and enjoying the view back to shore is very rewarding.

Eat and drink

Picnic: under $20; Snacks: $20–35; Real meal: $35–70; Family treat: over $70 (based on a family of four)

PICNIC Gourmet Garage *(155 West 66th St, between Broadway & Amsterdam Ave, 10023; 212 595 5850)* offers prepared salads, cold cuts, baguettes, and a great selection of cheeses. Stock up on food, then set up camp on Cherry Hill, a gentle slope overlooking the lake.
SNACKS Express Café *(Loeb Boathouse, East 72nd St & Park Drive North, 10021; 212 517 2233; www.thecentralparkboathouse. com/express-cafe.php)* serves burgers, hot dogs, soups, salads, and soft-serve ice cream.
REAL MEAL Candle Cafe *(1307 Third Ave between 74th and 75th St, 10021; 212 472 0970; www. candlecafe.com)* offers organic

Gourmet Garage, for all the picnic essentials

vegan cuisine founded on eco-friendly practices. A menu of salads and soups, plus mains such as veggie burgers, risottos and curries.
FAMILY TREAT Lakeside Restaurant *(Loeb Boathouse, East 72nd St & Park Drive North, 10021; 212 517 2233; www.thecentralparkboathouse.com/lakeside.php)* is an upscale place open year-round for brunch on weekends, when it serves jumbo lump crab cakes, waffles, and omelets. The lunch menu has beet-cured salmon, lobster roll, and sautéed chicken breast. Dinner, which is a seasonal affair, can feature Scottish salmon, pork loin, and pan-seared Colorado rack of lamb.

Find out more

FILM With its *Angel of the Waters* fountain, carved sandstone and granite steps and landings, and evocative arcade, Bethesda Terrace is a popular film location. It has appeared in several children's movies, including *Enchanted* (2007), *Elf* (2003), *Stuart Little 2* (2002), and *Home Alone 2* (1992).

Next stop...

STRAWBERRY FIELDS The memory of Beatle John Lennon lives on at Strawberry Fields *(West Side, between 71st St & 74th St, 10024)*, across the street from the Dakota Building where he lived with his wife Yoko Ono. It was here, walking into his home on December 8, 1980, that the singer, songwriter and peace activist was shot and killed by Mark David Chapman. The centerpiece of the memorial is a circular mosaic with the word "Imagine" in the center.

② The Ramble

Urban trails in wild woods

On the northern side of Central Park Lake, across the elegant Bow Bridge, a whole new world awaits – a huge patch of wilderness called The Ramble. It is filled with towering trees, a tangle of hiking trails, rocky cliffs, and quiet glades that look like something out of *Bambi*. However wild these woods are today, they were actually planted when the park was built. It was a carefully thought-out element of Olmsted's vision and one of the first to take shape. It is a great spot to wander in, but should be avoided after dark. Hikers should bring along water and snacks.

A family sailing model boats on Conservatory Water

Taking a stroll through the tree-shaded Ramble, Central Park

The Lowdown

🌐 **Map reference** 15 D6
Address Mid-Park, from 73rd St to 79th St, 10022

🚇 **Subway** B & C to 72nd St; 6 to 77th St. **Bus** M10, M72 & M79

🕐 **Open** 6am–1am daily

🚩 **Guided tours** The Central Park Conservancy hosts family-friendly tours, including Art & Architecture, Movie & TV Sites, and Hidden Secrets; call 212 772 0210.

👫 **Age range** 4 plus

⏱ **Allow** 1 hour

🍴 **Eat and drink** *Snacks* Le Charlot (19 East 69th St, 10021; 212 794 6419) offers French bistro fare and excellent mussels. *Real meal* Patsy's Pizzeria (61 West 74th St, 10023; 212 579 3000) serves antipasti, pasta, salads, and pizzas.

👫 **Restrooms** Ramble Shed, mid-Park at 79th St

Thanks to the nearby lake, the secluded 38-acre (15-ha) area is practically a bird sanctuary, especially near the water. About 250 species live or fish here, including herons and egrets. Many of them are migratory birds stopping on their way north for the summer or south for the winter. Among the best parts of The Ramble are a stream known as the Gill, which flows along it until it reaches the lake, the Point – a piece of land in the shape of a raven's beak protruding into the lake – and Azalea Pond, right in the middle of The Ramble. Keep a lookout for flowering azaleas and countless songbirds here in spring.

Take cover

Try and catch a puppet theater matinée at the **Swedish Cottage** (*see p142*) Marionette Theatre at the northwest edge of The Ramble. Reservations required (*www.cityparks foundation.org/arts/swedish-cottage-marionette-theatre*).

③ Conservatory Water

Model boats and a miniature lake

Among the most memorable scenes in E. B. White's classic children's book *Stuart Little* comes when the adventurous mouse volunteers to sail a toy boat called the *Wasp* in a sailboat race. The setting for this scene was based on the oval pond known as Conservatory Water, sometimes called the Boat Basin, originally modeled on a similar pond in Paris's Jardin du

The Lowdown

🌐 **Map reference** 16 E6
Address East Side from 72nd St to 75th St, 10021

🚇 **Subway** 6 to 77th St. **Bus** M1, M2, M3, M4 & M79

🕐 **Open** 6am–1am daily

💲 **Price** Sailboat rental: $11 per hour

🚩 **Guided tours** Range of tours, some free; call 212 772 0210 for details.

👫 **Age range** 3 plus

🏃 **Activities** Boat race: 10am Sat; call 212 874 0656 for info.

⏱ **Allow** 1 hour

🍴 **Eat and drink** *Snacks* Outside Bar at the Loeb Boathouse (*East 72nd St and Park Drive North*) offers cocktails and a café. *Real meal* Patsy's Pizzeria (*see The Ramble*).

👫 **Restrooms** In the Kerbs Memorial Boathouse

Luxembourg. In warmer months, it becomes a mini raceway for model boats, big and small, most of which are radio-controlled by people on the waterside.

Despite the number of regulars at the pond's edges, it is not a club, and visitors can rent remote-controlled boats on the weekend. They take a bit of getting used to, but are lots of fun. Many aficionados store mini-boats in the boathouse, and take them out for the weekly race.

Letting off steam

One of the best-equipped play spaces in Central Park, the **East 72nd Street Playground** (*Fifth Ave at 72nd St, 10021*) is the perfect place to burn energy. It is spacious, with climbing structures such as a giant spider web and a pyramid along with swings and a sandbox.

④ Alice in Wonderland and Hans Christian Andersen Statues

Climbing and storytelling

On the northern edge of Conservatory Water is a brass sculpture of Lewis Carroll's beloved *Alice in Wonderland* foursome: the White Rabbit, the Cheshire Cat, the Mad Hatter and, of course, Alice. Philanthropist George Delacorte Jr. came up with the idea to honor his wife, who loved both kids and Carroll's work. He hired Spanish-American artist José de Creeft to create it. De Creeft modeled the characters after the illustrations in the first edition of Carroll's book, and completed the sculpture in 1959. Its polished, gleaming surface is the result of all the little hands and bodies that have made their way up the statue over the years. It is proof that Delacorte's wish came true, as the statue, a gift to the children of the city, was built to be climbed.

Just opposite the boathouse, on the other side of the pond, is another kids' classic: a sculpture of master storyteller Hans Christian Andersen, who wrote unforgettable tales such as *The Ugly Duckling*, *The Little Mermaid*, and *The Princess and the Pea*. The work of sculptor Georg Lober, the statue was commissioned

Children and their parents frolic at East 72nd Street Playground

to celebrate the Dane's 150th birthday. Ever since it was unveiled in 1954, it has hosted a children's story hour.

Letting off steam

James Michael Levin Playground *(East 77th St, 10021)* has another *Alice in Wonderland* statue that kids can seek out. Here, Alice is dwarfed by the Mad Hatter and the Duchess.

The Lowdown

- 🌐 **Map reference** 16 E6
  Address Eastern edge of the Park at 74th St & 75th St, 10021
- 🚗 **Subway** 6 to 68th St-Hunter College. **Bus** M1, M2 & M72
- ☀ **Open** 6am–1am daily
- 👫 **Age range** All ages
- 👫 **Activities** 11am & 2pm Mon–Fri Sandbox Stories at playgrounds
- ⏱ **Allow** 1 hour
- 🍴 **Eat and drink** *Family treat* Sant Ambroeus *(1000 Madison Ave, 10021; 212 570 2211)* offers pasta, risotto, tiramisu, and cheesecake, plus an extensive selection of Italian wines.
- 👫 **Restrooms** In the Kerbs Memorial Boathouse

Bronze statue of Hans Christian Andersen and the Ugly Duckling

Belvedere Castle and around

Mid-Central Park offers broad swathes of nature, such as Turtle Pond and the Great Lawn, and even a teeming wildlife habitat: the Jacqueline Kennedy Onassis Reservoir. There are plenty of kid-centric attractions here as well. Belvedere Castle houses the Henry Luce Nature Observatory, where kids can borrow nature kits and take in some of the park's most striking views, while the Swedish Marionette Theater hosts children's productions year-round. Bringing along water and snacks is not essential, but they may come in handy for all the outdoor exploring that's in store here.

Central Park

Belvedere Castle
Bethesda Terrace p132
Central Park Zoo p126

Places of interest

SIGHTS
1. Belvedere Castle
2. Swedish Cottage
3. Shakespeare Garden
4. Great Lawn and Jacqueline Kennedy Onassis Reservoir

● EAT AND DRINK
1. Zingone Brothers
2. Shake Shack
3. Celeste
4. Nice Matin
5. Cafe Blossom
6. Calle Ocho
7. Café Frida
8. Kefi Restaurant
9. Coppola's West
10. La Mirabelle

● SHOPPING
1. Greenstones

● WHERE TO STAY
1. Hotel Wales
2. The Lucerne

Visitors outside Belvedere Castle, Central Park

Jogging track around the Jacqueline Kennedy Onassis Reservoir

M **96th St** B.C

97TH ST

TRANSVERSE ROAD

North Meadow Recreation Center

SOUTH MEADOW TENNIS COURTS

WEST DRIVE

EAST DRIVE

[4] Jacqueline Kennedy Onassis Reservoir

NSVERSE ROAD

PARK

Lawn

Jewish Museum

Cooper-Hewitt Museum

National Academy Museum

Solomon R. Guggenheim Museum

EAST DRIVE

Ancient Playground

belisk

Metropolitan Museum of Art

(MUSEUM MILE)

UPPER EAST SIDE

ANSVERSE ROAD

James Michael Levin Playground

FIFTH AVENUE

MADISON AVENUE

PARK AVENUE

LEXINGTON AVENUE

THIRD AVENUE

FIFTH AVENUE (MUSEUM MILE)

MADISON AVENUE

EAST 95TH ST
EAST 94TH ST
EAST 93RD STREET
EAST 92ND STREET
EAST 91ST ST
EAST 90TH ST
EAST 89TH ST
EAST 88TH ST
EAST 87TH STREET
EAST 86TH STREET
EAST 85TH STREET
EAST 84TH STREET
EAST 83RD STREET
EAST 82ND STREET
EAST 81ST STREET
EAST 80TH STREET
EAST 79TH STREET
EAST 78TH ST
EAST 77TH STREET

86th St M 4.5.6

77th St M 6

The Lowdown

🚇 **Subway** B & C to 81st St-Museum of Natural History or 86th St. **Bus** M10, M11, M72, M79 & M86

ℹ️ **Visitor information** Belvedere Castle, mid-Park at 79th St, 10024; 212 772 0210

⛴️ **Market** 79th Street Greenmarket, Columbus Ave, between 78th St & 81st St; 9am–5pm Sun

🎪 **Festival** Ice Festival at Central Park (Feb; *www.centralpark nyc.org/events*)

➕ **Pharmacy** Duane Reade, 380 Amsterdam Ave, 10024; 212 579 7246; 8am–10pm Mon–Fri, 9am–9pm Sat, 9:30am–7:30pm Sun

🧒 **Nearest playgrounds** Diana Ross Playground, 81st St, Central Park West, 10024 *(see p142)*. Ancient Playground, East 85th Street, 10028 *(see p143)*. James Michael Levin Playground, East 77th St, 10021 *(see p137)*.

0 meters 300

0 yards 300

Children on the Great Lawn in Central Park

① Belvedere Castle
Landmark lookout

The most majestic of Calvert Vaux's architectural creations, Belvedere Castle was completed in 1869. Erected on the second-highest point in the park, it could originally be seen rising from the distant woods when viewed from Bethesda Fountain. The Ramble's trees have now grown so tall that the castle is no longer visible from there, but it retains its fairy-tale charm and provides stunning vistas from its viewing platforms.

Exploring Turtle Pond

Key Features

Wooden pavilions Vaux planned to create another tower on the castle, but a lack of money led him to design viewing pavilions instead. The original pavilions fell into disrepair and were replaced in 1983.

Weather video For decades, the Central Park weather station was based inside the castle. Today, a video on the second floor relays up-to-date weather data gathered by a new, automated contraption nearby.

Papier-mâché birds On the second floor of the Henry Luce Nature Observatory is a collection of papier-mâché bird models showcasing all the bird species found in the park.

Facade The castle was built in Victorian-Gothic style from a stone known as Manhattan schist, which also makes up Vista Rock, on which the castle sits. The light-colored stone trim is granite.

Vista Rock Vaux singled out this 130-ft (10-m) tall rock outcrop, the second-highest natural elevation in Central Park, as the site for the castle, so that it could be seen from various vantage points.

Turtle Pond Surrounded by plants such as iris, bulrush, and turtlehead, this man-made pond is home to ducks, frogs, and large numbers of turtles, who lay their eggs on Turtle Island.

Observation deck Providing gorgeous views of the park, this open-air platform is one of the best places to watch the fall migration of birds of prey, between September and November.

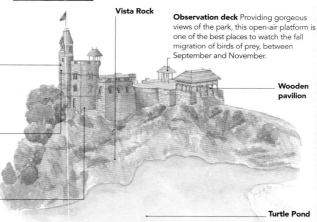

Vista Rock

Wooden pavilion

Turtle Pond

The Lowdown

🌐 **Map reference** 15 D5
Address Mid-Park at about 79th St, 10021; 212 772 0288; www.centralparknyc.org

🚗 **Subway** B & C to 81st St-Museum of Natural History; 6 to 77th St. **Bus** M1, M10 & M79

🕐 **Open** 10am–5pm daily; closed Dec 25, Jan 1 & Thanksgiving Day

💲 **Price** Free

🏴 **Guided tours** The Central Park Conservancy offers a "Belvedere's Kingdom" walking tour of Belvedere Castle and its environs; visit the park's website for details.

👫 **Age range** All ages

🤸 **Activities** On a Wing festival, in May, includes workshops and lectures; no advance registration but limited seating.

⏱ **Allow** 1–2 hours

♿ **Wheelchair access** Limited to the main floor only

☕ **Café** No

Theatrical performance in progress at the Delacorte Theater

Letting off steam

Borrow an explorer's backpack, complete with a birder's field guide, compass, and binoculars, from the **Henry Luce Nature Observatory** and let the kids see how many kinds of bird they can spy.

Eat and drink

Picnic: under $20; Snacks: $20–35; Real meal: $35–70; Family treat: over $70 (based on a family of four)

PICNIC Zingone Brothers *(471 Columbus Ave, between 82nd St & 83rd St, 10024)* has fresh bread, cheeses, and fruit. Stock up on food and then pick a spot near Turtle Pond, at the foot of the castle.

SNACKS Shake Shack *(366 Columbus Ave at 77th St, 10024; 646 747 8770)* offers burgers, including the vegetarian 'Shroom burger (portobello mushroom), fries, and excellent milkshakes.

REAL MEAL Celeste *(502 Amsterdam Ave, near 84th St, 10024; 212 874 4559)* serves fresh, inventive antipasti, salads, pasta, and wood-fired-oven pizzas.

FAMILY TREAT Nice Matin *(201 West 79th St, 10024; 212 873 6423; www.nicematinnyc.com)*, a cozy

French restaurant, whips up small plates and sizeable entrées, such as Atlantic cod with a horseradish crust. But it also offers bistro sandwiches, burgers, and even pizza, making it perfect for a family splurge.

Shopping

Head to **Greenstones** *(454 Columbus Ave, 10024; 212 580 4322; 10am–7pm)* for a well-selected mix of kids' wear (ages newborn to 14 years). They stock mostly European labels, Naturino shoes, and accessories such as hats, umbrellas, and backpacks.

Find out more

FILM The castle played an important role in the ongoing kids' TV show *Sesame Street*. It served as the home of Count von Count.

Next stop...

DELACORTE THEATER A typical New York City experience is taking in a Shakespeare in the Park production at the open-air Delacorte Theater *(Mid-Park at 80th St, 10023; www.centralparknyc.org)*, at the foot of Belvedere Castle. The actors are often big-name stars, and the shows are excellent. Tickets are free – they are distributed at noon (two tickets per person only) on the day of the performance – but there is always a long line. Plan to arrive by 8:30am on a weekday or 6:45am on the weekend. Alternatively, take a chance and sign up on the Virtual Line, a ticket lottery, at *www.publictheater.org*.

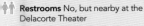

Restrooms No, but nearby at the Delacorte Theater

Good family value?
The fairy-tale look of the castle, along with its amazing vistas and the indoor displays at the Henry Luce Nature Observatory, make it an ideal stop for families.

KIDS' CORNER

Look out for...
1 Look above the doors leading into the castle and see if you can spy the cockatrice, a legendary creature that looks like a dragon. How is it different from other dragons?
2 To make Turtle Pond look like a natural lake, it was designed to curve so that you can't see the whole lakeshore in one go – except from one point. Can you guess where?
3 The castle seems almost to grow out of the rock it sits on. Why is this so?

Answers at the bottom of the page.

FEATHERY FACT
As many as 10,000 birds of prey, representing 15 different species, fly over Central Park each fall as they head south for the winter. Birders tallied thousands of broad-winged hawks, kestrels, ospreys, and bald eagles on a single September day as part of an organized hawk watch.

Spy on wildlife
On the side of Turtle Pond nearest to the Delacorte Theater is an unobtrusive spot where people can watch wildlife without being seen. Spot red-eared sliders, the most common of the pond's five turtle species.

Answers: 1 It has two feet, instead of the normal four. **2** You can see the entire pond from the castle's tower. **3** Because the castle is made of the same kind of rock as Vista Rock: Manhattan schist.

The fanciful facade of the Swedish Cottage, built in 1876

2 Swedish Cottage

Marionette magic

This rustic, dark-wooden house with Swedish and American flags flying on top really is Swedish – or perhaps Swedish-American is more accurate. The structure was built in Sweden from Baltic fir as a schoolhouse prototype. It was shipped over to the US to showcase Sweden's best indigenous architecture in the Centennial Exposition,

held in Philadelphia in 1876 to celebrate the centenary of the United States. When Frederick Law Olmsted caught sight of it in Philadelphia, he envisioned a permanent home for it in Central Park, and paid $1,500 to have it transported there after the show. It has served many functions since arriving here – as a tool shed, a cafeteria, and a center for the study of insects – before taking on its most distinguished role of all. In 1947, it became a children's marionette theater, home to a troupe that travels throughout the city to perform for schoolkids. The super-creative troupe is one of the few marionette companies left in the country that builds its own puppets and writes and produces its own shows. Most are fairy tales, which are a perfect fit for this little house in the woods.

Letting off steam

Head to the **Diana Ross Playground** *(81st St, Central Park West, 10024),* funded by the singer after her 1983

The Lowdown

- 🌐 **Map reference** 15 D5
- 🚗 **Address** West Side at 79th St, Central Park, 10023; 212 988 9093; www.centralparknyc.org
- 🚇 **Subway** B & C to 81st St-Museum of Natural History. **Bus** M10 & M79
- 🕐 **Open** Performances: 1pm Sat & Sun; call 212 988 9093 to check for additional timings.
- 💲 **Price** $34–44
- 👫 **Age range** Performances are aimed at kids aged 3 to 9.
- 🕐 **Allow** 1 hour
- ♿ **Wheelchair access** Yes
- 🍽 **Eat and drink** *Real meal* Cafe Blossom *(507 Columbus Ave between 84th St & 85th St, 10024; 212 875 2600)* serves fresh vegan dishes, such as crostini and roasted corn polenta with a tomato basil sauce. *Family treat* Calle Ocho *(45 West 81st St, 10024; 212 873 5025; www. calleochonyc.com)* offers a variety of ceviches (fresh, raw fish marinated in citrus juices and chilies), tapas, Caribbean entrées, and sides such as yucca fries and garlic spinach.
- 👫 **Restrooms** Swedish Cottage restrooms

concert on the Great Lawn. Kids can climb the giant wooden play structures, slide down a fire pole, scale the climbing net and, in summer, cool off in the sprinklers.

3 Shakespeare Garden

Green poetry

The Bard made ample mention of all kinds of plants, herbs, and flowers in his poetry and plays, and like other such plots around the world, this 4-acre (2-ha) Shakespeare Garden is a tranquil oasis planted with some of them. The greenery in the seasonal beds – bulbs in the spring, annuals in the summer – varies from year to year. However, one section, known as the Red Riding Hood bed, remains the same because it blooms with tulips of that name. Other plants referenced by Shakespeare that can be found here include garlic and onion, rosemary and thyme, potatoes, lavender, rhubarb, and camomile. Bronze plaques throughout mark noteworthy plantings, and inviting benches line the paths. One vegetable, the fragrant fennel mentioned in *Hamlet,* is a magnet for swallowtail butterflies.

The Lowdown

- 🌐 **Map reference** 15 D5
- 🚗 **Address** West Side, between 79th St & 80th St, Central Park
- 🚇 **Subway** B & C to 81st St-Museum of Natural History. **Bus** M10 & M79
- 🕐 **Open** 6am–1am daily
- 💲 **Price** Free
- 👫 **Age range** All ages
- 🕐 **Allow** 30 minutes
- 🍽 **Eat and drink** *Real meal* Café Frida *(368 Columbus Ave, between 77th St & 78th St, 10024; 212 712 2929)* offers fresh Mexican fare, such as enchiladas and fajitas. *Family treat* Kefi Restaurant *(505 Columbus Ave, between 84th St & 85th St, 10024; 212 873 0200; www. kefirestaurant.com)* serves rustic Greek specialties, including meze platters of crispy calamari, mussels, and grilled octopus at fairly reasonable prices.
- 👫 **Restrooms** No, but restrooms can be found at the Delacorte Theater *(see p141),* near Belvedere Castle.

Shady trees and seasonal plantings in the Shakespeare Garden

Letting off steam

Cross the Great Lawn, heading east, and look for the **Ancient Playground** (*East Side at 85th St near Fifth Ave, 10028; 8am till dusk daily*). Actually one of the park's newest play zones, this was inspired by the Egyptian art holdings of the Met (*see pp150–53*). Pyramid-shaped climbing equipment, slides, and tunnels are linked by concrete structures, and in summer, user-activated water jets can cool kids down. The playground also has tire and strap swings.

④ Great Lawn and Jacqueline Kennedy Onassis Reservoir

Obelisks and opera

If the Great Lawn seems curiously symmetrical, it is because this was originally the site of the Lower Reservoir, one of the city's main sources of water. When the Croton Aqueduct was established outside the city in 1842, the Lower Reservoir was no longer needed. In 1930, it was drained, filled in, and finally planted with grass in 1936. Today, the lawn is used in many ways, ranging from picnicking and sunbathing to use as an outdoor venue for summer concerts by the Metropolitan Opera and the New York Philharmonic. On the east side of the lawn is Cleopatra's Needle, the nickname for a 71-ft (22-m) tall Egyptian obelisk, made from a single shaft of red granite believed to have been cut in 1450 BC.

North of the 86th Street Transverse is another reservoir, which has not been emptied. City planners decommissioned the huge artificial lake in 1993, and in 1994 renamed it the Jacqueline Kennedy Onassis Reservoir after the former First Lady. The 2-mile (3-km) long path around the lake, a popular loop for joggers, is lovely and provides some truly unique views of the city. The lake also teems with birds, such as wood ducks, loons, cormorants, egrets, and herons.

Letting off steam

The **North Meadow Recreation Center** (*Mid-Park at 97th St, 10028; 212 348 4867*) allows visitors with photo ID to borrow Frisbees, bats, and assorted balls to play with on the many fields that dot the lawn.

The Lowdown

- 🌐 **Map reference** 15 D5
- **Address** Great Lawn: Mid-Park, between 79th St & 85th St. JKO Reservoir: Mid-Park, between 85th St & 96th St
- 🚗 **Subway** B & C to 81st St-Museum of Natural History. **Bus** M1–M4, M10, M79 & M86
- 🕐 **Open** Great Lawn: mid-Apr to mid-Nov, daily
- 💲 **Price** Free
- 👫 **Age range** All ages
- **Activities** Great Lawn: kite-flying and baseball (permit required)
- ⏱ **Allow** 2 hours
- 🍴 **Eat and drink** *Real meal* Coppola's West (*206 West 79th St, 10024; 212 877 3840*) has a warm, friendly atmosphere to match its Italian comfort food. *Family treat* La Mirabelle (*102 West 86th St at Columbus Ave, 10024; 212 496 0458*) serves French fare such as crêpes and sole *meunière* (in brown butter sauce).
- 🚻 **Restrooms** At the Ancient Playground

KIDS' CORNER

Find out more...

1 The Swedish Cottage was built with children in mind, but not as a theater. What type of building was it supposed to be?
2 One reason the gardeners in the Shakespeare Garden plant fennel is to attract a particular insect that finds it delicious. What creature is it?
3 Which monument was brought from the Egyptian city of Alexandria to the US by steamship in 1880?

....

Answers at the bottom of the page.

Heave ho!

It took a team of 32 horses to transport the Obelisk, which weighs 218 tons (198 tonnes), from the Hudson River to its destination in Central Park.

HIEROGLYPHIC WRITING

The top of the obelisk has three falcons, which are representations of the Egyptian god Horus. The hieroglyphs on each side of the ancient column begin by praising him.

Written in stone

The Obelisk in Central Park is one of a pair that originally stood in Alexandria in Egypt, where they were raised in 12 BC to decorate a temple built by Cleopatra to honor Mark Antony. They were toppled shortly thereafter, and lay buried for centuries, which is how their hieroglyphs remained intact.

....

Cleopatra's Needle.
butterfly **3** The Obelisk, also known as
Answers: 1 A school. **2** Swallowtail

Green expanses and a couple of baseball diamonds, Great Lawn

Upper East Side

One of New York City's most upscale areas, the Upper East Side is home to some of its greatest museums, several located on a compact strip of Fifth Avenue known as Museum Mile. The huge Metropolitan Museum of Art (the "Met") showcases superb Greek and Roman sculpture, while the Guggenheim is housed in a stunning Frank Lloyd Wright building. The Met borders Central Park, which allows for run-abouts in between sights.

Upper
West Side
and Harlem

Central
Park

**Upper
East Side**

Midtown

Downtown

Highlights

Metropolitan Museum of Art
Visit this grand museum and be amazed by its vast collection of art, sculpture, textiles, armor, and more (see pp150–53).

The Frick Collection
Wander around the magnificent mansion that houses this stunning collection, and marvel at the paintings, sculptures, and other works exhibited here (see p154).

Solomon R. Guggenheim Museum
Take a good look at Frank Lloyd Wright's most celebrated architectural creation and then

visit its galleries to view the excellent modern art collected by its founder (see pp158–9).

Jewish Museum
Discover an impressive assortment of paintings, sculptures, photographs, and archaeological artifacts, as well as Jewish-related films, in the Jewish Museum (see p160).

El Museo del Barrio
Savor the art and folklore of Latin America and the Caribbean and explore their influence on modern New York from pre-Columbian times to today, at El Museo del Barrio (see p161).

Left Grand staircase inside the Metropolitan Museum of Art
Above left Paintings, furniture, and decorative items displayed in the Living Hall at The Frick Collection

The Best of
Upper East Side

Art, architecture, lavish residences, and leafy avenues define the Upper East Side, which is the most affluent area of the city. Families will enjoy many of the museums here, from the impressive Metropolitan Museum of Art to the fascinating Museum of the City of New York. Along the western edge of the neighborhood lies lush Central Park, a great place to kick back with a picnic and cool off in the spray from stately fountains.

Art aficionado

This area has the highest concentration of art in the city. Peruse one of the world's greatest collections of European paintings, as well as ancient Egyptian temples and sculptures, at the **Metropolitan Museum of Art** (see pp150–53). For an overview of contemporary art, walk along the circular ramps of the **Solomon R. Guggenheim Museum** (see pp158–9). The **Whitney Museum of American Art** (see p87) features the city's premier collection of work by American artists, including Jackson Pollock and Georgia O'Keefe. Finally, sample the lifestyle of New York's elite among the antique furnishings and Old Masters at **The Frick Collection** (see p154).

Right Temple of Dendur in the Metropolitan Museum of Art
Below Floor mosaic in the Jewish Museum

Above *The fluted columns and graceful arches of the Metropolitan Museum of Art building*

Multicultural mishmash

New York's diverse cultures are showcased in several Upper East Side museums, including **El Museo del Barrio** *(see p161)*, which offers a peek into Latino culture – from the Taino Indians, who were the first settlers in Puerto Rico and the Dominican Republic, to contemporary Mexican and Nuyorican art. The renowned **Jewish Museum** *(see p160)*, housed in a French-Gothic chateau on Fifth Avenue, documents the evolution of Jewish culture over the centuries. The **Metropolitan Museum of Art** features elegant ceramics and calligraphy from Asia, plus vibrant masks and jewelry from

Africa and Oceania. It's also possible to follow the rich timeline of European culture here, by viewing paintings that span the continent, from Spain to Scandinavia.

Seasonal contrasts

Each season reveals a unique aspect of the Upper East Side. In spring, Central Park comes alive with flowers and butterflies. In summer, the museums' outdoor bars and restaurants open – including the rooftop sculpture garden at the **Metropolitan Museum of Art**, where patrons can enjoy a drink under the starry night sky. During warm weather, many museums also feature fun outdoor concerts and later openings on Fridays. In the fall and winter, galleries and museums often unveil new exhibits, while the whole neighborhood becomes a snowy wonderland, with plenty of outdoor spaces for kids to build snowmen and go sledding.

History buff

For a fascinating insight into the history of the city and its residents, visit the **Museum of the City of New York** *(see p160)*, set in a grand Neo-Georgian building. Many of the other Upper East Side museums, from **The Frick Collection** to **El Museo del Barrio**, also feature a rich array of historical artifacts, both from New York and around the globe. Central Park has a variety of historical treasures too, including the **Obelisk** *(see p143)*, which is the oldest man-made structure in the park.

Left *The facade of the Solomon R. Guggenheim Museum, an architectural landmark*

Metropolitan Museum of Art and around

Easy to reach by subway and very walkable, the neighborhood around the Metropolitan Museum of Art is a mix of museums, eateries, and quiet streets lined with upscale residences – it also includes the eastern section of Central Park. It is busiest on weekends, when tourists and locals arrive in droves to visit the museums. The crowds generally thin out during the week, especially in the late morning and mid-afternoon.

Engelhard Court, Metropolitan Museum of Art

The Lowdown

🚇 **Subway** 4, 5 & 6 to 86th St; 6 to 68th St-Hunter College. **Bus** M1, M2, M3, M4, M15, M72, M79, M101 & M102

🍜 **Supermarket** D'Agostino, 1233 Lexington Ave, at 83rd St, 10028; 212 570 6803

➕ **Pharmacies** Duane Reade, 1524 Second Ave, 10075; 646 422 1023; 8am–9pm Mon–Fri, 8am–7pm Sat, 9am–5pm Sun. CVS/pharmacy, 1241 Lexington Ave, 10028; 212 535 3438; 8am–9pm Mon–Fri, 9am–6pm Sat & Sun

🎋 **Nearest playground** Ancient Playground, East Side at 85th St near Fifth Ave, 10028

0 meters 400
0 yards 400

Places of interest

SIGHTS

1. Metropolitan Museum of Art
2. National Academy Museum
3. The Frick Collection
4. Asia Society

EAT AND DRINK

1. Eli's Manhattan
2. Shake Shack
3. Sfoglia
4. Café Boulud
5. Sarabeth's
6. Le Pain Quotidien
7. Fig and Olive
8. Heidelberg
9. Naruto Ramen

See also Asia Society (p155)

SHOPPING

1. Leo Castelli Gallery

WHERE TO STAY

1. Affinia Gardens
2. Courtyard New York Manhattan/Midtown East
3. Gracie Inn

Magnolia tree in
the garden, The
Frick Collection

Gallery of artworks,
The Frick Collection

① Metropolitan Museum of Art
Paintings, sculptures, and more

The treasures of the Met span thousands of years, embracing more than 2 million works of art from the Americas, Europe, Africa, and the Far East, as well as the classical and ancient worlds. The main entrance ushers visitors into the impressive Neo-Classical Great Hall. From here, the Grand Staircase leads to the museum's greatest attraction, the European Paintings galleries. The most popular exhibit with kids is the dramatic stone Temple of Dendur, from ancient Egypt.

An Egyptian statue next to the Temple of Dendur

Key Features

First Floor The museum's first floor features eight galleries: Egyptian Art; The American Wing; Arms and Armor; Medieval Art; European Sculpture and Decorative Arts; Modern Art; Arts of Africa, Oceania, and the Americas; and Greek and Roman Art.

First Floor

③ **Arms and Armor** The lavishly engraved wheellock of Holy Roman Emperor Charles V (1519–56) was the first self-igniting pistol. It can be viewed in this wing.

Entrance

④ **Medieval Art** This brightly colored stained-glass panel, titled *Angels Swinging Censers*, features flying angels set against an intricate background. It dates to around 1170 and was created for the Collegiate Church of Saint-Étienne in Troyes, France.

① **Egyptian Art** An astounding 36,000 exhibits make up this collection. Among them is the Temple of Dendur, a 15th-century BC temple that is lit up at night. It was moved here from Egypt, piece by piece, during the construction of the Aswan Dam in 1965. Also on display are splendid jewelry and tomb figures, including the jolly blue hippo that has become the museum's mascot.

② **The American Wing** Ralph Earl (1751–1801) was a self-taught, itinerant painter known mainly for his portraits. He painted royals and other notables in both England and America. This painting, *Elijah Boardman* (1789), portrays the richly dressed merchant (and later senator) in his dry-goods store in New Milford.

⑤ **European Sculpture and Decorative Arts** A 50,000-object collection is on view here, including striking statues by Rodin, French and Flemish tapestries, and period rooms such as the 18th-century Boiserie from the Hotel de Cabris, France, which features carved and gilded paneling.

Prices given are for a family of four

The Lowdown

 Map reference 16 E5
Address 1000 Fifth Ave, near 82nd St, 10028; 212 535 7710; www.metmuseum.org

🚗 **Subway** 4, 5 & 6 to 86th St.
Bus M1, M2, M3 & M4

🕐 **Open** 10am–9pm Fri & Sat, 10am–5:30pm Sun–Thu

💲 **Price** Suggested donation: $25 per adult; under 12s free

Cutting the line Tickets are available online.

Guided tours Free guided tours, daily; recorded audio tours of the major collections: adults $7, under 12s $5

👫 **Age range** 5 plus

Activities The museum features an array of family activities, including "How Did they do That?" and "Picture This!" family workshops, and storytime in the Children's Reading Room at the Nolen Library (Mon–Fri).

⏱ **Allow** A full day

♿ **Wheelchair access** Yes

☕ **Cafés** The museum cafeteria on the ground floor serves sandwiches, pizza, and salads. The Petrie Court Café in the Carroll and Milton Petrie European Sculpture Court has a range of light meals and desserts, from chicken salad to thick brownie sundaes.

🛍 **Shop** The Met Store is packed with everything from contemporary jewelry to unique puzzles.

🚻 **Restrooms** On multiple floors, including the first floor

Good family value?

A collection that includes some of the most famous paintings in the world, the amazing Egyptian wing, and an array of child-friendly activities and workshops make this a superb family outing.

⑥ **Modern Art** Since its foundation in 1870, the museum has been acquiring contemporary art, but it was not until 1987 that a permanent home for 20th-century art was built – the Lila Acheson Wallace Wing. The collection includes famous works such as *I Saw the Figure 5 in Gold* by Charles Demuth.

⑦ **Arts of Africa, Oceania, and the Americas** The best items in this collection include pre-Columbian gold, bronze sculptures, ceramics, and drums from Peru, such as this richly painted example featuring a serpent and killer whales.

⑧ **Roman Art** The *Badminton Sarcophagus* (AD 260–70) features the wine god Dionysus seated on a panther surrounded by devotees, the horned god Pan, and four youths representing winter, spring, summer, and fall.

① Metropolitan Museum of Art continued ▶

Metropolitan Museum of Art continued

Key Features

▓ **Second Floor** The second floor of the Metropolitan Museum of Art encompasses European Paintings; Modern Art; Drawings, Prints, and Photographs; Musical Instruments; The American Wing; Asian Art; and The Cantor Roof Garden.

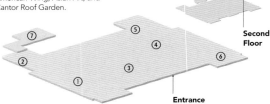

Second Floor

Entrance

The imposing facade of the Metropolitan Museum of Art

① European Paintings Within the European galleries is an amazing array of Impressionist and Post-Impressionist art, including 34 Monets and 18 Cézannes. The favorite theme of French artist Edgar Degas was ballet, as evidenced by his many beautiful paintings of dancers, including *Rehearsal on the Stage* (1874), showing lithe young girls on stage.

② Modern Art The Met's Modern Art collection is not the largest in New York, but it is considered to be one of the finest assemblages of European and American art from the 1900s onward. It includes Picasso's *Portrait of Gertrude Stein* (1906) and *The Blind Man's Meal* (1903), from his Blue Period. One entire section is devoted to the massive abstract works of Mark Rothko and Jackson Pollock, as well as Andy Warhol's *Mao* (1972), a silk-screen portrait of the Chinese leader.

③ Drawings, Prints, and Photographs This section includes photographs, historic advertisements, and illustrated books, and is especially rich in Italian and French art of the 15th to the 19th centuries. Featured below is *Lady Lilith* (1867) by English painter Dante Gabriel Rossetti.

④ Musical Instruments Among the museum's many historical musical instruments is a guitar (1937) that belonged to Andres Segovia (1893–1987), a guitarist from Andalucia, Spain, who is considered to be one of the finest classical guitarists of the 20th century.

⑤ The American Wing This section includes early Impressionist works such as *The Cup of Tea* (c.1880–81) by Mary Cassatt. Depictions of daily life, especially of women, were a signature of this artist.

⑥ Asian Art These galleries showcase Chinese, Japanese, Indian, and Southeast Asian sculpture, paintings, textiles, and ceramics.

⑦ The Cantor Roof Garden The Iris and B. Gerald Cantor Roof Garden (open: May–Oct) showcases sculpture, which changes regularly. The garden also offers a fine opportunity to enjoy a drink with a great view of Central Park and the surrounding skyline.

Prices given are for a family of four

Letting off steam

Climb up pyramids and discover a sundial at the charming **Ancient Playground** (see p143) in Central Park, just north of the Metropolitan Museum of Art. Despite its name, this is one of the park's newer playgrounds, and it was inspired by the Met's Egyptian Art collection. The playground offers fun water activities: observe how water flows from a central obelisk across two bridges, and then cascades like a mini waterfall. Kids will also enjoy the tire and strap swings.

A still from Percy Jackson and the Olympians: The Lightning Thief

Eat and drink

Picnic: under $20; Snacks: $20–35; Real meal: $35–70; Family treat: over $70 (based on a family of four)

PICNIC Eli's Manhattan *(1411 Third Ave at 80th St, 10028; 212 717 8100; www.elizabar.com; 7am–9pm daily)* sells specialty breads, imported cheeses, and fresh salads that can be enjoyed on Central Park's Great Lawn.
SNACKS Shake Shack *(154 East 86th St, 10128; 646 237 5035; www.shakeshack.com; 11am–11pm daily)* is the place for burgers, thick-cut fries, and frozen custards.
REAL MEAL Sfoglia *(1402 Lexington Ave, 10128; 212 831 1402; www.sfogliarestaurant.com; lunch noon–2:30pm Wed–Sun, dinner 5:30–10pm daily)* serves flavorful Italian cuisine, including fresh pasta, Calabrian chili, and creamy tiramisu.
FAMILY TREAT Café Boulud *(20 East 76th St at Madison Ave, 10021; 212 772 2600; www.cafe boulud.com/nyc; 7–10:30am, noon–2:30pm & 5:30–10:30pm*

Mon–Sat (till 11pm Fri & Sat), 8–11am, noon–3pm & 5:45–10:30pm Sun) delights with French fare by celebrity chef Daniel Boulud, from classic foie gras to creative dishes, such as roast duck with spiced Moroccan couscous.

Shopping

The nearby stretch of Madison Avenue features a range of art galleries, including the famous **Leo Castelli Gallery** *(18 East 77th St, 10075; 212 249 4470)*. The area also has upscale clothing boutiques for children and adults, espresso cafés, and flower shops.

Find out more

DIGITAL The museum's website, *www.metmuseum.org*, has a superb section for kids, with interesting trivia and facts about the museum's works along with downloadable activity packs.
FILM *Percy Jackson and the Olympians: The Lightning Thief* (2010) was set in the Met and features the Greek galleries and other parts of the museum.

Next stop...

OBELISK Head to Central Park to view the Obelisk *(see p143)*. The oldest man-made object in the park, it was one of two that were built on the banks of the Nile River in Egypt in 1450 BC. It was transported here in 1881.

Children skating around the impressive Obelisk in Central Park

(see p143)

KIDS' CORNER

Find out more...
1 Find the sculpture by Edgar Degas of *The Little Fourteen-Year-Old Dancer*. Do you know the name of the pose she is holding?
2 The museum does not just have paintings and sculptures, but also an amazing collection of musical instruments, including the world's oldest piano. Can you find out when it was made?
3 Paul Cézanne made a series of famous paintings of apples. Look for them, and see if you can identify all the different colors of the apples.

....

Answers at the bottom of the page.

NATURAL TALENT
Vincent van Gogh was a largely self-taught artist, with little formal training. He had an amazing memory, which helped him create many of his striking paintings from recall.

Post-Impressionist genius
A technique that artist Paul Cézanne used was to observe very closely everything around him, from apples and flowerpots to tablecloths and stools, so that he understood them as their basic shapes: spheres, cubes, cylinders, and cones. The objects in his paintings are based on these simple shapes.

Answers: 1 It is called the "casual fourth position." **2** In 1720. **3** Orange, red, yellow, and even some light green, all in varying shades.

Entrance to the National Academy Museum

② National Academy Museum

Visual journey of the arts in America

Modeled after the Royal Academy in London, the National Academy was formed in 1825 by a group of artists and architects with a mission of promoting the fine arts in

America. For years the Academy had no permanent home, until it took up residence at its current building, a Beaux Arts–style mansion that was once the home of philanthropist Archer Milton Huntington. The Academy's museum has an extensive permanent collection of paintings, prints, drawings, and sculptures from the 19th, 20th, and 21st centuries. Each of the more than 7,000 pieces in the permanent collection was donated to the museum by the artists themselves, and represents a wide range of work, from landscapes by 19th-century masters to contemporary abstracts. The Academy also hosts temporary exhibitions and holds weekly ARTalks to create a forum for discussing contemporary art in America.

Letting off steam

A great way to get a feel for the Upper East Side is by walking south on elegant **Park Avenue**, which is the epitome of the neighborhood and offers lovely views all the way down to the MetLife Building.

The Lowdown

- 🌐 **Map reference** 16 G5
  Address 1083 Fifth Ave (at 89th St), 10128; 212 369 4880; www.nationalacademy.org
- 🚇 **Subway** 4, 5 & 6 to 86th St Station. **Bus** M1, M2, M3 & M4
- 🕐 **Open** 11am–6pm Wed–Sun
- 💲 **Price** Pay what you wish; children under 12 free
- 🎫 **Guided tours** Free guided tours 1:30pm Sat & Sun. Call or email tours@nationalacademy.org.
- 👫 **Age range** 6 plus
- 🎨 **Activities** The museum offers programs and ARTalks; check the website for details.
- ⏱ **Allow** 2 hours
- ♿ **Wheelchair access** Yes
- 🍴 **Eat and drink** *Snacks* Naruto Ramen *(1596 Third Ave, 10128; 212 737 3533)* for slurping up traditional Japanese ramen noodles and soups. *Family treat* Sarabeth's *(1295 Madison Ave, 10128; 212 410 7335; www.sarabeth.com)* offers upscale American cuisine in a warm, friendly atmosphere. The weekend brunches (8am–4pm Sat & Sun) are deservedly popular, while the lunch and dinner menus will satisfy young and old alike .
- 🚻 **Restrooms** On the ground floor

③ The Frick Collection

Period furniture, paintings, and sculptures

As more and more condos and highrises sprout up across the city, it is easy to forget about New York's magnificent mansions of yesteryear. Touring the splendid home of American industrialist Henry Clay Frick (1849–1919) offers a glimpse into old New York.

The mansion sits on Fifth Avenue, fronted by a leafy garden with magnolia trees. Inside, Frick's impressive collection is beautifully displayed in 16 galleries, and includes 18th-century French furniture, Chinese porcelain vases, gilded clocks and pocket watches from the 16th to the 18th centuries, plus paintings by masters such as El Greco, Goya, Degas, Rembrandt, Velàzquez, and Vermeer. The mansion's sky-lit Garden Court has a gurgling fountain and is a great place to relax.

The Lowdown

- 🌐 **Map reference** 13 A1
  Address 1 East 70th St, near Madison Ave, 10021; 212 288 0700; www.frick.org
- 🚇 **Subway** 6 to 68th St-Hunter College. **Bus** M1, M2, M3 & M4
- 🕐 **Open** 10am–6pm Tue–Sat, 11am–5pm Sun
- 💲 **Price** $60; pay what you wish 11am–1pm Sun
- 👥 **Cutting the line** Lines are short on weekday mornings, right after the museum opens.
- 🎫 **Guided tours** Audio guides and group tours; details on website
- 👫 **Age range** strictly 10 plus
- 🎨 **Activities** "Sunday Sketch" sessions are held on scheduled Sun afternoons for children aged 10 and above.
- ⏱ **Allow** 2 hours
- ♿ **Wheelchair access** Yes
- 🍴 **Eat and drink** *Real meal* Le Pain Quotidien *(1131 Madison Ave, 10028; 212 327 4900)* serves hot soups, imported cheeses, and Mediterranean salads. *Family treat* Fig and Olive *(808 Lexington Ave, 10021; 212 207 4555)* offers rosemary-grilled lamb chops, lemon sole *papillote*, and warm marzipan cake served with olive oil *gelato*.
- 🚻 **Restrooms** On the first floor

Paintings and 18th-century furniture, Fragonard Room at The Frick Collection

Letting off steam

Swim, do gymnastics, and even try martial arts at the well-run **Asphalt Green** (www.asphaltgreen.org), a child-friendly fitness center in the middle of the Upper East Side.

④ Asia Society

Colorful traditions and Oriental treasures

Discover the vibrant arts and culture of Asia at this elegant museum, founded by John D. Rockefeller III in 1956. The museum provides a beautiful visual overview of Asian art, from Japan to Iran. Particularly striking is the personal collection of Rockefeller and his wife. Although it only encompasses 300 objects, it is considered one of the most notable Asian art collections in the US, and includes delicate Chinese ceramics from the Song and Ming periods (960–1279 and 1368–1644) and a copper Bodhisattva statue, inlaid with precious stones, from Nepal. Equally fascinating are the museum's other cultural offerings, including Asian films – keep an eye out for screenings of lively Bollywood movies – and dance performances, concerts, and theater.

Letting off steam

Explore the neighborhood of Yorkville, which is the only part of Manhattan that still retains vestiges of New York's German and Austro-Hungarian immigrant history. Around 1900, this was a lively locality that stretched from East 79th Street to 89th Street between Lexington and the East River. Today, the area has several traditional German cafés and delicatessens that serve everything from wiener schnitzel (breaded veal escallops) to gooey pastries.

Red banner marking the entrance of the Asia Society

The Lowdown

- 🌐 **Map reference** 13 B1
  Address 725 Park Ave at 70th St, 10021; 212 288 6400; www.asiasociety.org
- 🚇 **Subway** 6 to 68th St-Hunter College. **Bus** M1, M2, M3, M4, M30, M66, M101, M102 & M103
- 🕐 **Open** 11am–6pm Tue–Sun, until 9pm Fri (except Jul & Aug)
- 💲 **Price** $24–48; 6–9pm Fri free; under 16s free
- 👫 **Age range** 6 plus
- 🎨 **Activities** The society organizes family days that include arts and crafts, storytelling, and educational workshops to teach children and their parents about Asian traditions and holidays.
- 🕐 **Allow** 1 hour
- ♿ **Wheelchair access** Yes
- 🍽 **Eat and drink** Real meal Heidelberg (1648 Second Ave, 10028; 212 628 2332) features German specialties, from dumpling soup to juicy sausages. Family treat The lovely on-site Garden Court Café serves delicious Asian-accented fare, from herb-crusted salmon with lemongrass to roast chicken with jasmine rice.
- 👫 **Restrooms** The third floor gallery

The art of dance

Edgar Degas was a French artist known for his depictions of ballerinas. At the Frick Collection, find his painting *The Rehearsal*. It features three young ballerinas, each with a leg high in the air, and an older male violinist. Look at the contrast between the expressions and the outfits of the ballerinas and the violinist. What do you think Degas wanted to convey?

Chinese porcelain and ceramics on display at the Asia Society

Picnic under $20; **Snacks** $20–35; **Real meal** $35–70; **Family treat** over $70 (based on a family of four)

Solomon R. Guggenheim Museum and around

It is hard to miss the Guggenheim Museum, with its distinctive spiral architecture rising elegantly over Fifth Avenue. The surrounding area is an inviting blend of colorful boutiques, leafy residential streets, restaurants, and cafés. The biggest draw for kids, of course, is Central Park, which lies a short walk from the museum, and abounds with outdoor activities. The fragrant Conservatory Garden is perfect for a stroll among flowers and fountains. It is best to negotiate this area on foot, but for quick hops between sights, taxis are readily available.

Upper East Side

Solomon R.
Guggenheim
Museum

Metropolitan
Museum of Art
p148

Places of interest

SIGHTS
1. Solomon R. Guggenheim Museum
2. Jewish Museum
3. Museum of the City of New York
4. El Museo del Barrio

● **EAT AND DRINK**
1. Sarabeth's
2. Lexington Candy Shop
3. Ithaka
4. Demarchelier

5. Barking Dog Luncheonette
6. Jackson Hole
7. Paola's Restaurant
8. Joy Burger Bar

See also Jewish Museum (p160) & El Museo del Barrio (p161)

● **SHOPPING**
1. H&M
2. Ricky's NYC

● **WHERE TO STAY**
1. The Carlyle
2. Hotel Wales

0 meters 300
0 yards 300

TRANSVERSE

Jacqueline
Kennedy
Onassis
Reservoir

Cooper-H
Mu

National Acad
Mus

Solomon R.
Guggenheim
Museum 1

86TH ST (TRANSVERSE RD)

GREAT
LAWN

Ancient
Playground

Delacorte
Theater

CENTRAL
PARK

Belvedere
Castle

79TH STREET (TRANSVERSE ROAD)

Metropolitan
Museum
of Art

THE
RAMBLE

Loeb
Boathouse

Alice in
Wonderland
Statue

Bethesda
Terrace

Hans Christian
Andersen
Statue

CHERRY HILL

Conservatory
Water

EAST 86

EAST 85TH

EAST 84TH

EAST 83RD

EAST 82ND

EAST

81ST

EAST 80TH

EAST 79TH

EAST 78TH

EAST 77TH

EAST 76TH

EAST 75TH

MILE

MUSEUM

FIFTH AVENUE

MADISON AVENUE

PARK AVENUE

M 77th S
6

Mosaic detail inside the Jewish Museum

Scrutinizing the art at El Museo del Barrio

Display window at the Lexington Candy Shop, Upper East Side

① Solomon R. Guggenheim Museum
Splendid architecture and inspiring art

Housed in what looks like a giant inverted spiral shell, the Guggenheim Museum is as famous for its building, designed by Frank Lloyd Wright in 1959, as for its stunning collection of art by painters such as Kandinsky, Picasso, and Chagall. To explore both, head to the top via an elevator, then walk down the continuous spiraling ramp for temporary exhibitions on one side and dizzying glimpses of the ground floor on the other.

The museum's spiraling walkway

Permanent Collection

GALLERY GUIDE
The Guggenheim showcases its permanent and temporary exhibits across all its spaces. The Rotunda is often the site of celebrated temporary shows in addition to displaying parts of the permanent collection, while smaller galleries also feature works from the permanent collection, which ranges from splendid Impressionist pieces to contemporary paintings.

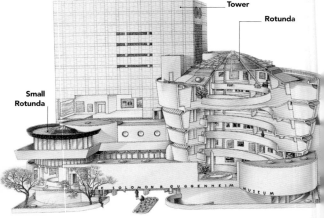

Tower

Rotunda

Small
Rotunda

Before the Mirror (1876) Edouard Manet captures a 19th-century courtesan viewing herself in the mirror.

Yellow Cow (1911) Franz Marc loved animals, as can be seen in this painting of a joyfully cavorting cow.

Paris Through the Window (1913) Marc Chagall depicts Paris as an illuminated cityscape with mysterious figures.

The Lowdown

🌐 **Map reference** 16 E4
Address 1071 Fifth Ave at 89th St, 10128; 212 423 3500; www.guggenheim.org

🚗 **Subway** 4, 5 & 6 to 86th St.
Bus M1, M2, M3 & M4

🕐 **Open** 10am–5:45pm Mon–Wed, Fri & Sun, 10am–7:45pm Sat

💲 **Price** $68–86; under 12s free; pay what you wish 5:45–7:45pm Sat, last ticket issued at 7:15pm

👫 **Cutting the line** The museum is busiest on weekends, so come during the week to avoid the big crowds. Advance tickets are sold online and allow visitors to bypass the ticket line.

🚩 **Guided tours** Free, 2pm daily; free multimedia guide with Guggenheim app; family activity guides and workshops Sun

👫 **Age range** 5 plus

👫 **Activities** The museum hosts art workshops, open studios, and activities for children of all ages; check www.guggenheim.org/familyprograms

⏱ **Allow** 2 hours

♿ **Wheelchair access** Yes

🍴 **Café** The Wright Restaurant offers seasonal fare as well as light bites; Café 3 on annex level 3 has sandwiches and pastries.

Prices given are for a family of four

Letting off steam

Paying homage to the Metropolitan Museum of Art's *(see pp150–53)* Egyptian collection, the **Ancient Playground** *(see p143)* in Central Park has chain bridges, pyramid-like structures, and tire swings for kids.

Counter dining at the Lexington Candy Shop, an old-fashioned diner

Eat and drink

Picnic: under $20; Snacks: $20–35; Real meal: $35–70; Family treat: over $70 (based on a family of four)

PICNIC Sarabeth's *(1295 Madison Ave, near 92nd St, 10128; 212 410 7335; www.sarabethseast.com; 8am–10:30pm Mon–Sat, 8am–10pm Sun)* stocks delicious baked treats, from pecan tarts to blueberry corn muffins and cookies; find a bench in nearby Central Park to enjoy them.

SNACKS Lexington Candy Shop *(1226 Lexington Ave at 83rd St, 10028; 212 288 0057; www. lexingtoncandyshop.net; 7am–7pm Mon–Sat, 8am–6pm Sun)* is a delightful luncheonette that offers classic diner fare, including pancakes, burgers, and traditional New York "egg creams" *(see p31)*.

REAL MEAL Ithaka *(308 East 86th St,10028; 212 628 9100; 4–10:30pm Mon–Fri, 12:30–10:30pm Sat & Sun)* offers an authentic Greek experience in the Upper East Side. A menu of tasty specialties, from

spicy meatballs and grilled octopus to stuffed eggplant and baklava.

FAMILY TREAT Demarchelier *(50 East 86th St, near Madison Ave, 10028; 212 249 6300; www. demarchelierrestaurant.com; 11:30am–10pm Mon, Tue & Sun, 11:30am–10:30pm Wed–Sat)* is a French bistro: try the French onion soup and roast duck, followed by the delicious chocolate mousse.

Shopping

The Upper East Side neighborhood features plenty of excellent stores – within a few blocks of the Guggenheim there is **H&M** *(150 East 86th St, 10028; 212 289 1724; www.hm.com)*, with a range of clothing for adults and kids, and **Ricky's NYC** *(1574 Third Ave, (between 88th & 89th St, 10128; 212 996 7030; www.rickysnyc.com)*, for all your hair, make-up, nail and skincare needs, along with a fun assortment of gadgets and gizmos.

The entrance of H&M, a popular clothing brand for adults and children

Find out more

DIGITAL The website *www. guggenheim.org* details information on art workshops, tours, and classes for kids. Check out *http://media. guggenheim.org/content/pdf/ education/familyguide_architecture. pdf* for family-friendly suggestions.

Next stop...

LITTLE SHOP OF CRAFTS Kids will be delighted by the craft center Little Shop of Crafts *(711 Amsterdam Ave,10025; 212 531 2723; www.little shopny.com)*, where they can paint pottery, string beads into necklaces, and assemble mosaics. They can also make plaster casts of favorite characters, from princesses to unicorns, and create stuffed animals.

(see pp150–53) *(see p143)* *(see p31)*

KIDS' CORNER

Look out for...
1 As you walk around Frank Lloyd Wright's famous spiral building, what sea creature are you reminded of?
2 Look at Marc Chagall's famous painting *Paris Through the Window*. What famous building do you see depicted in the painting? Also, can you spot the heart?
3 Observe the exterior and interior of the Guggenheim Museum building. What shapes can you see?

Answers at the bottom of the page.

IN A STROKE
Look closely at Picasso's famous painting *Woman with Yellow Hair*. He used continuous, fluid lines in many parts of the painting, most notably on the woman's face, from forehead to chin.

A deserving home

Frank Lloyd Wright initially resisted building the Guggenheim in New York. He wrote, "I can think of several more desirable places in the world to build this great museum, but we will have to try New York." To Wright, the city was overbuilt, but in the end it became the ideal showcase for the museum.

Answers: **1** The spiral design is similar to a nautilus shell. **2** The Eiffel Tower; the two-faced man has the shape of a heart imprinted on his hand. **3** The shapes include triangles, ovals, arcs, circles, and squares.

 Shop The museum's superb gift shop sells books and lots of fun items for kids.

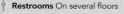 **Restrooms** On several floors

Good family value?

From its unique spiral building to its iconic contemporary paintings, this museum dazzles children and adults alike.

Children's art project in full swing at the Jewish Museum

② Jewish Museum

Jewish art from around the world

New York City, with its rich Jewish heritage, is a fitting home for the renowned Jewish Museum. The museum came into being in 1904, and moved to its current location, a lovely French-Gothic chateau on Fifth Avenue, in 1947, putting it in the middle of Manhattan's famed "museum mile." In addition to its

The Lowdown

🌐 **Map reference** 16 E3
Address 1109 Fifth Ave at 92nd St, 10128; 212 423 3200; www.thejewishmuseum.org

🚇 **Subway** 6 to 96th St. **Bus** M1–M4

🕐 **Open** 11am–5:45pm Sat–Tue, till 8pm Thu & 4pm Fri; closed Wed

⑤ **Price** $30; under 18s free; pay what you wish 5–8pm Thu

Guided tours Tours (Mon, Tue, Thu, Fri), free with admission; check website for details.

👫 **Age range** 5 plus

Activities For art workshops, theatrical performances and storytelling for kids, check website; Archaeology Zone: 11am–5:45pm, closed on Sat.

⏱ **Allow** 2 hours

♿ **Wheelchair access** Yes

Eat and drink *Picnic* The on-site café, Russ & Daughters, serves up kosher salads, bagels, and knishes. *Real meal* Barking Dog Luncheonette (1678 Third Ave at 94th St, 10128; 212 831 1800) has sandwiches, salads, and pasta.

Restrooms Off the fourth-floor lobby

collection of more than 28,000 pieces, from paintings, sculptures, and decorative arts to photographs and archaeological artifacts, the museum houses classrooms, an auditorium, and an inviting café.

The central exhibit, Culture and Continuity: The Jewish Journey, explores the myriad ways in which Jewish culture has evolved over the centuries. The museum also co-hosts the well-known Jewish Film Festival in January, showcasing a range of movies on the Jewish experience.

In Archaeology Zone, kids can dress up in period costumes and try their hand at being an archaeologist by exploring methods used to conserve artifacts after a dig.

Letting off steam

Enjoy the outdoors at the **Jacqueline Kennedy Onassis Reservoir** *(see p143)*. Let the kids have a run around, take a stroll on the path that rings the reservoir or go bird-watching, keeping an eye out for herons and loons.

③ Museum of the City of New York

All about NYC

The small but appealing Museum of the City of New York, housed in a 1930 Neo-Georgian building, features an eclectic mix of exhibits, including the New York Toy Stories, with dollhouses and sports equipment from the early 19th century. There are a number of exhibitions, ranging from the city's history to fashion, photography,

The Lowdown

🌐 **Map reference** 16 E2
Address 1220 Fifth Ave at 103rd St, 10029; www.mcny.org

🚇 **Subway** 6 to 103rd St.
Bus M1–M4 & M106

🕐 **Open** 10am–6pm daily; extended hours in summer

⑤ **Price** $28; under 19s free

Cutting the line Though the museum is generally busiest on weekends, the lines never get very long, so one rarely has to wait to enter.

👫 **Age range** 5 plus

Activities A 22-minute audio-visual presentation on the second floor runs every 30 minutes, offering an overview of the city's history, from the area's Iroquois Indians to the 9/11 attacks.

⏱ **Allow** 2 hours

♿ **Wheelchair access** Yes

Eat and drink *Real meal* Jackson Hole (1270 Madison Ave, near 91st St, 10128; 212 427 2820) is a cowboy-themed restaurant offering juicy burgers. *Family treat* Paola's Restaurant (1295 Madison Ave, 10128; 212 794 1890) serves classic Italian and Roman fare, with fresh-rolled pasta daily.

Restrooms Off the lobby

and fine art, while the Trade exhibit focuses on New York's role as a port from the 17th century. Northside galleries are closed for extensive renovations.

Letting off steam

Stroll the leafy shoreline of nearby **Harlem Meer** *(East Side from 106th St to 110th St, 10029)* in Central Park and spot birds such as the black-crowned night heron.

Grand facade of the Museum of the City of New York

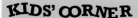

④ El Museo del Barrio

Latin American art and culture

Reflecting the heritage of its neighborhood, Spanish Harlem, El Museo del Barrio opened here in 1969. It covers more than 800 years of Latino, Caribbean, and Latin American art and culture. Walk through a colorful visual timeline, beginning with pre-Columbian objects of the Taino people, who first settled in Puerto Rico and the Dominican Republic. Ancient artifacts include carved amulets of small figurines, said to bring luck or protection to their owners.

Also on display are modern art and photography, with many pieces revealing the powerful connection between Latino artists and their adopted New York home. Look out for Roger Cabán's 1970 photographs of New York street scenes, featuring sidewalk vendors and barber shops. The Nexus New York exhibit showcases the pioneering Caribbean and Latin

American artists who helped shape the avant-garde movement in the 1920s and 1930s, and includes vibrant works by Mexican muralists such as Diego Rivera and paintings by Frida Kahlo.

Letting off steam

A man-made lake surrounded by trees, **Harlem Meer** (see p160) is the perfect setting for outdoor play. In summer, kids can go swimming in the **Lasker Pool** (11am–3pm & 4–7pm daily).

The Lowdown

- 🌐 **Map reference** 16 E1
  Address 1230 Fifth Ave at 104th St, 10029; 212 831 7272; www.elmuseo.org
- 🚇 **Subway** 6 to 103rd St. **Bus** M1
- 🕐 **Open** 11am–6pm Tue–Sat; closed Sun
- 💲 **Price** Suggested donation $9; under 12s free; free every third Sat of the month
- 👫 **Cutting the line** It is best to visit during the week (Tue–Fri) to avoid crowds.
- 👫 **Age range** 5 plus
- 👫 **Activities** Every third Sat of the month is called "Super Sabado!" with many activities geared to children, including free concerts, gallery tours, art workshops, film screenings, and recitals; timings vary.
- ⏱️ **Allow** 2 hours
- ♿ **Wheelchair access** Yes
- 🍴 **Eat and drink** Snacks El Café (on site) offers a taste of Latino cuisine and street food, from warm empanadas to fresh, tangy ceviche (seafood marinated in citrus). Real meal Joy Burger Bar (1567 Lexington Ave, 10029; 212 289 6222) serves burgers topped with special sauces, from pesto to garlic mayonnaise.
- 👫 **Restrooms** Near the café

Above A family walking past El Museo del Barrio on Fifth Avenue
Below Super Sabado! Children's program at El Museo del Barrio

KIDS' CORNER

Look out for...
1 During Hanukkah, the Jewish festival of light, a special lamp is lit. The Jewish Museum has a version featuring eight candleholders. Can you find it?
2 In the Museum of the City of New York you can find out everything about the city's history, including the first people to settle here. Do you know who they were?
3 Look for Mexican artist Diego Rivera's paintings at El Museo del Barrio. What kind of work was he most famous for creating?

Answers at the bottom of the page.

JEWISH HERITAGE
The Jewish Museum has artworks and other objects from around the world, spanning 4,000 years. Each tells a story about what it means to be Jewish.

On the menu
At El Museo del Barrio's café, you can sample lots of delicious Latino cuisine, including empanadas (a type of pastry stuffed with different ingredients, from chicken to ground beef). The menu also features sopa de plátano verde (green plantain soup) from the Dominican Republic, almondegas (meatballs) from Brazil, drizzled with guava sauce, and aguacate relleno con ensalada de atún (avocado filled with tuna salad) from Bolivia.

Answers: 1 "Miss Liberty", by Mae Rockland Tupa is in the Ceremonial Art section. **2** The Iroquois Indians, who are said to have arrived around 800 BC. **3** Large murals, which often depict simple figures in bold colors.

Upper West
Side and Harlem

A friendly neighborhood, the Upper West Side is full of gracious, old-fashioned, residential blocks, fascinating museums for young visitors, cultural centers offering family entertainment, and a fabulous park that overlooks the Hudson. In addition, the area is home to St. John the Divine, one of the world's largest cathedrals, and a renowned university campus. Farther north lies the vibrant African-American district of Harlem.

Upper
West Side
and Harlem

Central
Park

Upper
East Side

Midtown

Downtown

Highlights

Museum of Arts and Design
Admire over 2,000 innovative exhibits and watch artists at work at this unique museum, which runs great workshops (see pp168–9).

American Museum of Natural History
Encounter dinosaurs, see lifelike animal dioramas, and journey into outer space at this incredible museum (see pp174–5).

Riverside Park
Go wild at playgrounds themed on elephants, hippos, and dinosaurs, and take a leisurely stroll along the scenic Hudson River (see p176).

Children's Museum of Manhattan
Enter a world of fun at this wonderful kid-centric museum, which offers imaginative activities and art classes (see p176).

Cathedral Church of St. John the Divine
Marvel at this massive cathedral, with its inspiring mix of Romanesque and Gothic architectural styles (see pp176–7).

The Cloisters
View a wide range of medieval treasures at this world-famous museum (see pp186–7).

Left Life-size model of a blue whale suspended from the ceiling in the Milstein Hall of Ocean Life at the American Museum of Natural History
Above left Role play at the Children's Museum of Manhattan

The Best of
Upper West Side and Harlem

Beginning at Columbus Circle, the family-friendly Upper West Side is busy with attractions, including two kid-centered museums and the terrific Riverside Park. Beyond 96th Street is Morningside Heights, home to Columbia University and the Cathedral Church of St. John the Divine. The energetic Harlem district bustles around 125th Street, and at the very top of Manhattan Island, The Cloisters beckon with two lovely parks.

Cultural delights

One of the world's largest performing arts centers, **Lincoln Center** (see pp170–71) is home to opera, ballet, symphony and chamber music, theater, and film shows. The Nutcracker, performed by the **New York City Ballet** (see pp170–71) each December, is a beloved family tradition. **Jazz at Lincoln Center** hosts concerts for young people, while rock fans will find their favorites playing at the Beacon Theatre. **Symphony Space** (see p38), a smaller cultural center, features a variety of programs for children such as storytelling and book clubs. The **Vital Theater Company** (see p41) offers musicals and theater camps for children every weekend, almost all the year round.

Left Jurassic giants, American Museum of Natural History
Below A ballet performance in progress at the Lincoln Center

Above US Navy ships arriving in New York City for Fleet Week, as seen from Riverside Park

The great outdoors

Stretching 4 miles (6 km) from 72nd Street to 158th Street, along the Hudson River, **Riverside Park** *(see p176)* is spectacular. Designed by Frederick Law Olmsted in 1875, it offers delightful surprises: rocky precipices, green lawns, boulevards for strolling, paths beside the river, and delightful playgrounds. The park includes a colorful marina filled with sailboats and a restaurant with views of 79th Street. Grant's Tomb at West 122nd Street in the park is truly grand. The largest tomb in North America, it is a memorial to Civil War hero General Ulysses S. Grant, the 18th president of the United States. Olmsted's other famous creation, **Central Park** *(see pp122–31)*, runs along the eastern edge of the neighborhood from 59th Street to 110th Street.

Kids' day out

Younger kids will have a great time at the **Children's Museum of Manhattan** *(see p176)*, while the **American Museum of Natural History** *(see pp174–5)* satisfies lovers of gigantic dinosaurs, live butterflies, and jewels and gems. Older children are wowed by its Hayden Planetarium space shows, lectures, and astronomy programs. Anyone old enough to ride a bicycle will enjoy cycling in **Riverside Park**, with its river views. The college sports played at **Columbia University** *(see p177)* may interest teens: football beckons in the fall, basketball in winter, and baseball in spring.

Right Children dressed in firefighters' uniforms prepare for action, Children's Museum of Manhattan

History and food

The **American Museum of Natural History** is an important landmark of the city. It extends north to 81st Street and west to Columbus Avenue, a street filled with tempting shops and eateries. Nearby, Broadway between 70th Street and 89th Street is known for its giant food emporiums, while 96th Street is lined with lively cafés and interesting bookstores.

Peaceful Sunday mornings are the best time to discover Harlem's lures: church services with great gospel choirs, a walk to see the many fine buildings and historic sights – such as the **Abyssinian Baptist Church** *(see p182)* and the **Hamilton Heights Historic District and Sugar Hill** *(see p183)* – and a delicious soul food brunch of fried chicken and all the fixings, often with a gospel music accompaniment.

Museum of Arts and Design and around

The eclectic Museum of Arts and Design (MAD) is located in bustling Columbus Circle. To the west are the twin glass towers of the Time Warner Center, which houses upscale shops, restaurants, and the popular Jazz at Lincoln Center. The roundabout at Columbus Circle is always busy, as several major avenues intersect here, but the surrounding sidewalks make it safe and easy to get around. The area north of Columbus Circle is busiest on weekends, when Broadway's giant food stores attract shoppers from all over the city. There's also the city's largest flea market in this area, the GreenFlea Market on Columbus Avenue, which throngs with visitors.

Upper West Side & Harlem

The Cloisters
p184

125th Street, Harlem
p178

American Museum of Natural History
p172

Museum of Arts and Design

Places of interest

0 meters 200

0 yards 200

SIGHTS
1. Museum of Arts and Design
2. Time Warner Center
3. Museum of Biblical Art
4. Lincoln Center

● EAT AND DRINK
1. Whole Foods Market
2. Maison Kaiser
3. Bouchon Bakery & Café
4. Robert
5. 'wichcraft
6. The Coliseum Bar & Restaurant

See also Time Warner Center (p170)
& Lincoln Center (p171)

● SHOPPING
1. The Store
2. Time Warner Center

● WHERE TO STAY
1. Empire Hotel
2. Hotel Beacon
3. Mandarin Oriental Hotel

Shops in the Time Warner Center

Asaf and Yo'ah sculpture by Boaz Vaadia, Time Warner Center

The Lowdown

🚇 **Subway** 1, A, B, C & D to 59th St-Columbus Circle; 1 to 66th St-Lincoln Center. **Bus** M5, M7, M10, M11, M20 & M104

ℹ️ **Visitor information** NYC & Company at 810 Seventh Ave, 10019; 212 484 1200; *www.nycgo.com*

🛒 **Supermarkets** Whole Foods Market, Time Warner Center, 10 Columbus Circle, 10019; 212 823 9600.
Markets 57th Street Greenmarket, Ninth Ave between 56th St & 57th St; 8am–5pmWed & Sat. Tucker Square, West 66th St & Columbus Ave; 8am–5pm Thu. GreenFlea Market, 100 West 77th St at Columbus Ave, 10024; 10am–5:30pm Sun

🎪 **Festivals** Lincoln Center Festival (Jul to Aug). Lincoln Center Out of Doors (Jul to Aug)

➕ **Pharmacy** Rite Aid, 210-20 Amsterdam Ave, 10023; 212 787 2903; 7am–10pm Mon–Fri, 9am–6pm Sat, 10am–5pm Sun.

🛝 **Nearest playgrounds** Little Engine Playground, (see p171). Classic Playground, West 74th St & Riverside Drive, 10023. Neufeld Playground, West 76th St & Riverside Drive, 10023. Hecksher Playground, Central Park (see pp131)

Map labels: 77TH STREET, 76TH STREET, 5TH, AMSTERDAM AVENUE, AVENUE, WEST 77TH STREET, New-York Historical Society, VERDI SQUARE, 72nd St 1.2.3, SHERMAN SQUARE, The Dorilton, WEST 75TH STREET, WEST 74TH STREET, WEST 73RD STREET, The Dakota, WEST 72ND STREET, 72nd St B.C, WEST 71ST STREET, BROADWAY, COLUMBUS, WEST 70TH STREET, WEST 69TH STREET, WEST 68TH STREET, WEST 67TH STREET, 66th St-Lincoln Center, LINCOLN SQUARE, Hotel des Artistes, Museum of American Folk Art, Tavern on the Green, H. Coch, WEST 63RD STREET, eum of cal Art, WEST 62ND ST, 61ST STREET, Central Park Lake, STRAWBERRY FIELDS, CHERRY HILL, TRANSVERSE ROAD, Mineral Springs, WEST DRIVE

CENTRAL PARK

SHEEP MEADOW, WEST 65TH STREET, HECKSCHER BALLFIELDS, WEST DRIVE, Friedsam Memorial Carousel, 59th St-Columbus Circle 1.A.B.C.D, COLUMBUS CIRCLE, Heckscher Playground, CENTRAL PARK SOUTH (OLMSTED WAY), Museum of Arts and Design

Fountain in front of the Metropolitan Opera House

① Museum of Arts and Design

Creative crafts and artists at work

Crafts become art at the one-of-a-kind Museum of Arts and Design (MAD), which focuses on the creativity of contemporary artists. Nothing is too avant-garde for display - look out for the realistic knight on horseback created from strips of paper, a quilt in the shape of a kimono, and a quirky, hand-blown wine bottle. The museum's collection of 2,500 objects, in an array of media including clay, glass, metal, and wood, is frequently rotated to form the changing displays. One exception is the remarkable selection of jewelry, much of which is on permanent display.

Key Features

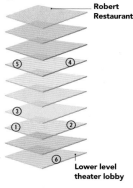

Robert Restaurant

⑤ ④

③ ① ②

⑥

Lower level theater lobby

① **Stained-glass window** With patterns as colorful as a kaleidoscope, *Seeing is Believing* (2008), by Judith Schaechter, brightens the third-floor stairwell.

② **Tiffany Jewelry Gallery** Part of the museum's permanent collection, Mary Lee Hu's jewelry is a study of opposites. She uses the delicate technique of weaving to create some of the boldest designs in contemporary metalwork.

③ **From the prosaic to the sublime** Everyday objects, including a collection of goblets made by artists from around the world, are displayed in the window of the third-floor stairwell to take advantage of the natural light.

④ **Artists' studios** The sixth floor of the museum houses three open artists' studios, where visitors can see the creative process in action.

⑤ **Children's workshops** "Studio Sundays" invite children aged 6 and above, and their adult companions, to make their own creations alongside professional artist-educators.

⑥ **Abstract relief** Bands of stoneware in varying shades make up the unusual ceramic wall relief *Untitled 1991*, by Ruth Duckworth, in the lower level theater lobby. The Modernist sculptor was known for her original use of ceramics in sculptural forms.

The Lowdown

🌐 **Map reference** 12 F4
Address 2 Columbus Circle, 10019; 212 299 7777; www.madmuseum.org

🚗 **Subway** A, B, C, D & 1 to 59th St-Columbus Circle.
Bus M5, M7, M10, M20 & M104

🕐 **Open** 10am–6pm Tue–Sun, until 9pm Thu & Fri; closed Mon & major holidays

💲 **Price** $32; under 18s free; pay what you wish 6–9pm Thu

🚩 **Guided tours** Free cell-phone audio tours; free guided gallery tours by docents: 11:30am & 3pm daily, plus 1:30pm Fri–Sun

🚻 **Age range** 6 plus

🧑‍🤝‍🧑 **Activities** Studio Sundays: intergenerational workshops, 6 plus, 2–4pm, one Sun a month. MAD Saturday: interpretative activities for kids and their adult companions, plus films, $30 per family. Check for upcoming dates on the museum's website.

⏱ **Allow** 2 hours

♿ **Wheelchair access** Yes

☕ **Café** Robert, on the 9th floor, is open for lunch, cocktails, coffee, and dinner.

🚻 **Restrooms** On the lower level

Good family value?
The offbeat artworks on display and the chance to watch artists at work make this museum an enjoyable place to visit.

Prices given are for a family of four

Fountains at Columbus Circle with Time Warner Center in the background

Letting off steam

Just outside the museum, **Columbus Circle**, with its wooden benches and fountains encircling the marble statue of Christopher Columbus, is a great place to relax with kids. The sound of splashing water masks the noise of this busy traffic circle and is a delight on a hot summer day.

Eat and drink

Picnic: under $20; Snacks: $20–35; Real meal: $35–70; Family treat: over $70 (based on a family of four)

PICNIC Head to **Whole Foods Market** *(Time Warner Center, 10 Columbus Circle, 10019; 212 823 9600)* to stock up for a picnic. The benches next to the splashing fountains in Columbus Circle are ideal for alfresco eating.
SNACKS Maison Kayser *(1800 Broadway at 58th Str, 10019; 212 245 4100; www.maison-kayser-usa. com)* is a Parisian boulangerie with delicious fresh-baked breads (from baguettes to sourdough to sweet breads), croissants, pastries, and baked goods. Good coffee, too.
REAL MEAL Bouchon Bakery & Café *(3rd floor, Time Warner Center, 10 Columbus Circle, 10019; 212 823*

9366; www.thomaskeller.com/ time-warner-new-york/bouchon-bakery-café) is the best bet nearby for a sit-down lunch of sandwiches, soups, salads, and yummy desserts.
FAMILY TREAT Robert *(on site, 9th floor)* serves an upscale American menu; lunch options include burgers, sandwiches, pasta, salad, or a three-course prix fixe meal. The view is a big draw.

Shopping

The Store at MAD sells creative books, fun gifts, and irresistible craft and design objects. The **Time Warner Center** *(see p170)* has a host of upscale shops as well as the as the Moleskin store. La Maison du Chocolat, on the ground floor, sells a variety of chocolates, pastries, ganache, and hot cocoa.

Find out more

DIGITAL Check the website for the Jamba Juice store, *www.jambajuice. com*, for interactive games for kids.
FILM Columbus Circle featured in the zany Hollywood comedies *Home Alone 2* (1992) and *Ghostbusters* (1984).

Next stop…

MERCHANT'S GATE The Merchant's Gate entrance to Central Park is at the northeast corner of 59th Street and Central Park West, just across from the Museum of Arts and Design. Located near Columbus Circle, it has plenty of room for running around and climbing. There are several playgrounds nearby as well. The park's vintage carousel, with its 57 handsome horses, is located mid-Park at 64th Street.

Gift and craft items for sale at The Store, Museum of Arts and Design

② Time Warner Center

City views, shopping, and all that jazz

This glittering 80-story twin-tower skyscraper hugging Columbus Circle offers free entertainment for people of all ages. Take the escalator up to the second and third floors and savor the superb views of the city and Central Park.

Afterwards, stop by the Samsung Experience on the third floor and try the latest and coolest in computers, don glasses to watch TV in 3D, and check email for free. There is often a sports event or TV show playing on the giant screen at the back.

Get to know all about the great jazz musicians at Jazz at Lincoln Center, a performing arts complex located on the 60th Street side of the Time Warner Center. There are photography and art exhibits in its fifth-floor arcade and photographs of legends adorn the Jazz Hall of Fame. The complex also includes an upscale shopping center with dozens of stores, a collection of gourmet restaurants and more informal eateries, and the Mandarin Oriental Hotel (see p249).

Letting off steam

Walk to the nearby **Lincoln Center** (see right), which has a pleasant, grass-covered hillside called the Illumination Lawn. It provides plenty of open space to roam around, picnic, or relax with a book. It is also open to visitors at night.

The Lowdown

- 🌐 **Map reference** 12 F3
- **Address** 10 Columbus Circle, 59th St, 10019; 212 823 6300; www.jalc.org.www.theshopsat columbuscircle.com
- 🚇 **Subway** A, B, C, D & 1 to 59th St-Columbus Circle. **Bus** M5, M7, M10, M20 & M104
- 🕐 **Open** 10am–9pm Mon–Sat, 11am–7pm Sun
- 🕐 **Allow** 1 hour
- ♿ **Wheelchair access** Yes
- 🍴 **Eat and drink** *Real meal* Bouchon Bakery & Café (see p169) serves soups and sandwiches. *Family treat* Landmarc (on site) has a full range of American dishes.
- 🚻 **Restrooms** On the second floor

Columbus Circle with the Time Warner Center in the background

③ Museum of Biblical Art

Divine art

This small museum shows the profound influence the Bible has had on art. It began as a gallery of the American Bible Society and, in 2005, grew into a fully fledged museum. This is the first institution in the US to be dedicated to art inspired by the Bible, both historical and contemporary. Exhibits change every three months, and show the enormous legacy of the Bible in Judeo-Christian culture. Themed exhibitions range from medieval paintings and folk art to movie posters and modern art; from stained glass by Louis Comfort Tiffany to prints by the German artist Albert Dürer.

The museum also preserves and displays items from the society's Rare Bible Collection, one of the foremost in the world. It includes scriptures in more than 2,000 languages spanning six centuries, including many rare manuscripts. Bibles of all kinds and in many languages are available in the shop on the ground floor.

The Lowdown

- 🌐 **Map reference** 12 E3
- **Address** 1865 Broadway at 61st St, 10023; 212 408 1500; www.mobia.org
- 🚇 **Subway** A, B, C, D & 1 to 59th St-Columbus Circle. **Bus** M5, M7, M10, M20 & M104
- 🕐 **Open** 10am–6pm Tue–Sun; closed Mon & public holidays
- 💲 **Price** $48
- 🕐 **Allow** 1 hour
- ♿ **Wheelchair access** Yes
- 🍴 **Eat and drink** *See* Time Warner Center
- 🚻 **Restrooms** On the first floor

Letting off steam

The **Merchant's Gate** (see p169) entrance to Central Park has space to run and climb, and there are playgrounds nearby. The vintage carousel, with its 57 handsome horses, is located mid-Park at 64th Street.

④ Lincoln Center

Ballet, music, and a dancing fountain

In the early 1960s, a slum area was transformed into one of the largest performing arts centers in the world – it draws five million people annually. A number of eminent companies, including the Metropolitan Opera, the New York City Ballet, the New York Philharmonic Orchestra, Lincoln Center Theater, and the Library for the Performing Arts, now have their head-quarters here. Each season, the Philharmonic conducts a few Young People's

Fine art on display at the Lincoln Center

Concerts for children aged between 6 and 12, preceded by Kidzone Live!, an interactive music fair where kids can try out instruments, play musical games, and check out the theme of the day's concert. The New York City Ballet also schedules regular programs for children, plus popular ballets such as *Sleeping Beauty* and *The Nutcracker*. The modernization program completed in 2011 has given the whole campus a bright look, including a stunning new glass facade on the Alice Tully Hall. Kids will be intrigued by the central fountain with its columns of water that jet higher and higher.

Lincoln Center has many artworks of note. The most famous are the giant Marc Chagall murals in the foyer of the Metropolitan Opera House building. Created in 1966, they are known as *The Triumph of Music* and *The Sources of Music*. Alexander Calder's steel sculpture *Le Guichet* (*The Box Office*, 1963), near the entrance to the Library for the Performing Arts, stands like a playful giant spider, inviting kids to walk under, through, and around it. The North Plaza in front of the theater is a nice place to relax, with its peaceful reflecting pool and a dramatic Henry Moore sculpture, *Reclining Figure* (1965).

Letting off steam

Besides the center's outdoor spaces, the **Little Engine Playground** (*Riverside Blvd, between West 67th St & West 68th St, 10023*) will delight children. Central Park and Riverside Park are also within walking distance. If it rains, head to the Apple Store (*see pp108–109*).

Entrance to the Alice Tully Hall, Lincoln Center

The Lowdown

🌐 **Map reference** 12 E2

📍 **Address** 10 Lincoln Center Plaza, 10023; 212 875 5000; lc.lincolncenter.org

🚗 **Subway** 1 to 66th St. **Bus** M104, M5, M7, M11 & M20

💲 **Price** Half-price tickets from David Rubenstein Atrium, east side of Broadway on 62nd St; weekly free performances

🕐 **Open** 8am–10pm Mon–Fri, 9am–10pm Sat & Sun

♿ **Wheelchair access** Yes

🍽 **Eat and drink** *Snacks* 'wichcraft (*David Rubenstein Atrium, 61 West 62nd St at Broadway, 10023; 212 780 0577*) serves light meals and snacks. *Real meal* The Coliseum Bar & Restaurant (*312 West 58th St, 10019*), an Irish pub, serves standard pub fare with mostly American options such as burgers and steaks.

🚻 **Restrooms** In the Avery Fisher Hall and David Rubenstein Atrium

KIDS' CORNER

Look out for...

1 How many floors are there in the Time Warner Center?

2 Which famous ballet about toys is performed every year at Lincoln Center?

3 Look at the fountain jets in Lincoln Center – how high do you think they can go?

4 Can you find the big spider-like sculpture in Lincoln Center? What is it made of?

Answers at the bottom of the page.

The Nutcracker ballet
The ballet is an adaptation of The Nutcracker and the Mouse King by E. T. A. Hoffmann. The story is about a young girl, Marie Stahlbaum, whose toy, a Nutcracker prince, comes to life and defeats an evil, seven-headed mouse.

MUSICAL NOTE

A typical symphony orchestra has 90 members playing 13 kinds of instruments. The instruments fall into four categories: string, woodwind, brass, and percussion.

Whale hunt

The Museum of Biblical Art shows works inspired by the Bible. The familiar stories pictured include Noah and the Ark and Jonah and the Whale.

Steps leading to the showstopping entrance of the Lincoln Center

Picnic under $20; **Snacks** $20–35; **Real meal** $35–70; **Family treat** over $70 (based on a family of four)

American Museum of Natural History and around

Set along Central Park West, the vast American Museum of Natural History is full of fascinating exhibits. Close by, the New York Historical Society has a center for children, while younger kids can attend art workshops at the Children's Museum of Manhattan. Farther north is the lively college district around Columbia University and the Cathedral Church of St. John the Divine. Broadway is the main artery in this busy area, filled with shops and cafés. The leafy side streets, lined with typical New York townhouses known as "brownstones," are ideal for a stroll.

Upper West Side & Harlem

The Cloisters
p184

125th Street, Harlem
p178

American Museum of Natural History

Museum of Arts and Design
p166

The Lowdown

Subway 1 to 79th St; B & C to 81st St-Museum of Natural History; 1 to 110th St-Cathedral Parkway; 1 to 116th St-Columbia University. **Bus** M4, M5, M7, M10, M11, M20, M79, M86 & M104

Supermarkets Zabar's, 2245 Broadway at 80th St, 10024; 212 787 2000. Gristedes, 251 West 86th St & Broadway, 10024; 212 721 0745. Gristedes, 504 Columbus Ave & 84th St, 10024; 212 721 3077. Food Emporium, 2415 Broadway at 90th St, 10024; 212 873 4031 **Markets** 79th St, Greenmarket, Columbus Ave (between 78th & 81st St); 9am–5pm Sun. West 97th St, between Amsterdam & Columbus; 8am–2pm Fri. Columbia Greenmarket, Broadway, between 114th St & 116th St; 8am–5pm Thu & Sun.

GreenFlea Market, 100 West 77th St at Columbus Ave; 10am–5:30pm Sun

Pharmacies CVS/pharmacy, 540 Amsterdam Ave, 10024; 212 712 2821; 24 hours daily. Duane Reade, 2522 Broadway at West 94th St, 10025; 212 663 1580; 24 hours daily. Duane Reade, 2864 Broadway, 10025; 212 316 5113; 24 hours daily

Nearest playgrounds River Run Playground, West 83rd St & Riverside Drive, 10024. Hippo Playground, West 91st St & Riverside Drive, 10024. Dinosaur Playground, West 97th St & Riverside Drive, 10025. Skate Park, West 109th St & Riverside Drive, 10025. Diana Ross Playground, 81st St & Central Park West, 10024

Massive Barosaurus skeleton, American Museum of Natural History

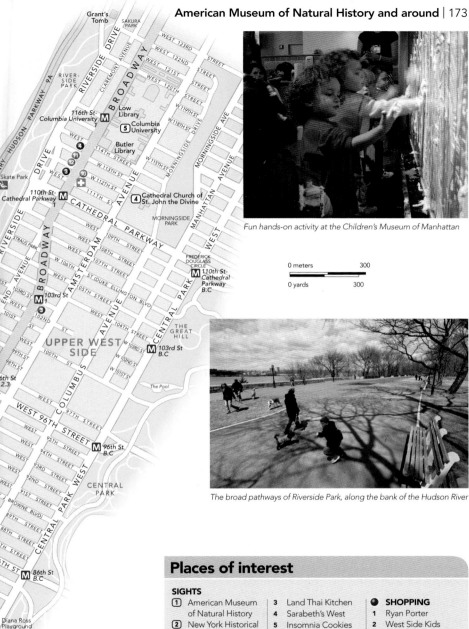

Fun hands-on activity at the Children's Museum of Manhattan

0 meters	300
0 yards	300

The broad pathways of Riverside Park, along the bank of the Hudson River

Places of interest

SIGHTS

① American Museum of Natural History

② New York Historical Society

③ Children's Museum of Manhattan

④ Cathedral Church of St. John the Divine

⑤ Columbia University

● EAT AND DRINK

1 Andy's Deli

2 Caesar's Palace Pizza

3 Land Thai Kitchen

4 Sarabeth's West

5 Insomnia Cookies

6 Alice's Teacup

7 Famous Original Ray's Pizza

8 Artie's Delicatessen

9 Café Lalo Patisserie

10 Tom's Restaurant

11 Nussbaum and Wu

12 Le Monde

● SHOPPING

1 Ryan Porter

2 West Side Kids

3 Bank Street Books

4 Book Culture

● WHERE TO STAY

1 Hotel Belleclaire

2 Hotel Newton

3 Marrakech

4 The Excelsior Hotel

5 The Milburn Hotel

① American Museum of Natural History
Dinosaur bones, huge meteorites, and fluttering butterflies

Ever since its founding in 1869, the American Museum of Natural History has led the way to important finds on expeditions from the North Pole to the Gobi Desert, filling its many galleries with treasures of all kinds. An exceptional dinosaur fossil collection, a suspended life-size model of a blue whale, fabulous meteorites and gems, and amazingly realistic animal dioramas make this perhaps the most kid-centric museum in the city. Learn about Earth's place in the solar system in the Hayden Planetarium and look out for the Discovery Room, a hands-on center for children.

Key Features

Fourth Floor Vertebrate Origins, Saurischian Dinosaurs, and Primitive Mammals

Third Floor Hall of Pacific Peoples, Primates, and Reptiles and Amphibians

Second Floor Birds of the World, African Peoples, and Mexico and Central America

First Floor Human Origins, Hall of Ocean Life, and Hall of Planet Earth

Rose Center for Earth and Space The Big Bang, a multisensory re-creation of the first moments of the universe, and the Hayden Planetarium

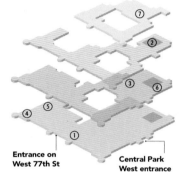

Entrance on West 77th St

Central Park West entrance

③ **Akeley Hall of African Mammals** Take in the life-size dioramas of animals from the rain forests and savannahs of Africa in realistic settings.

④ **Arthur Ross Hall of Meteorites** Marvel at the Ahnighito, the largest meteorite on display in the world.

⑤ **Morgan Memorial Hall of Gems** Gaze at the world's largest blue star sapphire, the 563-carat Star of India, and the 632-carat Patricia Emerald.

⑥ **Butterfly Conservatory** Open from October to May, this conservatory has more than 500 live butterflies. It features three out of the five butterfly families.

⑦ **Fossil Halls** The world's largest collection of dinosaur fossils, including the giant Tyrannosaurus rex, is a big attraction for families. More than 100 specimens are on display, and most are fossils rather than replicas.

① **Discovery Room** Hunt for animals in a replica of an African baobab tree or explore the minerals, arthropods, and skulls in cabinets full of fascinating specimens.

② **Hayden Planetarium** Take a voyage from Earth to the edge of the universe at the Space Theater, which has a custom-made Zeiss Mark IX Star Projector and a Digital Dome Projection System.

The Lowdown

🌐 **Map reference** 15 C6
Address Central Park West at 79th St, 10024; 212 769 5100; www.amnh.org

🚗 **Subway** B (weekdays only) & C to 81st St-Museum of Natural History; 1 to 79th St. **Bus** M7, M10, M11, M79, M86 & M104

🕐 **Open** 10am–5:45pm daily

💲 **Price** $57–69

👪 **Cutting the line** Purchase online tickets (extra $4 service charge).

Combination tickets are ideal for extra-cost IMAX movies, special exhibits, or space shows. Check museum website for details.

🚩 **Guided tours** Spotlight tours: check information desk for timings and topics; Museum Highlights Tours: hourly from 10:15am to 3:15pm daily

👫 **Age range** 2 plus

Activities Kids can watch IMAX movies and space shows, and participate in science activities.

⏱ **Allow** 3–4 hours

♿ **Wheelchair access** Yes

☕ **Cafés** The Museum Food Court at the lower level, Café on 1 and the first floor, and Café on 4 on the fourth floor

🚻 **Restrooms** On every floor

Good family value?
Although expensive, there are plenty of engaging activities for children here, making the museum a memorable experience.

Prices given are for a family of four

Strolling in Theodore Roosevelt Park, which surrounds the museum

Letting off steam

The museum's Theodore Roosevelt Park is ideal for quiet walks, while the summer fountains on Arthur Ross Terrace, next to the Hayden Planetarium, offer cooling jets to run through in summer. The closest play area, the **Diana Ross Playground** (see p142), is in Central Park at 81st Street.

Eat and drink

Picnic: under $20; Snacks: $20–35; Real meal: $35–70; Family treat: over $70 (based on a family of four)

PICNIC Andy's Deli (418 Columbus Ave at 80th St, 10024; 212 799 3355) makes tasty sandwiches and salads to be packed and enjoyed on a picnic at Riverside Park (see p176).
SNACKS Caesar's Palace Pizza (493 Amsterdam Ave, between 82nd St & 84th St, 10024; 212 724 7886; www.caesarspalacepizza.com) offers appetizers, shrimp, and slices of tasty pizza.
REAL MEAL Land Thai Kitchen (450 Amsterdam Ave, 10024; 212 501 8121; www.landthaikitchen. com) serves tasty, traditional Thai cuisine that is stylishly presented and reasonably priced. The two-course *prix fixe* lunch is a particularly great deal.
FAMILY TREAT Sarabeth's West (423 Amsterdam Ave, between 80th St & 81st St; 10024; 212 496 6280; www.sarabethsrestaurants.com/ upper-west-side) is a family-friendly restaurant that whips up delicious omelets, sandwiches, and innovative American dishes. A *prix fixe* menu is available.

Shopping

The museum's shop is full of scientific wonders, toys, books, and clothing. **Ryan Porter**, just south of

the museum, does cute beaded jewelry, and **West Side Kids** (498 Amsterdam Ave at 84th St, 10024) is a terrific toy store. **Bank Street Books** (4780 Broadway at West 107th St, 10025) and **Book Culture** (2915 Broadway at 114th St, 10025) are the city's best bookstores for kids.

A library of new worlds to discover at Book Culture

Find out more

DIGITAL Check out www. enchantedlearning.com for information about dinosaurs, and watch dinosaur videos on www.discovery.com/videos.
FILM This was the setting for the movie *Night at the Museum* (2006), where a security guard discovers that everything comes to life at night, including an enormous T. rex skeleton.

Next stop...

MORNINGSIDE HEIGHTS
Head north along Broadway to Morningside Heights for a taste of the neighborhood's historic highlights. Here, explore the campus of **Columbia University** (see p177), monuments such as Grant's Tomb, and the huge **Cathedral Church of St. John the Divine** (see pp176–7).

Sarabeth's West is a top spot for a family-friendly feed

② New York Historical Society

Gleaming lights and watercolor birds

The city's oldest museum, founded in 1804, has had a $60 million renovation, and now includes the DiMenna Children's History Museum on the lower level, which focuses on the lives of New York's kids in times past. It tells of famous figures, such as the statesman Alexander Hamilton, who came to New York as a teenage orphan to attend college, but also recounts the stories of the many poor children who hawked newspapers to earn a living. Interactive features include touch screens and a place to videotape your own history. The adult museum has a complete set of watercolors from James Audubon's *Birds of America* series and one of the world's largest caches of Tiffany lamps. Elsewhere, art and exhibits trace the city from its founding to the present day.

Letting off steam

Riverside Park *(between West 75th St & West 77th St, 10024)* is a great place for kids to fly kites.

The Lowdown

- 🌐 **Map reference** 15 C6
- **Address** 170 Central Park West, between 76th St & 77th St, 10024; 212 873 3400; www.nyhistory.org
- 🚇 **Subway** B & C to 72nd St; B & C to 81st St-Museum of Natural History. **Bus** M10 & M79
- ☺ **Open** 10am–6pm Tue–Sat, until 8pm Fri, 11am–5pm Sun
- 💲 **Price** $44–70; $6 ages 5–13; under 5s free
- 🚩 **Guided tours** Free tours 2pm & 3:30pm Tue–Sun
- 👫 **Age range** 8–13 for DiMenna Children's History Museum
- ⏱ **Allow** 2–3 hours
- ♿ **Wheelchair access** Yes
- 🍽 **Eat and drink** *Snacks* Insomnia Cookies *(405 Amsterdam Ave, 10024; 877 632 6654)* has a selection of cookies, brownies, and ice creams. *Real meal* Alice's Teacup *(102 West 73rd St at Columbus Ave, 10023; 212 799 3006)* serves breakfast, lunch, and dinner.
- 🚻 **Restrooms** On each floor

Prices given are for a family of four

Children playing at the popular Hippo Playground, Riverside Park

③ Children's Museum of Manhattan

Dora and Diego, a huge digestive system, and a hungry dragon

Learning through play is the goal at this museum, filled with fun activities for young children. Playworks, the third floor zone devoted to kids aged 4 and under, includes Alphie – a talking dragon who gobbles letters – a mock MTA bus, a fire truck, sand play, and a soft space for babies. At EatSleepPlay: Building Health Every Day, visitors learn about making healthy choices in food, exercise, and sleep. Kids can crawl through a giant digestive system and meet a team of super-powered vegetable heroes. Interactive exhibits use themes from popular children's books, movies, or TV shows such as *Dora the Explorer* to engage kids. In warm weather, City Splash teaches kids the unique qualities of water as they launch boats down a winding stream and test objects for their flotation properties in a tub of water.

Alphie the talking dragon, Children's Museum of Manhattan

The Lowdown

- 🌐 **Map reference** 15 B5
- **Address** 212 West 83rd St, 10024; 212 721 1223; www.cmom.org
- 🚇 **Subway** 1 to 86th St; 1 to 79th St. **Bus** M11 & M104
- ☺ **Open** 10am–5pm Tue–Sun, till 7pm Sat
- 💲 **Price** $44; free 5–8pm first Fri of the month; under 1s free
- 👬 **Cutting the line** Visit on Wed & Thu afternoons for fewer crowds.
- 👫 **Age range** All ages
- ⏱ **Allow** 2 hours
- ♿ **Wheelchair access** Yes
- 🍽 **Eat and drink** *Snacks* Famous Original Ray's Pizza *(462 Columbus Ave, 10024; 212 873 1720)* has classic New York pizza. *Real meal* Artie's Delicatessen *(2290 Broadway at 83rd St, 10024; 212 579 5959)* features a wide menu.
- 🚻 **Restrooms** On the lower level and third floor

Letting off steam

The **Hippo Playground** *(West 91st St & Riverside Drive, 10024)* offers swings and a sand pit, while the **Dinosaur Playground** *(West 97th St & Riverside Drive, 10024)* has fiberglass dinosaurs that kids will love.

④ Cathedral Church of St. John the Divine

An awe-inspiring cathedral

Begun in 1892, the construction of the Cathedral Church of St. John the Divine has been delayed by world wars, finances, and fire. Although still incomplete, the church is an amazing sight. Measuring 601 ft (183 m) in length, the building is longer than two soccer grounds put together. Gaze up at its 124-ft (38-m) high Gothic-style nave and admire the 40-ft (12-m) wide Great Rose Window which, with more than 10,000 pieces of glass, is the largest stained-glass window in the US. The adjoining garden is home to the impressive Ring of Freedom, which features plaques honoring famous writers, and 24 small animal sculptures that were made by school children in 1985. At the center of the Ring is the *Peace Fountain* sculpture, a towering statue of the Archangel Michael and Satan in battle atop a fountain. Children can learn about the plants mentioned in the Bible at the nearby Biblical Garden.

Letting off steam
Nearby **Morningside Park** *(Morningside Parkway, from 110th St to 123rd St)* has scenic cliffs, playgrounds and basketball courts.

The Lowdown
- 🌐 **Map reference** 17 B6
- **Address** 1047 Amsterdam Ave at 112th St, 10025; 212 316 7540; www.stjohndivine.org
- 🚇 **Subway** 1 to 110th St-Cathedral Parkway. **Bus** M11, M60 & M104
- 🕐 **Open** 7.30am–6pm daily
- 🎫 **Guided tours** 11am & 2pm Mon, 11am & 1pm Tue–Sat, 1pm select Sun; $8 per person
- 🧑‍🤝‍🧑 **Age range** All ages
- ⏱ **Allow** 1 hour, without the garden
- ♿ **Wheelchair access** Yes
- 🍽 **Eat and drink** *Snacks* Café Lalo Patisserie *(201 West 83rd St, 10024; 212 496 6031)* is famous for its desserts, especially the cheesecake. *Real meal* Tom's Restaurant *(2880 Broadway at 112th St, 10025; 212 864 6137)* has a typical New York diner menu, with a wide range on offer.
- 🚻 **Restrooms** In the north transept

⑤ Columbia University
Going to school

A walk through the campus of one of America's oldest and most prestigious universities will stretch little legs and interest everyone. Columbia was founded as King's College by the royal charter of King George II of England in 1754. The name was changed in 1784 after America's independence. Its fine

Peace Fountain, *created by Greg Wyatt, Cathedral Church of St. John the Divine*

Classical-style buildings were designed by famous architect Charles McKim, with the Low Library as the centerpiece. Look out for the three stained-glass windows and the Peace Altar at St. Paul's Chapel. The campus is a lively place, with students mingling in the expansive plaza near the Low Library, and participating in activities and sporting events. For a glimpse into college life, check the schedule before visiting.

Letting off steam
Head to **Skate Park** *(West 109th St & Riverside Drive, 10025)* to watch skateboarders in action. In spring, relax beneath Japanese cherry trees at **Sakura Park** *(Claremont Ave, above West 122nd St, 10027).*

The Lowdown
- 🌐 **Map reference** 17 B5
- **Address** 2960 Broadway, 10027; 212 854 1754; www.columbia.edu
- 🚇 **Subway** 1 to 116th St-Columbia University. **Bus** M4, M11, M60 & M104
- 🎫 **Guided tours** Free self-guided tour between 9am and 5pm Mon–Fri.
- 🧑‍🤝‍🧑 **Age range** All ages, but of special interest to teens
- ⏱ **Allow** 1 hour; longer for the tour
- ♿ **Wheelchair access** Yes
- 🍽 **Eat and drink** *Snacks* Nussbaum and Wu *(2897 Broadway at 113th St, 10025; 212 280 5344; www.nussbaumwu.com)* offers light meals, great pizza, and yummy desserts. *Real meal* Le Monde *(2885 Broadway, between 112th St & 113th St, 10025; 212 531 3939)* serves French cuisine plus pasta or burgers for kids.
- 🚻 **Restrooms** Downstairs from the Visitor Center

125th Street, Harlem and around

Extending from 116th Street to 155th Street, Harlem offers a tantalizing slice of African-American culture, past and present. It was the setting for the famous Harlem Renaissance, which saw black artists, writers, and musicians generating creative fireworks here in the 1920s and '30s. The area was slow to recover from the Depression but is now flourishing again, in what some call a "new renaissance." Best visited in the daytime, Harlem is suited for older children who can appreciate its fine architecture and lively streets.

Upper West Side & Harlem

The Cloisters p184

125th Street, Harlem

American Museum of Natural History p172

Museum of Arts and Design p166

Painting on a metal shutter by street artist Franco Gaskin

Places of interest

SIGHTS
1. 125th Street, Harlem
2. Schomburg Center for Research into Black Culture
3. Abyssinian Baptist Church
4. St. Nicholas Historic District
5. Hamilton Heights Historic District & Sugar Hill

EAT AND DRINK
1. 285 St. Nicholas Gourmet Deli
2. Presidential Pizza

3. Amy Ruth's
4. Sylvia's
5. Hadman Gourmet Deli
6. Dinosaur Bar-B-Que
7. Manna's Restaurant
8. Londel's
9. Best Yet Market
10. Queen Sheba
11. Sunshine Kitchen
12. Charles' Country Pan Fried Chicken

SHOPPING
1. Grandma's Place
2. Malcolm Shabazz Market

0 meters 300

0 yards 300

The Lowdown

🚗 **Subway** 2 & 3 to 125th St (Lenox Ave); 2 & 3 to 135th St (Lenox Ave); A, B, C & D to 145th St. **Bus** M2, M7 & M10

🍔 **Supermarkets** Best Yet Market, 2187 Frederick Douglass Blvd, between 118th St & 119th St, 10026; 212 377 2300. Fine Fare, 136 Lenox Ave, between 116th St & 117th St, 10026; 212 828 9951. 285 St. Nicholas Gourmet Deli, 285 St Nicholas Ave, 10027; 212 865 0830.
Market HERBan Farmers' Market, Marcus Garvey Park North at 124th St & Fifth Ave, 10027; Jul–Nov: 10am–5pm Sat; *www.herbanfarmers market.org*

🎪 **Festival** Annual Harlem Week/ Harlem Jazz & Music Festival: food tastings, art, music, and street entertainment (Aug)

➕ **Pharmacies** CVS/pharmacy, 105 West 125th St, near Lenox Ave, 10027; 212 864 5431; 8am–9pm Mon–Fri, 9am–6pm Sat & Sun. Duane Reade, 300 West 135th St at Frederick Douglass Blvd, 10030; 212 491 6015; 9am–9pm Mon–Fri, 9am–8pm Sat, 9am–6pm Sun

🛝 **Nearest playgrounds** Marcus Garvey Park, Madison Ave, 120th St to 124th St,10035. Three playgrounds in St. Nicholas Park, at 129th St, 133rd St & 140th St

City College of New York, Hamilton Heights Historic District

① 125th Street, Harlem

History, jazz, and soul-food restaurants

America's largest and most famous African-American district lures visitors with a heady cocktail of historic buildings, music – from jazz to hip hop to gospel – and sinfully delicious food. The heart of Harlem, 125th Street, between Fifth and Eighth Avenues, is the perfect place to feel the energy and appreciate the vibrant cultural scene. Sunday is the best day to hear a gospel choir, either at a church service or tasty brunch.

Apollo Theater

Key Sights

Apollo Theater Harlem's most famous showcase still hosts the Amateur Night that helped launch musical greats such as Michael Jackson and James Brown.

Street art Work by street artist Franco Gaskin adorns the steel security gates on 125th Street, between Frederick Douglass Boulevard and Adam Clayton Powell Jr. Boulevard.

Studio Museum This small museum exhibits the work of contemporary black artists in changing shows.

Mount Morris Historic District The prosperous Harlem of the past lingers on in the once-grand churches and residences here.

55 West 125th Street This modern 15-story office tower is where former president Bill Clinton has his offices.

Lenox Lounge One of the few surviving 1930s clubs that made Harlem famous. Jazz greats such as Billie Holiday and Miles Davis have performed here.

Marcus Garvey Park Named for the formidable black activist (1887–1940), the park *(see p181)* offers panoramic views from its lookout, The Acropolis.

The Lowdown

Map reference 17 D4
Address Apollo Theater: 253 West 125th St, between Adam Clayton Powell Blvd & Frederick Douglass Blvd, 10027; www.apollotheater.org. Studio Museum: 144 West 125th St, between Lenox Ave & Adam Clayton Powell Blvd, 10027; www.studio museum.org. Lenox Lounge: 288 Lenox Ave, between 124th St & 125th St, 10012; www.lenoxlounge.com

Subway 2 & 3 to 125th St (Lenox Ave); A, B, C & D to

125th St (Frederick Douglass Blvd). **Bus** M2, M7 & M10

Open Apollo Theater: Amateur Night 7:30pm Wed. Studio Museum: noon–9pm Thu–Fri, 10am–6pm Sat, noon–6pm Sun. Lenox Lounge: live music and dinner nightly; not recommended for kids under 10

Price Apollo Theater: Amateur Night $20–32 per person, depending on show; Studio Museum: $14; under 12s free; free on Sun

Age range 8 plus

Allow Studio Museum 30 minutes–1 hour

Shop The Studio Museum shop has interesting arty wares.

Restrooms On the first floor of the Studio Museum

Good family value?
Packed with historic buildings, gospel churches, jazz and blues clubs, and great food options, there is plenty here to entertain all.

Amy Ruth's, one of the city's popular neighborhood restaurants

Letting off steam

Marcus Garvey Park *(Madison Ave, East 120th St to 124th St, 10035)* has three playgrounds for kids, but be aware that homeless people sometimes come here. The park dates back to the early colonial period, when Dutch settlers called it Slangberg, or Snake Hill, because of its large reptile population. Luckily, the snakes are all gone today. Previously known as Mount Morris Park, it was renamed in honor of Marcus Garvey who founded the Universal Negro Improvement Association. Further west, St. Nicholas Park has a playground between 128th Street and 129th Street.

Eat and drink

Picnic: under $20; Snacks: $20–35; Real meal: $35–70; Family treat: over $70 (based on a family of four)

PICNIC 285 St. Nicholas Gourmet Deli *(285 Saint Nicholas Ave, 10027; 212 865 0830)* offers fresh sandwiches, burgers, and other classic deli fare.
SNACKS Presidential Pizza *(357 West 125th St,10027; 212 222 7744; 11am–10pm Mon–Sat, till 9pm Sun)* offers tasty pizza by the slice, as well as wraps, pastas, and salads.

Entrance to the colourful Malcolm Shabazz Market

REAL MEAL Amy Ruth's *(113 West 116th St, between Lenox Ave & Seventh Ave, 10026; 212 280 8779; www.amyruthsharlem.com)* is a popular choice for soul food such as fried chicken and ribs.
FAMILY TREAT Sylvia's *(328 Lenox Ave/Malcolm X Blvd at 126th St, 10027; 212 996 0660; 8am–10:30pm Mon–Sat, 11am–8pm Sun; www. sylviasrestaurant.com)* is Harlem's best-known soul-food restaurant. Its legendary Sunday brunch treats diners to a gospel choir along with their smothered pork chops, chicken, and waffles.

Shopping

The record stores on 125th Street are a great source of rap and soul music. **Grandma's Place** *(84 West 120th St, 10027; 212 360 6776)* has an array of educational books and toys, while Harlem's most unusual place to shop is the **Malcolm Shabazz Market** *(see below)*.

Find out more

DIGITAL The website *www. biography.com/people/groups/ movement/harlem-renaissance* has information and games on the Harlem Renaissance.

Next stop...

MALCOLM SHABAZZ MARKET
The Islamic section of Harlem is centered on 116th Street, site of the green dome of the Malcolm Shabazz Mosque. Turn east from here and enter the minaret gates of the **Malcolm Shabazz Market** *(52 West 116th St, between Lenox & Fifth Ave, 10027; 212 987 8131)* to find stalls offering art, masks, and fabrics.

A musical performance at Schomburg Center for Research into Black Culture

The Lowdown

🌐 **Map reference** 17 D2
Address 132 Odell Clark Place (formerly 138th St), 10030; 212 862 7474; www.abyssinian.org

🚗 **Subway** 2, 3, B & C to 135th St.
Bus M2, M7, M10 & M102

♿ **Wheelchair access** Yes

🍽 **Eat and drink** *Real meal* Manna's Restaurant *(486 Lenox Ave at 134th St, 10030; 212 234 4488)* serves southern specialties buffet-style and has a good salad bar. *Family treat* Londel's *(2620 Frederick Douglass Blvd, 10030; 212 234 6114)* serves southern, Continental, and Cajun cuisine.

🚻 **Restrooms** On every floor

② Schomburg Center for Research into Black Culture
Bringing black history to life

The Schomburg Center opened in 1926 with an incredible collection of 5,000 books, 3,000 manuscripts, and 2,000 etchings and paintings on the life, culture, and history of black people everywhere. They had been amassed by the Puerto Rican activist and scholar Arturo Schomberg (1874–1938), an influential figure in the Harlem Renaissance. The collection continues to grow, and

today changing themed exhibits in the center's two galleries may feature art, rare books, letters, tools, carvings, or photography. Four colorful murals, *Aspects of Negro Life* (1934), in the main Reading Room, are by a Harlem Renaissance artist, Aaron Douglas (1899–1979). Stop in the small shop for unusual jewelry from Africa plus music, posters, and carvings.

Letting off steam
There are three playgrounds along St. Nicholas Avenue in **St. Nicholas Park** *(West 128th St to West 141st St, 10027)*. Forged by nature in rugged masses of rock, the narrow park also has basketball and handball courts.

③ Abyssinian Baptist Church
A choir of heavenly voices

New York's oldest black church was founded in 1808 by a group of African Americans and Ethiopian sea merchants, who refused to accept the racially segregated seating in other churches. It was named for Abyssinia, the old name for Ethiopia. In 1923, the congregation built this fine Neo-Gothic stone building, which has imported stained-glass windows and a marble pulpit. The church gained prominence when a charismatic pastor, Adam Clayton Powell Jr. (1908–72), took over in 1937. Stop by to listen to the superb gospel choir *(9am & 11am Sun)*. Outside, vendors cluster on the corner selling fresh produce and African dolls.

Letting off steam
The **St. Nicholas Park** playgrounds *(129th St, 133rd St & 140th St)* are ideal for families with young kids. Another good option is the hilly campus of the **City College of New York** *(160 Convent Ave, 10031; 212 650 7000)*, which borders the west side of the park.

④ St. Nicholas Historic District
Houses of the rich

This well-preserved enclave of townhouses along two blocks, 139th and 138th, was built in 1891 at the height of Harlem's heyday as an upscale residential area. Although designed by three different architects, the varied buildings blend into a harmonious whole. Behind are alleyways where horse-drawn carts used to deliver groceries. A sign on the gateposts

The Lowdown

🌐 **Map reference** 17 D2
Address 515 Lenox Ave/Malcolm X Blvd, 10037; 917 275 6975

🚗 **Subway** 2 & 3 to 135th St.
Bus M7 & M102

🕐 **Open** 10am–6pm Mon, Fri & Sat, 10am–8pm Tue–Thu

⑤ **Price** Free

👫 **Age range** 10 plus

⏲ **Allow** 1 hour

♿ **Wheelchair access** Yes

🍽 **Eat and drink** *Picnic* Hadwan Gourmet Deli *(2445 Frederick Douglass Blvd at 131st St, 10027; 212 862 3145)* has fixings for a fine picnic lunch. *Real meal* Dinosaur Bar-B-Que *(700 W 125th St, 10027; 212 694 1777)* has a menu rooted in Southern barbecue – ribs, pulled pork, and buffalo wings.

🚻 **Restrooms** On the main floor

Stained-glass window inside the Abyssinian Baptist Church

between numbers 251 and 253 says, "Private Road. Walk Your Horses," warning cart drivers not to go too fast.

In the 1920s the subway arrived here, making all of Harlem more accessible. But overbuilding led to many vacant apartments and thus an opportunity for black tenants to move in. Successful black lawyers and musicians were among those who lived here, accounting for the nickname Strivers' Row.

Letting off steam

Kids may enjoy watching the action at the **St. Nick's Dog Run** *(St. Nicholas Park, near 136th St, 10027)*, a shady expanse where small and large dogs have separate areas to run and play. Known as the "Point of Rocks," the park's southern edge was a military camp in the Battle of Harlem Heights.

The Lowdown

- **Map reference** 17 C2
- **Address** 138th St & 139th St, between Adam Clayton Powell Jr. Blvd & Frederick Douglass Blvd
- **Subway** B & C to 135th St. **Bus** M2, M7, M102 & M10
- **Eat and drink** *Picnic* Best Yet Market *(2187 Frederick Douglass Blvd, 10026)* is good for picking up lunch supplies. *Real meal* Queen Sheba *(134 Edgecombe Ave, 10030)* is an unassuming hole-in-the-wall joint that serves excellent Yemeni food.

⑤ Hamilton Heights Historic District and Sugar Hill
The sweet life

Some of the handsomest residential blocks in New York are in this district, the former site of Founding Father Alexander Hamilton's 1801 country estate, Hamilton Grange. From the subway stop at 145th Street, walk for a short distance and turn right onto Edgecombe Avenue to see some of the lovely buildings. Handsome stone row houses and elegant apartment blocks in the Queen Anne, Romanesque Revival, and Neo-Renaissance styles were built here from the 1880s through

to the 1920s. When black people began moving into Harlem, many professionals chose this area, and it became known as Sugar Hill, because it represented the sweet life.

Among the elite addresses were No. 409 Edgecombe, home to Thurgood Marshall, the first African-American Supreme Court Justice; and 555 Edgecombe, whose tenants included actor Paul Robeson and jazz great Count Basie. Many of these homes are now occupied by faculty members of the nearby City College.

Letting off steam

Take the BR19 bus heading west on 145th Street to the **Riverbank State Park** *(679 Riverside Drive, 10031)*. Riverbank is a man-made park atop a wastewater treatment plant above the Hudson River, with fabulous views. The park includes two playgrounds, an Olympic-size pool, and a covered rink for summer roller-skating and winter ice-skating.

Stone row houses in the Hamilton Heights Historic District

The Lowdown

- **Address** West 141st St to 145th St & Convent Ave
- **Subway** 3 to 145th St; A, B, C & D to 145th St. **Bus** M3, M100 & M101
- **Eat and drink** *Snacks* Sunshine Kitchen *(695 St Nicholas Ave at 145th St, 10031; 212 368 4972)* is recommended for its Jamaican fare, including jerk chicken. *Real meal* Charles' Country Pan Fried Chicken *(2839–2841 Frederick Douglass Blvd, 10039; 212 281 1800)* is reputed to serve Harlem's best fried chicken.

Picnic under $20; **Snacks** $20–35; **Real meal** $35–70; **Family treat** over $70 (based on a family of four)

The Cloisters and around

All it takes is a 30-minute ride on the subway to leave the skyscrapers behind and get a new perspective on Manhattan. Here, the island's northernmost neighborhoods, Washington Heights and Inwood, boast extensive tracts of parkland, a fairy-tale building, a lighthouse, a 1780s farmhouse, and wooded grounds with views of the New Jersey Palisades, the vertical cliffs across the Hudson River.

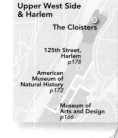

Upper West Side & Harlem

The Cloisters

125th Street, Harlem
p178

American Museum of Natural History
p172

Museum of Arts and Design
p166

Dyckman Farmhouse Museum, a vestige of 18th-century New York

Places of interest

SIGHTS

1. The Cloisters
2. Inwood Hill Park
3. Dyckman Farmhouse Museum
4. Little Red Lighthouse

● **EAT AND DRINK**

1. Frank's Market
2. Fivo's Pizza
3. Next Door Restaurant
4. New Leaf
5. Grandpa's Brick Oven Pizza
6. Indian Road Café
7. Rico Chimi
8. 809 Bar & Grill
9. Como Pizza
10. El Galicia Restaurant

● **SHOPPING**

1. The Cloisters gift shop

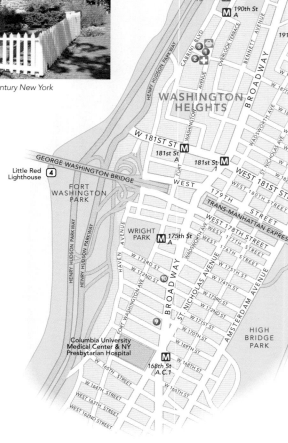

Laid-back dining at the Indian Road Café

0 meters		400
0 yards		400

The Little Red Lighthouse, with George Washington Bridge overhead

The Lowdown

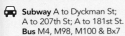 **Subway** A to Dyckman St; A to 207th St; A to 181st St. **Bus** M4, M98, M100 & Bx7

Supermarket Frank's Market, 807–809 West 187th St, near Fort Washington Ave, 10040; 212 795 2929
Markets Fort Washington Greenmarket, 168th St at Fort Washington Ave, 10033; Jun–Nov: 8am–4pm Tue. 175th St. Greenmarket; Jun–Nov: 8am–5pm Thu

Festivals Little Red Lighthouse Festival, Fort Washington Park (Sep or Oct); Medieval Festival, Fort Tryon Park (Sep or Oct); Commemoration of the Battle of Fort Washington, Fort Tryon Park (Nov)

Pharmacies Hilltop Pharmacy, 593 Fort Washington Ave at 187th St, 10033; 212 923 7176; 8am–8pm Mon–Fri, 9am–7pm Sat, 10am–7pm Sun. Rite Aid, 4910 Broadway, between 204th

St & 207th St, 10034; 212 569 2512; 8am–9pm Mon–Fri, 8am–6pm Sat, 10am–5pm Sun

Nearest playgrounds Jacob K. Javits Playground, Fort Washington Ave & Margaret Corbin Plaza, 10040. Anne Loftus Playground, Broadway & Dyckman St, 10034; Emerson Playground, Seaman Ave, between Isham St & West 207th St, 10034

① The Cloisters
Unicorns, gardens, and a trip into the past

With a prime location overlooking the Hudson, The Cloisters has a fairy-tale quality about it. A branch of the Metropolitan Museum of Art, it was acquired through the generosity of John D. Rockefeller Jr., who financed the land purchase and building works, and donated the amazing art collection so that it could open to the public in 1938. Step back in time among the medieval paintings and sculptures, and spot real and mythical animals in the Unicorn Tapestries.

Stained-glass window

Key Features

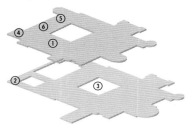

■ **Main Level** Unicorn Tapestries, Nine Heroes Tapestries, Romanesque Hall

■ **Lower Level** Sculptures, stained glass, paintings, and gardens

① **Palmesel** Kids love this multicolored wooden statue of Christ on a donkey, mounted on a wheeled platform. It comes from Germany and was once part of a Palm Sunday procession and pageant.

② **The Trie Cloister** Offering a little taste of French history, this marble cloister is made with capitals from the Carmelite Monastery of Trie-sur-Baïse, near Toulouse.

③ **Cuxa Cloister Garden** The peaceful main garden has a fountain in its center. Its pink columns and capitals, carved in the 12th century, feature strange creatures with two bodies and a single head.

④ **The Virgin Mary and Five Standing Saints** These glowing stained-glass windows (c. 1440–46) came from a former Carmelite church in Germany.

⑤ **Nine Heroes Tapestries** A rare tapestry series made in the early 15th century, this portrays heroes from Classical, Hebrew, and Christian history, but all dressed in medieval garb.

⑥ **Unicorn Tapestries** Woven around 1500, these show the hunt and capture of a unicorn. In medieval times, people thought unicorns were real and possessed magical powers.

The Lowdown

🌐 **Address** 99 Margaret Corbin Drive, Fort Tryon Park, 10040; 212 923 3700; www.metmuseum.org

🚗 **Subway** A to 190th St. **Bus** M4

🕐 **Open** Mar–Oct: 10am–5:15pm daily; Nov–Feb: 10am–4:45pm daily; closed Jan 1, Thanksgiving Day & Dec 25

💲 **Price** $50–75 (recommended admission); under 12s free; fee includes entry into main building

👫 **Cutting the line** School groups visit on weekday mornings; it is rarely crowded at other times.

🚩 **Guided tours** 3pm Tue–Fri & Sun; garden tours: 1pm Tue–Sun

👫 **Age range** 8 plus

👫 **Activities** Free gallery talks and programs on Sat & first Sun of the month at noon & 2pm. Free family workshops on most weekends; check website for schedule

⏱ **Allow** Half a day (including train ride and visit to Fort Tryon Park)

♿ **Wheelchair access** Yes, limited

🍵 **Café** Trie Café on the lower level; open Apr–Oct

🏷 **Shop** The Cloisters gift shop on the main floor

👫 **Restrooms** On the lower level

Good family value?
A trip to The Cloisters is a great experience, especially if combined with exploring the surrounding Fort Tryon Park.

Children playing among fountains, Anne Loftus Playground

Letting off steam

The nearest playgrounds are in Fort Tryon Park. The **Jacob K. Javits Playground** (*Fort Washington Ave & Margaret Corbin Plaza, 10040*) has really good play equipment and water sprinklers for warm days. The **Anne Loftus Playground** (*Broadway & Dyckman St, 10034*) at the northern end of the park also has swings.

Eat and drink

Picnic: under $20; Snacks: $20–35; Real meal: $35–70; Family treat: over $70 (based on a family of four)

PICNIC Frank's Market (*807–809 West 187th St, near Fort Washington Ave, 10040*) stocks an array of goodies that can be enjoyed while soaking up the awesome river view in Fort Tryon Park.
SNACKS Fivo's Pizza (*804 West 187th St, near Fort Washington Ave, 10033; 212 568 9050*) is sure to make kids happy, offering a range of pizza slices to munch on.
REAL MEAL Next Door Restaurant (*811 West 187th St, 10033; 212 543 2111; www. 107west.com*) is a local favorite serving American cuisine, from seafood to soul food and Cajun, as well as tempting desserts.

FAMILY TREAT New Leaf (*1 Margaret Corbin Drive in Fort Tryon Park, 10040; 212 568 5323*), set in a 1930s stone house, offers New American fare such as duck confit hash, portobello mushroom wrap, and bacon-wrapped scallops.

Shopping

The Cloisters gift shop (*Mar–Oct: 10am–5:15pm daily; Nov–Feb: 10am–4:45pm daily*) is a wonderland for kids. Pick up a mock suit of armor, medieval building blocks, or mugs featuring unicorns.

Find out more

DIGITAL For information about medieval times geared to kids of all ages, check *www.42explore2.com/medieval.htm*.

Next stop...

FORT TRYON PARK One of the highest points above the Hudson River, Fort Tryon Park (*Riverside Drive to Broadway & West 192nd St to Dyckman St, 10040*) was originally a fort, becoming a choice spot for estates in the 19th century. In 1917, John D. Rockefeller Jr. bought the land and had it transformed, adding promenades, terraces, wooded slopes, and 8 miles (13 km) of pedestrian paths, before finally presenting it to the city in 1935. The park's Heather Garden was built into the side of the rocky ridge as a series of terraces lining a promenade overlooking the Hudson. In the Alpine Garden, thickly wooded paths snake up and down the park's rocky eastern slope.

The leafy Fort Tryon Park

Inwood Hill Park with Henry Hudson Bridge in the background

A variety of savory and sweet treats on display, Indian Road Café

② Inwood Hill Park

A forest in the city

Native trees, a salt marsh, and Indian caves await in this rambling 196-acre (80-ha) park. During the colonial era this land was known as Cock or Cox Hill, probably inspired by the Native American name for the area, *Shorakapok* ("the edge of the river"). Created in 1916, much of the park is thickly wooded, with hiking and nature trails curving up the hill. Set out on foot to explore its Shorakapok Preserve, which boasts dense forests of mature red oaks, and large tulip trees. Spot the waterfowl that are attracted here by the salt marsh, and admire the natural rock caves once used for shelter by Native Americans.

Take cover

In case of rainy weather, take shelter in the **Inwood Hill Nature Center** *(near the 218th St at Indian Rd entrance; closed for renovation)*. Located on Manhattan's only saltwater marsh, this interesting center has dioramas of topographical features such as meadow, forest, and salt marsh. An exhibit has highlights of the various historical epochs the park has seen, from 2000 BC to the present day.

③ Dyckman Farmhouse Museum

A remnant of old New York

A farmhouse from 1784 perched on a hill above busy Broadway, this museum is a rare find in the city.

Parlor at Dyckman Farmhouse Museum

The Lowdown

- 🌐 **Address** Entrances at Dyckman St, Seaman Ave at West 207th St & 214th St, Indian Rd at 218th St, 10034
- 🚇 **Subway** A to Dyckman St; A to 207th St; 1 to 215th St. **Bus** M100
- 🕐 **Open** Dawn–dusk daily
- 💲 **Price** Free
- 👪 **Age range** All ages
- 🏃 **Activities** Hiking and bike trails
- ⏱ **Allow** 1–2 hours
- 🍴 **Eat and drink** *Snacks* Grandpa's Brick Oven Pizza *(4973 Broadway at 211th St, 10034; 212 304 1185)* offers thin-crust pizzas as well as salads, buffalo wings, and lasagne. *Real meal* Indian Road Café *(600 West 218th St at Indian Rd, 10034; 212 942 7451; www.indianroadcafe.com)* serves good American fare, such as Maine lobster rolls.
- 👫 **Restrooms** Near the basketball courts and in the nature center

The Lowdown

- 🌐 **Address** 4881 Broadway at 204th St, 10034; 212 304 9422; www.dyckmanfarmhouse.org
- 🚇 **Subway** A to 207th St. **Bus** M100
- 🕐 **Open** 11am–5pm Fri–Sun; Mon–Thu groups by appointment only
- 💲 **Price** $4; under 10s free
- 👪 **Age range** 8 plus
- 🏃 **Activities** Educational crafts and concerts
- ⏱ **Allow** 1 hour
- ♿ **Wheelchair access** No
- 🍴 **Eat and drink** *Snacks* Rico Chimi *(111 Dyckman St, 10040; 212 390 0464)* does Latin American fast food. *Family treat* 809 Bar & Grill *(112 Dyckman St, 10040; 212 304 3800)* serves Latin-American dishes such as *empanadas* (stuffed pastries).
- 👫 **Restrooms** In the grounds

Built by William Dyckman in the Dutch-Colonial style, the house has a porch, a gambrel roof, and decorative brickwork. It remained in the family until the 1870s, after which it fell into disrepair. Dyckman's descendants bought back the home in 1915, restored it and donated it to the city in 1916. Today, it offers a fascinating glimpse of rural life in 19th-century Manhattan.

Visitors can see the authentically furnished period bedrooms, the winter kitchen, and parlors for socializing and dining. The garden has a reproduction smokehouse and a cherry tree to represent the orchards that once stood here. There is also a reconstructed military hut of the kind that was used as a shelter during the American Revolutionary War (1776–83).

Letting off steam

Head to **Emerson Playground** *(Seaman Ave, between Isham Ave & West 207th St, 10034)*, named for nature-loving poet Ralph Waldo Emerson. It has space to run around in as well as a spray shower in the form of a frog and an iron sculpture of a wolf created in bas-relief.

④ Little Red Lighthouse

The unlikely hero of a classic children's book

The bright-red 40-ft (12-m) high lighthouse that stands proudly in Fort Washington Park has a story to tell. It was erected in 1880 and moved to its current site along a treacherous section of the Hudson in 1921. When George Washington Bridge opened above the lighthouse in 1931, the gleaming lights of the bridge's 600-ft (183-m) high towers overpowered the small lighthouse. In 1942, Hildegarde Swift wrote *The Little Red Lighthouse and the Great Gray Bridge*, in which the lighthouse learns one foggy night that it still has an important job to do.

In 1948, when the Coast Guard planned to dismantle the lighthouse, thousands of children who loved Swift's book started a nationwide campaign to save it. Today, it is a National Historic Landmark and a literary landmark for kids. Each September, the Little Red Lighthouse Festival brings hundreds to celebrate the proud little survivor.

Letting off steam

Fort Washington Park *(Riverside Drive, West 155th St to West 179th St, 10033)* has two playgrounds, at West 162nd Street and Riverside Drive, and at West 165th Street at Henry Hudson Parkway. It is also a great place to spot high-flying peregrine falcons, which nest on the towers of George Washington Bridge.

KIDS' CORNER

Find out more…

1 Native Americans once used the natural rock caves in Inwood Hill Park as shelter. Do you know the Native American name for the area and what it means?

2 When Dyckman Farmhouse was restored in 1916, a particular tree was planted to represent the farm's original orchards. Can you guess what tree it is?

3 Which famous children's book is about a certain lighthouse in Fort Washington Park? Do you know who wrote it?

·····································

Answers at the bottom of the page.

WEATHER UPDATES

In colonial times, many homes such as Dyckman Farmhouse had an inside kitchen to help keep the house warm in winter, and an outside kitchen for use in summer.

Money matters

A plaque in Inwood Hill Park marks the location of the legendary sale of Manhattan. This is where, in 1626, Dutch Governor Peter Minuit supposedly bought all of Manhattan Island from the Lenape Indians in exchange for beads and goods estimated to be worth a mere $24 today.

·····································

Answers: 1 It was Shorakapok, which means "the edge of the river." **2** A cherry tree. **3** *The Little Red Lighthouse and the Great Gray Bridge*, written by Hildegarde Swift and illustrated by Lynd Ward.

George Washington Bridge, with the Little Red Lighthouse on the Hudson

Beyond
Manhattan

New York was formed in 1898, when five boroughs (the Bronx, Brooklyn, Manhattan, Queens, and Staten Island) came together as one city. Each of the outer boroughs has a unique personality and something compelling to offer. While Queens is an up-and-coming center for the arts, the Bronx is the birthplace of hip hop, and Brooklyn boasts a botanical garden and seaside amusement parks.

Highlights

Brooklyn Museum
Admire one of the world's finest Egyptian collections, as well as modern and Asian art galleries, at this magnificent museum *(see pp202–203)*.

Prospect Park
Visit this verdant expanse for its zoo, carousel, hiking trails, and birding tours, which offer an instant antidote to urban confinement *(see pp204–209)*.

The Noguchi Museum
Step into the mind and work of an exceptional 20th-century sculptor, Isamu Noguchi, at this museum *(see p220)*.

Long Island City
Experience the emerging contemporary art scene in southern Long Island City, centered on MoMA PS1 *(see pp220–21)*.

Wave Hill
Enjoy art workshops for kids and explore the grounds of this public garden, with its spectacular views of the Hudson River *(see p232)*.

City Island
A seaside town with the feel of a tiny New England fishing village, this is a hidden treasure in the Bronx *(see p233)*.

Left Visitors to Luna Park enjoying a ride on a flying carousel, Coney Island, Brooklyn Above left Block Statue in the Egyptian Gallery, Brooklyn Museum

The Best of
Beyond Manhattan

Visitors who venture beyond the borders of Manhattan are amply rewarded. The outer boroughs are off the beaten path, but their mix of homegrown character, stellar cultural sights, and parks make them great child-friendly destinations. They offer a chance to mingle with local families while enjoying the bounty of the Bronx's zoo, Queens' and Brooklyn's museums, and Long Island City's bastion of contemporary art.

A dose of culture

Head north to the **Bronx Museum of the Arts** *(see p238)* for contemporary urban, often Bronx-themed, exhibits on such topics as civil rights and the huge transformations underway in the borough. Out in Queens, the **The Noguchi Museum** *(see p220)*, built by sculptor Isamu Noguchi to house his life's work, is an ode to simplicity, while the **Museum of the Moving Image** *(see pp218–19)* provides an insight into the history of cinema. Admire the world-class contemporary art at MoMA PS1 in **Long Island City** *(see p220–21)* or jump on the train to Flushing to take a look at *The Panorama*, an astonishing scale model of all five boroughs, at the **Queens Museum of Art** *(see p226)*.

The great outdoors

Venture across **Brooklyn Bridge** *(see pp196–7)*, one of the greatest architectural feats of modern times. Make a beeline to Prospect Park's **Audubon Center** *(see p209)* and, weather permitting, hop aboard an electric boat for an unforgettable bird-watching tour. Afterward, take a hike into the wilderness of the park's Ravine, visit **Prospect Park Zoo** *(see pp204–205)*, with its nature trail and copious activities for kids, or cross the street to admire the elegant Japanese Hill-and-Pond Garden at the **Brooklyn Botanic Garden** *(see p206)*. Up in the Bronx, explore the myriad animal habitats of the **Bronx Zoo** *(see pp236–7)*, the city's largest zoological garden.

Below Pebble beach near Brooklyn Bridge, with the Manhattan skyline in the background

Above Panoramic views of the Hudson River from the grounds of Wave Hill in the Bronx *Center* Entrance to the Museum of the Moving Image in Astoria, Queens *Bottom* Steps leading to the Beaux-Arts building of the Brooklyn Museum

House-hunting

New York's historic houses are like portals into the city's past, illuminating the lives of its former inhabitants. **Wave Hill** *(see p232)* in the Bronx, with spectacular views of the Hudson River, counts Teddy Roosevelt and writer Mark Twain among its former residents. Farther east is the **Edgar Allan Poe Cottage** *(see p232)*, where the poet spent the last two years of his life tending to his infirm wife and writing poetry. Time-travel back to the 17th century at **Lefferts Historic House** *(see p208)* in Brooklyn's Prospect Park, where kids can engage in old-fashioned pastimes such as churning butter. Finally, stop at **Brooklyn Museum** *(see pp202–203)* to see Schenck House, a Dutch homestead dating from about 1775.

By season

The winter months are ideal for a trip to the **New York Hall of Science** *(see pp224–5)* in Queens, where mind-bending exhibits such as Seeing the Light are designed especially for kids. In April and May, head to the blossoming cherry trees in the **Brooklyn Botanic Garden**, which are celebrated at the Japanese-inspired Sakura Matsuri festival. When the weather warms up, take the train to **Coney Island** *(see p214)*, where amusement park rides, a boardwalk strewn with arcades, and a genuine ocean beach await. And come fall, seek out the last pocket of the city's original forest in the **New York Botanical Garden** *(see pp230–31)* as it transforms into a canopy of fiery colors.

Brooklyn Bridge and around

The astonishing Brooklyn Bridge is beautiful to look at from a distance, but crossing it on foot makes for an exciting aerial adventure. Although it can be blustery at times, the elevated pedestrian walkway in the center is quite safe. It makes sense to start on the Manhattan side and arrive, after a 1-mile (2-km) walk, among the wealth of places to see on the Brooklyn side – including Dumbo's outstanding waterfront parks. Small or tired legs can opt to cross by subway or water taxi.

Downtown
Brooklyn Bridge
Brooklyn
Brooklyn Museum
p200

Water taxi on the East River

City Hall
R
City Hall
Chambers St
J,Z
CITY HALL PARK
Brooklyn Bridge-City Hall
4,5,6
Police Headquarters
MADISON STREET
PARK ROW
BROADWAY
Pace University
Fulton St
A,C,4,5
ANN STREET
OLD STREET
BROOKLYN BRIDGE
Fulton St
J,Z
MAIDEN LANE
Fulton St
2,3
Southbridge Towers
PEARL
PECK SLIP ST
Chase Manhattan Bank
WILLIAM
WATER
FRONT
South Street Seaport
FRONT
VIADUCT
PINE
PEARL
STREET
Brooklyn Bridge
WATER
STREET
STREET
SOUTH
PIER 17
South Street Seaport
South
PIER 15
Rive
PIER 14
PIER 13
Pier 11/Wall Street Ferry Terminal
PI
PIER 9
BROOKL
BRID
PA
East
PIER 2
PIER 3
PIER 4
FURMAN ST
BROOKLYN-QUEENS EXPRE
COLUMBIA PL

Places of interest

SIGHTS
1. Brooklyn Bridge
2. Dumbo
3. Jacques Torres Chocolate Shop
4. Brooklyn Ice Cream Factory
5. New York Transit Museum

● **EAT AND DRINK**
1. Peas and Pickles
2. Ignazio's Pizza
3. Grimaldi's Pizzeria
4. River Café
5. Almondine Bakery
6. Henry's End
7. AlMar
8. Vinegar Hill House
9. Brooklyn Roasting Company
10. Superfine
11. Pedro's Bar & Restaurant
12. Iris Café

● **WHERE TO STAY**
1. Best Western Plus Seaport Inn
2. Marriott Brooklyn Bridge

River Café in Brooklyn, over-looking the water

Pedestrian walkway on Brooklyn Bridge with views of the Financial District

0 meters 300

0 yards 300

PIKE ST

RUTGERS ST

MARKET STREET

bocker
age

ERRY STREET

RUTGERS
PARK

SOUTH STREET

VIADUCT

UTH STREET

SOUTH STREET

MANHATTAN BRIDGE

PIER 35

Fulton Ferry
Water Taxi
Landing

MAIN
STREET PARK

EMPIRE-
FULTON
FERRY PARK

WASHINGTON ST

MAIN ST

JOHN STREET

PEARL ST

JAY ST

PLYMOUTH STREET

WATER STREET

STREET

STREET

AVENUE

4

5

Brooklyn
Ice Cream
Factory

Jacques Torres
Chocolate Shop

3

2

Dumbo Arts
Center

Dewey's Candy

Dumbo

FRONT STREET

BRIDGE ST

GOLD ST

HUDSON

8

York St
F

VINE ST

BROOKLYN

YORK STREET

QUEENS EXPRESSWAY

MIDDAGH STREET

CRANBERRY STREET

ORANGE STREET

APPLE STREET

HICKS STREET

Clark St
2.3

SANDS STREET

TRINITY
PARK

High St
A,C

NASSAU ST

ADAMS STREET

PEARL STREET

JAY STREET

CONCORD STREET

CADMAN PLAZA WEST

MONROE PLACE

CLINTON STREET

BROOKLYN
HEIGHTS

PIERREPONT STREET

MONTAGUE STREET

HENRY STREET

CADMAN PLAZA E

CADMAN PL E

TILLARY STREET

MANHATTAN BRIDGE

Court St
R

JOHNSON STREET

COLUMBUS
PARK

Borough Hall
2.3.4.5

2

Jay St-
Metro Tech
A,C,F,R

JORALEMON STREET

LIVINGSTON STREET

New York
Transit
Museum

5

COURT ST

STATE STREET

The Lowdown

🚇 **Subway** Manhattan-side: R to City Hall; 4, 5 & 6 to Brooklyn Bridge-City Hall; 2 & 3 to Fulton St. Brooklyn-side: A & C to High St; F to York St. **Bus** M9, M15, M22, B25 & M103. **Water taxi** Between Manhattan's Pier11 & Brooklyn's Fulton Ferry Landing; New York Water Taxi: *www.nywatertaxi.com*; 212 742 1969

ℹ️ **Visitor information** Brooklyn Tourism & Visitors Center, 209 Joralemon St, Brooklyn, 11201; 718 802 3846

🛒 **Supermarkets** Brooklyn: Peas & Pickles, 55 Washington St, between Front St & Water St, 11201; 718 488 8336 **Markets** Manhattan: City Hall Park Greenmarket, Broadway at Chambers St; 8am–4pm Tue & Fri. Brooklyn: Brooklyn Borough Hall Greenmarket, Court St at Montague St; 8am–6pm Tue, Thu & Sat.

🎉 **Festivals** BKLYN Designs (May). Brooklyn Hip-Hop Festival (Jul).

➕ **Pharmacies** Manhattan: Duane Reade, 200 Water St, 10038; 212 825 0761; 7:30am–8pm Mon–Fri, 9am–6pm Sat & Sun. Brooklyn: Rite Aid, 168 Montague St, 11201; 718 522 2991; 7am–9pm Mon–Fri, 9am–6pm Sat, 9am–5pm Sun

🏊 **Nearest playgrounds** Brooklyn Bridge Park, foot of Brooklyn Bridge *(see pp196–7)*. Pierrepont Park, Pierrepont St, at the Promenade, Brooklyn, 11201. Main Street Park, Washington St *(see p198)*

Interior of the Jacques Torres Chocolate Shop

The Lowdown

 Map reference 2 G3

 Subway J & Z to Fulton St; 4, 5 & 6 to Brooklyn Bridge-City Hall; 2 & 3 to Fulton St; R to City Hall. **Bus** M9, M15, & M22. Pedestrian access to the bridge is near City Hall Park at Park Row & Central St.

 Guided tours Many companies, including Big Onion Walking Tours, offer guided tours of the bridge; check *www.bigonion.com* for details. Bike and Roll offers a 3-hour bike tour that traverses the bridge; check *www.bikeandroll.com* for details.

 Age range All age groups, but bring a stroller for toddlers, who may need a rest on the way.

⏱ **Allow** 1 hour

👫 **Restrooms** The nearest are at Au Bon Pain *(80 Pine St, 10005)* on the Manhattan side, and at Pier 1 *(see below)*.

Good family value?
The structure's architectural beauty and fascinating history, coupled with the open-air thrill of a crossing, make this one of the must-see attractions for families visiting the city.

① Brooklyn Bridge
A majestic span

An architectural wonder, Brooklyn Bridge was built across the East River between 1870 and 1883 to connect what were then America's two biggest cities, New York (now Manhattan) and Brooklyn. Many believed that the steel suspension bridge – the first in the world – was not safe. To prove them wrong, showman P. T. Barnum walked 21 elephants, led by one named Jumbo, across the bridge.

Key Features

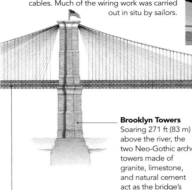

Central span 1,595 ft (486 m) in length, the span is held up by a graceful curve of steel cables. Much of the wiring work was carried out in situ by sailors.

Brooklyn Towers Soaring 271 ft (83 m) above the river, the two Neo-Gothic arched towers made of granite, limestone, and natural cement act as the bridge's main supports.

Roadway An elevated train ran on the two central lanes, with trolley cars and other vehicles alongside. Today, only cars are allowed.

Steel cables Four steel cables, each 3,579 ft (1,091 m) long, support the span of the bridge.

Brooklyn Bridge Park, an urban oasis along the East River

Letting off steam
Pier 1 of **Brooklyn Bridge Park** *(www.brooklynbridgeparknyc.org)*, with a playground at its northern edge, two large lawns, and a waterfront promenade, is the perfect place to enjoy a picnic or a stroll along the water.

Prices given are for a family of four

Eat and drink
Picnic: under $20; Snacks: $20–35; Real meal: $35–70; Family treat: over $70 (based on a family four)

PICNIC Peas & Pickles *(55 Washington St, 11201; 718 488 8336; 24 hours daily)* has sandwiches, grilled panini, and sushi. Pick up supplies and head to one of the lawns in Brooklyn Bridge Park.
SNACKS Ignazio's Pizza *(4 Water St, 11201; 718 522 2100; www. ignaziospizza.com)* offers pizza with shrimp, clams, or pineapple and ham toppings. Salads and a variety of drinks also feature on the menu.
REAL MEAL Grimaldi's Pizzeria *(1 Front St, 11201; 718 858 4300; www.grimaldis.com)* serves delicious brick-oven pizzas, salads, and desserts that make it well worth the wait for a table.

FAMILY TREAT River Café
(1 Water St, 11201; 718 522 5200; 5:30–11pm daily, plus 11:30am– 2:30pm Sat & Sun; www.theriver cafe.com), one of the city's most scenic dining spots, enjoys a lovely location at the foot of Brooklyn Bridge. It features classic New American cuisine prepared using fresh ingredients.

River Café offers fantastic views of the Manhattan skyline

Necklace of lights Set along the bridge's cables is a string of 904 lights meant to resemble a pearl necklace. The lights are only turned on when there is deemed to be enough money in the city's coffers to afford the electricity.

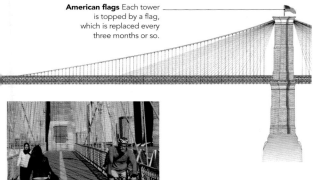

American flags Each tower is topped by a flag, which is replaced every three months or so.

Pedestrian walkway Brooklyn Bridge was the first bridge in the world to have a separate pedestrian walkway built into it, above the road. Today, cyclists and walkers share it, and are separated by a white line.

KIDS' CORNER

Look out for...
1 Steel wires were spun into cables to support the span of the bridge. Can you guess why the bridge company hired sailors to string the wire from the cable high up in the air?
2 Why is there a white line in the middle of the pedestrian walkway?
3 Which two original types of transportation no longer run on the bridge?
4 Which major New York landmark can you see from the bridge?

Answers at the bottom of the page.

HIDDEN FACT
In 2006, secret supplies were discovered inside one of the bridge's towers. The cache had been stored there in 1957 so that the tower could serve as a bunker if the Soviet Union attacked New York City with a nuclear bomb.

Tragic past
The German-born engineer John Augustus Roebling, who designed Brooklyn Bridge, did not live to see it built. He died of an injury during its construction. His son, Washington Roebling, took over, but he too was injured, so his wife Emily took on the daily supervison and site visits on his behalf.

Find out more
FILM Acclaimed documentarian Ken Burns made *Brooklyn Bridge* for the Public Broadcasting Service (PBS) in 1981. The film looks at the building of the bridge and its historical significance to New York City. The bridge is also featured in the BBC film *Seven Wonders of an Industrial World* (2003). In *Godzilla* (1998), starring Matthew Broderick and Jean Reno, the giant lizard that terrorizes New York is finally killed on Brooklyn Bridge.

Take cover
Head to the spacious **Dumbo** arts center *(see p198)* for a look at its current exhibits, or to the gigantic Dewey's Candy at 141 Front Street, stacked with colorful confections.

Brooklyn Heights Promenade has a great playground and knockout views

Next stop...
BROOKLYN HEIGHTS PROMENADE The Brooklyn Heights Promenade has terrific views of the bridge. Its Pierrepont playground is good, while tree-lined streets behind give an idea of what this area was like 100 years ago.

Answers: 1 Sailors were used to working up a tall ship's mast. **2** The line separates walkers from cyclists. **3** Elevated trains and trolley cars. **4** The Empire State Building.

Jacques Torres Chocolate Shop, filled with tempting goodies

② Dumbo

Artsy and green

Once an industrial area filled with warehouses, this part of Brooklyn is now one of the most charming neighborhoods in the city. Down Under the Manhattan Bridge Overpass, or Dumbo as it is commonly known, refers to the neighborhood's dramatic location at the foot of the looming Brooklyn Bridge. Its well-preserved architecture and Belgian-block cobblestoned streets have played muse to some of the city's greatest photographers, including Berenice Abbott and André Kertész, as well as filmmaker Sergio Leone, who relished its historic character and moody atmosphere.

Today, Dumbo is best known for its proliferation of artists and its stunning waterfront parks, among the most child-friendly in the city.

The Lowdown

🌐 **Map reference** 19 A3

🚇 **Subway** A & C to High St;
F to York St. **Bus** B25, B67 & B69

👫 **Age range** All ages

⏱ **Allow** 1–2 hours

🍴 **Eat and drink** *Real meal* Almondine Bakery (85 Water St, near Main St, 11201; 718 797 5026) offers cookies, breads, and classic and "fancy" French pastries. *Family treat* Henry's End (44 Henry St, 11201; 718 834 1776) uses seasonal ingredients sourced from local suppliers to create its New American menu.

🚻 **Restrooms** In nearby cafés, and on the second floor of the Dumbo Arts Center

Artists came to the area in droves in the 1970s and 1980s, and their influence is felt to this day in such institutions as the not-for-profit Dumbo Arts Center, with its galleries and children's workshops. Galapagos Art Space hosts video installations, performance art and theater, while St. Ann's Warehouse is renowned for its cutting-edge theater and rock concerts. Front Street and Water Street are lined with galleries, bookstores, design ateliers, and culinary establishments such as Jacques Torres Chocolate Factory.

Letting off steam

A nautically themed playground, great views of Manhattan, broad steps leading to the water, lush lawns, and a dog run make **Main Street Park**, a part of Brooklyn Bridge Park (see p196), one of this area's most treasured gems.

③ Jacques Torres Chocolate Shop

The chocolate factory

There is only one man in New York City whose name conjures up all the allure and decadence of excellent chocolate – Jacques Torres. Born in a fishing village in France, Torres came to New York to follow his passion for sweet treats and rose to the position of pastry chef at Le Cirque, one of the city's legendary restaurants. He eventually left the bright lights behind to convert an old brick warehouse at the edge of the East River into this world-renowned chocolate factory. A great variety of mouth-watering treats, including champagne truffles,

Brooklyn Ice Cream Factory, popular with locals and visitors alike

pralines, and straightforward chocolate bars, are available here. Inside, a glass window allows a delightful view of it all being made, à la Willy Wonka.

Letting off steam

Head to **Empire-Fulton Ferry Park**, also a part of Brooklyn Bridge Park (see p196), and take a whirl on Jane's Carousel, which now has a permanent home inside a weather-proof glass structure. The carousel, with its 48 horses and all-original platform, was made in Philadelphia in 1922. Named for its previous owner, who gave it to the city, it took 20 years to restore.

The Lowdown

🌐 **Map reference** 2 H3
Address 66 Water St, 11201; 718 875 1269; www.mrchocolate.com

🚇 **Subway** A & C to High St; F to York St. **Bus** B25 & B69

⏰ **Open** 9am–8pm Mon–Sat, 10am–6pm Sun

⏱ **Allow** 30 minutes

♿ **Wheelchair access** Yes

🍴 **Eat and drink** *Snacks* AlMar (111 Front St, 11201; 718 855 5288) serves sandwiches, panini, salads, and burritos. *Family treat* Vinegar Hill House (72 Hudson Ave, 11201; 718 522 1018), a top-notch New American brunch and dinner spot, serves classics with a twist.

🚻 **Restrooms** On the main floor

④ Brooklyn Ice Cream Factory

Creamy delights

The city's decision to preserve a 1924 fireboat house at Fulton Landing has proved to be a good one – the building's simple, cheerful architecture has been saved for posterity and it provides a delightful home for one of the best ice-cream parlors in New York. The plan was set in motion in 2001 by Mark Thompson, at the time a manager at the iconic River Café restaurant. His decision to limit the number of flavors – there are usually about eight – and use only the freshest ingredients has paid off in spades. Brooklyn Ice Cream Factory ranks high on most ice-cream aficionados'

The Lowdown

🌐 **Map reference** 2 H3

Address Corner of Old Fulton & Water St, 11201; 718 246 3963; www.brooklynicecreamfactory.com

🚗 **Subway** A & C to High St; F to York St. **Bus** B25 & B69

🕐 **Open** noon–10pm daily

👫 **Age range** All ages

⏱ **Allow** 1 hour

♿ **Wheelchair access** No

🍽 **Eat and drink** Snacks Brooklyn Roasting Company (25 Jay St, 11201; 718 855 1000) mostly serves free-trade, freshly roasted coffee, with a huge selection of flavors and varieties. There are also pastries from top local bakers. Real meal Superfine (126 Front St, 11201; 718 243 9005) offers Mediterranean-inspired brunch and dinner.

👫 **Restrooms** No

New York list. People queue up throughout the day for the privilege of tasting its icy treats.

Letting off steam

Just beyond the ramparts of Brooklyn Bridge (see pp196–7) from the ice-cream factory is the edge of **Empire-Fulton Ferry Park**. Start by walking to the foot of the bridge for panoramic vistas of Manhattan. This perfect view has found its way into just about every other movie set in New York City. Then visit the magnificent former Tobacco Warehouse. Built in the 1870s as a tobacco customs inspection center, the roofless brick building, punctured by arched windows, is a vivid reminder of Dumbo's past as a shipping hub.

⑤ New York Transit Museum

Trolleys, trains, and more

Located in the old Court Street subway station, abandoned in 1946, this museum is dedicated to the history of the city's public transit system. Three long-term exhibits occupy the mezzanine: Steel, Stone, and Backbone looks at the construction of the subway system; On the Streets: New York's Trolleys and Buses showcases above-ground

Items for sale in the store at the New York Transit Museum

transportation, and includes a 12-seat bus and child-size trolley that kids can board. The Fare Collection highlights the various toll collection devices used over the years. On the lower level, two working subway tracks house vintage subway and elevated train cars, which visitors can board. Most of the subway cars are operational, and occasionally make "Nostalgia Train" excursions.

Letting off steam

Just north of the museum is **Columbus Park** (Cadman Plaza West, Brooklyn, 11201), a flagstone-covered park with beautiful gardens and myriad sculptures to explore. The greenmarket at Brooklyn Borough Hall (see p195) sells all kinds of goodies.

The Lowdown

🌐 **Map reference** 19 A4

Address Boerum Pl & Schermer horn St, 11201; web.mta.info

🚗 **Subway** 2, 3, 4 & 5 to Borough Hall. **Bus** B25, B57, B61 & B103

🕐 **Open** 10am–4pm Tue–Fri; 11am–5pm Sat & Sun

👫 **Age range** All ages

💲 **Price** $24–28; under 2s free

🎏 **Activities** Numerous family-friendly programs; see web.mta.info/mta/museum/programs or call 718 694 1792.

⏱ **Allow** 1 hour

♿ **Wheelchair access** Yes

🍽 **Eat and drink** Snacks Pedro's Bar & Restaurant (73 Jay St, 11201; 718 797 2851) serves traditional Dominican and Mexican food. Real meal Iris Café (20 Columbia Pl, 11201; 718 722 7395) has sandwiches and all-day breakfast offerings.

👫 **Restrooms** On the main floor

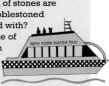

Brooklyn Museum and around

Brooklyn was an important city in its own right during the 19th century, and the proof is the grand complex of sights at the edge of Prospect Park, the borough's largest green space. The park itself is full of things to do, while a short walk away is the hands-on Brooklyn Children's Museum, a dream for kids. The Brooklyn Museum and its neighbor, the idyllic Botanic Garden, near to Prospect Park, are extremely accessible to families, too. Get here by subway, then explore the area on foot.

Places of interest

SIGHTS

1. Brooklyn Museum
2. Prospect Park Zoo
3. Grand Army Plaza
4. Brooklyn Botanic Garden
5. Brooklyn Children's Museum
6. Prospect Park
7. Lefferts Historic House
8. Audubon Center

● EAT AND DRINK

1. BKLYN Larder
2. Counter Café
3. Tom's Restaurant
4. Flatbush Farm
5. Bark
6. Carlton Park
7. James
8. Dizzy's Diner
9. Cheryl's Global Soul
10. Bareburger
11. Breukelen Coffee House
12. Applebees
13. Pony Express Snack Bar
14. Gino's Trattoria & Brick Oven Pizza
15. Scoops & Plates Eatery
16. King of Tandoor
17. Sushi Tatsu III

See also Brooklyn Botanic Garden (p206) & Audubon Center (p209)

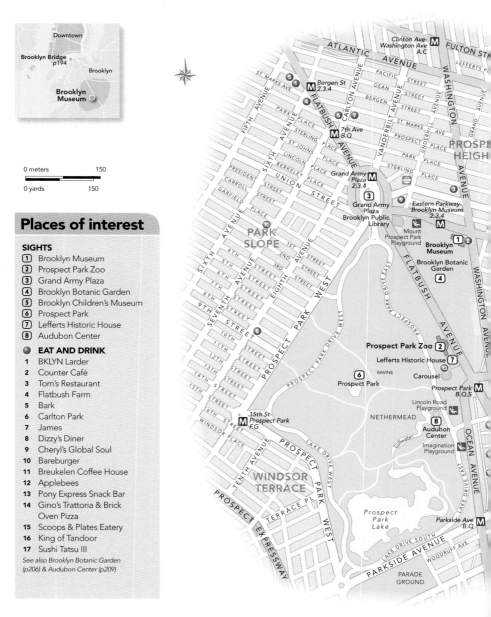

Prospect Park Lake, the only freshwater lake in Brooklyn

The Lowdown

🚗 **Subway** 2 & 3 to Eastern Parkway-Brooklyn Museum; B, Q & S to Prospect Park. **Bus** B41, B45 & B69

🍴 **Supermarket** St John's Marketplace, 323 St Johns Place, Brooklyn, 11238; 718 783 6950
Market Grand Army Plaza GreenMarket, Prospect Park W & Flatbush Ave, Brooklyn, 11238; 8am–4pm Sat

🎎 **Festivals** Sakura Matsuri Festival, Brooklyn Botanic Garden (Apr); Celebrate Brooklyn – concerts, dance & film, Prospect Park (Jun– early Aug)

➕ **Pharmacies** CVS/pharmacy, 1249 Nostrand Ave, Brooklyn, 11225; 718 282 6614; 8am–8pm Mon–Fri, 9AM–6PM Sat & Sun. Rite Aid, 1679 Bedford Ave, between Montgomery Place & Sullivan St, Brooklyn, 11225; 718 282 7476; 9am–9pm Mon–Fri, 9am–6pm Sat, 9am–5pm Sun

🛝 **Nearest playgrounds** Mount Prospect Park Playground, Eastern Parkway, between Washington Ave & Flatbush Ave, Brooklyn, 11238. Lincoln Road Playground (see p205). Imagination Playground (see p209)

Lefferts Historic House in Prospect Park

① Brooklyn Museum
Awesome art and mysterious mummies

The borough's main cultural magnet, Brooklyn Museum had its origins in 1823 when it was founded as an Apprentices Library. It evolved into the Brooklyn Institute of Arts and Sciences by the mid-19th century. In 1897, the museum opened in a massive Beaux-Arts building, designed by the city's star architects McKim, Mead, and White. Today, it is known for exhibits that challenge the definition of art, such as a display on the *Star Wars* movies and a photographic history of rock 'n' roll.

Sculpture outside the Brooklyn Museum

Key Features

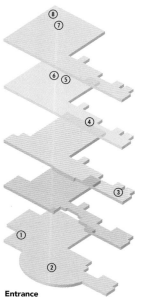

■ **Fifth Floor** Luce Center for American Art and Cantor Gallery

■ **Fourth Floor** Contemporary Arts Galleries, Decorative Arts Galleries and Elizabeth A. Sackler Center for Feminist Art

■ **Third Floor** Egyptian Galleries, Kevorkian Gallery and Beaux-Arts Court

■ **Second Floor** Asian and Islamic Galleries (currently closed for renovation)

■ **First Floor** African Galleries, Robert E. Blum Gallery, and Steinberg Family Sculpture Garden

① **Beaded Crown** This late 19th-century crown was made by a Yoruba craftsman for Onijagbo Obasoro Alowolodu, the oba (king) of Ikere (in present-day Nigeria) who reigned from 1890 to 1928.

② **Monument to Balzac** Auguste Rodin's sculpture (1898) honors the great French novelist and playwright, Balzac. It took the sculptor seven years to research the writer, who had died almost 50 years earlier.

③ **The Mummy of Hor** Encased in a cartonnage, this 2,700-year-old mummy was long believed to be that of a woman, until a CT scan in 2009 determined that Hor was in fact a man.

④ *The Dinner Party* Judy Chicago's symbolic installation (1974–9) features a gigantic triangular table with personalized settings for 39 influential women, from both history and myth.

⑤ **Decorative Arts Galleries** Twenty-three American period rooms, from the 17th to the 20th century, interspersed with galleries displaying American and European decorative arts.

Entrance

Letting off steam

Kids can run up and down the stairs outside the museum and across its spacious front yard. In summer, the dancing fountain here provides endless entertainment and a welcome chance to cool off.

Visitors admire the dancing fountains outside the Brooklyn Museum

Prices given are for a family of four

Eat and drink

Picnic: under $20; Snacks: $20–35; Real meal: $35–70; Family treat: over $70 (based on a family of four)

PICNIC BKLYN Larder *(228 Flatbush Ave, between Bergen St & Sixth Ave, 11217)* stocks fresh bread, cheeses, and charcuterie, which can be eaten in Prospect Park.

SNACKS Counter Café *(1st floor, Brooklyn Museum; 11am–5pm Wed–Sun)* offers a good selection of soups, salads, sandwiches, and desserts.

REAL MEAL Tom's Restaurant *(782 Washington Ave, 11238; 718 636 9738; 6am–4pm daily)* is an old-school diner that serves eggs, pancakes, and waffles for breakfast,

BKLYN Larder on Park Slope, a popular store for handcrafted cheeses

and sandwiches, burgers, and salads for lunch. Soda drinks and ice creams are also available.

FAMILY TREAT Flatbush Farm *(76 St Marks Ave, 11217; 718 622 3276; www.flatbushfarm.com)* uses

The Lowdown

🌐 **Map reference** 19 C5
Address 200 Eastern Parkway, 11238; 718 638 5000; www.brooklynmuseum.org

🚗 **Subway** 2 & 3 to Eastern Parkway-Brooklyn Museum. **Bus** B41, B48 & B69

🕐 **Open** 11am–6pm Wed, Sat & Sun, 11am–10pm Thu, 11am–11pm first Sat of the month

💲 **Price** $40–50; under 12s free

🚩 **Guided tours** Free tours frequently available; check the museum's website for schedule; Ask app also available.

👫 **Age range** All ages

⏱ **Allow** 2 hours

♿ **Wheelchair access** Yes

☕ **Café** The Museum Café is on the first floor.

🛍 **Shop** Brooklyn Museum Shop, on the first floor, sells jewelry, stationery, toys, and books.

🚻 **Restrooms** On the first and third floors

Good Family value?
The museum has an eclectic mix of artworks, outdoor space, and on-site eating facilities. It is a perfect day out for families.

⑥ **Nicholas Schenck House**
The cedar-shingled farmhouse is a remarkable vestige of American history. It was built by Dutch farmer Nicholas Schenck in the late 1770s.

⑦ ***The Peaceable Kingdom***
Painted by Edward Hicks, who started out as a sign painter, this mystical work from 1833–4 explores a passage from the Bible's Book of Isaiah.

⑧ **Spacelander Bicycle** The prototype of this extraordinary bicycle was designed in 1946 by Benjamin B. Bowden, an English-born American. It could store energy created by downhill motion and use it later to power uphill riding.

fresh, locally sourced ingredients to create dishes such as mushroom and duck confit and pork chop.

Next stop...
GRAND ARMY PLAZA Take the subway (line 2 or 3) to Grand Army Plaza, where a buzzing shopping scene awaits.

Actor Robert Redford in a scene from the film The Hot Rock

Find out more
DIGITAL Go to *www.brooklyn museum.org* to check out the excellent archive of pieces from the museum's vast collection. An interview about the Mummy Chamber, along with videos that are part of the exhibit, can be found at *www.archaeology.org/online/ interviews/edward_bleiberg*.
FILM In *The Hot Rock* (1972), Robert Redford plays a master thief who plans to steal a rare diamond from the museum's collection.

Life, Death & Transformation in the Americas
Themes of regeneration and spiritual transformation are explored through pre-Columbian and historical Native American artworks. On display is the Kwakwaka'wakw *Thunderbird Transformation Mask*, a carved wood mask of an ancestral being that opens to reveal a second, human face.

② Prospect Park Zoo
Small animal kingdom

A treat for children, the 11-acre (5-ha) Prospect Park Zoo abounds with little animals such as wallabies, pygmy goats, and porcupines. Run by the Wildlife Conservation Society, the zoo was revamped in the 1980s and dedicated to educating kids. There is lots to keep them busy, from feeding friendly barnyard animals to petting the cute alpacas and giggling at the antics of playful river otters and baboons.

Indian peacock with long tail feathers, Discovery Trail

Star Attractions

① Sea Lion Court California sea lions regale audiences no matter what time it is, but feeding time is not to be missed for the polished moves of these agile swimmers.

Entrance

Entrance (seasonal)

③ ② ① ④ ⑤ ⑥ ⑦

② Animals in Art This is one of the zoo's best-loved sections, home to scops-owls and meerkats. Kids can draw them and create animal-themed crafts.

③ Barn & Garden The semi-enclosed barn is home to alpacas, pygmy goats, a friendly short-horned dairy cow, and geese. Feeding and petting are encouraged.

④ Pallas's cats These mysterious, fluffy creatures live in mountainous and desert regions, from Tibet to Siberia.

⑤ Hamadryas baboons Watch baboons frolic in a natural outdoor enclosure. Births are frequent, so look out for tiny simians.

The Lowdown

🌐 **Map reference** 19 D5
Address 450 Flatbush Ave, near Empire Blvd, 11225; www.prospectparkzoo.com

🚗 **Subway** B, Q & S to Prospect Park. **Bus** B41

🕐 **Open** Apr–Oct: 10am–5pm Mon–Fri, 10am–5:30pm Sat, Sun & holidays; Nov–Mar: 10am–4:30pm daily

💲 **Price** $26–32; under 3s free

🚩 **Guided tours** Zoo Highlight Tours on weekdays

👫 **Age range** All ages

🏃 **Activities** Animal Encounters, on weekends at 12.30pm, 1pm,

2.30pm & 3pm teach kids about selected animals and how to care for them. Feed a sea lion at 11:30am, 2pm or 4pm.

⏱ **Allow** 2–3 hours

♿ **Wheelchair access** Yes

☕ **Café** No, but there are vending machines on site

👫 **Restrooms** At the north end of the zoo behind the Sea Lion Court

Good family value?
The nature trail, barnyard exhibit, sea lion exhibit, and interactive sessions with zookeepers make this an ideal family outing.

⑥ Discovery Trail Visit an interactive prairie dog habitat, a marshland with bullfrogs and turtles, and a grassy expanse for dingoes.

⑦ North American river otters Delight in the riveting antics of the playful river otters. They are known to use a dozen or more calls to communicate.

Prices given are for a family of four

Children enjoying the sandpit, Lincoln Road Playground

Letting off steam

The large **Lincoln Road Playground** inside Prospect Park, at the Lincoln Road/Ocean Avenue entrance, has swings of varying sizes, jungle gyms, monkey bars, and a tire swing. Bonuses include chess and checkers tables, and bronze frogs that spout water in the warmer months.

Eat and drink

Picnic: under $20; Snacks: $20–35; Real meal: $35–70; Family treat: over $70 (based on a family of four)

PICNIC Bark (474 Bergen St, 11217; 718 789 1939; www. barkhotdogs.com) sells hotdogs, burgers, fries, and a variety of sandwiches made from local and organic ingredients. Enjoy lunch at the zoo's picnic area.
REAL MEAL Carlton Park (636 Carlton Park Ave, 11238; 347 915 2222) has an Asian-inspired, eco-modern design, with wood-paneled walls and tables, and a sleek modern bar. It offers a limited, but excellent, menu of modern American cuisine.
FAMILY TREAT James (605 Carlton Ave, 11238; 718 942 4255; www.jamesrestaurantny. com) is a cozy eatery that focuses on dishes made with locally sourced, seasonal ingredients, such as beef burgers with Vermont cheddar, and lavender crème brûlée.

Find out more

DIGITAL Check out www. prospectparkzoo.com for details of current exhibits, latest zoo births, and

kid-oriented sessions with animals and their trainers. Its slide shows, podcasts, and videos introduce the zoo's residents. A detailed map of the zoo can also be downloaded from the website.

Take cover

The zoo has many indoor exhibits, making this a perfect refuge if the weather turns wet. A 10-minute walk from the zoo, **Brooklyn Museum** (see pp202–203) is also a fine place to spend a rainy day.

Next stop...

WATERFALL TRAIL A 5-minute walk from the zoo is the Waterfall Trail, beginning at the Audubon Center (see p209), where visitors can trace the source of Prospect Park Lake. Fallkill Falls is the first of six waterfalls along the footpath.

Cascade on the Waterfall Trail, Prospect Park

Memorial Arch at the Grand Army Plaza

③ Grand Army Plaza

A splendid arch and a horse-drawn chariot

A National Historic Landmark, this oval plaza was designed by the creators of Prospect Park, Olmstead and Vaux, in 1867. It is best known for its Soldiers and Sailors Arch, built in 1892 to commemorate the Union Army's victory over the Confederate South in the American Civil War (1861–5). This striking, intricately carved arch, probably modeled after Paris's Arc de Triomphe, is topped by the *Quadriga*, a bronze sculpture of Columbia, a female personification of the US, in a horse-drawn chariot.

Today, the plaza is the location for the city's second-largest outdoor farmers' market, and also the place where residents of Brooklyn welcome each New Year with fireworks.

Take cover

Head to the **Central Library** *(10 Grand Army Plaza, 11238; 718 230 2100)*, a massive building designed in the shape of an open book. Study the inlaid gold figures at the entrance, then check out the vast collection of children's books in many languages and the slew of "kids only" computers.

④ Brooklyn Botanic Garden

Magical garden and mini-trees

Completed in 1910, this urban oasis is full of fascinating botanical collections and gardens of all sizes. Its original mission, to teach city kids about the natural world so often absent from their lives, continues today in the Children's Garden, where they can plant and harvest flowers, herbs, and vegetables.

Another highlight is the beloved Japanese Hill-and-Pond Garden, built by landscape architect Takeo Shiota in 1915. An artificially contoured hill hugs the garden's lovely pond, which is adorned by a small island and full of ducks and turtles, with blue herons and snowy egrets stopping by. A wooden footpath reveals several natural set-pieces: sudden views of stone lanterns, a waterfall, a Shinto shrine, wooden bridges and, most dramatically, the orange Torii

The Lowdown

🌐 **Map reference** 19 C5
Address 150 Eastern Parkway, 990 Washington Ave, 11225; 718 623 7200; www.bbg.org
🚇 **Subway** B, Q & S to Prospect Park; 2, 3 & 4 to Eastern Parkway-Brooklyn Museum; S to Botanic Garden. **Bus** B16, B41, B43 & B45
🕐 **Open** Mar–Oct: 8am–6pm Tue–Fri, 10am–6pm Sat & Sun; Nov–Feb: 8am–4:30pm Tue–Fri, 10am–4:30pm Sat & Sun; closed Mon & some major holidays
💲 **Price** $24–36; under 12s free
🚩 **Guided tours** Free guided tours Sat & Sun; check website for seasonal Highlights Tour.
👫 **Age range** All ages
🤾 **Activities** Check www.bbg.org/ learn/children for children's and family programs.
⏱ **Allow** 1–2 hours
🍽 **Eat and drink** *Snacks* Terrace Café *(on site)* serves sandwiches, salads, and baked goods. *Real meal* Bareburger *(170 Seventh Ave, 11215; 718 768 2273; www.bareburger.com)* offers local, grass-fed beef burgers and sumptuous milkshakes made from organic, hormone-free milk, as well as salads and wraps.
👫 **Restrooms** In the Conservatory

The Lowdown

🌐 **Map reference** 19 C5
Address Intersection of Flatbush Ave, Eastern Parkway, and Prospect Park West
🚇 **Subway** 2, 3 & 4 to Grand Army Plaza; B & Q to Seventh Ave. **Bus** B41, B69 & B71
👫 **Age range** All ages
🤾 **Activities** GreenMarket, Grand Army Plaza; 8am–4pm Sat
⏱ **Allow** 30 minutes
🍽 **Eat and drink** *Snacks* Dizzy's Diner *(511 9th St, 11215; 718 499 1966; www.dizzys.com)* offers a classic diner menu. *Real meal* Cheryl's Global Soul *(236 Underhill Ave, 11238; 347 529 2855; www.cherylsglobalsoul.com)* serves dishes using locally sourced and seasonal ingredients.
👫 **Restrooms** No

The striking Torii gateway in Brooklyn Botanic Garden

gateway. Kanzan cherry trees can be seen in bloom in late April, when the Sakura Matsuri Festival is celebrated here. The Shakespeare Garden is planted with more than 80 botanical species mentioned in the Bard's sonnets and plays. The Steinhardt Conservatory showcases three environmental climates: desert, subtropical, and warm temperate, while the Bonsai Museum has more than 350 miniature trees.

Take cover

On the lower level of the **Steinhardt Conservatory**, itself a perfect refuge when it rains, is a gallery with regular rotating exhibits of botanical art, including two-dimensional, three-dimensional, and multimedia works.

⑤ Brooklyn Children's Museum

Interactive treasure trove

Founded in 1899, the Brooklyn Children's Museum was the first to be designed expressly for kids. A massive renovation in 2010 doubled its exhibition space and created a new area called Collections Central, which displays a changing selection of its 30,000-object collection. Here, little minds will be fascinated by cultural artifacts – masks, dolls, sculptures, and household items such as kitchen utensils – and natural history specimens, including stuffed animals, fossils, and minerals.

Interactive stations invite kids to explore the objects through drawing, puzzle-solving, games, and role-play – an approach that is also

Visitors at the colorful Kids Café, Brooklyn Children's Museum

adopted by the museum's excellent website. The museum's principal exhibit, Neighborhood Nature, re-creates a beach, urban woodlands, a freshwater pond, and a community garden. Here, kids can hone their field science skills with cameras and special listening devices, and touch animals such as horseshoe crabs and starfish at hands-on stations. World Brooklyn is a kid-sized cityscape where children are introduced to the borough's cultural diversity by visiting various shops, such as the Mexican Bakery and the West African Import Store, each with activities exploring the cultural background it represents.

Letting off steam

Get some fresh air at the outdoor garden and greenhouse near the Neighborhood Nature exhibit, which is filled with common and exotic plants, insects, and animals.

The Lowdown

🌐 **Map reference** 19 D4
Address 145 Brooklyn Ave, 11213; 718 735 4400; www.brooklynkids.org

🚗 **Subway** A & C to Nostrand Ave; A & C to Kingston Ave-Throop Ave; 2, 3, 4 & 5 to Kingston Ave.
Bus B43, B45 & B65

🕐 **Open** 10am–5pm Tue–Sun

💲 **Price** $36

👫 **Age range** All ages

🧗 **Activities** Interactive displays can be found throughout the museum.

⏱ **Allow** 1–2 hours

♿ **Wheelchair access** Yes

🍽 **Eat and drink** Snacks Breukelen Coffee House (764a Franklin Ave, 11238) offers bagels and pastries along with a wide variety of options for coffee. Real meal Applebees (1360 Fulton St in Restoration Plaza, 11216) has a kids' menu and lunch and dinner options including fish and chips, burgers, and wraps.

🚻 **Restrooms** On the first and second floors

KIDS' CORNER

Look out for...

1 The arch at Grand Army Plaza is modeled on another famous arch. Do you know which one and where is it?

2 The Union of the North and the Confederates of the South fought against each other in the American Civil War. Which army does Grand Army Plaza honor?

3 Which animals can often be seen in the Japanese Hill-and-Pond Garden?

4 In which museum can you find a beach?

Answers at the bottom of the page.

A PEEK INTO JAPAN

Staged in late April, the Sakura Matsuri Festival at the Botanic Garden is not only a great place to look at cherry blossoms, but also to check out what Japanese kids are wearing and their favorite games.

Out of the ordinary

The architect of the Japanese Hill-and-Pond Garden came to America in 1907 with the ambition to create, in his own words, "a garden more beautiful than all others in the world." The result was the first public Japanese garden in the US.

Answers: 1 The Arc de Triomphe in Paris. **2** The Union of the North. **3** Ducks, turtles, egrets, and herons. **4** Brooklyn Children's Museum.

Riding on the carousel in Prospect Park

⑥ Prospect Park

Rolling meadows and twirling horses

This enormous green oasis in the middle of Brooklyn is home to a man-made lake, a forest, a zoo, and the country's first urban-based Audubon Center, a branch of the Audubon Wildlife Conservation Society. It offers visitors a diverse pastoral landscape: the open fields of Long Meadow, the wooded hiking trails of the Ravine, waterfalls, and two bodies of water – the Lullwater and Prospect Park

The Lowdown

🌐 **Map reference** 19 C5
   Address Between Prospect Park West & Flatbush Ave and Eastern Parkway & Parkside Ave, 11215; www.prospectpark.org
🚇 **Subway** B, Q & S to Prospect Park. **Bus** B41, B68 & B71
🕐 **Open** 5am–1am daily; playgrounds and woodlands close at sunset; attractions' hours vary
💲 **Price** Free for park; $2 per ride, $9 for 5 tickets
👫 **Age range** 2 plus for carousel; small children should ride with an adult.
⏱ **Allow** 1 hour
♿ **Wheelchair access** Yes
🍴 **Eat and drink** *Picnic* Pony Express Snack Bar *(in front of the carousel)* sells popcorn, ice cream, and other treats (Apr–Nov). *Real meal* Gino's Trattoria & Brick Oven Pizza (548 Flatbush Ave, 11225; 718 287 1277) serves pizzas, pasta, and delicious tiramisu.
👪 **Restrooms** At several locations throughout the park

Lake – which can be explored from the shore or by pedal boat.

The park is also home to a vintage carousel, located on its eastern edge, right outside the Prospect Park Zoo *(see pp204–205)*. The horses and other animals that twirl on it were carved in 1912 by Russian immigrant Charles Carmel, considered one of the city's master carousel makers. Its Wurlitzer organ is notable for its loud, cheerful tunes. The carousel was renovated in 1990 and as many as 20 layers of paint were removed to reveal the bright original colors.

Take cover

The **Steinhardt Conservatory** in Brooklyn Botanic Garden *(see pp206–207)* is a perfect refuge when it rains. Look out for the regular botanic-themed exhibits – two-dimensional, three-dimensional and multimedia.

⑦ Lefferts Historic House

A blast from the part

This late-18th-century wooden house was built by Pieter Lefferts. In 1917, his descendant, John Lefferts, offered the house to the city so that it could be preserved. Today, this museum serves as a kind of colonial time capsule. Exhibits showcase the history of Brooklyn through the eyes of its many inhabitants over the past

The Lowdown

🌐 **Map reference** 19 D5
   Address Children's Corner, near the Park's Willink Entrance; 718 789 2822; www.prospectpark.org/visit-the-park/places-to-go/lefferts-historic-house
🚇 **Subway** B, Q & S to Prospect Park. **Bus** B41 & B48
🕐 **Open** Check website for hours.
💲 **Price** $3 suggested donation
🚩 **Guided tours** About once a month; $10 suggested donation
👫 **Age range** 4 plus
🧑‍🌾 **Activities** Craft and farming activities on weekends
⏱ **Allow** 1 hour
♿ **Wheelchair access** Yes
🍴 **Eat and drink** *Snacks* Scoops Ice Cream Parlor (624 Flatbush Ave, 11225; 718 282 5904) serves vegan Caribbean dishes along with vegan ice cream. *Real meal* King of Tandoor (600 Flatbush Ave, 11225; 347 533 6811) has excellent Indian fare and very friendly staff.
👪 **Restrooms** At the Lincoln Road Playground

500 years: native Americans; the Dutch, who settled the area in the 17th century; and African Americans, many of whom were owned as slaves.

Undertake farming activities in the working garden, play with traditional toys and games, and participate in activities such as candle-making, sewing, and butter-churning. Seasonal planting and harvesting activities and festivals are held throughout the year. Check the website for details of upcoming events.

Children playing in the grounds at Lefferts Historic House

Playing with toys and donning cloth wings at the Audubon Center

Letting off steam

Located near the center of Prospect Park, the **Nethermead** is a remote clearing surrounded on all sides by hills, water, and forest. It is a perfect place to have a picnic, run around, and perhaps kick a soccer ball or throw a Frisbee.

⑧ Audubon Center

Exotic birds and giant snails

Nearly destroyed by the city in 1964, today the elegant, low-slung Boathouse is Prospect Park's architectural gem. It was modeled after the 16th-century St. Mark's Library in Venice, Italy. In 1992, the beautifully restored building welcomed a new resident: the first urban branch of the famous Audubon Society, a wildlife education and preservation group. Its aim is to get city kids excited about nature.

On the first floor, children can get cozy in a human-sized bird's nest and use a magnifying contraption to study insects and plants. Upstairs, in the Discover Nature theater, rangers introduce kids to the center's resident animals, such as snakes, via live demonstrations. In another corner, kids can don cloth wings and become giant bats or swans. Occasionally rangers even let kids "fish" for giant freshwater snails in the Lullwater – the snails are thrown back in, of course.

Audubon's best offering, however, is its series of summer bird-watching tours on the Lullwater and Prospect Park Lake by electric boat. The boat's motor is quiet, so it does not disturb the migratory birds – green

and blue herons, snowy egrets, and 18 duck species – that live on the lake's islands, which are otherwise inaccessible to people.

Letting off steam

Imagination Playground (170 Ocean Ave, Brooklyn, 11225) lacks swings, seesaws, or jungle gyms, but that is the point. A multi-tiered stage for acting out stories, niches for reading books or storytelling sessions, and animal face cutouts all encourage children to let their imaginations run wild.

The Lowdown

- 🌐 **Map reference** 19 D5
  Address Located just inside the Lincoln Rd/Ocean Ave entrance to the Park; 718 287 3400; www.prospectpark.org/visit-the-park/places-to-go/audubon-center
- 🚇 **Subway** B, Q & S to Prospect Park. **Bus** B41 & B43
- 🕐 **Open** Check the Prospect Park website for current hours
- 💲 **Price** Free
- 🚻 **Age range** All ages
- 🏃 **Activities** Bird-watching tours; Lakeside Nature Stroll; Nature's Helpers; and Junior Naturalists. Discovery Pack kits with family-friendly activities
- ⏲ **Allow** 1–2 hours
- ♿ **Wheelchair access** Yes
- 🍴 **Eat and drink** Snacks Bluestone Lakeside Café (on site) serves light bites as well as more hearty fare. Real meal Sushi Tatsu III (644 Flatbush Ave, 11225; 718 282 8890) offers sushi and other traditional Japanese fare, including bento-box lunches.
- 🚹🚺 **Restrooms** On the ground floor

Look out for...
1 All kinds of animals, not only horses, can be found on the Prospect Park Carousel. Can you spot the mythical ones? What are they?
2 The Audubon Center has an electric boat for bird-watching. Can you guess why this boat was chosen over other kinds?
3 Which Italian city has a structure similar to the Audubon Center Boathouse?

Answers at the bottom of the page.

Once upon a time
When Prospect Park was built, Brooklyn was the second-largest city in the US; the largest was New York City, also known as Manhattan.

BIRDING BONANZA

Prospect Park Lake is an important feeding ground for thousands of migratory birds along the Eastern Seaboard. Many of these nest on islands very close to the city.

Answers: 1 The dragons. **2** Because electric boats are the quietest and will not scare away the birds. **3** Venice.

New York Aquarium, Coney Island, and around

From New York Aquarium's fascinating marine exhibits to the carnival atmosphere of the seaside boardwalk, Coney Island is a virtual children's playground. However, the crowds can get heavy on weekends. Summer is the best time to visit, as most attractions, including Luna Park, the Wonder Wheel, and, of course, Coney Island Beach, are outdoors – although the aquarium is worth the trip alone, even in winter.

Brooklyn Museum
p200

Brooklyn

New York
Aquarium

Walrus feeding time at the Sea Cliffs habitat, New York Aquarium

0 meters — 400
0 yards — 400

Bay 50 S

Gravesend
Bay

BAY 30TH STREET
WEST 16TH STREET
BAY 34TH ST
BAY 53RD ST
CROPSEY AVENUE
HART

BAY VIEW AVENUE
WEST 33RD STREET
NEPTUNE AVENUE
WEST 28TH STREET
WEST 23RD STREET
WEST 22ND STREET
WEST 21ST STREET
WEST 20TH STREET
WEST 19TH STREET
WEST 17TH STREET

NEPTUNE AVENUE
WEST 37TH STREET
WEST 36TH STREET
WEST 35TH STREET
WEST 33RD STREET
WEST 32ND STREET
WEST 31ST STREET

MERMAID AVENUE
WEST 30TH STREET
WEST 29TH STREET
WEST 28TH STREET
WEST 25TH STREET
WEST 27TH STREET

MCU
Park

Abe Stark Rink

Poseidon
Playground

BOARDWALK

WEST

Coney Island Beach

Places of interest

SIGHTS
1. New York Aquarium
2. Coney Island
3. Brighton Beach

● EAT AND DRINK
1. Coney Island Bagels
2. Kashkar Café
3. Gargiulo's Restaurant
4. Nathan's Famous
5. Totonno's Pizzeria Napolitano
6. Kiev Bakery
7. Café Glechik

● SHOPPING
1. Williams Candy

Visitors building sand castles and relaxing on the beach, Coney Island

Brighton Beach boardwalk lined with shops and restaurants

Café Glechik at Brighton Beach, the city's go-to place for Ukrainian cuisine

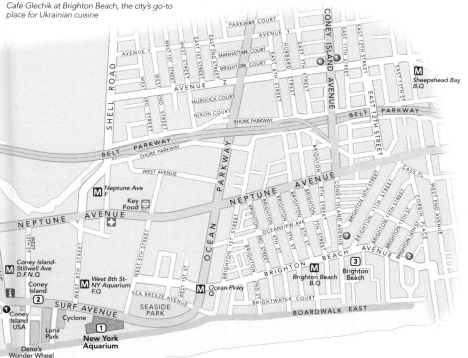

The Lowdown

🚇 **Subway** F & Q to West 8th St-NY Aquarium; D, F, N & Q to Coney Island-Stillwell Ave.
Bus B36, B68, B74, B82, X28 & X38

ℹ️ **Visitor information** Coney Island cultural center: Coney Island USA, 1208 Surf Ave, Brooklyn, 11224; www.coneyisland.com

🍴 **Supermarket** Key Food, 505 Neptune Ave, Brooklyn, 11224; 718 714 6049; www.keyfood.com
Market Coney Island Farmers' Market, Surf Ave and West 16th St at MCU Park, Brooklyn, 11224; Jul–Nov: Sun

🎭 **Festivals** Mermaid Parade (mid- to late Jun). Nathan's Famous Hot Dog Eating Contest (Jul 4)

➕ **Pharmacies** CVS/pharmacy, 512 Neptune Ave, Brooklyn, 11224; 718 996 2233; 8am–9pm Mon–Sat, 9am–6pm Sun

🛝 **Nearest playground** Poseidon Playground, Surf Ave, between West 25th St & West 27th St, Brooklyn, 11224

① New York Aquarium
Come see the sea

Located on Coney Island *(see pp214–15)*, the New York Aquarium opened in 1896, making it the oldest continuously operating aquarium in the US. Here, walruses practice water ballet, penguins torpedo through the water, and glowing jellyfish float like aliens in outer space. The aquarium is currently undergoing a major transformation and some areas are closed, but there are still many wonders of the sea to enjoy.

Entrance to the New York Aquarium, Coney Island

Star Attractions

① **Glover's Reef** This exhibit is home to stingray, which stay near the tank's surface, schools of exotic fish, and moray eels lurking among the coral fronds at the bottom.

② **Sea lion show** Four sea lions regale visitors to the open-air Aquatheater with tricks such as flipperstands and dancing to music.

③ **Explore the Shore** Kids and adults alike can stroke sea stars and horseshoe crabs in the touch pool (outdoors in summer and indoors in winter) and feel the thrill of a crashing tidal wave at this exhibit.

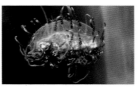

④ **Alien Stingers** A quiet, darkened building houses an array of tanks filled with elegant jellyfish, sea nettles, and other *cnidarians* (a group of stinging invertebrates) that catch the light in such a way that they seem to glow.

⑤ **Sharks and turtles** Sand tiger sharks, nurse sharks, and reef sharks – which, like bloodhounds, can detect the presence of minute quantities of blood – live side by side in a deep-ocean tank with stingrays and endangered loggerhead sea turtles.

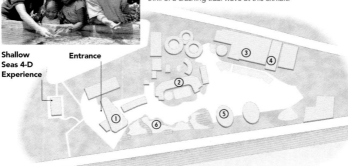

Shallow Seas 4-D Experience

Entrance

⑥ **Sea Cliffs** The three Pacific Northwest exhibits showcase sea otters, walruses, and black-footed penguins. These agile swimmers can be viewed from different vantage points.

The Lowdown

🌐 **Address** 602 Surf Ave, Brooklyn, 11224; 718 265 3474; www.nyaquarium.com

🚇 **Subway** F & Q to West 8th St-NY Aquarium; D, F, N & Q to Coney Island-Stillwell Ave. **Bus** B36 & B68

🕐 **Open** Daily; hours vary by season

💲 **Price** $48; under 3s free

👪 **Cutting the line** Check website for schedules or purchase online tickets in advance.

🚩 **Guided tours** Yes

👫 **Age range** All ages

🤸 **Activities** Watch an octopus solve puzzles at the daily Octopus Chats. Kids can feed penguins, sea otters, and sharks. Check the website for information about free and fee-based programs and family workshops.

⏱ **Allow** 2 hours

♿ **Wheelchair access** Yes

☕ **Café** Seaside Café, near the Alien Stingers exhibit

🛍 **Shops** The aquarium has two gift shops: one by the entrance and the other near the Explore the Shore exhibit.

🚻 **Restrooms** At Explore the Shore and Conservation Hall

Good family value?
More than 12,000 fish and marine mammals, indoor and outdoor exhibits, and interactive learning make the aquarium ideal for families.

Visitors at the entrance of Central Park Zoo

Take cover

Families can head indoors to kick back and enjoy an aquatic-themed "4-D" movie, like *Happy Feet* or *Spongebob Squarepants: The Great Jelly Rescue.*

Opposite the Glover's Reef tank in the Conservation Hall is a series of enclosures where endangered amphibians make their home. Look out for the striking, nocturnal Malagasy tomato frog, which inflates to resemble a tomato when threatened, and the Oriental fire-bellied toad.

Eat and drink

Picnic: under $20; Snacks: $20–35; Real meal: $35–70; Family treat: over $70 (based on a family of four)

PICNIC Coney Island Bagels *(2829 Coney Island Ave, 11235; 718 332 1906; www.coneyislandbagels.com)* is a great stop for breakfast or lunch. Pick up sandwich bagels, wraps, or a salad and head to the outdoor tables at the aquarium.
REAL MEAL Kashkar Café *(1141 Brighton Beach Ave, 11235, 718 743 3832)* serves delicious Uzbek and Uygur fare, such as kebabs, salads, soups and hot appetizers.
FAMILY TREAT Gargiulo's **Restaurant** *(2911 West 15th St, 11224; 718 266 4891; www.gargiulos.com)* offers classic Neapolitan fare. The seafood dishes are especially popular. Try the baked clams and calamari. The restaurant has a strict dress code so be sure to avoid wearing shorts or sandals.

Shopping

Worth a stop for its extraordinary candy treats, **Williams Candy** *(1318 Surf Ave, 11224; 718 372 0302; www.candytreats.com)* specializes

in old-fashioned candy such as candy apples, popcorn, cotton candy, and salt water taffy.

Find out more

DIGITAL The aquarium's website has exhibit and animal directories with photos, videos, and fun facts. The World Conservation Society, which runs the aquarium, has a research station on Glover's Reef, which lies off the coast of Belize in Central America: *www.wcsglovers reef.org.* Kids can also play the Wii video games Endless Ocean: Blue World and Endless Ocean 2.
FILM Young fish fans will enjoy the following movies: *Popular Mechanics for Kids: Super Sea Creatures and Awesome Ocean Adventures* (2004) and *Finding Nemo* (2003).

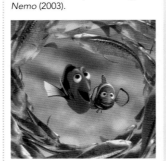

A still from Finding Nemo, *the popular Pixar movie about a cute clownfish*

Next stop...

CENTRAL PARK ZOO For a more urban take on marine animals, head to Central Park Zoo *(see pp128–9)*, where many cousins of the aquarium-dwelling species can be found, including gentoo, king penguins, and another community of California sea lions.

Above The Air Race ride, Luna Park, Coney Island
Below right Nathan's Famous hot-dog stand, Coney Island

② Coney Island

Circus tricks and thrilling rides

At the edge of the Atlantic Ocean, the spit of land known as Coney Island is one of the city's most iconic locales. The beachside resort rose to prominence in the early 20th century and was often called the poor man's Atlantic City. Coney Island is famous for its wide boardwalk peppered with marine mosaics, gaming arcades, concession stands hawking souvenirs and prizes, amusement park rides, and freaky sideshows.

Those looking for a thrill can head to the 150-ft (46-m) high **Deno's Wonder Wheel**, which was built in 1918, and the 1927 **Cyclone**, one of the country's oldest working wooden roller coasters (kids must be at least 54 inches, or 137 cm, tall to ride). For more amusement-park fun, visit **Luna Park**, which opened with much fanfare in 2010. It offers a huge range of rides, from tame

kiddie fare, such as the Happy Swing and the Mermaid Parade, to mega-thrills such as the Tickler, a twister coaster/teacup combo, and the Brooklyn Flyer, a nearly 100-ft (30-m) tall, high-speed ride. Most rides strike a balance between the extremes, making them perfect for all ages, but be prepared to wait in more than one long line.

For a taste of Coney Island's quirky past, visit Coney Island Circus Sideshow, housed in a 1917 building, and run by **Coney Island, USA**. On the second floor is the tiny Coney Island Museum, dedicated to the history and culture of the neighborhood (*see Take cover*).

Baseball fans should not miss an afternoon in Coney Island's **MCU Park**, home to the Brooklyn Cyclones, a minor-league team brought to the city in 2000 and affiliated with the New York Mets. Quality game play, affordable seats (from $10) with unobstructed views, and manageable crowds make it a great alternative to a day with the Yankees or the Mets.

Children on the Cyclone rollercoaster at Luna Park, Coney Island

Prices given are for a family of four

Among Coney Island's best-loved seasonal events are Nathan's Famous Hot Dog Eating Contest, held each July 4 at the 1916-built fast-food mecca; and the ocean-themed Mermaid Parade in June that heralds the start of the summer season. To the delight of adults and kids alike, fireworks light up the sky every Friday evening in summer.

Take cover

Indoor offerings being scarce here, head to the centrally located **Coney Island USA** (*1208 Surf Ave, 11224; 718 372 5159*) and visit its Circus Sideshow and Museum. The circus enthralls with such acts as sword-swallowing, fire-eating, snake-charming, magic, and more. In the small museum there are rotating exhibits on the history of Coney Island, plus a permanent collection

The Lowdown

🌐 **Address** Luna Park, 1000 Surf Ave, Brooklyn, 11224; 718 373 5862; www.lunaparknyc.com. Coney Island Circus Sideshow & Coney Island Museum, 1208 Surf Ave, Brooklyn, 11224; 718 372 5159; www.coneyisland.com

🚌 **Subway** F & Q to West 8th St-NY Aquarium; D, F, N & Q to Coney Island-Stillwell Ave. **Bus** B36, B68, X28 & X38

🕐 **Open** Luna Park: times vary, check website for opening and closing timings; Coney Island Circus Sideshow & Coney Island Museum: times vary, check website for opening and closing timings

💲 **Price** Luna Park: free entry; check website for price details and deals for rides; Coney Island Circus Sideshow: $30–40, under 12s $5; Coney Island Museum: $16–20; under 12s $3

🎫 **Guided tours** Two-hour walking tour of Coney Island; call 347 677 3962 to arrange; $25 per person

👫 **Age range** All ages

🎢 **Activities** Amusement park rides, arcade games, and swimming

🕐 **Allow** 4–5 hours

🍴 **Eat and drink** *Snacks* Nathan's Famous (*1310 Surf Ave, 11224; 718 946 2202*) offers delicious hot dogs year-round. *Real meal* Totonno's Pizzeria Napolitano (*1524 Neptune Ave, 11224*) serves coal-oven pizzas.

🚻 **Restrooms** At the beach and in Coney Island Museum

Books for sale at St. Petersburg Bookstore, Brighton Beach

of memorabilia that includes parts of old amusement rides. This great little hub of activity is sure to keep the gang amused and dry.

③ Brighton Beach
Eastern Europe in New York

Coney Island Beach's next-door neighbor, Brighton Beach, is a multiethnic enclave nicknamed Little Odessa, after the Ukrainian city from which many immigrants came in the 1970s. Several waves of Eastern European immigrants have made this area their home, from Jewish people fleeing the Holocaust to a whole generation of post-USSR arrivals in the 1990s. Explore the boardwalk, where it is possible to relax at a café and enjoy Eastern European treats such as *pierogi* (stuffed dumplings, boiled or fried) and *blintzes* (pancakes). Another

good strip to explore is Brighton Beach Avenue. This trellis-canopied thoroughfare is home to a fascinating mix of delicacy shops, restaurants, and stores. For a taste of what the neighborhood was like in the mid-1930s, watch *Brighton Beach Memoirs* (1986).

Take cover

Head to **St. Petersburg Bookstore** *(230 Brighton Beach Ave, 11235; 718 891 6778)*, which bills itself as the largest Russian bookstore outside Russia. The shop caters, of course, to Brighton Beach's huge immigrant community, with rows of Russian books, CDs, and DVDs. Kids will get a kick out of toys such as nesting dolls and decorative eggs. There are Russian crafts, too.

The Lowdown

🌐 **Address** Between Ocean Parkway & Corbin Place, 11235

🚇 **Subway** B & Q to Brighton Beach; Q to Ocean Parkway.
Bus B1, B36 & B68

👫 **Age range** All ages

🤸 **Activities** Building sand castles and swimming

⏱ **Allow** 2 hours

🍴 **Eat and drink** *Picnic* Kiev Bakery *(2666 Coney Island Ave, 11223; 718 648 1905)* offers Eastern European cakes, pastries, and bread. *Real meal* Café Glechik *(3159 Coney Island Ave, 11235; 718 616 0494; www.glechik.com)* has Ukrainian dumplings, stews, and kebabs.

🚻 **Restrooms** Along the boardwalk

KIDS' CORNER

Find out more...
1 Along Coney Island Boardwalk there's a mosaic showing marine creatures. Can you find it?
2 Brighton Beach is nicknamed after a place in Ukraine. What is the beach popularly known as?
3 See how long it takes you to comfortably eat one Nathan's Famous hot dog, then figure out how long it would take to eat 62 of them. That is how many Joey Chestnut ate in 10 minutes to win his fifth straight title in 2011.

Answers at the bottom of the page.

Island only in name
Did you know that Coney Island is no longer an island but a peninsula? It used to be separated from the Brooklyn mainland by a creek, but this was filled in for construction before World War II.

CHILLY THRILL
Every New Year's Day, the Coney Island Polar Bear Club invites the public to join its members for a swim in the stone-cold Atlantic Ocean, where the water temperature can be as low as 33°F (1°C).

Holidaymakers unwinding on Brighton Beach

Picnic: under $20; **Snacks:** $20–35; **Real meal:** $35–70; **Family treat:** over $70 (based on a family of four)

Museum of the Moving Image and around

Astoria and Long Island City, the two Queens neighborhoods closest to Manhattan, are in some respects a world away. Their industrial past is evident in their quiet, warehouse-lined streets, but a burgeoning art and restaurant scene and revitalized green spaces are making them a popular destination. The area is somewhat off the beaten path, so it is wise to plan ahead of time and have a map handy. Start with the multifaceted Museum of the Moving Image – in addition to its vast collection of movie artifacts, the museum often screens films for kids on weekends.

The Lowdown

🚗 **Subway** N & Q to 36th Avenue; M & R to Steinway St; N & Q to Broadway **Bus** Q69 & Q102

ℹ️ **Visitor information** Queens Economic Development Corporation's online visitor center, It's In Queens (www.itsinqueens.com)

🍽️ **Supermarket** Bravo Supermarket, 34-12 34th Ave, between 34th St & 35th St, 11106; 718 784 8420
Market Brooklyn Grange Market, 37–18 Northern Blvd at 38th St, 11101; www.brooklyngrangefarm.com/markets; mid-May–Oct; 11am–4pm Sat

➕ **Pharmacy** Rite Aid, 32–87 Steinway St, Astoria, 11103; 718 278 2100; 8am–9pm Mon–Fri, 9am–6pm Sat, 9am–5pm Sun

🌿 **Nearest playgrounds** Thirty-five Playground (see p219). Sean's Place (see p219)

Visitors browsing through items at The Moving Image Store

Children creating animation films at the museum

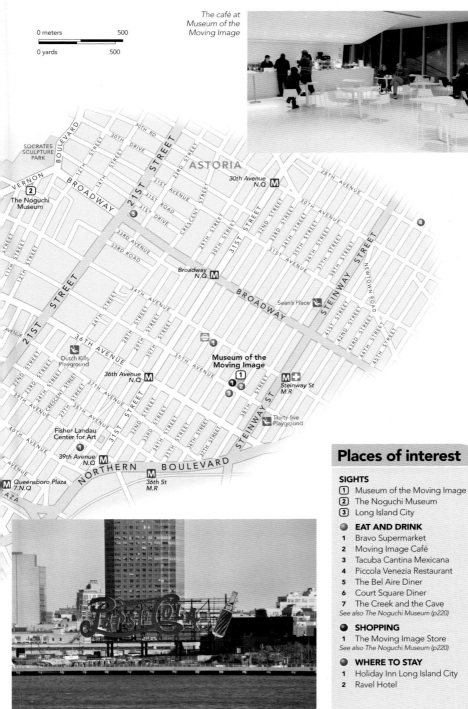

0 meters 500

0 yards 500

The café at Museum of the Moving Image

SOCRATES SCULPTURE PARK

ASTORIA

BOULEVARD

30TH RD

30TH DRIVE

12TH STREET

14TH STREET

31ST STREET

23RD STREET

30th Avenue N.Q

VERNON

BROADWAY

2 The Noguchi Museum

21ST STREET

31ST STREET

31ST ROAD

31ST DRIVE

CRESCENT STREET

31ST AVENUE

29TH STREET

30TH STREET

31ST STREET

32ND STREET

33RD STREET

30TH AVENUE

34TH STREET

35TH STREET

36TH STREET

37TH STREET

38TH STREET

28TH AVENUE

31ST AVENUE

STEINWAY STREET

NEWTOWN ROAD

4

33RD AVENUE

33RD ROAD

Broadway N.Q

BROADWAY

Sean's Place

41ST STREET

42ND STREET

43RD STREET

44TH STREET

45TH STREET

11TH STREET

12TH STREET

21ST STREET

24TH STREET

28TH STREET

29TH STREET

30TH STREET

34TH AVENUE

35TH STREET

35TH AVENUE

36TH AVENUE

Dutch Kills Playground

36TH AVENUE

36th Avenue N.Q

Museum of the Moving Image

1

1
2
3

Steinway St M.R

22ND STREET

23RD STREET

24TH STREET

CRESCENT STREET

27TH STREET

38TH AVENUE

31ST STREET

32ND STREET

33RD STREET

38TH STREET

STEINWAY ST

Thirty-five Playground

39TH AVENUE

40TH AVENUE

Fisher Landau Center for Art

1

39th Avenue N.Q

NORTHERN BOULEVARD

Queensboro Plaza 7.N.Q

PLAZA

36th St M.R

Places of interest

SIGHTS
1 Museum of the Moving Image
2 The Noguchi Museum
3 Long Island City

EAT AND DRINK
1 Bravo Supermarket
2 Moving Image Café
3 Tacuba Cantina Mexicana
4 Piccola Venezia Restaurant
5 The Bel Aire Diner
6 Court Square Diner
7 The Creek and the Cave
See also The Noguchi Museum (p220)

SHOPPING
1 The Moving Image Store
See also The Noguchi Museum (p220)

WHERE TO STAY
1 Holiday Inn Long Island City
2 Ravel Hotel

Long Island City waterfront as seen from Manhattan

① Museum of the Moving Image
Moviemakers and flip-book stations

Tucked away in Astoria, Queens, the glossy, high-tech Museum of the Moving Image is one of the most exciting museums in the city. Located next to a working TV and film studio, the museum celebrates the art of cinema as well as the wonders of video, television, and digital media. Temporary exhibits on the third floor explore the interface between art and technology, while the action-packed permanent exhibit, Behind the Screen, wows with its collection of movie memorabilia. There is also a spaceship-like theater where families can enjoy a movie matinee.

Entrance of the Museum of the Moving Image

Key Features

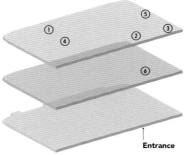

▬ **Third Floor** Rotating exhibits and installations and part of the "Behind the Screen" exhibit

▬ **Second Floor** Part of the "Behind the Screen" permanent exhibit and an amphitheater for video screenings

▬ **First Floor** Lobby, café, museum store, 267-seat movie theater, screening room, and education center

Entrance

① **Optical Toys** Don't miss the Victorian zoetrope, a cylinder with vertical slits, which when spun creates the illusion that the figures painted inside it are moving.

② **Automated Dialogue Replacement Studio** Children can pick a movie clip, then practice and record the dialogues of movie characters such as Dorothy from *The Wizard of Oz* in their own voice.

③ **Sound Effects Display** Here, kids can learn all about sound effects and experiment with prerecorded sounds and a clip from *The Simpsons*, to see their impact on a scene.

Prices given are for a family of four

④ **Flip-book Station** Dance or mime in front of a camera that captures movement as a succession of still photos. Then buy the results as a flip book.

⑤ **Live TV Control Room** Watch a director at work choosing shot after shot from a huge number of cameras to make sense of a baseball game.

⑥ **Merchandising Exhibit** Look at shelf upon shelf of tie-in merchandise, from Star Trek dolls to Batman lunchboxes, to understand how movies are marketed.

The Lowdown

🌐 **Address** 36-01 35th Ave, Astoria, 11106; 718 777 6888; www.movingimage.us

🚗 **Subway** M & R to Steinway St; N & Q to 36th Ave. **Bus** Q101 departs from Second Ave, between 60th St & 61st St

🕐 **Open** 10:30am–5pm Wed & Thu; 10:30am–8pm Fri; 11:30am–7pm Sat & Sun

💲 **Price** $36–46; under 3s free (admission price includes film screening); 4–8pm Fri free (film screenings not included)

🚹 **Cutting the line** No online ticket bookings

🚩 **Guided tours** $48–58, tours of the permanent exhibit; groups of 10 minimum

👫 **Age range** 4 plus

🏃 **Activities** Besides many interactive displays, a drop-in mediamaking studio session (for ages 7 plus) takes place noon–5pm most Sat.

⏱ **Allow** 2 hours without a movie, 3–4 hours with one

♿ **Wheelchair access** Yes

☕ **Café** The Museum Café

🛍 **Shops** The Moving Image Store has a great selection of books, DVDs, T-shirts, and cinema-related toys and gifts. Visitors can also purchase their flip books here (see left).

🚻 **Restrooms** By coat check and in education center

Good family value?
With excellent exhibits, a state-of-the-art theater, and lots of hands-on activities, this museum appeals to both adults and kids.

Letting off steam

Head to the **Sean's Place** playground (*38th St, between Broadway & 31st Ave, 11103*) and let the kids run riot among the sandpits, sprinklers, jungle gym, and swings. Closer to the museum is the tiny **Thirty-five Playground** (*35th Ave, between Steinway St & 41st St, 11101*).

Eat and drink

Picnic: under $20; Snacks: $20–35; Real meal: $35–70; Family treat: over $70 (based on a family of four)

PICNIC Bravo Supermarket (*34-12 34th Ave, between 34th St & 35th St, Astoria, 11106; 718 784 8420; www.bravosupermarkets.com*) sells cheeses, sausages, breads, and fruit – devour them in the Thirty-five Playground.

SNACKS Moving Image Café (*36-01 35th Ave at 37th St, Astoria, 11106; 718 777 6888*), on the museum's first floor, offers small bites such as baked goods, soups, salads, and a selection of sandwiches.

REAL MEAL Tacuba Cantina Mexicana (*35–01 36th St, Astoria, 11106; 718 786 2727; noon–10pm daily; www.tacubanyc.com*), right across the street from the museum, dishes up traditional Latin food with a gourmet flair. Kids will love the tacos and nachos.

FAMILY TREAT Piccola Venezia Restaurant (*4201 28th Ave Astoria, 11103; 718 721 8470; noon–10pm Mon–Fri, 4:30–11pm Sat, 2–9pm Sun; www.piccola-venezia.com*) is an elegant family-run restaurant offering northern Italian cuisine. The menu features homemade pasta, fresh seafood, and a high-quality wine selection.

Visitor browsing at the well-stocked Moving Image Store

Shopping

The Moving Image Store (*718 777 6800; www.movingimage.us/visit/shop*) sells whimsical T-shirts and stylish notepads. A wide range of books for movies buffs and video-gamers is also on offer. Look out for unusual DVDs such as Ruth Orkin and Morris Engel's *The Little Fugitive*, a short fictional tale of a boy who runs away to Coney Island, shot in the style of a documentary.

Find out more

DIGITAL The website *www. movingimage.us/families* gives information on workshops, films, and other events at the museum.

Next stop...

PALEY CENTER FOR MEDIA A TV- and radio-centric spot in Midtown, the Paley Center for Media (*see p115*) has individual consoles that let kids and adults choose from a huge archive of radio broadcasts and TV show episodes such as *The Pilot* (*Seinfeld*).

Archival footage on display at the Paley Center for Media

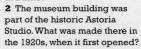

KIDS' CORNER

Find out more...

1 Many cameras are used at once to capture live events such as sports games. Why does the television viewer see only one picture at a time?

2 The museum building was part of the historic Astoria Studio. What was made there in the 1920s, when it first opened?

3 A man named Jack Foley pioneered the art of creating sound effects for motion pictures in 1927. What is this art called today?

4 The station at which visitors can dub their voices into famous movie scenes is called ADR. What do the letters stand for?

Answers at the bottom of the page.

WHAT'S IN A NAME?

Originally called Hallet's Cove, the Queens neighborhood of Astoria was renamed for John Jacob Astor. The millionaire gave $400,000 for building the Astor Library, but never set foot in Astoria himself.

Video games

The Video Arcade is on the second floor of the museum, filled with a variety of working consoles in their original format. Visitors are encouraged to interact with many of these games.

Answers: 1 Because a director is at work deciding which camera view should follow another. **2** It was used to make movies. **3** Foley art. **4** They stand for Automated Dialogue Replacement.

Red-brick facade of the Noguchi Museum

② The Noguchi Museum
Nature transformed

Born in Los Angeles to an American journalist mother and a Japanese poet father, Isamu Noguchi (1904–88) was one of the 20th century's premier sculptors. He spent his life traveling between Japan and the US, breaking down many barriers: between the natural and the man-made, between the earthly and the spiritual, and between various artistic disciplines. Although primarily a sculptor (his principal materials were stone, wood, and marble), Noguchi undertook many collaborations. He designed stage sets for choreographers Martha Graham, George Balanchine, and Merce Cunningham, created furniture with the Herman Miller company, and designed playgrounds with the renowned American architect Louis Kahn.

One of his most enduring creations is the Noguchi Museum, which he built both to house the bulk of his output and as a work of art in itself. The outdoor sculpture garden seems to have a magical life of its own. The museum's seven ground-level galleries showcase the permanent exhibition, which consists mostly of the artist's monumental stone and marble works. These include the powerful *Void* and *Walking Void 2*, sculptures exploring form and formlessness, and the *Slide Mantra* – the model of a work he designed for a park in Miami. Its elegant slab of marble features a spiral slide for children, encircling a central staircase.

Ever-changing curated exhibits of Noguchi's work are mounted in the galleries on the second floor. The highlight for kids is bound to be the tree-canopied, open-air sculpture garden. Massive works such as *Sea Stone* and *Helix of the Endless*, which grapple with destruction and creation, invite exploration.

Letting off steam
Continue the art theme at **Socrates Sculpture Park** (*Broadway at Vernon Blvd, 11106; 718 956 1819; www.socratessculpturepark.org; 10am to sunset*), which was once an abandoned landfill and illegal waste dump site. A coalition of artists and community members turned it into an outdoor museum and public recreation space in 1986. Most of the sculptures and multimedia installations here are created on site, meaning families can often meet artists at work. The artworks are often tactile and interactive, and children are encouraged to explore, and even touch, the works on view. Temporary group shows and installations are mounted regularly.

Intruder by Lauren Ewing on display in Socrates Sculpture Park

③ Long Island City
Cutting-edge art spaces

Just a couple of subway stops from Grand Central Terminal (*see pp100–101*), the Hunters Point section of Long Island City (LIC), Queens, has become a major destination for

The Lowdown

🌐 **Address** 9-01 33rd Rd, between Vernon Blvd & 10th St, Long Island City, 11106; 718 204 7088; www.noguchi.org

🚇 **Subway** N & Q to Broadway, then take the Q104 bus to 11th St; 7 to Vernon Blvd-Jackson Ave, then take the Q103 bus to 10th St.

🕐 **Open** 10am–5pm Wed–Fri; 11am–6pm Sat & Sun

💲 **Price** $30–40; under 12s free; pay what you wish first Fri of the month.

🚩 **Guided tours** Free 1-hour tours are available for groups of 10 or more and must be scheduled in advance; call 718 204 7088, ext. 203. Free gallery talks take place at 2pm Wed–Sun, open to all individual visitors.

🏃 **Activities** Open Studio: first Sun of the month; 11am–1pm; $10 per family, includes museum admission; no registration required. Themed family art workshops on most weekends; pre-registration required; aimed at kids between the ages of 2–4 (Art for Tots) and 5–11 (Art for Families); $10 per family

⏱ **Allow** 2 hours

♿ **Wheelchair access** Yes

🍴 **Eat and drink** *Snacks* The on-site Noguchi Café offers sandwiches, snacks, and beverages. *Real meal* The Bel Aire Diner (31-91 21st St, Astoria, 11101; 718 721 3160) offers fresh fish, burgers, and salads.

🛍 **Shop** The Noguchi Museum Shop sells Akari light sculptures from the 1950s, Akari prints, and Noguchi furniture.

🚻 **Restrooms** On the main floor

Gantry Plaza State Park along the East River, Long Island City

contemporary art-lovers thanks to its cluster of world-class galleries and arts centers. Foremost among them is **MoMA PS1** *(22–25 Jackson Ave, 11101; 718 784 2084; www. ps1.org)*, an exhibition space that is now permanently affiliated to MoMA *(see pp106–107)* in Manhattan. Devoted solely to contemporary art, it actively involves innovative and experimental artists, highlighting their work through solo retrospectives and site-specific installations. Several long-term installation pieces are worth seeking out, among them Sol LeWitt's *Crayola Square*, and James Turrell's *Meeting*, an open-air space that radically changes visitors' perception of the sky (open for viewing an hour before sunset, weather permitting).

Nearby are two more inspiring places for cutting-edge art: **SculptureCenter** *(44-19 Purves St, 11101; 718 361 1750; suggested donation: $5 per person)* and the **Fisher Landau Center for Art** *(38-27 30th St, 11101; 718 937 0727; free)*, in a former parachute-harness factory.

Founded by a group of artists in 1928, SculptureCenter moved into its building from the Upper East Side in 2001. Its dramatic exhibition spaces are ideal for fulfilling the group's mission to give exposure to contemporary sculpture.

The Fisher Landau Center for Art, a more refined exhibit space and study center, is devoted to the holdings of Emily Fisher Landau, a collector who has amassed a significant body of modern and contemporary pieces, including works by Kiki Smith, John Baldessari, Robert Rauschenberg, and Cy Twombly.

Letting off steam

Head to the East River for **Gantry Plaza State Park** *(Center Blvd, between 47th Rd & 49th Ave, Long Island City, 11101; www. nysparks.com/parks/149/fees-rates.aspx)*, which has curved chaise longue benches for taking in the spectacular views of the midtown Manhattan skyline. The park includes four piers (one for recreational fishing), playgrounds, manicured gardens, basketball and handball courts, and a mist fountain. Restored gantries – once used to load and unload barges – take center stage as a monument to the waterfront's industrial past. In warmer months the plaza becomes an occasional concert venue.

The Lowdown

- 🌐 **Address** Newtown Creek to East River Waterfront & Queensboro Bridge to railyards, 11101
- 🚇 **Subway** E & G to 23rd St-Ely Ave; 7 to 45 Rd-Court House Sq. **Bus** M60, Q32, Q67, Q69 & Q103
- 👫 **Age range** All ages
- 🏃 **Activities** MoMA PS1: Warm Up, an all-ages experimental music series-cum-dance party in its courtyard; Sat in summer; $20 (includes museum admission; $18 if booked in advance).
- ⏱ **Allow** 3 hours
- 🍴 **Eat and drink** *Snacks* Court Square Diner *(45–30 23rd Ave, 11101; 718 392 1222)* offers good diner fare; kids' meals cost $7.45 apiece. *Real meal* The Creek and the Cave *(10–93 Jackson Ave, 11101; 718 706 8783; www. creeklic.com)* is a Tex-Mex spot offering a range of burritos, tacos, and entrées.
- 🚻 **Restrooms** At various restaurants and cafés along the way

New York Hall of Science and around

Two World's Fairs and a constellation of family-friendly cultural attractions have put Flushing Meadows-Corona Park on the tourist map. From the New York Hall of Science, with its awesome outdoor Science Playground, to the Queens Museum of Art's Panorama of the City of New York, an architectural scale model of all five boroughs, the complex is abuzz with things to discover. It's about a 40-minute ride on the 7 subway from Midtown to the park; once there, be prepared for quite a bit of walking to reach the sights.

Places of interest

SIGHTS

1. New York Hall of Science
2. Queens Zoo
3. Queens Museum of Art
4. Queens Botanical Garden

● EAT AND DRINK

1. Pollo Campero
2. Park Side Restaurant
3. Asian Jewels Seafood Restaurant
4. Empanadas Café
5. Leo's Latticini Mama's
6. Tortillería Nixtamal
7. Nan Xiang Dumpling House
8. New Bodai Vegetarian

See also Queens Museum of Art (p226)

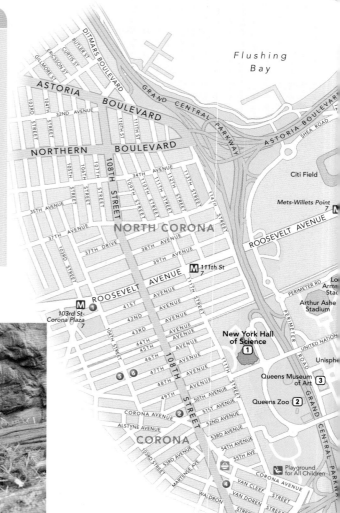

Endangered Andean bear at Queens Zoo

Mini-golf course demonstrating the science of spaceflight, at the New York Hall of Science

0 meters 500

0 yards 500

The Lowdown

🚗 **Subway** 7 to 111th St, Mets-Willets Point & Flushing-Main St
Bus Q23, Q44 & Q58

ℹ️ **Visitor information** Online visitors' center: *www.itsinqueens.com*

🏪 **Supermarket** Fine Fare Supermarket, 108-02 Otis Ave, Corona, 11368; 718 271 8600
Markets Queens Botanical Garden's Down to Earth Farmers' Market, Dahlia Ave off Main St, Queens, 11355; Jun–mid-Nov: 8:30am–4pm Fri. Corona Greenmarket, Roosevelt Ave at 103rd St; Jul–Nov: 8am–3pm Fri; *www.grownyc.org/greenmarket/queens/corona*

🎊 **Festivals** Cinco de Mayo Festival (early May). Colombian Independence Day Festival (mid-Jul). Dragon Boat Festival (early Aug)

➕ **Pharmacy** Duane Reade, 13602 Roosevelt Ave, Flushing, 11354; 718 886 3212; 24 hours daily

👶 **Nearest playground** Playground for All Children (PAC), 111-01 Corona Ave, Flushing, 11368; 718 699 8283

① New York Hall of Science
Rockets and optical illusions

New York City's only science museum is all the way out in Queens for a reason. It was originally an exhibition hall at the 1964 World's Fair, which took place in Flushing Meadows-Corona Park. The hall continued to draw crowds after the fair was over, surprising everyone, and even spurring other cities to build their own science meccas. In 1979, it was converted into a true museum and has gone on to expand and modernize with the times. The best of the original exhibits survive, including Mathematica and the fun-filled Science Playground.

Star Attractions

Second Floor North Wing: Sports Challenge

First Floor North Wing: Search for Life Beyond Earth; Central Pavilion: Hidden Kingdoms, Mathematica, and Seeing the Light

Rocket Park Spacecraft, rockets

Ground Floor Design Lab

① **Search for Life Beyond Earth** Various exhibits here look at the most likely places life might exist beyond Earth, including Mars and Europa, one of Jupiter's moons.

② **Design Lab** In the Design Lab visitors can experiment with engineering structures, using simple materials at five different activity areas.

Auditorium

Science Playground entrance

⑤ **Seeing the Light** In this section, kids can uncover the secrets behind optical illusions such as holograms, and explore how shadows influence perception.

⑥ **Sports Challenge** This set of exhibits focuses on principles of physics – balance, reaction time, trajectories – through sports activities such as mock-surfing, wall climbing, and a simulated wheelchair race.

③ **Hidden Kingdoms** Look at living microbes through special microscopes called Wentzscopes, and learn more about the lives of species such as amoebae and paramecium.

④ **Mathematica** Created by world-renowned designers Charles and Ray Eames, Mathematica brings math to life with such exhibits as a cube of lights that acts as a multiplication machine.

⑦ **Rocket Park** Authentic spacecraft and rockets are on display here. Visitors can get inside a replica of the *Mercury Atlas D* capsule that carried US astronaut John Glenn into orbit in 1962.

The Lowdown

🌐 **Address** 47th Ave & 111th St Flushing Meadows-Corona Park, 11368; 718 699 0005; *www.nysci.org*

🚗 **Subway** 7 to 111th St, then walk three blocks south. **Bus** Q23, Q48 & Q58

🕘 **Open** 9:30am–5pm Mon–Fri, 10am–6pm Sat & Sun

💲 **Price** $42–60; Science Playground additional $5 per person. Free admission year-round 2–5pm Fri, 10–11am Sun

(except during World Maker Faire weekend in September).

👫 **Cutting the line** Combination ticket includes entry to Rocket Park and Science Playground.

👫 **Age range** 3 plus

⏱ **Allow** 2 hours

♿ **Wheelchair access** Yes

☕ **Café** The New York Hall of Science café offers a selection of pre-made salads, sandwiches, and pizzas.

🏷 **Shop** The Science Shop is an on-site gift shop selling science kits, games, and books, among other offerings.

👫 **Restrooms** On the first and ground floors

Good family value?
The combination of fun and educational activities makes the science museum an excellent option at any time of the year.

Prices given are for a family of four

Play equipment with a scientific touch at the Science Playground

Letting off steam

Designed to encourage children to explore aspects of science with their bodies as well as their minds, the outdoor **Science Playground** is an enormous enclosed space packed with fun, interactive stations, offering the chance to run and play freely. Among the best are a water table with Archimedes Screw, a thrillingly long slide, a standing spinner, a giant seesaw, and a 3-D spiderweb to climb.

Eat and drink

Picnic: under $20; Snacks: $20–35; Real meal: $35–70; Family treat: over $70 (based on a family of four).

PICNIC Pollo Campero (103–26 Roosevelt Ave, Corona, 11368; 718 205 6943) offers delicious Latin-style grilled and fried chicken that can be picked up before heading to Flushing Meadows-Corona Park for a picnic.

REAL MEAL Park Side Restaurant (107-01 Corona Ave, Corona, 11368; 718 271 9871) is an Italian restaurant serving a range of pasta, seafood, and meat entrées.

FAMILY TREAT Asian Jewels Seafood Restaurant (13330 39th Ave, 11354; 718 359 8600) is a massive Chinese dim sum emporium with an extensive menu that includes specialties such as noodles with dry shredded pork and fried chive dumplings.

Find out more

DIGITAL The New York Hall of Science has a fairly in-depth website, *www.nysci.org*, covering its exhibits. Also, *www.learningscience. org* offers interactive, science-related games and activities to spark curiosity after a visit.

Next stop...

UNISPHERE Another authentic relic of the 1964 World's Fair is the iconic Unisphere in Flushing Meadows-Corona Park, between Grand Central Parkway and Van Wyck Expressway. A 140-ft (43-m) tall stainless-steel representation of the Earth, the Unisphere was designed to celebrate the Space Age. Those who have seen the film *Men in Black* (1997) will recognize this giant hollow ball of green steel surrounded by fountains and the three observatory towers behind it.

The Unisphere at Flushing Meadows-Corona Park

② Queens Zoo

Alligators, giant rabbits, and acrobatic sea lions

Just beside the New York Hall of Science is the Wildlife Conservation Society's small and inviting Queens Zoo, the only zoo in the city devoted to wildlife from North and South America. It was built after the 1964 World's Fair to add another visitor magnet to the newly popular Flushing Meadows-Corona Park. Pathways wind through its assorted habitats, including the Great Plains, with bison and prong-horn antelopes, and the Woodland Trail, with pumas, owls, and elks.

Do not miss the South American Trail, home to endangered spectacled bears, which look as if they are wearing glasses. The Waterfowl Marsh contains an array of ducks, cranes, and American alligators. The zoo's most historic building houses one of its best exhibits, the aviary, which occupies the huge geodesic dome built for the World's Fair. Inside, a steep pathway takes visitors from the forest floor all the way up to the treetop perches of egrets and porcupines – yes they really do live in trees. At the Domestic Animals corner, kids can buy a handful of

The Lowdown

🌐 **Address** 53-51 111th St, Flushing, Queens, 11368; 718 271 1500; www.queenszoo.com

🚗 **Subway** 7 to 111th St. **Bus** Q58, Q23 & Q88

🕑 **Open** Mar–Nov: 10am–5pm Mon–Fri, 10am–5:30pm Sat, Sun & holidays; Nov–Mar: 10am–4:30pm daily

Ⓢ **Price** $26–32; under 3s free

🚩 **Guided tours** $150 for groups up to 30 people

👫 **Age range** All ages

🕐 **Allow** 2 hours

♿ **Wheelchair access** Yes

🍽 **Eat and drink** Snacks Empanadas Café (56-27 Van Doren St, 11368; 718 592 7288; www.empanadascafe.com) offers its signature in entree and dessert versions. Real meal Leo's Latticini Mama's (46-02 104th St, Corona, 11368, 718 898 6069) sells sandwiches that can be eaten in the picnic area of the zoo.

🚻 **Restrooms** In the Discovery Center

A flock of thick-billed parrots brighten the scene at Queens Zoo

grain to feed the inhabitants. Among them are Flemish giant rabbits, llamas, and a pig. Not to be missed are the California sea lion feedings (check website), when these acrobatic creatures perform various tricks.

Letting off steam

The **Playground for All Children** (111-01 Corona Ave, Flushing, 11368) has slopes to run down, swings, a basketball court, and a play-and-pretend section with props.

③ Queens Museum of Art

Mini-NYC and other treasures

The Queens Museum of Art is a cultural center with strong ties to the multi-ethnic community that surrounds it. It is housed in the New York City Building, which began life as the New York City pavilion for the 1939 World's Fair. When the next World's Fair rolled around, in 1964, the building was spruced up for the same purpose. This time it had

The Lowdown

🌐 **Address** New York City Building, Flushing Meadows-Corona Park, 11368; 718 592 9700; www.queensmuseum.org

🚗 **Subway** 7 to 111th St. **Bus** Q23 & Q58

🕑 **Open** Noon–6pm Wed–Sun

Ⓢ **Price** $24–34; under 5s free

🚩 **Guided tours** Free museum tours at 2pm, 3pm & 4pm Sun; recommended age: 12 plus

👫 **Age range** All ages

👪 **Activities** Drop-in family art workshops for children ages 5 plus, 1:30–4:30pm Sun; special-event days with tours of the museum and live music, second Sun of each month

🕐 **Allow** 1 hour

♿ **Wheelchair access** Yes

🍽 **Eat and drink** Snacks Unisphere Café (on site; open Wed–Sun) serves sushi, desserts, and drinks. Real meal Tortillería Nixtamal (104-05 47th Ave, Corona, 11368; 718 699 2434) offers tacos with delicious fillings.

🚻 **Restrooms** On the first floor

something phenomenal to offer: the Panorama of the City of New York – a 9,335-sq-ft (868-sq-m) architectural model of the city depicting every building in all five boroughs to scale. Updated several times, the Panorama now includes all buildings built before 1992, including the World Trade Center.

Letting off steam

The sprawling grounds of **Flushing Meadows-Corona Park** (see pp222–3) have plenty of activities to keep kids busy, such as mini-golf and bike trails.

Panorama of the City of New York scale model at Queens Museum of Art

Herb Garden on a sunny winter afternoon, Queens Botanical Garden

④ Queens Botanical Garden

Red roses, green design

What began as a 5-acre (2-ha) exhibit at the 1939 World's Fair and moved a short distance away for the next World's Fair is now an extensive 39-acre (16-ha) urban oasis. Among the highlights are the largest rose garden in northeastern USA, the Bee and Herb Gardens, the Fragrance Walk, the Cherry Circle, and a cluster of diverse habitats, including the Woodland and

The Lowdown

⊕ **Address** 43-50 Main St, 11355, Flushing, Queens; 718 886 3800; *www.queensbotanical.org*

🚗 **Subway** 7 to Flushing-Main St. **Bus** Q44, Q58 & Q20

🕐 **Open** Apr–Oct: 8am–6pm Tue–Sun; Nov–Mar: 8am–4:30pm Tue–Sun

⑤ **Price** Apr–Oct: $12–16, under 3s free; 3–6pm Wed, 4–6pm Sun free; Nov–Mar: always free

🚶 **Guided tours** For tours of the garden call 718 886 3800 ext 230

👫 **Age range** All ages

⏲ **Allow** 1–2 hours

♿ **Wheelchair access** Yes

🍴 **Eat and drink** *Snacks* Nan Xiang Dumpling House (38-12 Prince St, Flushing, 11354; 718 321 3838) specializes in pork dishes, with great pork-and-crab soup dumplings. *Real meal* New Bodai Vegetarian (59-08 Main St, Flushing, 11355; 718 939 1188) serves vegetarian (and kosher) Chinese meals.

👥 **Restrooms** In the Visitors' Center

Wetland gardens, the Pinetum (for cone-bearing species), and the Meadow. Garnering even more attention than the blooms, though, is the Visitors & Administration Building, which opened in 2007. It is the first platinum-certified eco-friendly structure to be built in New York City. Among its features are a planted green roof to minimize water run-off, solar panels, and graywater recycling, by which water from sinks, showers, and dishwashers is purified for use in its toilets.

At nearby Flushing Meadows-Corona Park, seek out the sculptures *Rocket Thrower* by Donald Delue and *Freedom of the Human Spirit* by Marshall M. Fredericks, both commissioned for the 1964 World's Fair.

Take cover

The garden's QBG Store is stocked with something for everyone to browse: toys and books for kids and an array of crafts, jewelry, and stationery for adults.

Landscaped Rose Garden at Queens Botanical Garden

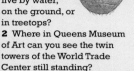

New York Botanical Garden and around

Despite being a bit off the beaten path, the Bronx is home to some of the city's loveliest and most fun cultural gems, none of which is overcrowded. The city's most populous borough is easily accessible via the Metro-North commuter rail which connects it to Wave Hill, a nature center with breathtaking views of the Hudson, and the fantastic New York Botanical Garden, among others. Visit Edgar Allan Poe's cottage, where the writer spent the last years of his life, and City Island, a tiny seaside spot, and kids will feel they have discovered some genuine secrets.

New York Botanical Garden

Bronx Zoo
p234

Bronx

Entrance of Sugar and Spice, a popular bakery

Places of interest

SIGHTS
1. New York Botanical Garden
2. Edgar Allan Poe Cottage
3. Wave Hill
4. City Island

● EAT AND DRINK
1. Pioneer Supermarket
2. Webster Café
3. Great Wall Chinese Restaurant
4. Garden Café
5. Roma Luncheonette
6. Mario's
7. Riverdale Greentree
8. Sugar and Spice
9. Sammy's Fish Box

See also Wave Hill (p232)

● SHOPPING
1. NYBG Shop in the Garden

See also Wave Hill (p232)

Part of the grounds at Wave Hill, with the Hudson River in the background

The Lowdown

 Train Metro-North Harlem local line from Grand Central Terminal to Botanical Garden.
Subway B & D to Bedford Park Blvd; 4 to Bedford Park Blvd-Lehman College, then take the Bx26 bus east to Mosholu Gate entrance; B & D to Kingsbridge Rd; 1 to Van Cortlandt Park-242nd St; 6 to Pelham Bay Park

i **Visitor information** Leon Levy Visitors' Center at NYBG,

2900 Southern Blvd, Bronx, 10458; 718 817 8700

Supermarket Pioneer Supermarket, 2870 Webster Ave, 10458; 718 364 0101
Market New York Botanical Garden Greenmarket, Mosholu Gate on Southern Blvd, Bronx, 10458; mid-Jun through mid-Nov: 9am–3pm Wed

Festivals Annual Orchid Show (Feb–Apr). Holiday Train Show (mid-Nov through Jan)

Pharmacy Walgreens, 5564 Broadway, Bronx, 10463; 718 548 5884; 24 hours daily

Nearest playgrounds Bronx Park-French Charley Playground, East 204th St at west side of Bronx Park, 10467. Poe Park, East Kingsbridge Rd & Grand Concourse, 10468. P. S. 175's nautical-themed playground, 200 City Island Ave, 10464.

Edgar Allan Poe Cottage, the writer's last home

NYBG Shop in the Garden, Leon Levy Visitors' Center

① New York Botanical Garden
Ancient forest and tropical blooms

Bursting with flowers, meadows, and forest, the New York Botanical Garden (NYBG) feels like a world unto itself, and certainly not part of central Bronx. Its outdoor landscapes are magnificent in the warmer months, and the stellar conservatory is great in any weather. In winter the garden puts on its famous Holiday Train Show, featuring an amazing miniature world made of botanical materials. In the Everett Children's Adventure Garden, kids can have a hands-on garden experience.

Peggy Rockefeller Rose Garden

Key Sights

① Enid A. Haupt Conservatory
This Victorian-style glasshouse showcases a tour through 11 of the world's ecospheres, from African deserts to two types of rain forest.

② Rock Garden An Alpine habitat, the garden has rocks punctuated by flowering plants, a stream running through it, and a waterfall that spills into a flower-encircled pond.

③ Ruth Rea Howell Family Garden
Open from April through November, this garden teaches children all about horticulture, from digging for worms to planting seeds.

④ Cherry Valley A must-visit in April and May, this area has the majority of the garden's 200 flowering cherry trees.

⑤ Peggy Rockefeller Rose Garden Among its 3,500 varieties are EarthKind roses, hybrids that can survive with few or no pesticides.

⑥ Benenson Ornamental Conifers This zone is dedicated to trees with needles (like pines) or scale-like leaves, like cedars.

⑦ Everett Children's Adventure Garden Designed for kids from 2 to 12, it offers indoor and outdoor attractions, such as a touch tank filled with aquatic plants.

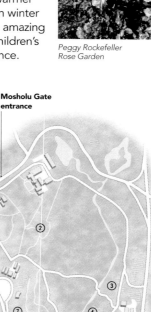

Mosholu Gate entrance

Garden Café

Entrance

Letting off steam

The New York Botanical Garden's greatest treasure is also its oldest: the 50-acre (20-ha) Thain Family Forest that is the largest remaining tract of New York City's indigenous woodlands. Its original inhabitants were American Indians of the Lenape tribe.

Extensive trails lead through the woods, which are made up of oak, beech, birch, tulip, ash, and cherry trees – some more than 200 years old. They are open year-round, so

Prices given are for a family of four

children can ramble through them while exploring whatever the season brings.

Eat and drink

Picnic: under $20; Snacks: $20–35; Real meal: $35–70; Family treat: over $70 (based on a family of four)

PICNIC Pioneer Supermarket (2870 Webster Ave, 10458; 718 364 0101) is good for picking up supplies to eat in the designated

picnic area near the Everett Children's Adventure Garden.
SNACKS Webster Café (2873 Webster Ave, Bronx, 10458; 718 733 9634) is a popular neighborhood spot to munch on a hot dog, salad, or sandwich after touring the garden.
REAL MEAL Great Wall Chinese Restaurant (3003 Webster Ave, 10458; 718 584 5488; 11am–11:30pm daily) offers tasty, authentic Chinese fare at a good price.

The Lowdown

🌐 **Address** 2900 Southern Blvd, Bronx, 10458; 718 817 8700; *www.nybg.org*

🚃 **Train** Metro-North Harlem local line from Grand Central Terminal to Botanical Garden. **Subway** B, D & 4 to Bedford Park-Lehman Blvd station, then the Bx26 bus to Mosholu Gate

🕐 **Open** 10am–6pm Tue–Sun; till 5pm (winter)

💲 **Price** $24–34 (grounds only); under 2s free; free Wed

👫 **Cutting the line** Book tickets online in advance for the Holiday Train Show.

👉 **Guided tours** Weekend "expert" tours; hop-on tram tour; bird-walks (Sat, seasonal); daily docent-led tours; audio tours

👫 **Age range** 2 plus

🧍 **Activities** Ongoing at the Everett Children's Adventure Garden and the Family Garden; check website

⏱️ **Allow** 2–3 hours

♿ **Wheelchair access** Yes

☕ **Cafés** Garden Café; Pine Tree Café in Leon Levy Visitors' Center

🛍️ **Shop** Just right of the conservatory entrance

🚻 **Restrooms** In Leon Levy Visitors' Center

Good family value?
Lush gardens, where kids can learn about gardening, and tropical hothouses make it a great favorite with families.

largely upscale goods, from housewares and gardening tools to botanical prints, jewelry, and food.

Find out more
DIGITAL The garden's website, *www.nybg.org*, has a wealth of information about its botanical collections and special events. It also highlights what's in bloom.

Café at Leon Levy Visitors' Center, New York Botanical Garden

FAMILY TREAT Garden Café (2900 Southern Blvd, 10458; 718 817 8700; 10am–4pm Tue–Sun) has an extensive menu, including grilled and vegetarian fare.

Shopping
Far more than a typical gift shop, **NYBG Shop in the Garden**, next to Leon Levy Visitor Center, offers an eclectic, nature-themed array of

Next stop...
BROOKLYN BOTANIC GARDEN Less vast than the NYBG, the Brooklyn Botanic Garden (see p206–207) offers a more intimate set of gardens. Highlights include the serene Japanese Hill-and-Pond Garden, teeming with koi (giant goldfish) and ducks; it sometimes also harbours rare migratory birds who have stopped by to fish.

(see p206–207)

Plants and colorful pots for sale at the NYBG Shop in the Garden

Facade of the Edgar Allan Poe Cottage

② Edgar Allan Poe Cottage
Home of a tortured soul

The writer Edgar Allan Poe led a largely itinerant life up and down the Atlantic seaboard, touching down in Richmond, Virginia, Baltimore, Philadelphia, and New York to seek fame and fortune. One of the first writers in the US to make a living solely by his craft, he struggled financially all his life. He married his cousin Virginia Clemm in 1835, when he was 26 and she 13. When she became increasingly ill with tuberculosis 11 years later, Poe moved with her to this cottage, hoping the country air would restore her health.

Set in the then bucolic rolling hills of the Bronx, with an unobstructed view to the shores of Long Island,

the house would be the last home of both Poe and his young wife. Virginia died in the cottage less than a year after moving here, in 1847. Poe remained in the Bronx for another two years before undertaking a trip to Baltimore that would be his last; he died a mysterious death there at the age of 40. The writer penned some of his finest works in this house, among them *The Bells* and *Annabel Lee*, his last complete poem, about the tragic death of a loved one.

Letting off steam
The cottage is set in **Poe Park**, named for the writer, with a fine play-ground and a gazebo that acts as a fort to play in, and also makes for a good picnic spot.

③ Wave Hill
Gorgeous views

The best thing about this 28-acre (11-ha) public garden and cultural center is its awe-inspiring views of the Hudson River, which it overlooks, and the Palisades, a steep line of cliffs on the New Jersey side. Enjoy them from the balustraded, flower-decked pergola in the middle of the grounds.

The oldest building in the grounds, **Wave Hill House**, was built in 1843 as a jurist's country home and has an impressive array of former residents. In the summers of 1870 and 1871, the future president Teddy Roosevelt (then 12–13 years old) lived here with his family. The appreciation of nature

and the outdoors that he gained here was probably instrumental in his efforts to preserve America's wilderness through the creation of a national parks system. Another illustrious resident was the writer Mark Twain, who built a tree house in a chestnut tree on the lawn.

The center aims to connect visitors with nature, not only by providing

The Lowdown

🌐 **Address** West 249th St at Independence Ave, Bronx, 10471; 718 549 3200; www.wavehill.org

🚗 **Train** Metro-North train to Riverdale Station, then free Wave Hill shuttle bus; 9:45am–3:45pm hourly. **Subway** 1 to Van Cortlandt Park-242nd St, then free Wave Hill shuttle bus

🕐 **Open** mid-Mar–mid-Oct: 9am–5:30pm Tue–Sun; Nov–mid-Mar: 9am–4:30pm Tue–Sun

💲 **Price** $20–32, $4 students, $2 ages 6 plus, under 6s free; 9am–noon Tue & Sat free year-round; parking on site $8 per vehicle

🔫 **Guided tours** Free garden and conservatory tours: 2pm Sun. Group tours of the garden and the conservatory must be scheduled in advance.

🚻 **Age range** All ages

🎨 **Activities** Art workshops (for adults) weekends, year-round

⏱ **Allow** 2 hours

🍽 **Eat and drink** Snacks The Wave Hill Café (on site) offers light meals and refreshments. *Real Meal* Riverdale Greentree (5693 Riverdale Ave, Bronx, 10471; 718 601 2572) offers main courses.

🚻 **Restrooms** In the Perkins Visitor Center and Wave Hill House

The Lowdown

🌐 **Address** 2640 Grand Concourse at 192nd St, Bronx, 10458; 718 881 8900; www.bronx historicalsociety.org

🚇 **Subway** B, D (at Grand Concourse) & 4 (at Jerome Ave) to Kingsbridge Rd

🕐 **Open** 10am–3pm Thu & Fri, 10am–4pm Sat, 1–5pm Sun

💲 **Price** $16–20

🔫 **Guided tours** Yes

🚻 **Age range** 4 plus

⏱ **Allow** 1 hour

♿ **Wheelchair access** Yes

🍽 **Eat and drink** Snacks Roma Luncheonette (636 East 187th St at Belmont Ave, Bronx, 10458; 718 367 9189) serves Italian fare. *Real meal* Mario's (2342 Arthur Ave, between 184th St & 186th St, Bronx, 10458; 718 584 1188) offers traditional Italian meals.

🚻 **Restrooms** In the cottage

Family working on an art and craft project at Wave Hill House

View toward Long Island Sound from City Island

stunning views, but through an array of different gardens, a trio of glasshouses, and nature-themed exhibits. Wave Hill also hosts great art workshops throughout the year, which are aimed mostly at kids.

Letting off steam

Stop in at the **Perkins Visitor Center** *(www.wavehill.org)*, home to the Shop at Wave Hill, which sells fun and educational toys, books, jewelry, and accessories. Also on offer here are handmade arts and crafts, ceramics, gardening products, and even honey from on-site hives. Do not forget to check out artist Maira Kalman's colorful mural, too.

④ City Island

Marinas and seafood restaurants

This tiny island, a part of the Bronx, is likely to be a pleasant surprise to first-time visitors. Its small-town charm, fresh seafood and aromas of

The Lowdown

🚇 **Subway** 6 to Pelham Bay Park, then Bx29 bus to City Island

👫 **Age range** All ages

🏃 **Activities** Hire a fishing boat for 10 hours, $60 on weekdays, $70 on weekends; *www.jacks baitandtackle.com*

⏱ **Allow** 4 hours

🍴 **Eat and drink** *Snacks* Sugar and Spice *(536 City Island Ave, City Island, Bronx, 10464; 718 885 9229)* offers breakfast and brunch. *Real meal* Sammy's Fish Box *(41 City Island Ave, City Island, Bronx, 10464; 718 509 6367)* serves seafood and free kids' meals.

👫 **Restrooms** In various restaurants

the ocean are immeasurably different from the rest of New York City. The island has been home to sailmakers, oystermen, fishermen, and shipyards, and has played a big part in the city's naval defense since being settled by Europeans in 1761.

Visit the City Island Historical Society and Nautical Museum *(190 Fordham St, 10464; www. cityislandmuseum.org)* to explore the island's past. The best way to take in the present is on foot, along City Island Avenue, the island's main drag. Shops, seafood restaurants, and marinas vie for attention, along with a fascinating array of houses. If the ocean beckons, visitors can hop aboard a charter fishing vessel, or even hire one of their own to try their luck offshore.

Letting off steam

Take a break at the **P. S. 175** nautical-themed playground *(200 City Island Ave, Bronx, 10464; 718 885 1093)*, where kids can splash around in an anchor-shaped sprinkler or steer a model ship; younger kids can play on swings.

City Island Avenue is lined with characterful shops and eateries

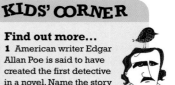

Bronx Zoo and around

The contrast between the sprawling swathe of nature that is the Bronx Zoo and the largely residential neighborhood that surrounds it is somewhat stark, but nothing to be concerned about. It is helpful, however, to plan a trip to the zoo or any other South Bronx destination carefully, as this part of town lacks amenities such as taxis. Dining options in and around the zoo are few; but not far away is the Bronx's Little Italy, which has a cluster of excellent restaurants ideal for lunch or dinner.

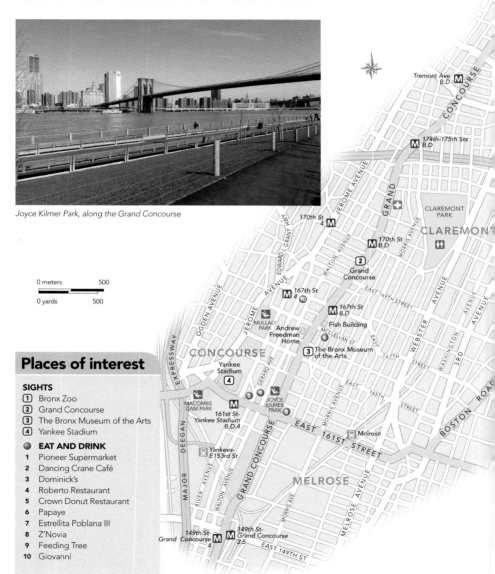

Joyce Kilmer Park, along the Grand Concourse

0 meters 500

0 yards 500

Places of interest

SIGHTS

1. Bronx Zoo
2. Grand Concourse
3. The Bronx Museum of the Arts
4. Yankee Stadium

EAT AND DRINK

1. Pioneer Supermarket
2. Dancing Crane Café
3. Dominick's
4. Roberto Restaurant
5. Crown Donut Restaurant
6. Papaye
7. Estrellita Poblana III
8. Z'Novia
9. Feeding Tree
10. Giovanni

The Lowdown

🚗 **Subway** B, D & 4 for stops along Grand Concourse; 2 & 5 for Bronx Zoo. **Bus** BxM11, Bx1, Bx2 & BxM4A

ℹ️ **Visitor information** Online official guide to the Bronx, www.nycgo.com/the-bronx

🏪 **Supermarket** Pioneer Supermarket, 2044 Boston Rd, Bronx,10460; 718 378 5007 **Markets** Poe Park Greenmarket, East 192nd St, between Grand Concourse & Valentine, Bronx, 10462; Jun–Nov: 8am–3pm Tue. Bronx Borough Hall Greenmarket, between 161st St & Grand Concourse, Bronx, 10451; Jun–Nov: 8am–4pm Tue

🎏 **Festivals** Bronx River Festival, (mid-Jun). The Tour de Bronx cycling event (Oct; www.tourde bronx.org)

➕ **Pharmacy** Rite Aid, 1540 Grand Concourse, Bronx, 10457; 718 731 8733; 9am–8pm Mon–Fri, 10am–6pm Sat, 10am–5pm Sun

🛝 **Nearest playgrounds** River Park Playground (see p237). Joyce Kilmer Park, between East 161st St & East 164th St, Bronx, 10452. Mullaly Park, Jerome Ave, between 164th St & McClellan St, Bronx, 10452. Macombs Dam Park, between River Ave, 157th St, 161st St & Major Deegan Expressway, Bronx, 11102

Siberian tigers in a re-created woodland, Bronx Zoo

Entrance of The Bronx Museum of the Arts, a cultural landmark

① Bronx Zoo
Congo gorillas and hissing cockroaches

The largest city zoological park in the US, the Bronx Zoo opened to the public in 1899. Run by the Wildlife Conservation Society, it is home to around 4,000 animals, representing about 650 species, most of which live in cageless environments. Among the highlights are exhibits where visitors can go nose-to-nose with Siberian tigers and western lowland gorillas, and take a monorail ride through a range of Asian-type habitats.

Camel rides at the zoo

Star Attractions

① Congo Gorilla Forest Get close to the gorillas by walking through the glass passageway that runs alongside their habitat.

② Children's Zoo Kids can feed goats, climb into a bird's nest, and visit skunks, foxes, and owls here.

③ Madagascar! Nile crocodiles and hissing cockroaches share this space with ferocious fossas and four types of lemurs, whose antics are enchanting.

④ Tiger Mountain This exhibit re-creates the eastern Russian habitat of Amur (Siberian) tigers, with only a thick glass wall separating visitors and these gorgeous cats.

Asia Gate entrance

⑤ Himalayan Highlands Look out for stealthy red pandas, white-naped cranes, and endangered snow leopards in this mock mountainous terrain.

⑥ African Plains This sprawling re-creation of the African savannah has open-air enclosures that house African wild dogs, cheetahs, Grevy's zebras, giraffes, and a pride of lions.

⑦ Wild Asia Monorail Spy elephants and Przewalski's horses on a ride through and above the zoo's East Asian exhibits.

⑧ Jungle World Do not miss the endangered binturong and a water-and-land exhibit with otters and gibbons in this tropical rain forest.

The Lowdown

Address 2300 Southern Blvd, Bronx, 10460; 718 220 5197; www.bronxzoo.com

Subway 2 & 5 to West Farms Sq-E Tremont Ave. **Bus** BxM11, Bx9 & Bx19

Open Daily; Children's Zoo & African Plains: Apr–Oct

Price $60–70; additional fee for some attractions; pay-what-you-wish Wed

Cutting the line Buy tickets online at the zoo's website to avoid long lines, especially on summer weekends.

Guided tours Yes

Age range All ages

Activities Wild Asia Monorail rides, May–Oct. Feedings: sea lions 11am & 3pm, penguins 3:30pm; primate training 2:30pm daily; camel rides; the Bug Carousel (with bugs in lieu of horses); the Bee-eater Buffet: 2:45pm daily at the World of Birds exhibit – the birds feed on live crickets and kids can talk to zookeepers.

Allow 3–5 hours

Wheelchair access Yes

Cafés Dancing Crane Café (see p237); more cafés and stands are open in the warmer months throughout the zoo.

Shops The Bronx Zoo Store; smaller outposts are scattered throughout the park.

Restrooms At the Dancing Crane Café and near the Jungle World and Madagascar! exhibits

Good family value?
The zoo is a must-do day trip for families, with excellent animal habitats as well as indoor and outdoor exhibits and rides.

Letting off steam

Just a block south of the Asia Gate entrance is the **River Park Playground** (corner of East 180th St & Boston Rd, Bronx, 10460). This refurbished park is an excellent play spot, with sprinklers, a huge rock to clamber up, and a giant spiderweb perfect for energetic climbers.

Metal and rope spiderweb for climbing, River Park Playground

Eat and drink

Picnic: under $20; Snacks: $20–35; Real meal: $35–70; Family treat: over $70 (based on a family of four)

PICNIC Pioneer Supermarket (2044 Boston Rd, Bronx, 10460; 718 378 5007), by West Farms Square subway, stocks fruit, drinks, and deli wares. From here, head to River Park at 180th Street, which has picnic grounds as well as barbecues for public use.

SNACKS Dancing Crane Café (2300 Southern Blvd, Bronx Zoo, Bronx, 10460; 718 367 1010) is not the most exciting place, but it does offer decent burgers, hot dogs, fries, salads, and drinks.

REAL MEAL Dominick's (2335 Arthur Ave, Bronx, 10458; 718 733 2807) is an institution in a neighborhood New Yorkers often call the city's true Little Italy. The restaurant serves up huge portions of Italian family-style food.

The rustic, cozy interior of the Roberto Restaurant

FAMILY TREAT Roberto Restaurant (603 Crescent Ave, Bronx, 10458; 718 733 9503; www.robertos. roberto089.com) is a classic Italian spot just off Arthur Avenue. Its rustic charm and sumptuous cooking are well worth a detour. Homemade pasta, antipasti, and veal dishes are some of the highlights.

Find out more

DIGITAL The zoo's interactive website, www.bronxzoo.com, which includes links to YouTube videos to watch, gives visitors a preview of the exhibits, complete with some interesting animal facts and zoo feeding times.

FILM Jim Knox's Wild Zoofari at the Bronx Zoo is a children's wildlife documentary that captures a visit to the Bronx Zoo, featuring the lowland gorillas of the Congo Gorilla Forest exhibit, one of the world's premier big-primate habitats.

Rockefeller Rose Garden, New York Botanical Garden

Take cover

There are many indoor areas throughout the zoo, among them the Mouse House, with rodents of all shapes and sizes, the fascinating World of Reptiles, and the World of Birds, an ear-shattering riot of colors.

Next stop...

NEW YORK BOTANICAL GARDEN Bursting with flowers and fauna, the Bronx Zoo's stately neighbor, the New York Botanical Garden (see pp230–31), is best visited on a different day since both sites are enormous and entail a lot of walking.

KIDS' CORNER

Look out for...

1 Among the inhabitants of the Himalayan Highlands zone is one of the most endangered animals in the world. What is its name?
2 As you can see in the Madagascar! exhibit, there are many animals that exist only on that island and nowhere else. Why do you think this is so?
3 If you are lucky enough to catch a tiger-training session you might see the animals playing with toys and trying to figure out how to get at their food. What do you think is the purpose of this?

Answers at the bottom of the page.

FURRY FACT

Red pandas, found in the Himalayan exhibit of the Bronx Zoo, are not related in any way to China's giant, black-and-white pandas. Their closest relative is actually the raccoon.

Wild horses

Przewalski's horses – the only surviving breed of truly wild equines – are a different species from domesticated horses. Named after the Russian geographer and explorer Nikolai Przhevalsky, they are native to the steppes of Central Asia, are stockily built, and have shorter legs.

Answers: 1 The snow leopard. **2** Separated from Africa millions of years ago, Madagascar is ecologically unique and species have been able to develop there in isolation. **3** The purpose is to engage the tigers and stimulate their minds.

② Grand Concourse

Art Deco treasures and marvelous lobbies

The aptly named Grand Concourse, a 5-mile (8-km) boulevard that extends from 138th Street all the way up to the northern end of the Bronx, was designed by Louis Risse after Paris's Champs-Elysées in 1892, and opened to traffic in 1906.

Some of New York's most exceptional Art Deco apartment complexes and homes were built here during the Concourse's heyday, between the 1920s and 1940s. While the thoroughfare is a shadow of its former self, it is still worth exploring for the architectural gems that remain. Right across from the Bronx Museum of the Arts is the boulevard's most stately residence: the **Andrew Freedman Home**, a 1924 limestone mansion that was once the home of a millionaire subway contractor. He bequeathed much of his fortune to establish a home for needy elderly people in the mansion, which today houses a social services agency. At the corner of McClelland Place, two blocks north, is **1150 Grand Concourse**, an apartment complex often referred to as the "fish building" for the ocean-themed mosaic at its entrance. The restored lobby deserves a peek too, for its terrazzo floor, pastoral murals, and striking elevator doors.

The Lorelei Fountain in Joyce Kilmer Park

It is also worth walking the 23 blocks north of the museum to the landmark **Loew's Paradise Theater** at 2413 Grand Concourse, near 188th Street, once the largest movie theater in New York City.

Letting off steam

Just across the street from 888 Grand Concourse lies **Joyce Kilmer Park** *(between East 161st St & 164th St, Bronx, 10452)*. Here, kids can seek out the statue of Louis J. Heintz, who pioneered the construction of the Grand Concourse, and the Lorelei Fountain, which celebrates German poet Heinrich Heine. The park also has a playground.

③ The Bronx Museum of the Arts

Amazing architecture and art

This museum got it right when it called itself the "flagship cultural institution of the Bronx," for no other place in the borough is as devoted or tied to its surroundings as this one. Its focus is on contemporary art that has relevance to the district, either because of its urban themes or because it was created by local artists for whom the neighborhood has had a particular importance. All of its exhibits are temporary, which lends the museum a lively dynamic.

The Lowdown

◉ **Address** 1040 Grand Concourse, Bronx, 10456; 718 681 6000; www.bronxmuseum.org

🚇 **Subway** B & D to 167th St. **Bus** Bx1, Bx2 & BxM4

🕐 **Open** 11am–6pm Thu, Sat & Sun; 11am–8pm Fri

💲 **Price** Free

🚩 **Guided tours** On request. On the first Wed of the month, the Bronx Culture Trolley picks up and drops visitors for free at various art hot spots in South Bronx, including the Bronx Museum of the Arts (no tours in Jan or Sep). It is hop-on and hop-off (5:30pm, 6:30pm & 7:30pm); www.bronxarts.org.

👫 **Age range** 5 plus

🤸 **Activities** Periodic Family Affair afternoons feature a mix of performances, museum tours, and hands-on workshops for kids aged 5–11 and their caregivers; details on the museum website.

⏱ **Allow** 1 hour

♿ **Wheelchair access** Yes

🍽 **Eat and drink** *Snacks* Estrellita Poblana III *(2328 Arthur Ave, 10458)* serves authentic Mexican food. There's also a kids' menu. *Real meal* Z'Novia *(888B Grand Concourse at 161st St, 10451; 718 585 5550)* offers sophisticated soul food just two blocks from Yankee Stadium.

👫 **Restrooms** On every floor and in the north and south wings

The Lowdown

◉ **Address** Grand Concourse, Bronx, between 138th St & Mosholu Parkway

🚇 **Subway** B, D & 4 to 167th St. **Bus** Bx1, Bx2 & BxM4

👫 **Age range** All ages

⏱ **Allow** 1 hour

🍽 **Eat and drink** *Snacks* Crown Diner *(79 East 161st St, 10452; 718 538 0309)* is a popular, but cash only, diner with standard breakfast and lunch offerings such as omelets, waffles, and burgers. *Real meal* Papaye *(196 McClellan St, 10456; 718 681 3240)* features authentic Ghanaian fare including fish, soups, cassava-based fufu (thick starchy paste) and omo tuo (balls of cooked rice).

👫 **Restrooms** Inside the Bronx Museum of the Arts

Gallery displaying contemporary art at the Bronx Museum of the Arts

Though founded in 1971, the museum did not have its own address until 1982, when it moved into a former synagogue purchased for it by the City of New York. In 2006, a stunning extension was added, designed by the cutting-edge architecture firm Arquitectonica. All glass and steel, it looks like a hastily folded piece of origami. The contemporary art, Friday night special events (such as jazz and film nights), and periodic family-friendly programs make it worth the trek.

Letting off steam

Mullaly Park *(Jerome Ave to River Ave, between 164th St & McClellan St, Bronx, 10452)* was named for the so-called father of the Bronx parks system, John Mullaly. The refurbished complex is home to a skate park, sprinkler area, playground, ice-skating rink, soccer field, and basketball court – so families are spoilt for choice.

④ Yankee Stadium

Baseball fever

It is unclear whether anything was really wrong with the original Yankee Stadium, which opened in 1923, but the Yankees' late owner, George Steinbrenner, wanted a new arena, no matter what. His wish came true with the opening of this brand-new stadium in 2009, just a stone's throw from the old one. His team seemed to like it too: the Yankees went on to win the 2009 World Series that fall. If possible, take in a game here. Seeing baseball live, amid a devoted, exuberant crowd, is an electrifying experience. If that is not possible, take the tour, which covers the Yankees Clubhouse, Monument

Park, which honors retired Yankees, and the Yankees Museum, whose Ball Wall contains hundreds of baseballs signed by past and present Yankees.

Letting off steam

Relocated and rebuilt to make way for the new Yankee Stadium, **Macombs Dam Park** *(between Jerome Ave & Major Deegan Expressway, Bronx, 11102)* has playgrounds, a soccer field, and a state-of-the-art high-tech sports track where kids can do laps. It is also a perfect spot for a pre-game picnic.

The Lowdown

🌐 **Address** 1 East 161st St, Bronx, 10451; 718 293 4300; www.yankees.com

🚇 **Subway** B, D & 4 to 161st St-Yankee Stadium. **Bus** Bx6 & Bx13

☺ **Open** Varies (May–Oct)

☺ **Price** $5–370 plus for a game

Ⓢ ticket per person; Classic Tour $55–80 (family); under 4s free

👫 **Cutting the line** Buy game or tour tickets at www.yankees.com.

📢 **Guided tours** Classic Tours: noon–1:40pm daily

👫 **Age range** All ages

⏱ **Allow** 1 hour without game; 3–4 hours with game

♿ **Wheelchair access** Yes

🍴 **Eat and drink** *Real meal* Feeding Tree *(892 Gerard Ave, 10452; 718 293 5025)* is a Caribbean restaurant whose strong suit is jerk chicken, goat stew, and seafood dishes, served with rice and beans, cabbage, and sweet fried plantains. Popular with locals and baseball fans alike.

👫 **Restrooms** In the stadium

A packed house for a baseball game at the Yankee Stadium

Picnic under $20; **Snacks** $20–35; **Real meal** $35–70; **Family treat** over $70 (based on a family of four)

Where to Stay in New York

New York offers a wide range of accommodations for families, including budget, luxury, and intimate boutique hotels, and a variety of furnished apartments suitable for longer stays in the city. A number of hotels welcome children and have special packages for families.

AGENCIES

Abode Apartment Rentals
www.abodenyc.com
Manhattan Getaways
212 956 2010; www.manhattan getaways.com
Both agencies offer furnished apartments for short-term stays, ranging from small studios to three-bedroom suites, with the added convenience for families of self-catering facilities.

Elegant dining room in the Ritz-Carlton Battery Park

Downtown: Lower Manhattan

HOTELS
Best Western Seaport Inn   Map 2 F3
33 Peck Slip, 10038; 212 766 6600; www.seaportinn.com; Subway: 2 & 3
This 72-room hotel near South Street Seaport (*see pp66–7*) offers free breakfast, free Wi-Fi, and a 24-hour fitness center. Kids aged 12 and under stay free in their parents' room. Terrace rooms have whirlpool tubs and great views of Brooklyn Bridge (*see pp196–7*).
ℝ ⛟ $–$$

Cosmopolitan Hotel   Map 1 C2
95 West Broadway, 10007; 212 566 1900; www.cosmohotel.com; Subway: A, C, 1, 2 & 3
One of the city's oldest hotels, the Cosmopolitan is nothing fancy, but its furnishings are modern, it is

clean, and it offers good value for money. The location on a busy Tribeca corner is ideal for exploring downtown and also convenient for taking a subway for uptown.
ℝ P ⚐ $

DoubleTree by Hilton Hotel – Financial District   Map 1 D5
8 Stone St, 10004; 212 480 9100; http://doubletree3.hilton.com; Subway: N, R, 4 & 5
This 44-story downtown tower opened in 2010 and has all the amenities expected of a full-service hotel, including flat-screen TV and MP3 players in rooms. Family accommodations can be a room with two doubles or a junior suite with sofa bed. Cribs are available, as is a kids' menu.
ℝ ⛟ ⚐ ⚐ $$–$$$

Duane Street Hotel   Map 1 C2
130 Duane St, 10013; 212 964 4600; www.duanestreethotel.com; Subway: A, C, 1, 2 & 3
Minimalist is the word for the decor in this clean, intimate, 43-room Tribeca hotel, where kids are welcomed with a library of books that can be borrowed at the desk. Rooms are attractive, and have iPod plug-ins and free Wi-Fi. The hotel also offers free use of iPads.
ℝ ⚐ $$

New York Marriott Downtown   Map 1 C4
85 West St, 10006; 212 385 4900; www.marriott.com; Subway: N, R & 1
Rates are way below Midtown at this sleek, high-rise, 497-room hotel, especially on weekends, when business travelers are not around. The hotel has many amenities, including safe deposit boxes, Wi-Fi, a fitness center, and evening turndown service. The Brookfield Place/World Financial Center shops,

restaurants, and river terrace are close by, and the nearby subway takes visitors uptown.
ℝ ⚐ $$

The Wall Street Inn   Map 1 D5
9 South William St, 10004; 212 747 1500; www.thewallstreetinn.com; Subway: N, R
An alternative to the standard downtown high-rise, this warm, 46-room hotel with a classic Early-American decor offers good value for money. Rooms are not especially large, but are well furnished and include small refrigerators. The Continental breakfast is free.
ℝ $$

Millennium Hilton   Map 1 C3
55 Church St, 10007; 212 693 2001; www3.hilton.com; Subway: N, R, E & 4
A heated indoor pool overlooking the city is the best reason to consider this 569-room hotel. Amenities include big plasma-screen TVs and a fitness center. Room service with a kids' menu. Within walking distance of 17 museums and landmarks.
ℝ ⚐ ⊗ $$$

The Ritz-Carlton, Battery Park   Map 1 C5
2 West St, 10004; 212 344 0800; www.ritzcarlton.com; Subway: 4 & 5
Teddy bears, coloring books, and a child's guide to the city await young guests at this luxurious hotel. The

A guest room at the Millenium Hilton, with great views of downtown Manhattan

location, across the street from riverside parkland, offers plenty of space for kids to run around. The only downside is the long walk to the subway.

🔊 📶 🍽 $$$

Downtown: Chelsea, Meatpacking District & Gramercy Park

BED & BREAKFAST
Townhouse Inn of Chelsea Map 8 G5
131 West 23rd St, 10011; 212 414 2323; www.townhouseinnchelsea.com; Subway: 1, 2, A, C, E, N, Q & R
This charming townhouse has 14 guestrooms and apartment-style suites. Fully renovated with modern amenities. The brick and wood accents and classic furniture give it an old-fashioned, rustic feel. There is a library with newspapers, magazines, and books that guests can access.

🔊 $

HOTELS
Chelsea Lodge Map 8 E6
318 West 20th St, between Eighth Ave & Ninth Ave, 10011; 212 243 4499; www.chelsealodge.com; Subway: C, E & 1
A remodeled brick townhouse with 22 rooms and a pleasant decor, this is a reasonable budget choice. The lodge bedrooms have one double bed plus a sink and shower, and a shared toilet on each floor. Be aware that there is no elevator.

🔊 📶 🍽 $

Hotel 17 Map 9 C6
225 East 17th St, between Second Ave & Third Ave, 10003; 212 475 2845; www.hotel17ny.com; Subway: L, N, Q, R, 4, 5 & 6
This basic, 120-room budget choice is a short walk from Union Square, the East Village (see p82), and Gramercy Park. The rooms are plain, but neat and clean. Shared bathrooms are down the hall.

🔊 $

Larchmont Hotel Map 4 F2
27 West 11th St, between Fifth Ave & Sixth Ave, 10011; 212 989 9333; www.larchmonthotel.com; Subway: F & M
Although short on space and style, this hotel enjoys a great location in Greenwich Village (see pp80–81).

Family suite accommodations come with a private bathroom, kitchenette, and Continental breakfast.

🔊 📶 🍽 $

W New York – Union Square Map 9 A6
201 Park Ave South, between 17th St & 18th St, 10003; 212 253 9119; www.whotels.com; Subway: L, N, Q, R, 4, 5 & 6
A landmark 1911 Beaux-Arts building transformed into a hip contemporary hotel, this place is located near Union Square's many attractions and multiple subway connections. Rooms come with pillow-top mattresses, robes, and access to a library of films for the in-room DVD player.

🔊 🍽 $$–$$$

A comfortable guest room at the Hotel Gansevoort, Meatpacking District

Gansevoort Meatpacking NYC Hotel Map 3 D1
18 Ninth Ave at 13th St, 10014; 212 206 6700; www.hotelganse voort.com; Subway: A, C, E & L
A hip hangout, this luxury hotel invites families to join the other guests enjoying the rooftop pool. Play Station, video games, a lunch-box full of treats, and a cupcake at turndown are provided for kids.

🍽 P $$$

Gramercy Park Hotel Map 9 B5
2 Lexington Ave, between 21st St & 22nd St, 10010; 212 920 3300; www.gramercyparkhotel.com; Subway: 6
Eclectic and elegant best describe the luxurious reincarnation of this classic hotel dating back to 1925. The interiors are filled with artworks, grand chandeliers, tapestries, velvet drapes, and a Renaissance-inspired color scheme of deep red and blue. Rooms are of a good size, and guests have keys to the lovely, private Gramercy Park just outside.

🔊 📶 🍽 $$$

Standard, High Line Map 3 C1
848 Washington St at 13th St, 10014; 212 645 4646; www.standard hotels.com; Subway: A, C, E & L
Straddling the High Line (see pp86–7), this ultra-modern hotel has glass-walled rooms and easy access to the area's dining and nightlife scenes. However, it is better suited to older children and there is a limit of three people per room.

🔊 🍽 $$$

Downtown: Lower East Side

BED AND BREAKFAST
Union Square Inn Map 5 A1
209 East 14th St, 10003; 212 614 0500; www.unionsquareinn.com; Subway: L, 4, 5 & 6
Union Square Inn has 47 rooms that are geared towards extended stays. The rooms have basic amenities like private bathrooms, Wi-Fi, and a kitchenette. Although on the small side and not luxurious, the rooms are clean and comfortable. The different types include two twins and one queen.

🔊 🍽 $

HOTELS
Off SoHo Suites Map 5 B5
11 Rivington St, 10002; 212 979 9815; www.offsoho.com; Subway: F, J & Z
Modest but comfortable, this property in a trendy location offers two-room suites for four, plus full kitchens. Bedrooms come with twin or queen beds; living rooms have a queen-size sofabed. The best of the Lower East Side's art and dining scenes are just steps away.

🔊 📶 🍽 $–$$

St. Marks Hotel Map 4 H2
2 St. Marks Place, 10003; 212 674 0100; www.stmarkshotel.net; Subway: 6
This clean no-frills hotel, without an elevator, has decent rooms with private bathrooms. Conveniently located in East Village with the subway just a block away.

🔊 $

Key to symbols *see back cover flap*

The Gem Hotel SoHo Map 5 B4
135 East Houston St, 10002;
212 358 8844; www.thegemhotel.
com; Subway: F
This budget 45-room hotel is
located on the edge of the East
Village and the trendy Lower East
Side. Rooms are basic, but equipped
with pillow-top mattresses, robes,
upscale Gilchrist & Soames toiletries,
free Wi-Fi, and flat-screen LCD TV.
🌐 🍽️ $

Hotel on Rivington Map 5 C4
107 Rivington St, 10002; 212 475
2600; www.hotelonrivington.com;
Subway: F, J, M & Z
Spectacular views from floor-to-
ceiling glass walls are the hallmark
of the guest rooms in this cutting-
edge, 21-story tower, a dramatic
sign of the changing Lower East
Side. Adults and children will be
equally delighted with the
glass-enclosed bathrooms with
steam showers and soaking tubs.
The East Village, Nolita, and
Chinatown are all nearby.
🌐 🍽️ $$

Blue Moon Map 5 C5
100 Orchard St, 10002; 212 533
9080; www.bluemoon-nyc.com;
Subway: F, J, M & Z
The old and the new blend
beautifully in this elegant, 22-room
boutique hotel, which has been
transformed from a 19th-century
tenement. The accommodations,
named after celebrities of the 1920s
and 1930s, are roomy and include
family quarters with high ceilings,
offering a queen-sized bed and a
sofa bed with trundle. Amenities on
offer include free Wi-Fi and
Continental breakfast. All rooms
come with iPod docking stations.
🌐 🛎️ $$$

The dining room at the Hotel on Rivington with fine views of the city

Key to Price Guide *see p241*

The Bowery Hotel Map 5 A3
335 Bowery, 10003; 212 505
9100; www.theboweryhotel.com;
Subway: B, D, F, M & 6
Designed to blend in with the
old neighborhood, this stylish
hotel has retro-chic furnishings
in the lobby, with a porch facing
a green lawn. Rooms are airy,
with floor-to-ceiling windows.
Two people per room is the limit.
There is also a fitness center
and a spa.
🌐 🍽️ $$$

The Standard, East Village Map 5 A3
25 Cooper Square, Bowery at East
5th St, 10003; 212 475 5700; www.
standardhotels.com/east-village;
Subway: N, Q, R, 4 & 6
The Standard has a sleek, modern
decor, with floor-to-ceiling and
wall-to-wall windows. Room
types differ, from the Standard
Double to the Skyline Studio.
All have comfort-able beds with
Italian sheets and down pillows,
spacious modern bathrooms, and
free Wi-Fi.
🌐 🛎️ 🍽️ $$

Midtown: East

HOTELS
Carlton Arms Hotel Map 9 B5
160 East 25th St, 10010; 212 679
0680; www.carltonarms.com;
Subway: 6
Expect more art than amenities at
this hotel. The 52 rooms explode
with colorful works painted by
different artists. The rooms are
compact, with no TV or phones, and
the cheapest do not have private
bathrooms. This is a budget hotel,
but it has plenty of atmosphere.
🌐 $

*Hotel Giraffe, a stylish boutique hotel
on Park Avenue South*

Ramada Eastside Map 9 B4
161 Lexington Ave, 10016; 212 545
1800; www.applecorehotels.com/
ramada-eastside; Subway: 6
This 111-room, 12-story hotel is a
good budget choice. Rooms are a
little small and dated, but clean, with
comfortable beds. Amenities include
free Wi-Fi and phone calls, free
newspapers on weekdays, flat-screen
TV and a complimentary Continental
breakfast. Children under 13 stay for
free when sharing with adults. Cribs
are available on request.
🌐 🛎️ $

The Evelyn Map 9 A4
7 East 27th St, between Fifth Ave
& Madison Ave, 10016; 855 468
3501; www.theevelyn.com;
Subway: N, R & 6
A colorful, stylish boutique
hotel, the Evelyn boasts rooms
with luxurious Frette linens and
bathrobes, C.O. Bigelow toiletries,
walk-in rain showers, flat-screen
TVs, and free Wi-Fi. Complimentary
morning pastries, and coffee and
tea in the lobby add to the charm.
🌐 🛎️ 🍽️ $-$$

The MAve NYC Map 9 A4
62 Madison Ave at 27th St, 10016;
212 532 7373; www.themavehotel.
com; Subway: N, R & 6
Housed in a lovely mansard-roofed
building from around 1902, the
72-room MAve (for Madison Ave) is
tight on room space, but offers a
Continental breakfast and free
Wi-Fi. Pets are welcome with prior
notice. Madison Square Park (see
p83) is just a block away.
🌐 $

Affinia Dumont
Map 9 B3

150 East 34th St, 10016; 212 481 7600; www.affinia.com; Subway: 6
Part of the Affinia all-suite chain, this hotel has an emphasis on fitness. Guests are offered "Experience Kits" for yoga, running, and strength-training and there is a spa on site. The one-bedroom suites for four are spacious, with a sofa bed in the living room and a full kitchen.

📶 🛏 🍽 **$$**

Affinia Fifty NYC
Map 13 B5

155 East 50th St, 10022; 212 751 5710; www.affinia.com/fifty; Subway: M & 6
Another all-suite hotel, with two-room accommodations including a dining area and a full kitchen. The Midtown location is convenient, with nearby subway and bus connections to get around the city. The dream pillow menu gives six choices, from down and hyper-allergenic to a Swedish memory foam pillow.

📶 🚲 🛏 🍽 **$$**

Affinia Shelburne
Map 9 B2

303 Lexington Ave at 37th St, 10016; 212 689 5200; www.affinia.com; Subway: 4, 5, 6 & 7
Stylishly remodeled, the Shelburne has spacious rooms with modern decor. Suites offer pantries with microwave and refrigerator. The location in quiet Murray Hill and the seasonal rooftop terrace are added attractions.

📶 🛏 🍽 **$$**

Best Western PLUS Hospitality House
Map 13 B5

145 East 49th St, between Third Ave & Lexington Ave, 10017; 212 753 8781; www.bestwesternnewyork.com; Subway: 6
This renovated complex of 34 one- and two-bedroom suites offers full kitchens in each unit plus lots of freebies: complimentary full Continental breakfast, local calls, Wi-Fi, and use of a guest computer. There is an outdoor seating area.

📶 🚲 🖥 🛏 🍽 **$$–$$$**

Courtyard by Marriott New York Manhattan/ Midtown East
Map 13 B5

866 Third Ave at 53rd St, 10022; 212 644 1300; www.marriott.com; Subway: E, M & 6
Fluffy pillows, good mattresses, a big flat-screen TV, free high-speed

A suite at the New York Palace, with bedroom, living room, and kitchenette

Internet, and refrigerators are among the room amenities in this modern high-rise hotel. The best guest rooms for families come with two queen beds and a sofa bed.

📶 🚲 🍽 **$$**

Hotel Giraffe
Map 9 B4

365 Park Ave South at 26th St, 10016; 212 685 7700; www.hotelgiraffe.com; Subway: 6
Light, bright, and modern, with a spacious and welcoming sitting-room lobby, the Giraffe has good-sized rooms with two beds, iPod docking stations, DVD players, and a big-screen TV. Baby cribs are also available. Add a free breakfast buffet and evening wine and cheese, and there is good reason to consider this outpost just south of Midtown.

📶 🍽 **$$**

Kimberly Hotel
Map 13 B5

145 East 50th St, between Lexington Ave & Third Ave, 10022; 212 702 1600; www.kimberlyhotel.com; Subway: E, M & 6
For the price of an average hotel room, the Kimberly offers spacious suites with traditional decor. The largest is the two-bedroom, two-bathroom suite with a separate living room, a queen-sized pull-out sofa bed plus a dining area, and a kitchenette (no stove). There is also a rooftop lounge bar on the 30th floor.

📶 🛏 🍽 **$$**

Martha Washington Hotel
Map 9 A4

29 East 29th St, between Madison Ave & Park Ave, 10016; 212 689 1900; www.chelseahotels.com; Subway: N, Q, R, 4 & 6

Located in the area called NoMad, Martha Washington is just a few blocks between Madison Square Park and Penn Station, in the heart of Manhattan. Guestrooms range from the "Cozy Bedroom" to larger suites. They are not particularly spacious but they are comfortable, sleek, and newly renovated.

📶 🍽 **$$**

Marcel at Gramercy
Map 9 B5

201 East 24th St at Third Ave, 10010; 212 696 3800; www.themarcelatgramercy.com; Subway: 6
The Marcel has a sleek decor, with a Polar lounge for relaxing, which is open on Fridays and Saturdays. There is also a computer for guests with free Internet access. Nearby attractions that can be reached on foot include the Flatiron Building (*see p82*), Soho, Greenwich Village, and Chelsea.

📶 🍽 **$$**

New York Palace Hotel
Map 13 A5

455 Madison Ave at 50th St, 10022; 212 888 7000; www.newyorkpalace.com; Subway: E, M & 6
A luxury hotel with unusually large rooms, the Palace provides young guests with coloring books, teddy bears, child-size robes and slippers, and DVD players. Baby powders and lotions, cribs, high chairs, and cots are also available on request. There is also a free shuttle – only on weekday afternoons – to Broadway theaters. Considering the elegant setting and the many adult amenities, it is excellent value.

📶 🍽 **$$**

Key to symbols *see back cover flap*

Roger Smith Hotel
Map 13 B6

501 Lexington Ave, between 47th St & 48th St, 10017; 212 755 1400; www.rogersmith.com; Subway: 6

This 130-room hotel, with its plentiful art and New England decor, is a welcome alternative to the look-alike chains, and its rates are reasonable. Rooms are equipped with coffee-makers and small refrigerators. There is cable TV and movie rental is available. A seasonal rooftop bar features in-house art installations.

$$

The InterContinental New York Barclay
Map 13 B6

111 East 48th St, 10017; 212 755 5900; www.intercontinental nybarclay.com; Subway: 6

An updated landmark 1920s classic hotel, the Barclay is an oasis of quiet graciousness. It offers a unique package for American Girl doll fans that includes a DVD, and a souvenir doll bed. The junior suites are comfortable spaces for families, and refrigerators are available on request. The Grand Central Terminal *(see pp100–101)* is nearby.

$$

70 Park Avenue Hotel
Map 9 B2

70 Park Ave at 38th St, 10016; 212 973 2400; www.70parkave.com; Subway: 4, 5, 6 & 7

This classy pied-à-terre makes children especially welcome by offering the KimptonKids program, which includes a welcome gift, a list of nearby child-friendly activities, toilet latches, and a night light. Cribs are available on request.

$$–$$$

Waldorf Astoria
Map 13 B5

301 Park Ave at 50th St, 10022; 212 355 3000; www.waldorfastoria.com; Subway: 6

An Art Deco landmark with one of the city's grandest lobbies, the Waldorf Astoria occupies a full city block with 1,415 rooms, three restaurants, and two lounges. Guests should be aware that casual attire is not encouraged in the hotel's public areas. All rooms have high-speed Internet access. The room decor varies, and may disappoint after the opulent lobby, but there is a certain cachet to saying that you've stayed here.

$$–$$$

Wyndham Midtown 45 at New York City
Map 13 C6

205 East 45th St, between Second Ave & Third Ave, 10017; 212 867 5100, www.wyndhammidtown45. com; Subway: 4, 5, 6 & 7

Ideal for families, the two-bedroom suites here have a king- and a queen-size bed, two bathrooms, two TVs, and DVD players. Every suite in this hotel comes equipped with a Poggenpohl kitchen. Cribs are available on request.

$$$

Four Seasons Hotel
Map 13 B4

57 East 57th St, between Madison Ave & Park Ave, 10022; 212 758 5700; www.fourseasons.com; Subway: 4, 5, 6, N, Q & R

This modern, 52-story hotel is minimalist and opulent at the same time. It has some of the city's largest rooms and its most lavish bathrooms: walk-in closet, in-bathroom TV, glass-enclosed shower stall, and soaking tub that fills in 60 seconds.

$$$

Hotel Elysée
Map 13 A5

60 East 54th St, between Madison Ave & Park Ave, 10022; 212 753 1066; www.elyseehotel.com; Subway: E & M

Celebrity sightings are frequent at this opulent, antique-filled boutique hotel and its legendary Monkey Bar. Rooms are lavishly furnished and come with a free breakfast, cookies, fresh fruit, all-day coffee and tea, and evening wine and cheese. Free Wi-Fi and passes to a nearby health club are also included.

$$$

Library Hotel
Map 9 A1

299 Madison Ave at 41st St, 10017; 212 983 4500; www.libraryhotel. com; Subway: S, 4, 5, 6 & 7

A unique, luxury boutique hotel where floors are named for categories of the Dewey Decimal System: technology, philosophy, and the arts. Guests receive free Continental breakfasts and evening refreshments, and have access to a book-filled reading room, a garden, and a writer's den with a fireplace. However, only one child is allowed per suite. Larger families will need to book connecting rooms.

$$$

Omni Berkshire Place
Map 13 A5

21 East 52nd St at Madison Ave, 10022; 212 753 5800; www. omnihotels.com; Subway: E & M

Omni's special kids' program welcomes children with a backpack filled with games and books, and menu choices geared to young tastes. Located near the shops on Fifth Avenue, the hotel is also within walking distance of Broadway.

$$$

Midtown: West

B&B AND MOTELS

414 Hotel
Map 12 E6

414 West 46th St at Ninth Ave, 10036; 212 399 0006; www.414 hotel.com; Subway: A, C & E

A nice surprise in this busy area, this 22-room inn consists of two historic townhouses, one behind the other, separated by a garden courtyard. Continental breakfast, Wi-Fi, iPod and iPhone players, and big flat-screen TVs are included in the rate; all the rooms have refrigerators. Ask about family packages.

$–$$

Stylish marble lobby at the Four Seasons Hotel

Key to Price Guide *see p241*

A suite at the Hilton Garden Inn

Skyline Hotel
Map 11 D5

725 Tenth Ave at 49th St, 10019; 212 586 3400; www.skylinehotelny. com; Subway: C & E

The only Midtown hotel catering to motorists, with a low daily parking rate, the Skyline is close to the Theater District and has spacious rooms and a large heated indoor pool on the penthouse floor. Rooms come equipped with refrigerators, flat-screen TVs, and Wi-Fi. The location is a bit far west, but the crosstown bus is handy.

🔊 P ⊘ $

HOTELS
Broadway@Times Square
Map 12 G6

129 West 46th St, between Sixth Ave & Seventh Ave, 10036; 212 221 2600; www.applecorehotels.com; Subway: B, D, F & M

A family-friendly budget hotel, with perks such as free Continental breakfasts, free Wi-Fi and national phone calls, coffee-makers, in-room personal safes, iPod connections, Movies on Demand, and Nintendo video games for kids.

🔊 P $

Hilton Garden Inn Times Square
Map 12 F6

790 Eighth Ave at 50th St, 10019; 212 581 7000; www. hiltongardeninn.hilton.com; Subway: C, E, N, Q, R & 1

A good location and comfortable rooms are among the pluses of this hotel. Rooms are equipped with mini-refrigerators, coffee-makers, microwaves, and free Wi-Fi. It also offers a fitness center, a rooftop lounge, and an on-site, 24-hour mini-market.

🔊 ⊟ |◎| $

Hotel Edison NYC
Map 12 F6

228 West 47th St, between Eighth Ave & Broadway, 10036; 212 840 5000; www. edisonhotelnyc.com; Subway: N, Q & R

An Art Deco hotel with a mural-filled lobby, the Edison is a long-time budget favorite. The small but elegantly decorated rooms offer a choice of queen- or king-sized beds, and some of the hotel's packages include Broadway tickets. There is also a fitness center and airport transfers are available.

🔊 |◎| $

New York Manhattan Hotel
Map 8 H3

6 West 32nd St, near Fifth Ave, 10001; 212 643 7100; www.apple corehotels.com; Subway: B, D, F, M, N, Q & R

This 17-story, 171-room hotel is stingy with room space, but generous with benefits such as free Continental breakfast, Wi-Fi, free phone calls, cribs on request, and a small fitness center. Kids under 13 can stay for free when sharing a room with adults. Families can also shop at Macy's (see p95) nearby.

🔊 $

Salisbury Hotel
Map 12 G4

123 West 57th St, 10019; 212 246 1300; www.nycsalisbury.com; Subway: F, N, Q & R

There is nothing fancy about the Salisbury, but its location is first class. The decent-size rooms have private bathrooms and many also include a pantry with a coffee-maker, microwave, and refrigerator. The hotel serves a Continental breakfast at rates that are a steal in this area. Free stay for kids under 5.

|◎| ⊟ $

The Hotel @ Times Square
Map 12 G6

59 West 46th St, between Fifth Ave & Sixth Ave, 10036; 212 719 2300; www.applecorehotels.com; Subway: B, D, F & M

This budget option has a pleasant lobby and tastefully decorated, albeit small, rooms. Amenities include free Continental breakfast, free Wi-Fi and phone calls within the US, coffee-makers, Nintendo video

games, Movies on Demand, and a flat-screen TV.

🔊 P $

Room Mate Grace Hotel
Map 12 G6

125 West 45th St, between Sixth Ave & Seventh Ave, 10036; 212 354 2323; www.room-matehotels.com; Subway: B, D, F & M

A budget choice with a young vibe, minimalist decor, and a swimming pool in the lobby. Amenities include Continental breakfast and free Wi-Fi and DVD players in rooms. Cribs are also available. The lowest rates for families of four are for the rooms with bunk beds.

🔊 ⚡ ⤏ |◎| P ⊘ $-$$

Shoreham Hotel
Map 12 H4

33 West 55th St, 10019; 212 247 6700; www.shorehamhotel.com; Subway: E, F & M

This modern hotel offers state-of-the-art features. The spacious rooms include a penthouse, a junior suite, and one-bedroom suite rooms large enough to accomodate a family with children. The hotel is located close to The Museum of Modern Art (see pp106–107).

🔊 ⤏ |◎| $-$$$

414 Hotel, located in the heart of Midtown Manhattan

Affinia Manhattan
Map 8 F3

371 Seventh Ave at 31st St, 10001; 212 563 1800; www.affinia.com/ manhattan; Subway: A, C, E, N, Q, R, 1, 2 & 3

The 1929 Art Deco touches remain, but the Affinia Manhattan has been nicely modernized and offers suites with full kitchens. Ask for the iPod loaded with a walking tour and a deck of cards to amuse the kids.

🔊 |◎| ⊟ $$

Key to symbols *see back cover flap*

Algonquin Hotel
Map 8 G1

59 West 44th St, between Fifth Ave & Sixth Ave; 10036; 212 840 6800; www.algonquinhotel.com; Subway: B, D, F, M, S & 7

This 174-room literary landmark is New York's oldest operating hotel. The lobby is full of period atmosphere. Families can stay in suites with sofa beds in the living room, two flat-screen TVs, and free Wi-Fi.

$$

Belvedere Hotel
Map 12 F6

319 West 48th St, between Eighth Ave & Ninth Ave, 10036; 212 245 7000; www.belvederehotelnyc.com; Subway: C & E

All rooms have a kitchenette that includes a microwave, refrigerator, and coffee-maker at this stylish hotel.

$$

Best Western Plus President Hotel at Times Square
Map 12 F6

234 West 48th St, between Broadway & Eighth Ave, 10036; 212 246 8800; www.bestwestern. com; Subway: C, E, N, Q, R & 1

Located in the heart of the Theater District, this chain hotel has suites with a queen bed and queen sofa bed priced just above budget rates. Amenties include flat-screen TVs, free Wi-Fi and iPod docking stations.

$$

DoubleTree Suites by Hilton Hotel New York City – Times Square
Map 12 F6

1568 Broadway, 10036; 212 719 1600; www3.hilton.com; Subway: N, Q & R

This all-suite hotel is smack in the middle of Broadway. Each suite has a bedroom and a separate living room offering a double sofa bed, two flat-screen TVs, microwave, and mini-refrigerator.

$$

DoubleTree by Hilton Hotel New York City – Chelsea
Map 8 G4

128 West 29th St, 10001; 212 564 0994; www3.hilton.com; Subway: 1

This 26-story hotel offers fresh, modern decor, comfortable rooms with the usual amenities, a fitness room and an on-site restaurant with a children's menu. Rooms on higher floors have a view of the Empire State Building *(see pp94–5)*.

$$

Eventi
Map 8 G4

851 Ave of the Americas, between 29th St & 30th St, 10001; 212 564 4567; www.eventihotel.com; Subway: N, Q, R & 1

Convenient for Chelsea or Midtown, this 292-room boutique newcomer offers floor-to-ceiling windows, Frette linens, original artworks, and a fifth-floor veranda with seating, and evening wine and cheese. The trademark KimptonKids program offers special gifts and animal print robes for youngsters, and all necessary equipment for toddlers.

$$

Hilton Times Square
Map 8 F1

234 West 42nd St, between Broadway & Eighth Ave, 10036; 212 840 8222; www3.hilton.com; Subway: A, C, N, Q, R, S, 1, 2, 3 & 7

The accommodation at this Hilton hotel starts on the 23rd floor of a 44-story skyscraper. The rooms are spacious and the views impressive. Although 42nd Street is busy, the noise is lessened by the hotel's lofty setting. The location is close to Times Square *(see pp118–19)*.

$$

Hotel Metro
Map 8 H2

45 West 35th St, between Fifth Ave & Sixth Ave, 10001; 212 947 2500; www.hotelmetronyc.com; Subway: B, D, F, M, N, Q & R

This friendly 181-room hotel has much to recommend it. Family rooms have adjoining bedrooms and there is a generous complimentary Continental breakfast buffet that can be enjoyed in a library room. Wi-Fi is free and there's a rooftop terrace and fitness center.

$$

Intercontinental New York Times Square
Map 8 F1

300 West 44th St at Eighth Ave, 10036; 212 803 4500; www. interconny.com; Subway: A, C & E

One of the newer hotels in the neighborhood, this 36-story glass skyscraper towers above Times Square. Rooms are comfortable and bathrooms have walk-in rain showers. There is an inviting guest lounge and restaurant with a faux fireplace, a 24-hour fitness center, and a theater ticket desk.

$$

The opulent oak-panelled lobby and interior of the Algonquin

Mansfield Hotel
Map 8 H1

12 West 44th St, between Fifth Ave & Sixth Ave, 10036; 212 277 8700; www.mansfieldhotel.com; Subway: B, D, F, M, S & 7

There's a gracious feel to the Mansfield, a 126-room boutique hotel in a carefully restored 1903 building whose period charms have been retained. Rooms are small but comfortable and have flat-screen TVs. There is a fitness center and the paneled Club Room library has a fireplace, table games, and complimentary coffee all day.

$$

Novotel
Map 12 F5

226 West 52nd St, between Broadway & Eighth Ave, 10019; 212 315 0100; www.novotel.com; Subway: B, C, D, E & 1

Up to two kids under 16 can stay for free in their parents' room and the breakfast buffet is also free for them when they dine with their parents at this family-friendly hotel. The lobby is on the seventh floor, with views of Times Square.

$$

Residence Inn by Marriott-New York Manhattan
Map 8 G2

1033 Sixth Ave, between 38th St & 39th St, 10018; 212 768 0007; www. marriott.com; Subway: B, D, F & M

Designed to attract long-stay business travelers, this is a fine option for families. Studios and two-bedroom suites have kitchenettes with a microwave, a refrigerator, coffee-maker and dishwasher, plus pots, dishes, and cutlery. Free Wi-Fi and a buffet breakfast are included in the rates.

📶 🍽 **$$**

Renaissance New York Hotel Times Square Map 12 G6

Two Times Square, 714 Seventh Ave at West 48th St, 10036; 212 765 7676; www.marriott.com/renaissance hotels; Subway: N, Q & R

It is hard to beat the exciting location, smack in the heart of Times Square, or the dazzling views from the lounge and some of the guest rooms. This stylish hotel promises total sound-proofing and rooms have large flat-screen TVs and plug-in connectivity panels. Cribs are available.

📶 ♿ 🍽 **$$**

The Muse New York Map 12 G6

130 West 46th St, between Sixth Ave & Seventh Ave, 10036; 212 485 2400; www.themusehotel.com; Subway: B, D, M & F

The 200-room Muse, a Kimpton hotel, has a touch of whimsy and luxurious rooms with goose-down feather beds with Frette linens, 37-inch (94-cm) TVs, and animal-print robes in adult and kids' sizes. KimptonKids amenities, including a welcome gift, are offered here.

📶 🛏 🍽 **$$**

The Jewel Facing Rockefeller Center Map 12 H5

11 West 51st St, 10019; 212 863 0550; www.thejewelny.com; Subway: B, D, E, F & M

In a great location facing Rockefeller Center (see pp112–13) and reasonably priced, modern suite accommodations with kitchenettes make The Jewel an excellent family choice. Perks include free Wi-Fi, complimentary use of computers and printers, and discounts on

Outdoor seating area at the Peninsula New York

nearby attractions. Most rooms have floor-to-ceiling glass walls; some have fantastic views of St Patrick's Cathedral (see p114).

📶 🍽 **$$**

Le Parker Meridien Map 12 G4

119 West 56th St, 10019; 212 245 5000; www.parkermeridien.com; Subway: F, N, Q & R

The big indoor rooftop pool and a burger joint in the lobby are reasons enough to choose this hotel. When available, the Family Fun package includes a Junior Suite, and spa sessions. Rooms have big flat-screen TVs, and free Wi-Fi.

📶 🍽 P **$$$**

The Plaza Hotel Map 12 H3

768 Fifth Ave at Central Park South, 10019; 212 759 3000; www.fairmont .com/theplaza; Subway: N, Q & R

New York's grande dame lost a bit of its historic luster with the $450 million redo, which cut rooms and added condos, but it retains the fabulous Palm Court for afternoon tea. The rooms have luxurious amenities to match the price, including tablet-controlled drapes, lights and entertainment.

🍽 P **$$$**

The Westin New York at Times Square Map 8 F1

270 West 43rd St & Eighth Ave, 10036; 212 201 2700; www.westinny.com; Subway: A, C, E, N, Q, R, S, 1, 2, 3 & 7

The upscale 873-room Westin offers rooms with flat-screen TVs, iPod docking stations and coffee-makers. Young guests

receive backpacks filled with "toys and tools" to help them enjoy the city.

📶 🍽 **$$–$$$**

London NYC Map 12 G5

151 West 54th St, between Sixth Ave & Seventh Ave, 10019; 866 690 2029; www.thelondonnyc.com; Subway: B, D, E, F, M, N, Q & R

The London has spacious sitting areas in each bedroom, and provides all luxurious amenities. The two restaurants here are run by renowned British chef Gordon Ramsay. Tabs can be expensive since families of four are required to take two rooms, but when rates are on special, this is a handsome choice.

📶 🍽 **$$$**

Peninsula New York Map 12 H4

700 Fifth Ave at 55th St, 10019, 212 956 2888; www.peninsula.com; Subway: E & M

Among the luxuries at this hotel are an indoor pool and an outside sun terrace. The warm welcome for kids includes child-sized robes, DVDs, books, and suggestions for special outings. Suites and connecting rooms are great for families who can afford it.

🛏 🍽 P ⊙ **$$$**

Warwick New York Hotel Map 12 G4

65 West 54th St at Sixth Ave, 10019, 212 247 2700; www.warwickhotelny. com; Subway: F

A long-time choice of stars, from Cary Grant to Elvis Presley, the 1926 Warwick has large rooms and suites. Families are accommodated in rooms with two double beds, and rollaway beds are available.

📶 🛏 🍽 **$$$**

Imposing facade of the Plaza Hotel

Key to symbols see back cover flap

Homey yet elegant interiors at Hotel Wales

Upper East Side

BED AND BREAKFAST

Gracie Inn   Map 16 G5
502 East 81st St, 10028; 212 628 1700; www.gracieinnhotel.com; Subway: 6
An 100-year-old townhouse residence that is now a cozy inn, the Gracie is an affordable choice – even for its small duplex penthouse suites with a private sundeck. All rooms have private bathrooms and free Wi-Fi. Continental breakfast-in-bed is also on offer. Suites have kitchenettes. The Carl Schurz Park nearby is a bonus for families.

$–$$

HOTELS

Affinia Gardens   Map 13 C2
215 East 64th St, between Second Ave & Third Ave, 10065; 212 355 1230; www.affinia.com; Subway: F
A good choice for families, this all-suite property offers a one-bedroom suite with a kitchen. Kids will enjoy the amenities such as board games, coloring books and crayons, and other items through e-concierge, which are made available to guests. There is also a free tea bar.

$$

Courtyard New York Manhattan/ Midtown East   Map 16 G3
410 East 92nd St at First Ave, 10128; 212 410 6777; www.marriott. com; Subway: 4, 5 & 6
The 50-ft (15-m) indoor lap pool and the Carl Schurz Park, a short drive away, with a riverside walkway and playgrounds, are the main reasons to consider this basic 226-room-high rise lodging. Families with small children may

find this a worthwhile option, even though there is no subway station nearby.

$$

Hotel Wales   Map 16 E3
1295 Madison Ave, between 92nd St & 93rd St, 10128, 212 876 6000; www.hotelwalesnyc.com; Subway: 6
Step inside the Wales and a small European establishment comes to mind. It is a little dated, perhaps, and somewhat quirky, with rooms of various sizes, but it has a charm of its own. Families can stay in suites with sofa beds in the living room and two TVs. There is a rooftop terrace.

$$

The Carlyle   Map 16 E6
35 East 76th St, between Park Ave & Madison Ave, 10021; 212 744 1600; www.thecarlyle.com; Subway: 6
There is no hotel more exclusive than the Carlyle, a gracious old-world hideaway with 188 rooms. However, it does cater to families through its "Rose Buds for Children" program, making available baby monitors, cribs, child-size robes, changing tables, bed rails, and a children's menu for room service and in the restaurant. Expect spacious suite accommodations with traditional decor and a hefty tab.

$$$

Loews Regency   Map 13 B3
540 Park Ave at 61st St, 10065; 212 759 4100; www.loewshotels.com/en/ Regency-Hotel; Subway: F, N, Q & R
A top luxury hotel, the Loews Regency is known locally for business "power breakfasts," but like all Loews hotels, it welcomes families with gifts

and with packages that offer a 50 percent discount on a second room. There is also a kids' menu and lending libraries of games. The location is excellent, quiet, and close to Midtown.

$$$

Upper West Side

HOTELS

Marrakech Hotel   Map 15 B2
2688 Broadway at 103rd St, 10025; 212 222 2954; www.marrakech hotelnyc.com; Subway: 1
The Moorish decor doesn't disguise the fact that this is a basic, slightly scruffy budget choice with no elevator and little space. That said, rooms have private bathrooms, Wi-Fi is free in the lobby, the neighborhood is good, and a subway station is on the corner.

$

The Milburn Hotel   Map 15 B6
242 West 76th St, between Broadway & West End Ave, 10023; 212 362 1006; www.milburnhotel. com; Subway: 1
There is a lot to recommend at this budget accommodation, where family suites have kitchenettes with sink, microwave, refrigerator, dishes, and cutlery. Guests also have free use of the pool and facilities at a health club one block away. Wi-Fi is free.

$

Hotel Newton   Map 15 B3
2528 Broadway, 10025; 212 678 6500; www.thehotelnewton.com; Subway: 1, 2 & 3
Even the standard rooms come equipped with mini-refrigerators, microwaves, and coffee-makers at this 105-room budget hotel, and suites have kitchenettes. The decor may be dated and there is not a lot of space, but rooms are clean and well kept and express subway connections are on the corner.

$

Hotel Belleclaire   Map 15 B6
250 West 77th St, between Broadway & West End Ave, 10024; 212 362 7700; www.hotelbelleclaire. com; Subway: 1
Modest but attractive updated accommodations, including family suites, are found here in a classic,

Bright dining room, Mandarin Oriental Hotel

quiet West Side residential area. Free Wi-Fi and coffee, flat-screen HD TVs, iPod docking stations, and a fitness center are among the amenities. Good transportation options are available nearby.

$-$$

The Excelsior Hotel   Map 15 C5
45 West 81st St, between Central Park West & Columbus Ave, 10024; 212 362 9200; www.excelsiorhotel ny.com; Subway: B & C
Just across the street from the American Museum of Natural History (see pp174–5), and close to Central Park, the Excelsior has an old-world residential feel and good rates for decent-size rooms in a fine location. Downtown subways are on the corner.

$-$$

Hotel Beacon   Map 15 B6
2130 Broadway at 75th St, 10023; 212 787 1100; www.beaconhotel. com; Subway: 1, 2 & 3
The family suites for four at this popular 260-room hotel have modern furnishings, good-size rooms, separate living rooms with sofa beds, and full kitchenettes with stoves, microwaves and coffee-makers. Some of the city's best gourmet grocery shopping is available nearby, as is convenient transportation. Overall, this is good value for money.

$$

The Lucerne   Map 15 B5
201 West 79th St at Amsterdam Ave, 10024; 212 875 1000; www. thelucernehotel.com; Subway: 1
A 1904 classic building renovated to blend traditional charm with modern accommodations, the 200-room

Lucerne offers comfortable rooms with marble baths and two-room suites with kitchenettes including refrigerator, microwave, and fine china. Evening turndown service, in-room spa treatments, and complimentary Wi-Fi are also available. Nintendo game systems, iPod docks, and flat-screen TVs are in all rooms. The American Museum of Natural History and Central Park are nearby.

$$

Empire Hotel   Map 12 E3
44 West 63rd St, 10023; 212 265 7400; www.empirehotelnyc.com; Subway: A, B, C & 1
The 423-room Empire has a stylish, global chic lobby and comfortable modern rooms. There is free Wi-Fi, and an on-site fitness center. The outdoor pool is a great refresher in summer. The hotel's location next to Columbus Circle is handy when looking for transportation.

$$-$$$

Mandarin Oriental Hotel   Map 12 F3
80 Columbus Circle at 60th St, 10023; 212 805 8800; www.mandarin oriental.com; Subway: A, B, C, D & 1
Families who can afford the hefty tab will find a warm reception at this stunning, modernistic, five-star hotel with peerless city views. Kids receive welcome amenities or baby toiletries. Coloring books, crayons, kids' DVDs, video games, and high chairs and strollers are also available upon request, subject to availability. Cribs and rollaways are free.

$$$

Beyond Manhattan
HOTELS
Holiday Inn Long Island City – Manhattan View
39-05 29th St, Long Island City, Queens, 11101; 718 707 3700; www.holidayinn.com; Subway: N & Q
The decor is typical Holiday Inn, but the rates are good and the views of the city are great. Kids under 12 eat free in the hotel restaurant. The fitness center is another attraction. The subway to Manhattan is one block away. For those with cars, parking is cheaper, but limited.

$

Ravel Hotel
8-08 Queens Plaza South, Long Island City, Queens, 11101; 718 289 6101; www.ravelhotel.com; Subway: F
The modern 63-room Ravel accommodates families in large rooms with two queen beds. Bathrooms have a soaking tub and rain-shower heads; most have a balcony overlooking Manhattan too. Free shuttles take guests to subway stops for a quick trip to Midtown.

$

Marriott New York at the Brooklyn Bridge
333 Adams St, Brooklyn, 11201; 718 246 7000; www.marriott.com; Subway: A, C, F, N, R, 2, 3, 4 & 5
An indoor lap pool, inexpensive parking, and a nearby TKTS booth for Broadway shows are good reasons to cross the East River. Multiple subways are close by. Alternatively, walk across Brooklyn Bridge to Manhattan.

$$

Outdoor pool deck with great views at the Empire Hotel

Key to symbols *see back cover flap*

An aerial view of a part of Central Park, surrounded by New York's skyscrapers

NEW YORK CITY

Maps

New York City Maps

The map below shows the divison of the 19 pages
of maps in this section, as well as the main areas
covered in the sightseeing section of this book.
The smaller inset map shows Greater New York and
the area covered in Beyond Manhattan.

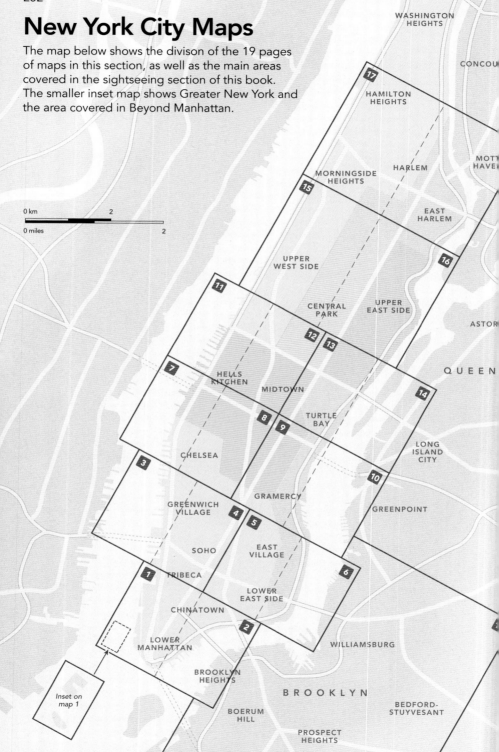

0 km   2

0 miles   2

WASHINGTON
HEIGHTS

CONCOU

HAMILTON
HEIGHTS

MOTT
HAVE

HARLEM

MORNINGSIDE
HEIGHTS

EAST
HARLEM

UPPER
WEST SIDE

UPPER
EAST SIDE

CENTRAL
PARK

ASTOR

QUEEN

HELLS
KITCHEN

MIDTOWN

TURTLE
BAY

CHELSEA

LONG
ISLAND
CITY

GRAMERCY

GREENWICH
VILLAGE

GREENPOINT

SOHO

EAST
VILLAGE

TRIBECA

LOWER
EAST SIDE

CHINATOWN

LOWER
MANHATTAN

WILLIAMSBURG

BROOKLYN
HEIGHTS

BROOKLYN

BEDFORD-
STUYVESANT

Inset on
map 1

BOERUM
HILL

PROSPECT
HEIGHTS

CLAREMONT
VILLAGE

ONX

HUNTS
POINT

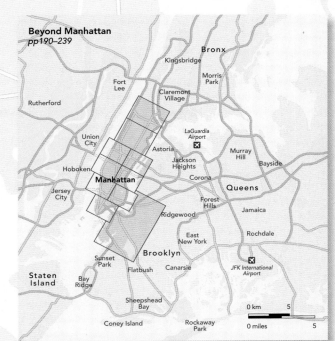

Beyond Manhattan
pp190–239

Bronx

Kingsbridge

Fort
Lee

Morris
Park

Rutherford

Claremont
Village

Union
City

LaGuardia
Airport

Astoria

Murray
Hill

Bayside

Hoboken

Jackson
Heights

Manhattan

Corona

Queens

Jersey
City

Forest
Hills

Jamaica

Ridgewood

Rochdale

East
New York

Staten
Island

Sunset
Park

Brooklyn

Canarsie

JFK International
Airport

Bay
Ridge

Flatbush

Sheepshead
Bay

0 km   5

0 miles   5

Coney Island

Rockaway
Park

JACKSON
HEIGHTS

KEY TO MAPS 1–19

- 🟩 Major sight
- ⬜ Place of interest
- ⬜ Other building
- 🚉 Train station
- 🚌 Bus station
- Ⓜ Subway station
- River boat boarding point
- Ferry terminal

- 🚁 Heliport
- 🅿 Parking
- ℹ Visitor information
- Police station
- Playground
- ▭ Highway
- ▭ Pedestrian road
- Railroad

SPETH

MAPS 1–14

0 meters   200

0 yards   200

MAP 19

0 meters   750

0 yards   750

RIDGEWOOD

MAPS 15–18

0 meters   200

0 yards   200

SHWICK

48TH AVENUE

GANTRY PLAZA STATE PARK

5TH STREET

49TH AVENUE

VERNON BLVD

AVENUE

JACKSON AVENUE

11TH STREET

1

Belmont Island

50TH AVENUE

51ST AVENUE

2ND STREET

AVENUE

M Vernon Blvd-Jackson Ave
7

BORDEN AVENUE

Pulaski Bridge

Queens - Midtown Tunnel 495

FRONT STREET

Long Island City Station

54TH (FLUSHING) AVENUE

2

AVENUE

55TH AVENUE

Newton Creek

MANHATTAN AVENUE

COMMERCIAL STREET

STREET

56TH AVENUE

BOX STREET

CLAY STREET

STREET

3

DUPONT STREET

STREET

FRANKLIN STREET

EAGLE STREET

STREET

E a s t

WEST STREET

FREEMAN STREET

GREEN STREET

STREET

4

STREET

HURON STREET

STREET

R i v e r

INDIA STREET

STREET

JAVA STREET

Manhattan Marina

KENT STREET

GREENPOINT AVE

5

PIER 70

FRANKLIN D ROOSEVELT DRIVE (EAST RIVER DRIVE)

AVENUE C

PIER 69

PIER 68

PIER 67

6

AVENUE C

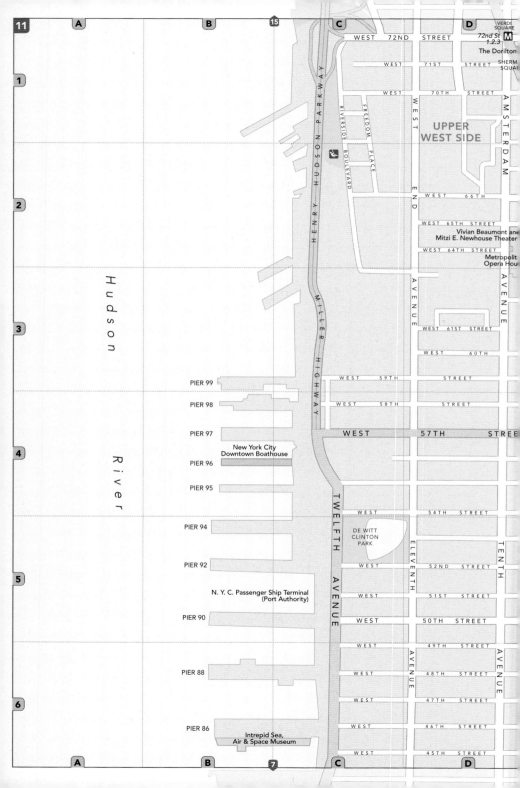

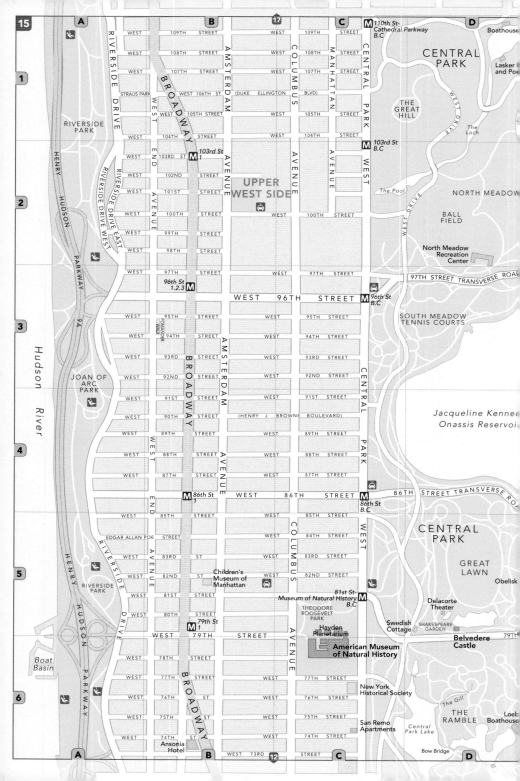

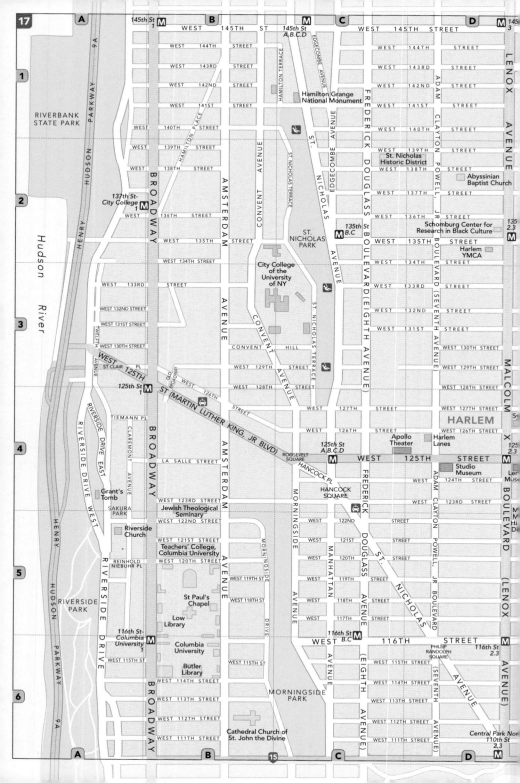

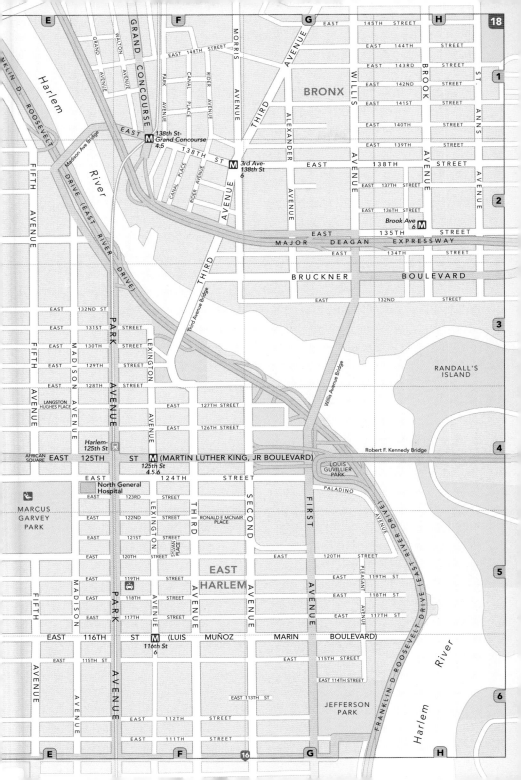

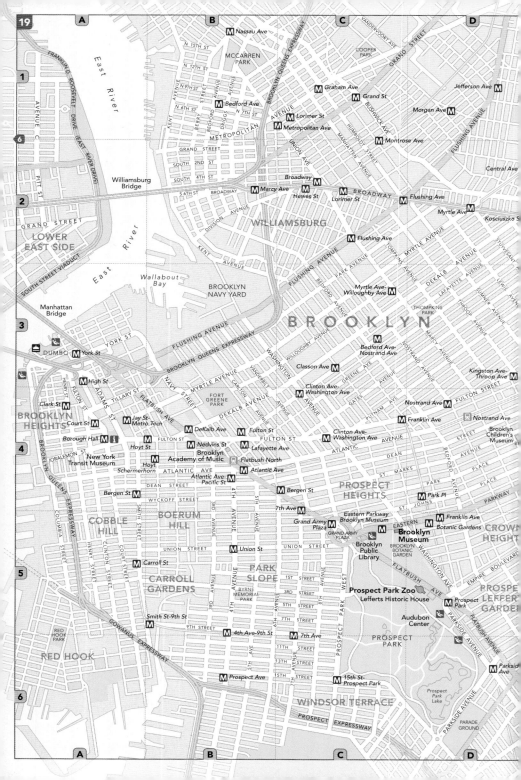

New York Maps Index

Index